SEA SENSE

Third Edition

Hans C. Engels

A passage under sail brings out in the course of days whatever there may be of sea love and sea sense in an individual whose soul is not indissolubly wedded to the pedestrian shore.

Joseph Conrad

SEA SENSE

Third Edition

Richard Henderson

International Marine Publishing
Camden, Maine

Other Books By Richard Henderson

Sailing at Night
Sailing in Windy Weather
Singlehanded Sailing, Second Edition
Understanding Rigs and Rigging, Revised Edition
53 Boats You Can Build

Published by International Marine

10 9 8 7 6 5 4 3 2

Library of Congress Cataloging-in-Publication Data

Henderson, Richard, 1924–
    Sea sense / Richard Henderson.—3rd ed.
        p.   cm.
    Includes bibliographical references and index.
    ISBN 0-87742-270-2
    1. Boats and boating—Safety measures.   I. Title.
VK200.H45 1991   90-48728
623.8—dc20   CIP

TAB BOOKS offers software for sale. For information and a catalog, please contact
TAB Software Department, Blue Ridge Summit, PA 17294-0850.

Questions regarding the content of this book should be addressed to:

International Marine Publishing
P.O. Box 220
Camden, ME 04843

Typeset by TAB BOOKS, Blue Ridge Summit, PA
Printed by Fairfield Graphics, Fairfield, PA
Design by Faith Hague, Watermark Design, Camden, ME

In Memory of My Mother
VERA P. HENDERSON
Who was always
a cautious sailor

CONTENTS

Preface

More than 2300 years ago, a Greek historian wrote the following description of his meeting with a Phoenician seaman: "I found the mate of the steersman, who is called the prow's man, so well acquainted with the location of each article that even when absent he could tell where everything lay and what their number was, just as a person who has learnt to read could tell the number and order of the letters in the name Socrates. I saw this man examining, at an unoccupied time, everything that is of use on board a ship; and on my asking him the reason, he replied, 'Stranger, I am looking to see whether anything is lacking or out of order; for it will be no time to look for what is missing or out of place when a storm comes up at sea.'"

Those exact words could be used today to describe a high degree of nautical competence. Sailors with that kind of careful proficiency possess a quality that might be called "sea sense," essentially a blending of common sense with seamanship. Sea sense has been a requirement aboard ships since before the time of the Phoenician sailor, but this quality was never so badly needed as it is today, because never have there been so many landsmen taking to the water, and so many non-seapeople involved in nearly all phases of the boating industry.

The primary and essential ingredient of sea sense is a thorough awareness of safety afloat. Every skipper has the responsibility of seeing that he or she is well informed in matters relating to safety in the selection and equipping of his vessel, preparedness for emergencies or accidents, and proper, seamanlike management of his vessel under adverse as well as favorable conditions. He owes this not only to himself and his crew, but to those aboard other vessels in his vicinity.

This book is a dissertation on safety in small craft, both sail and power, monohull and multihull, with emphasis on some points seldom found in a seamanship manual. Some of the topics discussed are controversial, particularly in the area of boat management in heavy weather offshore, but in those cases I have collected and collated the opinions of dozens of experienced seamen and established authorities, not only through their published writings but through personal letters and conversations.

For its third edition, *Sea Sense* has been completely updated and much expanded. The added material includes such wide-ranging topics as stability, roll inertia, and self-righting criteria for sailboats; construction standards, scantlings, and hull inspection procedures; a new section on multihulls; more information on powerboat design and handling; commentary on yacht and training-ship disasters; a section on proper and improper navigation practices; new information on safety gear, electrical protection, corrosion control, hypothermia, crew welfare, and man-overboard recovery; advice on stowage, rescue by helicopter, rigging and rig improvements, storm avoidance, and in-port storm protection; the latest thinking on weather bombs, microbursts, and heavy-weather management; a promising survival technique for the ultimate storm; and a glossary of terms. My intention has been to produce as complete a book as possible, one that I hope will stimulate forethought on just about all aspects of boating safety.

I sincerely hope this book will be helpful to boatmen and women, especially novices, but seasoned seamen as well. *Sea Sense* attempts to point out potential problems and suggests means of avoiding or overcoming them. In addition, it describes many actual experiences to show how problems have been handled, successfully or not, in the past. If *Sea Sense* helps prevent just one serious accident at sea, it will have been well worth the effort.

Richard Henderson
Gibson Island, Maryland
September 1990

Acknowledgments to the Second Edition

This book could not have been written without considerable advice from experienced seamen and experts in subjects related to boating safety. Most helpful of all has been my good friend Harold R. White, marine engineer and yacht yard manager, who not only supplied me with much information, but looked over those parts of the manuscript that dealt with mechanical matters. Also, I am especially grateful to Roderick Stephens, Jr. for his thoughts on boat management in heavy weather. The late naval architect-design critic Robert G. Henry was most generous in expressing his opinions on what constitutes a seaworthy boat. I am indebted to William T. Stone for advice in certain matters related to boating legislation and rules of the road. Victor Jorgensen, past publisher of *The Telltale Compass*, was most helpful in supplying me with safety-related information, and also I appreciate the suggestions made by Captain Sven T. Simonsen, director of the Coast Navigation School. William W. Robinson, past editor of *Yachting* magazine, was very helpful in the area of research suggestions, and David Q. Scott also made some valuable suggestions. Once again, Dr. Roger P. Batchelor was most encouraging and helpful, and Roger C. Taylor, president of International Marine Publishing Company, did a splendid job of helping with the planning and editing of the manuscript. In addition, I am grateful for information through letters or conversations from: John Guzzwell, Frank Casper, Eric C. Hiscock, Richard Page, Frik Pottgieter, Peter Spronk, Spaulding F. Dunbar, Scott Allen, Francis C. Stokes, Frederick B. Thurber, Harry C. Primrose, James L. Potter, Richard F. Jablin, Robert Peterman, Irving Groupp, Shaw Mudge, Richard C. Newick, Pete Hodgins, Dean H. Bergman, Otto C. Steinmayer, Jr., C. Henry Depew, Hal Roth, Walter H. Page, Sol S. Firman, Roger L. Woods, and John Hedden. Finally, I want to thank my typist, Patty M. Maddocks, not only for her competence, but also for her speed and dependability.

Acknowledgments to the Third Edition

Once again, I gratefully acknowledge my indebtedness to those named above. In addition, the following individuals furnished valuable technical insights, criticism, drawings, and photographs to the third edition of *Sea Sense*. To them, a sincere thank you:

Chris White, Dave Gerr, Donald J. Jordan, Dr. E. Franklin Tulloch, Jr., Forrest L. Griffith, Admiral William J. Kotsch (USN Ret.), Preston Kelly (Jr. and Sr.), Cecil E.S. Barclay, Admiral T.R. Weschler (USN Ret.), Captain Paul DeOrsay, Captain George E. White, Karl L. Kirkman, John Rousmaniere, William E. Brooks III, Edmund Cutts, Kaare Lindeman, John A. Kupersmith, and my editor, Jonathan Eaton.

Finally, I want to thank my son Rip Henderson for his photography, and my daughter Sarah Cramer for her help with research and typing.

Chapter 1
SAFETY IN HULL DESIGN

S ea sense begins with the selection of a safe, seaworthy, and soundly constructed vessel. Of course, the design concept and scantlings will depend largely on the purpose for which the craft is intended; a daysailer or cruising houseboat intended for protected waters is vastly different in design and construction from an offshore powerboat or sailing ocean racer. Nevertheless, in every vessel there should be an ample margin of safety, because any boat can be caught in heavy weather or subjected to stresses beyond those the builder, designer, or owner might expect. Even the most experienced boatmen make occasional mistakes in seamanship or weather forecasting that may put tremendous strains on a boat or her equipment, and enthusiastic racing skippers often throw caution to the winds, driving their craft beyond the limits of prudence.

A goodly number of boats produced today suffer glaring deficiencies in design, construction, and equipment. These deficiencies may not be as dangerous in a boat intended for navigating protected near-shore waters as in a boat intended for offshore use, but the near-shore craft is the one more often manned by the novice mariner who knows little of design, construction, or what to expect in the way of potential dangers. Furthermore, bad weather can be destructive even in sheltered waters. Marine historians remember that the great schooner *Mohawk* capsized, drowning five people, when only 500 yards from shore.

Several years ago I helped deliver a brand-new boat, produced by a noted builder, to her home port. After being underway for a few hours we noticed that the boat seemed sluggish, and peering down below, I saw water over the cabin sole. Some minutes later we discovered that the bilge pump was back-siphoning water into the bilge. The pump was neither looped nor vented, nor did it have a seacock. We found that by tacking and slowing the boat's speed to reduce the quarter wave, we could lift the pump's outlet from the water to stop the flow. Fortunately, the experience ended happily, but we might have sunk if we had been in a bad seaway, had not noticed the boat's logginess, had not been able to locate the source of the trouble, or had been unable to overcome the problem quickly. This story illustrates one of a great many examples of safety deficiencies seen today as a result of poor design, poor construction, corner cutting, or a combination of such factors.

Many design, construction, or equipment features that are desirable or essential for safety can be obtained on stock boats, but often only as optional extras at additional cost, while nonessential frills such as carpeting on the cabin sole are standard equipment. It should be the other way around, even if this means a higher base price, because many new boat buyers don't know what extras are important, and salesmen are often reluctant to inform them for fear of losing a sale from implications of possible dangers. One usually gets what one pays for in a boat. Although it is perfectly possible to buy a sound and safe boat at a moderately low price, with super-bargains the motto should be *caveat emptor*.

Faults seen on many stock boats include lack of or inadequate flotation in open boats; lack of rigidity or stiffness in vulnerable areas of fiberglass and aluminum boats; vulnerability to blistering and delamination in fiberglass hulls; insecurity of tanks, batteries, and other heavy installations; lack of internal ventilation and lack of access to areas that should be serviced or inspected periodically; improper protection from electrolysis and galvanic action; improper grounding and bonding for lightning protection; dangerous stove, fuel tank, or engine installations; lack of watertightness on deck (seat lockers without latches, non-closing ventilators, Dorades installed backwards, etc.); lack of seacocks on through-hull fittings; improper installation of toilet, bilge pump, or sink; inadequate installation of chainplates and weaknesses at the stemhead, under the mast heel, and at other stress points; improper rigging practices; fittings that are too light; breakable or vulnerable windows, windshield, or cabin trunk; a vulnerable companionway hatch posing the possibility of downflooding; cockpit drains that are far too small; lifelines that are too low; inadequate handrails; sharp edges on tables, counters, and partial bulkheads below; inadequate support at the mast step; weakness at and around the keel-to-hull bond of fin-keeled sailboats; weak juncture of the deck and topsides; vulnerable, ineffective, or inadequately secured rudder; and improperly bonded bulkheads. I am not saying that all boats have these or other defects. There are many well-made, properly designed boats on the market, but too many modern craft are carelessly designed and slapped together for the sake of making a fast buck. After a spell of heavy weather or a rough ocean race, one hears too many horror stories of gear failures, chainplates pulled out, dented bows on aluminum boats, stress cracks and delamination in fiberglass boats, lost centerboards, broken rudders and steering mechanisms, etc. I have even heard of a houseboat produced by a large, mainstream builder that cracked in half during fair weather in a very moderate seaway, because the plywood boat lacked the customary sheer clamp and shelf construction and was held together only by thin wooden battens and fiberglass cloth.

It is a pity that some boat producers do not feel more responsible for the safety of their customers. I would hate to see the adoption of rigid federal safety regulations, but it is becoming more and more apparent that the rapidly expanding boating public needs protection. I don't think many sailors want strict controls on the boating industry, but there is little doubt that the public needs to be made aware of the faulty craft and equipment produced by some manufacturers, who care little about what happens after the initial sale has been made.

The best general advice I can think of to aid the prospective buyer in his boat purchase is, first of all, to buy a boat designed by a reputable naval architect and built by an established and respected builder. Finding such designers and builders may take some research and involve questioning knowledgeable boatmen, but I think the effort will be worthwhile. In my opinion, it is important to pick a designer and a builder who are experienced seamen. The boats they produce should be the result not only of theory and professional experience, but also of knowledge gained at sea. It is customary for the buyer to hire a professional marine surveyor to examine a used boat before she is purchased. New boats are seldom surveyed, but I think is often wise to do so. A good professional surveyor may find faults or inadequacies that can be corrected before the owner takes delivery, thus preventing trouble later on. Unfortunately, finding a dependable, competent, completely impartial surveyor is not always easy. We will speak more of this difficulty in Chapter 3 when we discuss preparation and inspection for sea.

This chapter and the next attempt to point out basic design and construction features, both safe and unsafe, seen on modern stock boats. We will discuss safety in rigging and equipment in later chapters. Here we shall focus on the hull and most of its permanent fixtures (except plumbing and electrical systems and fittings related to fire hazards, which we also will discuss later).

Safe Design for Day Boats, Overnighters, and Other Small Craft

Very small boats designed for sheltered waters do not require the rugged construction and many safety features needed by larger boats that venture offshore. Nevertheless, small open boats, lacking size and weight, are often roughly handled, and this requires a certain robustness of construction. Then too, when considering safety features, one must give thought not only to the degree of protection offered by the waters of operation, but also to the time of year and the temperature of those waters. An easily capsizeable boat with ample flotation used near a well-populated area might be perfectly safe in warm summer waters, but a capsizing in the same boat could prove fatal in winter.

Perhaps the most glaring safety deficiency on many small boats is lack of flotation. Although this fault is not as common nowadays as it was formerly, there are still a great number of small, open (undecked)

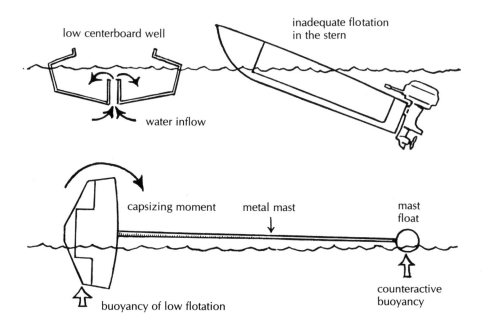

Figure 1-1. *Flotation.*

Figure 1-2. *Outboard well.*

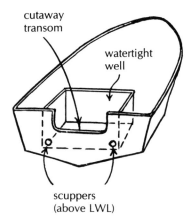

boats in production or use today that are capable of capsizing or swamping and yet lack adequate flotation. Nearly all boats except some built of wood will sink when filled with water unless flotation is added. Even wooden boats with heavy keels or engines need extra buoyancy to remain afloat and support their crew when swamped. Furthermore, many small boats in a swamped condition have so little freeboard, or height above the water's surface, that they cannot be bailed out; waves or even wavelets will slosh into the boat and fill her faster than she can be emptied. This problem is most critical in small sailboats with low centerboard wells that are open at the top (see Figure 1-1) and runabouts whose transoms are cut away to accommodate an outboard motor with a short shaft length.

Unless the stern is extremely buoyant, an outboard motorboat with a cutaway transom needs a self-bailing well just forward of the transom similar to the one illustrated in Figure 1-2. A wave sloshing over the transom cutout simply flows into and eventually drains out of the well without flooding the bilge. Designer Francis S. Kinney, in the book *Skene's Elements of Yacht Design*, points out the danger of a transom cutout when two people move aft in a small outboard runabout to fuss with a stalled motor in rough waters. Their weight aft will raise the bow and cause it to swing downwind, which will result in the cutout transom facing the waves. Water can quickly slosh in and perhaps swamp a boat that lacks a well.

Flotation may be in the form of a double skin (an inner and outer hull shell, the space between them being unfilled or filled with very light material), air tanks, watertight compartments, airbags, or expanded foamed-plastic materials. Air alone affords the greatest buoyancy, but airtight areas between skins, in tanks, or in compartments may allow water to enter through even the smallest undetected hole and thus reduce or destroy the buoyancy. Airbags are effective but difficult to secure and vulnerable to punctures. Flotation materials in motorboats must meet a number of federal requirements as set forth in the United States Code and the Code of Federal Regulations; these may be obtained from the Coast Guard, the American Boat and Yacht Council, or the Government Printing Office (addresses given elsewhere in this book).

Foamed plastics such as polyurethane, polyvinyl chloride (PVC), or Styrofoam (a polystyrene) make good flotation because the aerated foam contains a myriad of bubbles or closed cells and thus overcomes the danger of puncture or air leakage through one or a few holes. One cubic foot of this foamed material will support 50 to 62 pounds in fresh water. Polystyrene can be damaged by uncured polyester resin (used in most fiberglass boat construction), gasoline, and oil; therefore this type of foam usually should be protected with a coating of shellac or perhaps epoxy resin. Styrofoam comes in the form of rigid blocks and may be cut easily to fit under decks, seats, or any suitable space, but polyurethane in liquid form can be poured and expanded into solid foam inside an enclosed space. Some plastic foams are toxic during a fire; burning polyurethane foam gives off cyanide gas.

How much flotation is enough? In his book *Fibreglass Boats*, Hugo Du Plessis offers these approximations for fully crewed and well-equipped boats: 3 cubic feet of polystyrene foam for an 8-foot dinghy; 7.5 cubic feet for a 12-foot runabout; 3.5 cubic feet for a 14-foot sailing dinghy; and 30.5 cubic feet for a 20-foot sailing cruiser. The size of the boat, the construction material, and the weight of the engine, keel, and gear all affect the equation.

Proper buoyancy depends not only on the adequacy of the flotation material but also on its location. Flotation should be distributed fore and aft in such a way that the boat floats level when swamped, not bow up

Figure 1-3. *Although far from the best type to take on an extended offshore passage, this boat at least has a proper outboard motor well. These men were rescued by the Coast Guard after drifting for two days in the Straits of Florida when they attempted to reach Cuba in order to pick up relatives (Courtesy U.S. Coast Guard)*

and stern down or vice versa. Motorboats with their engines far aft will need considerably more flotation aft than forward. Flotation placed low in the bilge or under the cockpit sole will make a boat float high when she is swamped, but it may also increase her tendency to capsize or turn turtle, bottomside up (see Figure 1-1). This is especially true of a small centerboard sailboat. If she capsizes and lies on her beam ends, flotation located at the turn of her bilge will attempt to turn her completely over. Boats with this tendency, especially those with hollow metal masts that can fill with water, should carry air floats at their mastheads (see Figure 1-1). I believe further that the bottom of any boat with a strong tendency to turn turtle should be fitted with hand grips. These might be in the form of small apertures cut out of the skeg, an arrangement that will minimize harmful effects on boat speed. Turning turtle is not always dangerous, but it is inconvenient to say the least. In the bottom-up position, many boats are extremely difficult to right, and in shallow water the top of the mast might jam in a soft bottom and possibly break. One can often avoid turning turtle by promptly standing on the centerboard as a capsize unfolds, but even those who have practiced the maneuver repeatedly can be thrown to leeward, away from the board, in the early stages of a capsize.

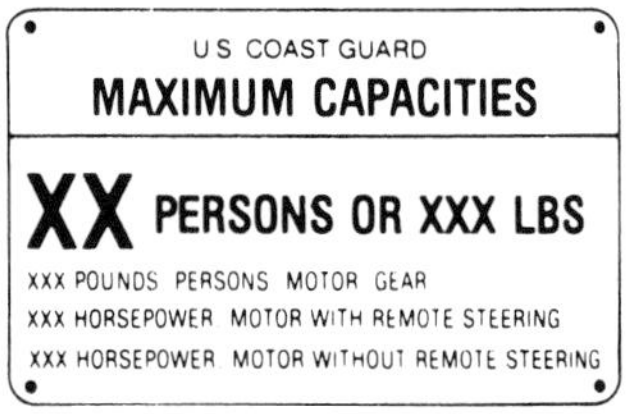

Other highly recommended design features for small craft are:

Figure 1-4. *Format of the U.S. Coast Guard capacity plate.*

- Ample beam and moderately low deadrise to provide high initial stability. Any boat larger than a dinghy should be sufficiently stiff to support, without heeling excessively, one or two people standing on her gunwale.

- Sufficient freeboard to keep out water in a chop. If the transom is drastically cut away for an outboard, it should be provided with a self-bailing well, as previously described.

- A small motorboat should be fitted with a capacity plate (a small, indelible information plate fastened to the inside of the transom or in some conspicuous location) that gives loading capacity, an estimate of maximum person capacity (pounds), and the total weight (including the weight of people, fuel, motor, and gear) the boat can safely carry in normal weather. On a boat propelled by an outboard motor, the plate should also specify the maximum horsepower. Such a plate is required by the U.S. Coast Guard for monohull boats less than 20 feet in length built on or after November 1, 1972, except sailboats, canoes, kayaks, and inflatable boats. It would not be a bad idea for the plate to give flotation information, an estimate of how much weight the boat can support in a swamped condition, and also whether the boat's permanently installed equipment meets federal requirements. Loading capacity should generally follow the formulas and standards developed by the Coast Guard and the American Boat and Yacht Council (ABYC) (P.O. Box 747, 405 Headquarters Drive, Suite 3, Millersville, MD 21108), as set forth in the book *Standards and Recom-*

Figure 1-5. *This hull shows a deep-V underbody with the deadrise carried aft toward the transom. The running strakes or spray strips (longitudinal ridges) help the hull break free of the water on a plane, thus enhancing lift and speed, but they have little to do with seakeeping ability. The chine flats (overhanging shelves at the chines, where the underbody meets the topsides) add stability, which is sometimes suboptimal in a deep-V hull at slow speed. See Figure 3-24 for a larger deep-V hull with pronounced flare forward.*

mended Practices for Small Craft. One simple, rule-of-thumb formula recommended by the ABYC and the Coast Guard for the maximum number of persons (P) to be carried in a rowing boat or small craft having a conventional shape is:

$$P = \frac{length \times beam}{15}$$

If no information plate is provided, the boat buyer should obtain the above information from the dealer or manufacturer.

- Open boats above dinghy size should have forward decks with washboards (on sailboats) or windshields (on motorboats) and also side decks with cockpit coamings to help prevent spray or waves from flooding the cockpit.

- Windshields on powerboats should be adequately braced; made of Plexiglas, Lexan, or safety glass; devoid of sharp corners or edges; of such a height that one's head will not strike the upper edge in a collision; and raked at the proper angle to avoid, as much as possible, distracting reflections. The helmsman's seat should be high enough to afford a view over the bow; more specifically, the ABYC used to suggest that the helmsman's eye height ensure an unimpaired view of the water directly ahead as determined by the formula: $X = L[3 - .02(L - 16)]$, where L is the boat's overall length and X is the distance on the water from the bow to the point ahead where the helmsman's view is obstructed by the bow. The formula yields 58 feet for a 20-foot boat, 82 feet for a 30-footer, and 100 feet for a 40-footer. I prefer these standards to the current, more relaxed ABYC recommendation of an X of 100 feet for all small powerboats.

- Some small motorboats designed for efficient planing at high speeds have steering difficulties or a tendency to bury their bows when operating at slow speeds. These faults are often present when the immersed hull volume forward is too small to balance the volume aft; when a large exposed transom creates more reserve buoyancy aft than the forward sections can balance; or when the bow sections have insufficient flare or freeboard to provide adequate reserve buoyancy. Reducing the amount of vee forward makes a boat pound terribly and can't be recommended. Instead, the buoyancy forward has to be increased while maintaining the vee—not an easy task for the designer, but one he usually tackles with some combination of ample flare and freeboard near the bow, which also helps keep spray out of the boat. Reducing the beam somewhat at the transom helps balance the buoyancy fore and aft, but the amount of deadrise from amidships aft has minimal bearing on a planing or semiplaning hull's ability to operate safely at moderate and low speeds in severe conditions. Probably the only way to tell for certain whether these factors are harmoniously combined and the vessel is suitable for rough conditions is to take her out in it and see how she does.

  Excessive stern squat can be counteracted with trim tabs (see Figure 1-6). The Coast Guard warns, however, that some boats, especially those with high-horsepower outboards, cannot always maneuver safely at high speeds when equipped with hydraulic trim tabs. A sudden turn may result in total loss of control. Boats that go faster than 35 or 40 mph and cannot negotiate a prescribed test course or a sudden extreme turn at full throttle should carry a warning label stating the maximum safe maneuvering speed. Veed sections aft usually require ample beam for sufficient stability at rest or at slow speeds. A skeg is a great help to directional stability, but if it is too close to a high-speed propeller it can cause cavitation. In this case, the skeg should end at least 9 inches ahead of the wheel, and its after edge should be well faired.

- It is essential that small ballasted keel sailboats without watertight compartments and self-bailing cockpits be fitted with sufficient flotation to buoy up the boat with a full crew aboard when she is swamped.

- To avoid personal injury from falls, all surfaces that will be walked on should be skidproofed with abrasive paint, pads, raw teak, molded textures in fiberglass, etc. Decks should not be excessively crowned, and there should be a low toerail at the deck's edge. Hand grips should be placed wherever feasible, especially on a high-speed boat. There should be no sharp corners anywhere that one could fall against. Falls often result when operators start their

Figure 1-6. *A starboard-side stern flap or trim tab. Though the drawing doesn't show it, there would be a duplicate tab on the port side of the transom. The simple mechanical linkage shown here is often superseded by more sophisticated hydraulic systems permitting convenient adjustment underway. The tabs not only aid fore-and-aft trim, but also enhance side-to-side stability in a deep-V hull.*

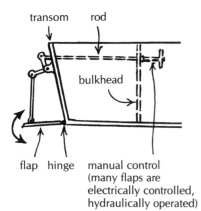

transom   rod

bulkhead

flap   hinge   manual control
(many flaps are
electrically controlled,
hydraulically operated)

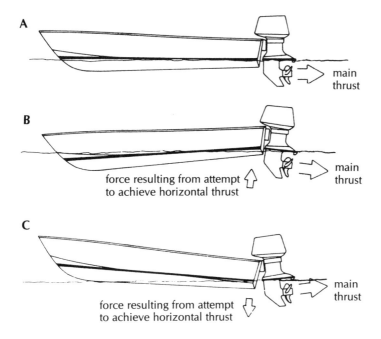

Figure 1-7. *Outboard motors and sterndrive engines can be trimmed in or out to affect the boat's fore-and-aft trim. In (A), with the main thrust parallel to the water surface, the boat runs on her lines. Trimming the drive unit in (B) tends to bury the bow but is useful to get a boat up on plane more quickly or to counteract the effect of excess weight in the stern. Trimming out (C) can add slight positive trim for optimum planing or counteract the effect of bow weight.*

outboard motors while a crewmember is standing. Crew should be sitting down and holding on, but it would also be highly desirable if all motors were made so that they would not start with their throttles wide open. This would prevent sudden acceleration while the operator is looking aft, having just pulled the starter cord on a small motor.

Designs for Open Waters

The primary design considerations for boats that navigate unprotected waters are stability, self-righting ability, and watertight integrity. A small- to medium-size monohull sailboat going offshore should be able to recover not merely from a mast-horizontal knockdown but also from a much greater angle of heel, such as would occur if she was rolled by a steep breaking sea striking her beam. This means that she must have ample ballast, normally in or on her keel, to self-right promptly from an extreme knockdown or rollover, and her decks and cockpit must be watertight to prevent swamping or downflooding into the hull's interior.

Prior to the 1980s many sailors and even some respected designers had come to equate sail-carrying power with stability, and very little concern was given to the possibility of an ocean racer/cruiser capsizing. Boats were given increasingly greater beam to support generous rigs and less displacement for greater speed under average racing conditions. Although a few yachts had capsized in heavy weather, it wasn't until 1979, after the gale-plagued Fastnet yacht race, that offshore sailors and designers became seriously concerned about ultimate stability. During that disastrous event in waters between England and Ireland, 77 ocean racers, boats supposedly designed for offshore conditions, suffered extreme (mast well submerged) knockdowns, and many of them rolled upside down. It was subsequently determined that more than a few IOR racers (boats designed to the International Offshore Rule) had dangerously short ranges of stability for the heaviest weather at sea.

As a result of the Fastnet tragedy, in which 15 sailors lost their lives, a number of scientific studies involving model testing investigated the phenomenon of capsizing. We now know that among several unseaworthy characteristics of modern ocean racers, two parameters—broad beam and light displacement—can combine to detract seriously from ultimate stability. Since these parameters can be easily obtained and utilized, a simple capsize screening formula was developed and is now promulgated by the USYRU (United States Yacht Racing Union). The formula divides the boat's maximum beam in feet by the cube root of her weight in pounds divided by 64 (to obtain displacement in cubic feet). Expressing it graphically:

$$\frac{B}{\sqrt[3]{D/64}}$$

The result should be 2 or, preferably, less for a boat to pass the screen.

Another rough guide to estimating a boat's resistance to capsize and her ability to recover from one is her static stability range, which is now calculated under the IMS (International Measurement System), a currently much-used yacht racing handicap rule. For most stock boats—at least those measured under the IMS—a stability curve such as the one in Figure 1-8 can be obtained from the USYRU or IYRU (International Yacht Racing Union). This curve, forming a hump above a baseline (where the righting arm is 0) and a smaller hump below the baseline, shows: the maximum righting moment (75 degrees in the illustration), the range or angle of heel at which the boat will capsize (134 degrees in the illustration), and the ratio of positive to negative stability. Represented by the

Figure 1-8. *Static stability curve for* Kelpie, *an Ohlson 38A, as calculated under the IMS (International Measurement System). Above the baseline the curve shows positive stability; below the line, negative stability. The ratio of positive to negative is shown in the upper right corner. (Courtesy USYRU)*

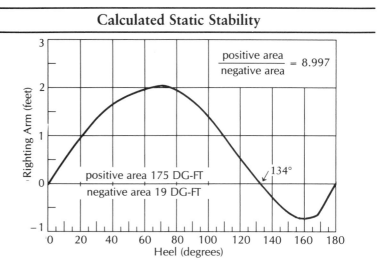

curve's hump below the baseline, negative stability shows the boat's stability in the inverted position and measures her lack of ability to self-right. According to one USYRU bar graph of stability comparisons (Figure 1-9), most boats in the IMS have stability ranges of about 120 degrees and ratios of 4, meaning that the area of the positive hump (above the baseline) is 4 times greater than that of the negative hump. These are minimal numbers for medium-size offshore sailing yachts;

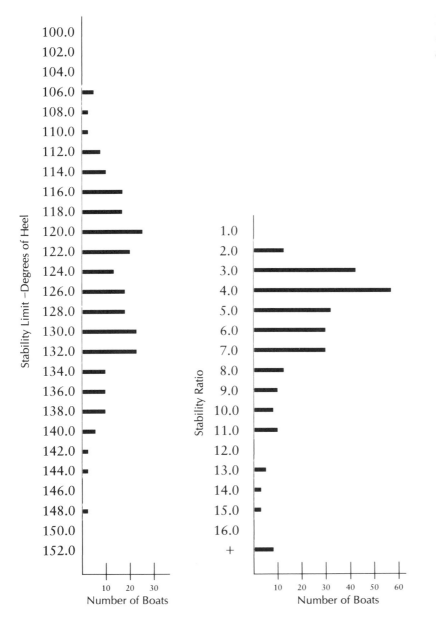

Figure 1-9. *IMS fleet distributions of stability limit and ratio.*

smaller seagoing boats need higher numbers to reduce the risk of capsize
and failure to right promptly.

Low negative stability, indicated by a small hump below the baseline,
is especially important if a boat is to right herself in the quickest possible
time after a capsize. Using stability data together with oceanographic
information on wave formation, a safety-at-sea committee sponsored
jointly by USYRU and SNAME (the Society of Naval Architects and
Marine Engineers) developed a graph relating inversion time to stability
range. This graph estimates that a boat having a range of 100 degrees is
apt to remain upside down for slightly more than five minutes before
being righted by another wave. But with a range of 120 degrees she is
likely to right in two minutes, which the committee considered significant since this is approximately how long a person can hold his breath
under water. When the capsize angle is greater than 130 degrees the boat
will probably right in a few seconds, and she should roll upright immediately with a range of 140 degrees or higher. The latter condition is obviously the most desirable.

The USYRU/SNAME investigation and other studies have verified
that vessel size, as well as beam and displacement, has a significant
effect on resistance to capsize. A small boat is more likely to roll over

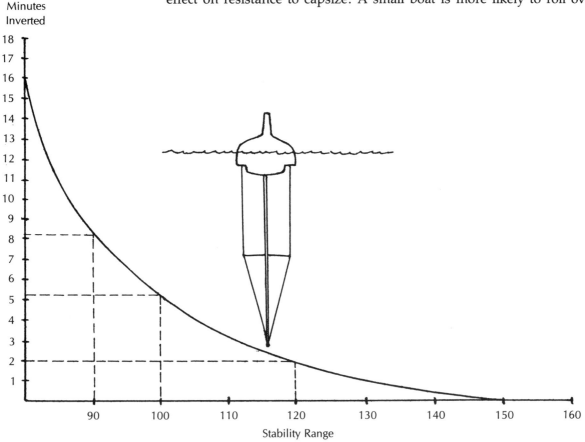

Minutes
Inverted

Stability Range

than a larger vessel of similar shape. The principal reason for this, aside from the effect of scaling laws, is that the larger vessel has the greater roll moment of inertia (resistance to rolling) and therefore more dynamic stability when struck by breaking waves. Partly for this reason, large craft such as sail training vessels and other so-called tall ships do not need the stability range of a small yacht. Nevertheless, some tall ships of former times and even modern replicas have less than adequate reserve stability and watertight integrity, a fact that became painfully apparent with the well-publicized sinkings of the sailing vessels *Marques* and the *Pride of Baltimore* during the mid 1980s.

These led to new Coast Guard regulations for sailing school vessels, which prescribe extended stability range and downflooding angles (heel at which water could flood the hull's interior). For example, the minimum required downflooding angle for the largest vessels increased from 45 to 60 degrees in partially protected waters, and from 50 to 60 degrees in exposed waters. Corresponding stability range requirements increased from 70 to 80 degrees and from 80 to 90 degrees, respectively. The text of the Sailing School Vessel Regulations (Code of Federal Regulations, Volume 46, Parts 169-199) must be read for a complete understanding. A multiplier based on displacement is applied to the required stability number to account for differences in vessel size.

When a boat lacks adequate stability, she can usually be improved with the addition of ballast to her keel or deep within her bilge. This will not only increase her displacement and roll inertia, but also lower her center of gravity to increase the righting moment. Ballast within the bilge must be placed as deeply as possible, and it must be firmly secured to resist shifting in the event of a knockdown or possible rollover. As an example of how effective deep ballast can be, a sister boat to the one whose stability curve is illustrated in Figure 1-8 had a thousand pounds of lead added to the bottom of a keel tank, and this increased her stability range to the "magic" number of 140 degrees, the range at which the boat will right immediately according to the USYRU/SNAME report. A word of caution, however: Lead should not be placed in a freshwater tank that will be used for drinking water unless it is certain that the ballast can be completely sealed off (usually with epoxy) to prevent any possibility of lead poisoning. Incidentally, a tall, heavy mast, though it adversely affects sail-carrying power, may improve a boat's capsize resistance by increasing her roll inertia and thus her dynamic stability.

Ballast is not normally needed in a fast powerboat used in semiprotected or coastal waters, because she carries no sail to cause significant heeling and, when bad weather threatens, can usually reach shelter before the seas kick up. Broad beam and flattish bilges provide great initial stability to a boat but make her vulnerable to capsizing in steep breaking waves. Anyone caught out in weather that produces such seas must take care to hold the boat end-to rather than broadside to the waves.

Another consideration is the boat's motion. A large powerboat must

Figure 1-11. *The author aboard the* Corwith Cramer, *the first vessel built to the new Sailing School Vessel Regulations. She has a stability range of 120 degrees and a downflood angle of 75 degrees, far in excess of the requirements. (Sarah Cramer photo)*

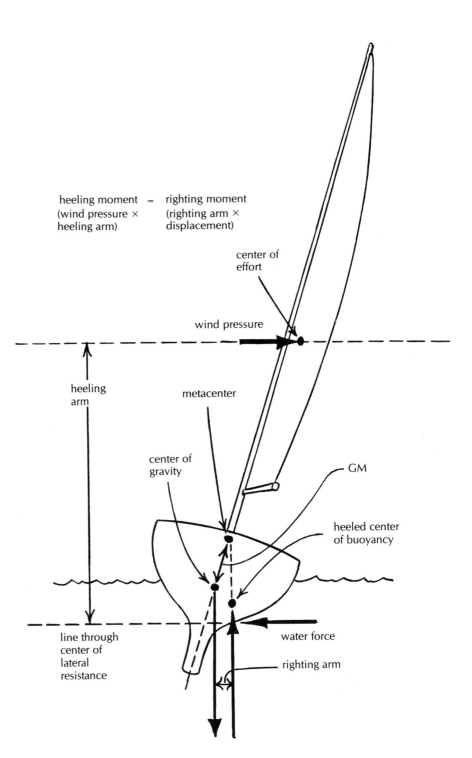

Figure 1-12. *The elements of stability and heeling motion.*

heeling moment = righting moment
(wind pressure × (righting arm ×
heeling arm) displacement)

center of effort

wind pressure

heeling arm

metacenter

center of gravity

GM

heeled center of buoyancy

line through center of lateral resistance

water force

righting arm

restrict its metacentric height (GM), the distance between the center of gravity and the metacenter (point M shown in Figure 1-12), for seakindly motion. The metacenter is the point at which a vertical line through the heeled center of buoyancy intersects the plane of the vessel's centerline. Adding or lowering ballast will lower the center of gravity and thus increase the GM, and a long GM will increase a boat's stiffness and give her a quick roll. Considerable stiffness is tolerable on a racing sailboat, because she should be stiff enough to carry a lot of sail and sails are effective roll dampers, but on a powerboat, whose hull form contributes to a relatively high metacenter, excessive or deeply located ballast could increase her GM to the point where a very quick, jerky rolling motion results. (Antiroll devices for powerboats are discussed in Chapters 3 and 13.)

On the other hand, displacement powerboats intended for extensive offshore work may well require ballast, because such craft often carry sail, even if only a small steadying sail. Another possible reason for ballast is that most seagoing powerboats have less beam than those intended to plane in protected waters, and of course, less beam means less initial stability. Then too, the very lofty superstructures seen on some powercraft are affected by wind pressure almost like sails. Of course, the need for ballast will depend on the vessel's hull form and center of gravity. A hull having flattish bilges with little deadrise and with her engines and fuel tanks placed extremely low will be stiff, but a narrower round-bottomed or deep V-bottomed boat with tall superstructures, higher tanks and engine, and steadying sails will undoubtedly need some ballast.

Ample freeboard is especially important on sailboats, because it extends the range of stability. Once a boat heels beyond the point where she begins to submerge her rail, the heeled center of buoyancy (as shown in Figure 1-12) begins to move inboard, with a resulting loss of stability. Freeboard should not be excessive, however, because this would raise the hull's center of gravity and cause harmful windage. Furthermore, keel-centerboard boats might suffer from excessive "rollout" (the tendency of a hull to lift when heeled), which would be harmful to the control of a shallow rudder.

Adequate freeboard forward, combined with proper flare and buoyancy, helps powerboats throw aside spray and seas. In his book *Seamanlike Sense in Powercraft* the late designer Uffa Fox described what he considered a dangerous practice, "the ramping down of the foredeck" of many sharp-bowed motorboats. These craft, designed to excel at high speeds, often lack proper freeboard far forward and buoyancy in the forefoot to negotiate a steep head sea at low speeds. With their "sloping down foredecks" scooping up the seas, such boats can be what Mr. Fox describes as "death traps." These boats might be safe for careful operation in protected waters, but when exposed runs are to be made, even just occasionally, it would seem prudent to choose a design with adequate freeboard, flare, and buoyancy forward. Proper flare will not only deflect spray but will add a reserve of buoyancy to the bow when it is immersed in a sea.

Let us now turn to some considerations of watertight integrity. Cockpits should have scupper pipes of large diameter, located reasonably high above the waterline (see Figure 1-13), and the volume of the cockpit well should be minimal, because a large well filled with water can reduce freeboard and stability to a dangerous degree. The Offshore Rating Council (ORC) recommends a cockpit volume (for sailing yachts in unprotected waters) derived from the following formula: 6% (length overall × maximum beam × freeboard aft) = maximum volume over lowest coamings. The ORC also recommends that the cockpit floor be at

Figure 1-13. *Cockpit well and details.*

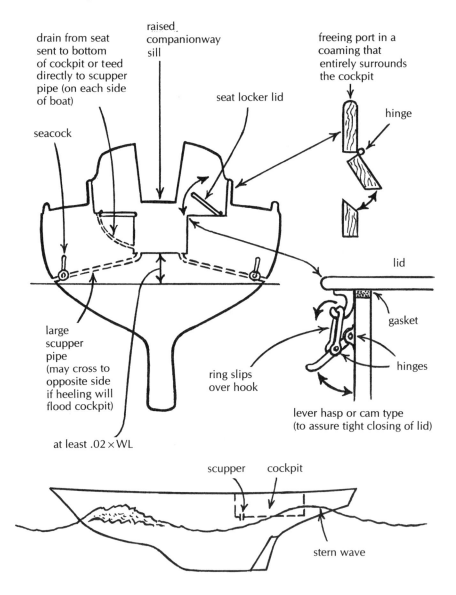

Sea Sense

least .02 times the load waterline length above the load waterline, and that the cockpit drains have a combined area not less than the equivalent of four 3/4-inch drains. The ABYC has recommended that scuppers or freeing ports be located on both sides of the boat and have a minimum total area determined by the formula: total area of scuppers in square inches = cockpit length in feet × cockpit width in feet ÷ 15. It is important that wide scuppers be covered with a coarse screen to prevent clogging. Scuppers should be located at the well's low points (which, on a non-planing sailboat, will usually be at both sides of the cockpit's forward end) in order that the well not be flooded by the boat's quarter wave at fast speeds (see Figure 1-13). On a planing powerboat or any boat that lifts her bow at high speeds, scuppers should usually be placed at the cockpit's after end. In some cases, usually on boats with abundant flotation, drains might be put through the transom. Quite often transom drains have outboard flaps that can be opened or closed with a cable leading to a control near the helmsman.

Though a self-bailing cockpit on a motorboat is desirable, it is no guarantee against swamping or capsizing. A heavy sea breaking aboard could seriously weigh down a boat and affect her stability before the water drains out. Furthermore, any rolling would cause the water to flow to the boat's low side, exacerbating her tendency to capsize. In many powerboats the need for comfort and convenience makes it impossible to reduce the size of the cockpit; such boats should have drains as large as possible and ample flotation, especially near the rails or gunwales, and care should be taken to avoid getting broadside to heavy breaking seas. (Management of powerboats in heavy weather will be discussed in Chapter 13.)

Common shortcomings of sailboat cockpits include seat locker lids that are not watertight and are not provided with latches; ventilating holes in the sides of cockpit wells; and companionway sills that are too low. Most cockpit seats containing lockers that are accessible from the top have hinged lids. At extreme angles of heel these lids can fall or float open, and since most lockers of this type allow water to drain into the bilge, the boat can quickly swamp or sink (see Figure 1-13). Thus it is important that locker lids be fitted with dogs, hasps, or some kind of secure latching device, and that they be well gasketed to prevent leaks even when completely submerged. In some cases seat locker openings are in the sides of cockpit wells, an arrangement that is seldom safe. The openings are often left unclosed, and many covers for these openings are not really watertight. Quite often one sees ventilating holes in the sides of a cockpit well. There must be a means of blocking these holes when underway if they can admit water to the bilge.

Perhaps the most serious cockpit design fault, and one seen on a surprisingly large number of production boats, is a low companionway sill. The sill height, the distance from the cockpit floor to the bottom of the companionway hatch opening, is often less than six inches. This distance is far from adequate for a boat sailing or especially racing in

Figure 1-14. *Example of a low companionway sill necessitating a lower dropboard in heavy weather. (Richard Nickel photo)*

Figure 1-15. *A high companionway sill and centerline hatch, as shown on this 23-foot Sea Sprite, are valuable safety features for windy-weather sailing. (Barbara Hatch photo)*

exposed waters, because a knockdown or sea breaking into the cockpit could flood the cabin. In fact, a low sill was responsible for the recent sinking of a 30-foot sailing cruiser in the middle of a protected Chesapeake Bay harbor when she was knocked down by a sudden squall before her sail could be lowered. On some boats companionway slides, or dropboards, can be inserted in rough weather to raise the sill level, but most such slides I have seen lack the strength to take the brunt of a heavy sea. European offshore boats are now fitted with sturdy Fastnet storm slides, which lock in place; these will be discussed briefly in Chapter 4. The ideal solution is a high bridge deck between the companionway and cockpit well for maximum strength and minimum cockpit volume, but in the absence of a bridge deck there should be a strong sill or slide at least as high as the point at which water would begin to flow onto the deck from the flooded cockpit.

Scuppers between the edge of the cockpit seats and the coamings of a sailboat will drain off water trapped in that area when the boat is heeled, thus greatly increasing comfort. These are often in the form of deep sloping gutters or pipes leading to the bottom of the well, as shown in Figure 1-13.

Watertight integrity below decks must be assured with the proper installation of sinks, head, permanent bilge pumps, and seacocks for all through-hull openings, whether intakes or outlets, below or near the waterline. Too many new stock boats are not fitted with seacocks or shutoff valves as standard equipment. They are usually offered as options only, and many boat owners don't appreciate their safety value. Three stock sailing auxiliaries of a well-known class sank in California waters when hoses slipped off through-hull fittings that lacked seacocks. Shutoff valves are especially important on underwater orifices such as those for the head and the engine's water intake, but usually there should also be a means of closing openings slightly above the waterline, such as scuppers, bilge pump outlets, and engine exhausts. Although some ocean racing requirements do not insist on seacocks on scupper outlets above the waterline, I know of a sailboat that nearly sank because such a scupper pipe ruptured while the vessel was heeled during an overnight race well offshore.

A common failing on many stock boats is the inaccessibility of sea-cocks or through-hull fittings that need servicing. There must be a reasonably convenient means of reaching all seacocks, and even if some are rarely used, they should be lubricated and opened or closed periodically in order to prevent corrosion and jamming (which usually happens during emergency use). The stuffing box, a gland (often bronze) with a large packing nut inside the boat through which the propeller shaft passes before penetrating the hull, is often difficult to reach. This fitting is intended to prevent water from leaking into the hull at the point of the shaft's penetration. Stuffing boxes need periodic inspections for leaks and occasional servicing in the form of repacking, tightening the nut, or lubrication of the type that has a grease fitting. When a grease fitting is hard to reach, some builders extend the grease cup with a copper tube to a readily accessible point. Such tubes can be vulnerable to damage, however, through corrosion, vibration fatigue, or being struck with a falling object, and more than one boat has developed a dangerous leak from a ruptured grease cup tube. Many stuffing boxes are the self-aligning type with a short length of rubber hose and two hose clamps that may need tightening or renewal. Clamps occasionally corrode, especially if they are not made of stainless steel, and the hoses have been known to tear. Naval architect Eric Steinlein has written that overtightening an unlubricated packing nut can cause the packing to bind on the shaft and tear or loosen the hose. One hears frequent warnings, by the way, against overtightening the stuffing box. A small drip while the engine is running is not serious, and such a leak will serve as a lubricant for flax packing.

Every part of the hull's interior should be accessible for inspection. This is especially important for wood boats with seams that can leak and for inspection of areas that can catch fresh water, which causes rot. Collisions with floating objects, broken-off fishnet stakes, and the like are not uncommon, and such accidents require immediate access to the damaged area for inspection and repairs. Other areas that must be reached for periodic inspection or servicing include tanks, limber holes, keel bolts, chainplates, bilge pump strainers, all parts of the engine and fuel line, steering mechanisms (cables, sheaves, quadrant, worm gears, etc.), and every part of the plumbing and electrical systems. Access is often blocked by solid continuous ceilings or headliners, by access openings or doorways that are too small, or by the building practice commonly referred to as "unitized construction," which means that a major part of the boat's interior is molded or otherwise permanently bonded into one unit to lower production costs. In most cases, unitized construction seriously impedes access to the hull shell, to fastenings such as the nuts for through-bolted fittings, and to piping, wiring, and many other important components that sooner or later may need to be reached. In my opinion, the nonremovable, structural part of ceilings should be constructed separately as longitudinal stringers spaced fairly wide to allow access to all parts of the hull, and deep lazarettes or lockers should have hatchways or openings large enough for a man to get his shoulders through.

In the earlier discussion of safe design for small craft, I mentioned the importance of skidproof decks, adequate handrails, and the danger of sharp corners anywhere on a boat. These features are even more important for larger craft designed for unsheltered waters. Sharp corners are often seen on tables, partitions, cupboards, stowage shelves, iceboxes, and elsewhere. Even in smooth water a crewmember can lose his balance and fall against a corner when the boat is rolled unexpectedly by the wake of a passing powerboat.

Additional safety features for boats in exposed waters include a hatch other than the companionway that is large enough to be used as an alternate exit; hatch covers fitted with strong dogs for secure latching; windows of safety glass, heavy Plexiglas, or preferably Lexan set in strong metal frames; a strong rudder of ample size located as far as possible abaft the vertical turning axis and preferably where it will receive propeller wash for effective steering under power; and, on a high-sided powerboat, a transom platform or ladder to assist a swimmer or man overboard to board the boat. The alternate hatch may be needed for entrance or exit should the companionway be blocked by water, wreckage, or fire. When English yachtsman Humphrey Barton was pooped by a heavy sea in the 25-foot sloop *Vertue XXXV*, the force of the sea jammed the companionway hatch cover, and a canvas cover over the forward hatch prevented escape there. Barton might have been trapped in the cabin were it not for the fact that a broken doghouse window was large enough for him to crawl through. The lesson in this case is hardly the value of large doghouse windows, but to have a forward hatch that will permit exit.

Important safety items such as bilge pumps, pulpits, and lifelines will be discussed in Chapter 5, "Safety Equipment," and we look at wiring, piping, and galvanic corrosion in Chapter 4. Fuel tank installation and engine ventilation will be dealt with in Chapter 6, in the discussion of fire prevention. Thus far we have pretty much neglected hull shape and underwater configuration with their effects on directional stability, balance, and performance, but we will cover or at least touch on these subjects in Chapter 3.

Chapter 2
SOUND CONSTRUCTION

It seems that hulls are becoming lighter and lighter as new boatbuilding techniques and materials are developed. The trend is desirable to a point, for it keeps down the cost (when superexotic materials are not used) and generally improves a boat's performance. A light sailboat, for example, can carry extra ballast on her keel for better stability, and she can perform well under a handy sail plan without compromising the all-important sail area-to-displacement ratio. Nevertheless, I worry that many of the cheaper stock boats are becoming too light for the greatest longevity and adequate rigidity, strength, and seakindliness in heavy weather.

Construction need not be heavy when the hull is properly reinforced in vital areas with such modern materials as epoxy resins, Kevlar, carbon fiber, and S glass, but the exterior skin should be sufficiently thick, strong, and well supported to resist panting, oil-canning (inverting), abrasions, weakening from blisters, and rupture from collisions with floating objects. Most sailors give little thought to running into flotsam or sealife, but more than a few boats have been sunk or damaged by semi-submerged objects such as logs or containers, and offhand, I can think of nine cruisers up to 46 feet that were sunk by whales. Such evidence argues for construction that is unquestionably strong and reasonably hefty.

This chapter will not attempt a detailed discussion of construction methods and scantlings; it will merely try to enumerate those commonly seen, modern construction practices that are generally considered good or not so good.

Stresses on the Hull

It is well to examine the principal stresses to which a vessel is subjected. The sizes of the arrows in Figure 2-1 show, in a very approximate way, degrees of stress. Exact loads vary according to conditions—i.e., whether or not the boat is moored or underway, how hard she is driven, wind and sea conditions, and so forth. The stress labeled H is caused by the propeller's thrust, and would be considerable on an accelerating, high-speed powerboat. Engine beds and longitudinal stringers should be ample to resist the thrust and vibration of a powerful engine.

The downward thrust of a mast and the upward pull of the rigging put considerable strain on a sailboat. The pull of the shrouds, which is not only considerable but is also concentrated on one side of the boat when she is heeled, tends to hog or bend her rail upward in the vicinity

Figure 2-1. *Hull stresses.*

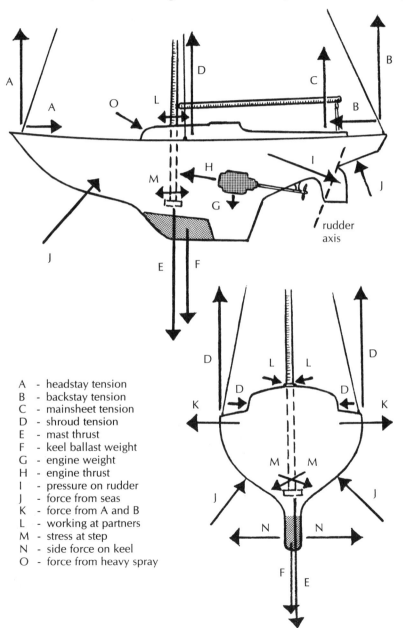

A - headstay tension
B - backstay tension
C - mainsheet tension
D - shroud tension
E - mast thrust
F - keel ballast weight
G - engine weight
H - engine thrust
I - pressure on rudder
J - force from seas
K - force from A and B
L - working at partners
M - stress at step
N - side force on keel
O - force from heavy spray

of the mast. The load on the windward shrouds is roughly equal to the boat's displacement. Chainplates must be carefully designed with sufficient length, a means of spreading the load over a considerable area, or both. The load might be spread by "beefing up" a large area surrounding the chainplates with additional fiberglass laminate or by attaching them to frames or a transverse bulkhead securely attached to the hull. The upward strain of stays at A and B can be enormous on a racing boat when she carries her jibstay tight for optimum windward efficiency. This strain not only causes the hull to bend up at her ends like a banana, but it may cause it to spread apart amidships as indicated by the K arrows. Here again, a securely attached bulkhead will help, as will the inward pull of lower shrouds shown at point D. The strains at K and D may vary and oppose each other alternately in a seaway, and they can cause the cabin-top to move slightly up and down; thus it is desirable to have a tie rod between the partners and mast step unless the mast is very close to the main bulkhead. The strain on the rigging tends to drive the mast through the bottom of a boat, so the mast step must be well supported and the load distributed over a wide area with adequate frames and floors in the vicinity of the step. This area is sometimes neglected, as boats with broken steps can testify. Boats with masts stepped on deck should have a sturdy post (or two posts with a strong metal spanner at the top) to transmit the mast's load to the floors and keel.

The stresses shown at J and even O in Figure 2-1 can be severe in a seaway. Flat surfaces are more vulnerable than convex surfaces. The thinnest eggshell derives surprising strength from its rounded shape. Thus, V-bottomed boats must be more strongly constructed than those with round bottoms to confront similar conditions. The angle of deadrise will also affect the stresses at J. Slack, easy bilges and deep, slightly rounded bow and stern sections will minimize harmful pounding.

The area in way of the entrance (surrounding J) is subject to a lot of stress, and dented-in bows on aluminum boats and broken furniture in the bows of fiberglass boats are not uncommon. There is, in addition, always the possibility of colliding with flotsam or sealife, so the entrance should be heavily reinforced. Before embarking on a transatlantic voyage in my 37-foot fiberglass sloop, I wrote to her molder, the Tyler Boat Company in England, explaining my intention and asking for recommendations for modifying and strengthening the boat to cope with any eventuality. The builders replied that no modifications were necessary, but they felt it might be desirable, depending on how the boat was finished, to add a bulkhead under the forward bunks. I followed their advice even though the boat already had a number of longitudinal stringers to strengthen her bow.

A source of weakness on many offshore boats is the shape of the cabin trunk. Flat, slab-sided deckhouses are vulnerable in heavy weather, and cabin trunks or similar structures on offshore boats must not only be strong, they should be slanted and curved or rounded to resist boarding seas or impact with the water during an extreme knockdown. Wood cabin trunk sides should usually be secured to the deck carlins or headers with long vertical bolts or tie rods. The cabintop should be well crowned and supported with bulkheads or posts to resist oil-canning. A few years ago a friend of mine capsized during a coastal passage in a 42-foot sloop built by the respected builder, Henry R. Hinckley & Company. Her cabintop inverted enough to pop out her windows, and without watertight integrity the boat had to be abandoned, as related in Chapter 12.

Arrows F and N in Figure 2-1 denote keel stresses. These can be considerable, especially in heavy seas, because of ballast weight and the side forces and twisting action imposed on the keel by leeway and the boat's yawing, swaying, and pitching while heeled. An integral keel faired into the hull, with the ballast bolted on or sealed inside the keel, normally is stronger than a bolted-on metal fin. When the forefoot is swept back and the keel's leading edge is raked, as in Figure 2-1, the boat will ride up on a submerged floating object and gradually dissipate energy rather than stopping abruptly with a consequent shock loading that could seriously strain the forepart of the boat or her keel.

Substantial floor timbers, web frames, or other structural members inside the hull at the base of any bolted-on underwater appendage not only support the bolts but also distribute the load evenly over a wide area. Fiberglass boats need extensive laminate reinforcement on either side of the keel extending an athwartships distance of about one-quarter of the keel's height, a recommendation suggestive of ABS (American Bureau of Shipping) scantlings. Figure 2-2, based on Lloyd's Register of Shipping recommendations, shows other areas of the hull that need reinforcement.

The ABS and Lloyds are the principal societies setting building standards and classifying or certifying vessels in the United States and England, respectively. An equivalent organization serving Scandinavia and other maritime countries is Det Norske Veritas of Norway. There can be reasonable assurance that construction is sound when a vessel is built and classed in accordance with the standards of any of these societies.

Figure 2-2. *Fiberglass hull reinforcement (suggestive of Lloyd's recommendations). The hull is gradually thickened from areas A to B, B to C, and C to D. The weight per square foot of D should be about 2½ times that of A.*

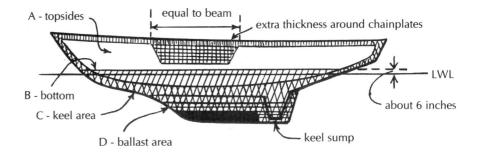

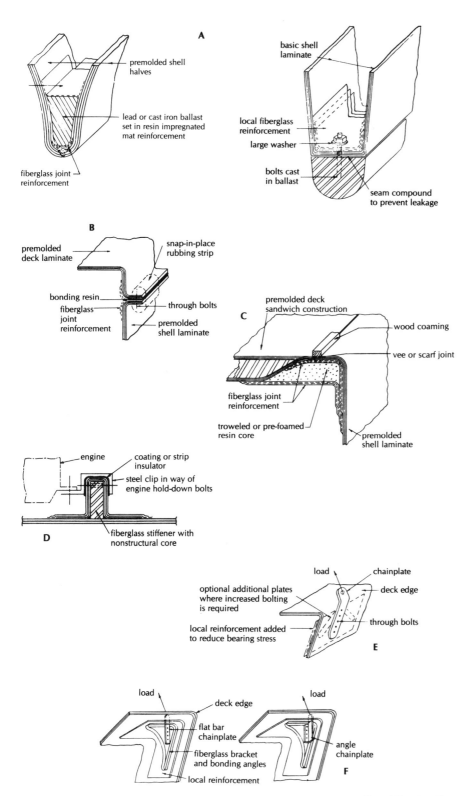

A

premolded shell halves

lead or cast iron ballast set in resin impregnated mat reinforcement

fiberglass joint reinforcement

basic shell laminate

local fiberglass reinforcement

large washer

bolts cast in ballast

seam compound to prevent leakage

B

premolded deck laminate

snap-in-place rubbing strip

bonding resin

fiberglass joint reinforcement

through bolts

premolded shell laminate

C

premolded deck sandwich construction

wood coaming

vee or scarf joint

fiberglass joint reinforcement

troweled or pre-foamed resin core

premolded shell laminate

engine

coating or strip insulator

steel clip in way of engine hold-down bolts

fiberglass stiffener with nonstructural core

D

load

chainplate

deck edge

optional additional plates where increased bolting is required

through bolts

local reinforcement added to reduce bearing stress

E

load

deck edge

flat bar chainplate

fiberglass bracket and bonding angles

local reinforcement

load

angle chainplate

F

Figure 2-3. *An assortment of fiberglass hull connections and fittings. Note the additional reinforcing layers of fiberglass on each. **A**: Ballast to hull connections. **B**: A common small-boat hull-to-deck joint, this one known as a "pout." Self-tapping screws are often used instead of through-bolts. **C**: Another hull-to-deck joint often seen on boats over 25 feet long, with or without sandwich-constructed decks. In one variation the deck laminate overlaps the inturned flange of the hull shell laminate rather than meeting it in a scarf joint, and the area of overlap may be pinched upward as a bulwark and covered with a caprail. Though not shown here, the toerail, coaming, or caprail should be screwed or bolted into the joint. **D**: A steel clip bolted to an engine bed, in this case a hat-shaped stiffener with a nonstructural core, to receive the engine hold-down bolts. **E**: An exterior shroud chainplate. **F**: Interior shroud chainplates, showing one made of flat bar and one of angle. The mounting brackets should be bolted to a transverse bulkhead or longitudinal frame. The chainplate should be bent or positioned to align with the direction of load. The construction details shown here are the minimum acceptable. (Courtesy Gibbs & Cox)*

Modern stock boats are made from a variety of materials, including aluminum, steel, wood, plywood, and ferrocement, but by far the greatest number of craft produced in the United States at the present time are of fiberglass.

Fiberglass Construction

The material known in the American vernacular as fiberglass is more accurately referred to as FRP (fiberglass-reinforced plastic) or GRP (glass-reinforced plastic). In much the same way that steel rods reinforce concrete, fiberglass uses glass filaments to strengthen the plastic, which is generally in the form of a thermosetting resin. The fiberglass skin of a boat is a laminate built up from alternating layers of woven or bonded glass materials stuck together with resin. In some cases, chopped glass fibers are sprayed with resin onto the hull or hull mold with a special gun. Glass materials used for reinforcement are in the form of mat (random glass strands loosely bonded together), cloth (a finely woven fabric of glass strands), and woven roving (a coarsely woven fabric). A typical laminate combination for a small hull laid up in a mold starts with a gelcoat (the thin, smooth outer layer of the hull composed of pure resin and pigment), followed by two layers of mat, a layer of woven roving, another mat, a layer of woven roving, and a final layer of mat or cloth. Well-constructed larger boats use more plies of roving, seven or more below the waterline in some cases. Resins are sometimes epoxy, which is expensive and extremely strong, but far more often the more economical, easier to work with, and weaker (but in most cases adequately strong) polyester. In recent years, builders of high-speed powerboats and high-tech sailboats have begun to use vinylester resin because of its high resistance to blistering and its tenacious bonding to core materials. Vinylester is intermediate in cost and strength between polyester and epoxy.

Although fiberglass boats are built by several different methods, the most usual one for the stock hull is to build it on the inside of a female mold. Gelcoat is sprayed or painted on the mold first, and then the alternating layers of fiberglass reinforcement and resin are applied. There is a good deal of controversy about the quality of the manufacturing method that uses chopped glass fibers sprayed on with a "chopper gun," as opposed to the "hand lay-up" method, which uses alternating layers of glass mat and roving. Most manufacturers extol their own systems and sometimes criticize those of competitors. It seems reasonably certain, however, that either the spray-on or lay-up method is satisfactory when properly done, though most authorities agree that it takes greater skill to use a chopper gun. Great care must be taken that chopped glass laminates have even, uniform thickness overall, with greater thickness in areas of extra stress. In the hand lay-up method, strength can be assured with the use of fabrics made of long, woven, twisted and untwisted fibers; the correct amount of resin must be applied (too much and the laminate is brittle; too little and it is resin starved), and voids and air bub-

Figure 2-4. *Rolls of woven roving (foreground) and chopped-strand mat (background). (Fenno Jacobs photo)*

bles must be removed as much as possible by thorough wetting and rolling. Many builders use a combination of chop and hand lay-up, substituting the chop for mat between layers of roving.

Fiberglass construction offers important advantages in compressive and tensile strength; freedom from corrosion, rot, and destruction from worms; and ease of repair. However, the material can blister, sometimes delaminate, and abrade, and it is highly flexible. To assure adequate stiffness, fiberglass hulls should be sufficiently thick especially in stress areas to inhibit excessive flexing (oil-canning), and stiffeners should be provided in the form of frames, bulkheads, longitudinal stringers, and stowage shelves, tanks, or furniture built in to serve double duty as stiffening members. Exotic materials such as carbon fiber and Kevlar 49 have been used effectively to strengthen and stiffen hulls. These materials are expensive, but they can be used in small amounts as reinforcement at areas of great stress. Bulkheads and other stiffeners must be securely attached to the hull shell, usually with continuous fiberglass tabbing of mat and roving on both sides of the stiffener where it meets the shell. I recently heard of a transverse bulkhead popping loose from a fiberglass hull due to excessive strains at points K in Figure 2-1, when the boat's headstay and backstay were carried extremely taut. Shrouds are often attached to a bulkhead, and their upward pull puts extra stress on the hull-bulkhead attachment.

Another potential source of weakness is "hardspots," small areas of stiffness surrounded by flexible areas. These spots are usually caused by the pressing of a rigid stiffener on a small area of the flexible shell. Hardspots can create serious stress concentrations or fatigue from constant bending where there is an abrupt transition from stiffness to flexibility, and the condition should be avoided by distributing the pressure of stiffeners over wide areas with the use of extra plies of laminate or, preferably, wide plates between the shell and stiffener to disperse the stress (see

Figure 2-5). A fillet of foam between the edge of a bulkhead and the hull will also ease that particular hardspot.

One of the great advantages of fiberglass construction is that it produces a nearly monolithic hull with minimal joints or seams. The few joints that do exist, such as where the deck joins the hull, require careful, strong connections, perhaps with epoxy resin in some cases. When the deck and hull laminates are butted and held together with layers of fiberglass reinforcement on the inside of the seam, there is a tendency for the hull and the deck laminate to peel apart near the outside of the seam. In some cases the hull laminate can be rolled over at its top edge so that the seam can be covered with a toerail to mitigate the tendency to peel, or the deck and hull edges can be flanged or given lips which may be bolted together and then covered with a rubbing strip (see Figure 2-3). The strongest and most leakproof hull-deck joints are usually bonded, fiberglassed, and mechanically fastened (preferably with bolts). Decks and other relatively flat surfaces, such as transoms or bulkheads, need to be quite rigid; thus they are often of plywood covered with glass cloth,

Figure 2-5. *Interior stiffeners can cause undesirable hardspots in the hull. A: This sequence shows bad, indifferent, and good ways of terminating a transverse frame. B: Good practice for tabbing a bulkhead or frame to the hull shell. Foam fillets and local reinforcement relieve the hardspot. A continuous foam fillet between the bulkhead and the shell (dashed line in drawing) is recommended when a rigid full bulkhead is tabbed to the hull. (Courtesy Gibbs & Cox)*

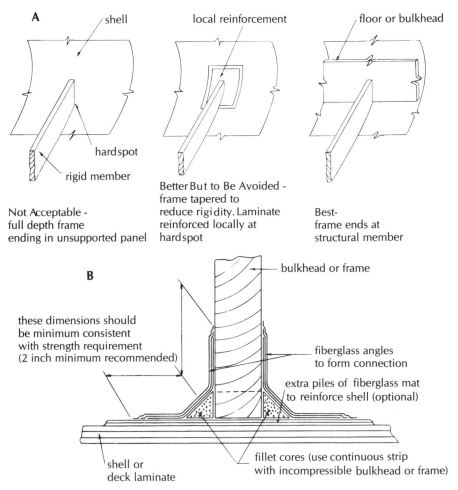

A
shell
hardspot
rigid member

Not Acceptable -
full depth frame
ending in unsupported panel

local reinforcement
Better But to Be Avoided -
frame tapered to
reduce rigidity. Laminate
reinforced locally at
hardspot

floor or bulkhead
Best-
frame ends at
structural member

B
these dimensions should
be minimum consistent
with strength requirement
(2 inch minimum recommended)

bulkhead or frame

fiberglass angles
to form connection

extra piles of fiberglass mat
to reinforce shell (optional)

shell or
deck laminate

fillet cores (use continuous strip
with incompressible bulkhead or frame)

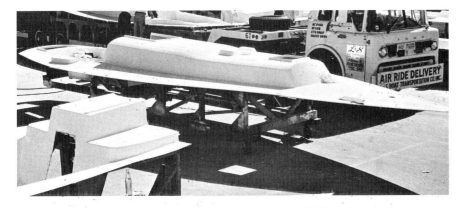

Figure 2-6. *A fiberglass deck, cockpit, and cabin trunk molded in one piece at Morgan Yachts. (Fenno Jacobs photo)*

plywood or balsa sandwiched between layers of fiberglass, or, in some cases, fiberglass with molded-in stiffeners.

Sandwich construction is often used for the hull. A good grade of marine plywood is a suitable core material when weight is not a factor, but solid hardwood should be avoided because it might swell and crack the laminate. By far the most common core materials are balsa wood and various foamed plastics, including PVC (polyvinyl chloride) foams such as Airex and Klegecell. Divinycell and Termanto 75, which are cross-linked PVCs and not so subject to heat softening from the sun, are sometimes used for the deck core. Sandwich construction provides rigidity with light weight and insulates interior spaces from extremes of temperature, condensation, and vibration noise. The core materials must have the strength to resist impact and shear stresses, and also the outer laminate skin must be sufficiently thick and strong to resist puncture or leakage of water through minute holes in the laminate. Water leaking into the core can sometimes cause serious problems, especially with balsa, which can rot. To avoid water migration in balsa, the core panels should be end grain (cut across the grain) and preferably precoated with polyester resin.

Ballast is secured to an integral (molded) fiberglass keel in one of two ways: by bolting the ballast to the outside of the keel (see Figure 2-3), or by placing the ballast inside the hollow keel. There are advantages and

Figure 2-7. *Bolted-on ballast is vulnerable at the keel bolts. (R.C. Henderson photo)*

disadvantages in each method. External ballast assures the lowest possible center of gravity for a given weight and affords good protection when grounding on rocks or hard bottoms, but it usually detracts from the keel's smoothness and fairness, and the keel bolts will corrode or erode in time. Access for the inspection, tightening, and replacement of the bolts and nuts is essential but sometimes lacking. Internal keel ballast assures smoothness and eliminates the keel bolts, but the keel is more vulnerable to groundings, and if the ballast is not tightly fitted and bonded in place it may shift, with any movement possibly leading to fatigue or abrasion. If the keel should be holed from a grounding, it may fill with water or even drop ballast if the ballast comprises small pieces of

Figure 2-8. *A: Bottom blistering. B: When blisters become this numerous, it's tempting to call them ''boat pox.'' C: Deep blisters with delamination of the underlying laminate. D: A close-in view of delamination. (R.C. Henderson photos)*

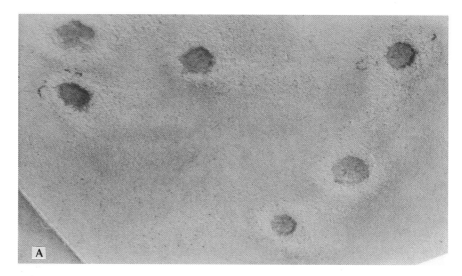

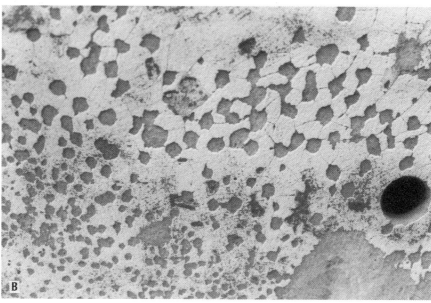

metal. This has happened on several occasions. Pockets of water allowed to remain between the keel shell and the ballast may freeze and swell in northern waters, possibly cracking the laminate. The most satisfactory internal ballast is a one-piece lead casting that exactly fits the hollow of the keel. Internal keel ballast requires ample laminate thickness at the garboards as well as in the keel itself, and the ballast should be sealed with fiberglass at its top to firmly hold it down and to prevent water from entering the hull should the keel be punctured.

A growing problem with fiberglass construction is boat pox or osmotic blistering, which may appear at any time during a boat's life. Whether a craft is affected depends on its construction and whether stor-

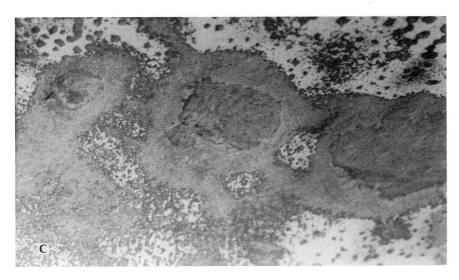

age is dry or wet during the winter season, but surveys show that anywhere from one-fifth to one-half of all fiberglass boats have the problem to some degree on their underwater surfaces. Boats left in the water year-round suffer the most, and there is some evidence that warm water and fresh water both aggravate the problem. Most blisters are cosmetic and only affect the gelcoat, but some are more deeply buried in the laminate and can affect hull integrity. The U.S. Coast Guard has been sufficiently concerned to fund a study of the causes of blistering, which was carried out at the University of Rhode Island.

The gelcoat acts as a barrier to inhibit the entrance of water into the laminate, but water may eventually work its way through the gelcoat and combine with water-soluble materials just above or in the top layers of the laminate. An acid solution is formed, and the resultant osmotic pressure draws in more water, forming blisters. The many possible causes of blistering or delamination start with the construction process and include dirty working conditions during hull lay-up, lack of temperature and humidity control, resin starvation, inadequate removal of air pockets with rollers or a vacuum bag, stress concentrations improperly built into the hull, overly catalyzed resin, improper curing, adulteration of the resin with pigments and fillers, gelcoat that is too thick or too thin, and particularly, an inferior quality of resin.

It is interesting that most of the early "overbuilt" boats of the late 1950s and 1960s seem to have less trouble with blisters, while in boats built from the early 1970s to the early 1980s blistering is epidemic. At least one authority attributes this to the fact that many boatbuilders began to use the cheaper orthophthalic-type polyester resins during the oil crisis of the 1970s. (Another theory blames the extensive use in the early 1970s of chromic chloride, which encourages osmosis in fresh water.) Since then, most builders have switched to isophthalic resin, which is stronger and more water resistant. A few builders are now using vinylester resin, while custom racers made with exotic materials are often stuck together with epoxy.

There is some disagreement over the best treatment for blisters. The University of Rhode Island study recommended sealing the hull with two or three coats of an alkyd-urethane-silicone blended marine paint, but this has been seriously questioned by many professional boat repairers. This blend, a topsides enamel-like paint, is not intended for underwater use, and it may be incompatible with antifouling bottom paints. A more popular method of treatment, one that has been successfully used for a number of years, is to apply barrier coats of epoxy. Some authorities recommend coal-tar epoxy, and many successful repairs have been made with the WEST system epoxy procedure as developed and marketed by Gougeon Brothers, Inc. of Bay City, Michigan. The U.S. Coast Guard has recommended coating the entire underwater surface with 10 to 12 mils (.010 to .012 inch) of two-part epoxy resin, 18 mils (.018 inch) if the gelcoat was removed. Some specialists in blister repair now prefer coating with vinylester resin.

Everyone agrees that the hull must be thoroughly dried out before the pox is treated. All blisters must be removed by puncturing, draining, washing with fresh water, and sanding. Remove any soft laminate near the blisters. In severe cases the entire gelcoat might need removal, often by sandblasting the bottom. Then the boat should be dried, perhaps for months, before the bottom is coated. The Gougeon Brothers have developed a more speedy method of drying the hull by vacuum bagging (i.e., sealing the hull in an airtight bag and removing the air with a vacuum pump, thereby drawing moisture out of the laminate).

When fiberglass boats were first built back in the early 1950s, they were expected to last forever, but we now know this is not true—certain components will degrade in time. Degradation takes place after water permeates the gelcoat or other barriers and wicks into the laminate, eventually dissolving soluble chemicals and ultimately causing delamination. The process will be exceedingly slow, however, when the boat is well built and well cared for. Conditions that promote longevity include a clean lay-up environment; temperature and humidity control when laminating the hull; the use of high-quality materials (for example, isophthalic resin when polyester is used); a glass-to-resin ratio (by weight) of at least $^{35}/_{65}$ for conventional construction ($^{50}/_{50}$ is ideal, while $^{65}/_{35}$ risks resin starvation); careful hand lay-up by skilled workers or use of such modern methods as vacuum bagging and prepreg (fiberglass cloth that is pre-impregnated with catalyzed resins) to assure proper saturation; thoughtful engineering in regard to reinforcement and orientation of woven materials; meticulous attention to curing and bonding; use of coated, closed-cell cores that are highly resistant to rot or heat softening; use of unpigmented and otherwise unadulterated gelcoat below the waterline; prompt repair to blisters even if they are only cosmetic; meticulous maintenance of the gelcoat or other barrier coating to delay the penetration of water; keeping the bilge dry; dry storage or at least periodic drying out of the hull during the off season; and periodic monitoring of hull saturation by someone familiar with the operation of an electronic moisture-detection meter. Some surveyors recommend that new fiberglass hulls be given a protective coating of epoxy before launching.

A few additional, miscellaneous thoughts on fiberglass construction: Sharp, right-angle corners should be avoided in favor of curved or rounded corners to mitigate cracking the laminate; stress areas at winches, cleats, chainplates, chocks, etc. should be thickened and reinforced with extra laminate plies; these plies should add thickness gradually, with the reinforcement laid in patches of increasing size, one on top of another; when strains are mostly in one direction, the reinforcing fabric should be aligned so that the stress is in the direction of the cloth's weave and not on the bias; and extra roving and stiffeners should be used when the laminate is subject to fatigue stress produced by continually alternating or repetitive loads. Fatigue stresses are most often produced by the pounding of seas under the bows of high-speed flat- or V-bottomed craft and by the vibration of powerful engines.

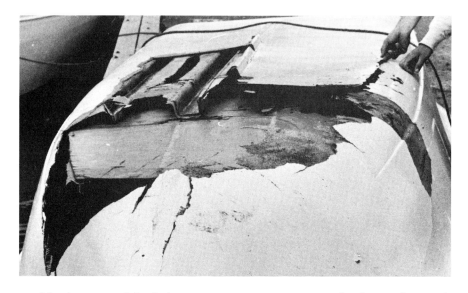

Figure 2-9. *Fiberglass is not indestructible. Prolonged pounding in head seas at high speeds can cause fatigue cracks and perhaps massive failure if the boat is not built to the highest standards. This boat was damaged in a race at Fond du Lac, Wisconsin. (Milwaukee Sentinel photo)*

Not long ago I had the opportunity to examine the bow of a stock fiberglass boat that was leaking from a crack near her stem. The crack resulted from an abrupt discontinuity of the stem reinforcement. The thick reinforcement should have been thinned at its edges gradually to minimize fatigue.

Many of the better-built European boats have longitudinal stringers inside the hull that provide extra stiffening, enhance hull fairness, resist oil-canning and fatigue stresses from head seas, and dissipate the strains imposed by taut rigging. Unfortunately, stringers are not very often found on mass-produced American sailing boats. Another method of adding longitudinal stiffness without excessive weight is with C-Flex fiberglass construction. Developed by Seemann Plastics of New Orleans, C-Flex uses "planks" consisting of closely spaced rigid glass rods held together with roving and cloth. Boats are planked with the rods running longitudinally the entire length of the hull, and when the material is saturated with resin, great fore-and-aft stiffness results. The method is most suitable for one-off (i.e., custom-built) hulls.

More will be said about inspections and looking for flaws in fiberglass and other forms of construction when we discuss preparations for sea in Chapter 4.

Wood Construction

A primary consideration with wood construction should be the inhibition of dry rot. Suitable woods such as teak, mahogany, Douglas fir, longleaf yellow pine, and white oak (for structural members) should be used, and they should be well dried and treated with a wood preservative. It is essential that adequate ventilation be provided below decks and that all dead air pockets be eliminated. There should be ventilation holes in all lockers and closed spaces, ceilings or inner skins should be open at

Figure 2-10. *C-Flex is a fiberglass construction method that uses ''planks'' made of rigid fiberglass rods. These long planks, stapled to a wood framework, are held together with resin-saturated roving. The principal advantages of this system are its flexibility in construction and its longitudinal strength. (Courtesy Seemann Plastics Inc.)*

the top or preferably slotted, and forepeaks and after lazarettes should be aired with cowl or venturi ventilators. Butt blocks, floor timbers, mast steps, and other such potential water traps should be beveled or provided with adequate drains or limber holes to prevent the collection of displaced bilgewater or fresh water from condensation or rainwater leakage.

An adequate ceiling inside a boat adds considerably to her longitudinal strength. For this reason and others, bilge stringers are often omitted from modern, ceiled boats of conventional wood construction. Yet Swedish designer-builder Gustav Plym believes that for the very roughest weather offshore a sailing yacht may need the extra support of a bilge stringer. In his book *Yacht and Sea*, Plym describes how his *Elseli IV* suffered broken frames and superficially split planks during the rough Fastnet race of 1957. He came to the conclusion that the planks and ribs had flexed on either side of a rigid bulkhead and that bilge stringers were needed to distribute the stress. Steel frames or floors are sometimes used for rigidity, but they may suffer from rust or galvanic corrosion, particularly when fastenings of dissimilar metals are used.

Boats with glued seams have rigid, almost monolithic, watertight hulls, but the builder must foresee the inevitable shrinking and swelling of the wood that results from drastic temperature and humidity changes and from the alternate drying out and saturating of the hull as it is hauled and launched. A conscientious, knowledgeable builder will use woods with low rates of shrinkage and the proper initial moisture content (approximately 12 percent). Square planking strips, oriented with the annual rings perpendicular rather than parallel to the side of the hull, and the use of semiflexible glues and edge nailing also help. When inflexible epoxy glue is used, the strips should not be fastened to continuous frames. The hull is best painted white in hot climates.

Since the advent of modern, waterproof glues after World War II, many boats have been built of laminated wood, either molded or in flat plywood sheets. Round-bottomed boats must usually be molded or built up in layers of thin veneer, bent either hot or cold over a mold or framing. This construction, using veneer strips laid diagonally with each layer crossing the one beneath at nearly right angles, provides one of the highest possible strength-to-weight ratios. A popular method of cold molding is the WEST System (Wood Epoxy Saturation Technique) developed by the Gougeon brothers of Bay City, Michigan. This method uses epoxy glues and coatings, which not only add strength and seal out moisture but also provide great stiffness and hull rigidity. Although there is unusual inherent strength in modern molded systems, they seldom justify ruthless abandonment of fastenings and framing, as is sometimes done with ultralight offshore racing boats. Also, the skin should be sufficiently thick to resist puncturing and possible wrinkling from diago-

Figure 2-11. *Wooden hull construction.*

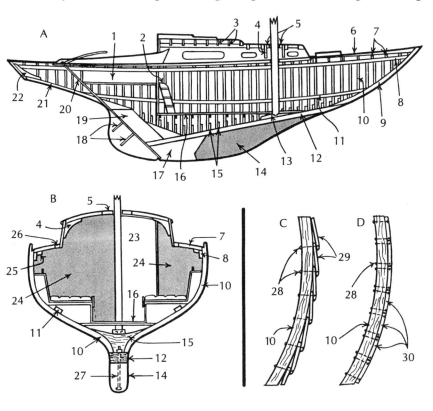

1 - cockpit well	9 - stem	17 - false keel	25 - deck shelf
2 - companion ladder	10 - rib or frame	18 - rudder straps	26 - carlin
3 - cabin beams	11 - bilge stringer	19 - deadwood	27 - keel bolt
4 - hanging knees	12 - keel	20 - rudder stock	28 - fastenings
5 - mast partners	13 - mast step	21 - horn timber	29 - clinker planks
6 - rail	14 - ballast keel	22 - stern knee	or lapstrake
7 - deck beams	15 - floor timbers	23 - doorway	30 - carvel planking
8 - clamp	16 - cabin sole	24 - bulkhead	

nal stress. Exterior epoxy coatings are subject to damage from sunlight, so the exposed surface should be protected with paint or varnish with an ultraviolet filter.

Sheet plywood has many advantages for the amateur builder, but the hull must be especially designed (usually with a hard-chine form) for the material, because the sheets cannot be bent into compound curves. Top-grade marine plywood should be used for boatbuilding, and the wood must be kept well painted, especially on any exposed edges, which are vulnerable to delamination from water seepage. Plywood is often covered with fiberglass cloth bonded with epoxy resin, which generally makes a tough, strong, and rigid construction, but the bonding of fiberglass to plywood is not as strong as that of fiberglass to fiberglass when subjected to stresses that tend to pull the laminations apart. Naval architect Robert Harris tells us that when the anticipated load is at 90 degrees to a fiberglass-plywood bonded surface, the glass should be through-bolted; otherwise the bond might fail as a result of the wood surface fibers pulling apart. Regardless of the hull material, sheet plywood is often suitable for stiffening and for structural members such as knees and bulkheads. Oval openings and doorways with rounded instead of square corners will avoid stress concentrations.

The blistering problems of many fiberglass boats and a renewed interest in classic yachts may help bring about a renaissance in wood construction. Wood is already reappearing in mainstream boatbuilding as conventional construction is modified to take advantage of modern materials and technology. Two examples of composite construction that use

Figure 2-12. *Strip-plank construction. Gluing and edge-nailing wood strips one on top of the other makes a strong, bottle-tight hull that requires a minimum of frames. (W.H. Ballard photo)*

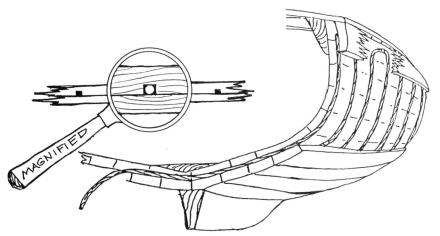

Figure 2-13. *The Cutts method of wooden boatbuilding reinforces the planks with athwartship cords of Kevlar. (Courtesy Cutts & Case)*

wood as the basic material are Durakore and the Cutts Patent Method. The latter, developed and patented by boatyard owner Edmund Cutts of Oxford, Maryland, reinforces wood with Kevlar windings. Laid into athwartship grooves routed out of a planked inner skin, the Kevlar cord is epoxy glued and then covered with a slightly thinner exterior planking. A boat built by this method is said to be extremely rigid, light, and impervious to rot.

Durakore is a sandwich system developed by the Baltek Corporation. Preformed strip planks are encapsulated within layers of fiberglass, carbon fiber, or Kevlar fabric. Composed of balsa and mahogany, the strips incorporate precut finger joints for end-to-end splicing and are edge fastened with epoxy resin. As with the Cutts method, Durakore construction requires minimal internal framing and therefore increases interior space while producing a light yet rigid hull. These methods are promising, but they must withstand the test of time with regard to water penetration, degradation from the sun, and exposure to temperature extremes.

Naval architect Ted Brewer sums up conventional wood construction well when he writes: "'Well built,' when applied to a wooden hull, means bronze, copper, mahogany, teak, and white oak. It does not mean red oak, birch, galvanized nails, black spruce, etc."

Metal Construction

Welded metal hulls are strong, abrasion-resistant, and free from rot, worm, and osmotic destruction. Their particular enemy, but one that can be overcome with proper care, is corrosion and deterioration by galvanic action and electrolysis. Close attention should be given to electric wiring (which should be done by a qualified marine electrician), and fastenings and other metals used in construction and the metal in bottom paints should be electrolytically compatible with the hull shell.

When it is necessary to use dissimilar metals, they should be close together on the galvanic scale (see Figure 4-1) or insulated with a barrier material such as neoprene. Metal hulls should be fitted with sacrificial zinc anodes or protective voltage systems, though according to some authorities such measures can be overdone and can lead to hydrogen embrittlement. Robert L. Kocher, technical editor of *National Fisherman* magazine, recommends for a steel hull a protective voltage no greater than 0.2 volt more negative than it would be without the protective systems. More will be said about this subject in Chapter 4.

Of conventional boatbuilding materials, steel is the most rugged, providing great strength and maximum puncture protection in collisions and groundings. But it has a number of drawbacks, the most obvious being rust and weight. Insulation against sound, condensation, and especially temperature is desirable, and correcting for compass deviation may be tricky. Welded steel construction is inexpensive, but designer Francis S. Kinney warns that careful welding in proper sequence is important to minimize hull distortion. He advises welding the shell and deck plating simultaneously, and welding the seams before the butts. Fairness is assured with close spacing of frames, but South African designer Dudley Dix, who has had much experience with steel, has endorsed widely spaced frames with closely spaced stringers. Hard-chine hulls are the most suitable for amateur building.

Some of the modern, high-strength steels such as Corten resist rust, but the hull must be carefully prepared and treated with protective coatings. The hull should first be shot- or sandblasted, then sprayed with hot zinc or coated with epoxy and finally finished with a proven painting system. Every effort should be made to eliminate remote and hidden pockets inside the boat that cannot be reached for inspection and maintenance.

Weight is not a serious problem for a steel cruising boat unless she is under about 35 feet. Anything smaller will probably be so heavy that the ballast weight will have to be compromised. The thinnest possible plating is often used to reduce weight, and the very experienced and skillful Dutch builders will sometimes use topside plating .116 inch thick on a welded hull. Lloyds requires .137-inch plating, although British authority Douglas Phillips-Birt tells us that the Society is concerned with allowance for wastage, which is not now the problem it once was. The thinnest limit suggested by Ted Brewer, an experienced designer of steel boats, is .125 inch, partly due to the adverse effect on hull fairness when thinner plating is used.

Aluminum construction is much more expensive but very light and strong, and the newest marine alloys stoutly resist saltwater corrosion. Its greatest disadvantages are high susceptibility to electrolysis or galvanic action and the need for insulation against sound, temperature, and condensation. The forward plating is not always adequately supported with structural members, and several ocean racers have had their bows dented by head seas. Aluminum is more susceptible than steel to fatigue in areas where there is continual vibration (in way of a severely vibrating engine or propeller shaft).

The electrolysis/galvanic action problem is best solved by using compatible metals (stainless steel, for example) and insulating necessary noncompatibles from each other with inert materials such as Micarta, Tuflol, or neoprene (more about galvanic corrosion in Chapter 4). Copper and bronze are particularly harmful in contact with aluminum in salt water. Care must be taken not to use damaging antifoulants, particularly copper and mercury paints. Det Norske Veritas warns against lead-based paint, but Francis Kinney writes that its use is permissible when the hull is well primed with zinc chromate. Tin-based antifouling paints have long been the first choice for aluminum hulls, but these paints are coming under increasing regulation for environmental reasons. Their use is now federally banned on non-aluminum hulls less than 80 feet long, and in the state of Florida they may be applied only by licensed personnel in yards authorized to handle toxic materials.

Some aluminum alloys can be weakened by welding; for example, an alloy strengthened by heat treatment will revert locally to the strength of a non-heat-treatable alloy when welded. Also, aluminum welds are not as strong as the metal (in contrast with steel welds). Although it may cause unfairness in the shell plating, welded joints can be strengthened by overlapping the plates as though they were to be riveted. Care must be taken to avoid creating pockets that can trap water.

Ferrocement Construction

A surprisingly old boatbuilding material, steel-reinforced concrete, commonly called ferrocement, has enjoyed a revival in recent years. In modern construction with this material, thin layers of cement are applied to both sides of a metal skeletal form of the boat comprising bent pipe frames connected with longitudinal steel rods and wire mesh. The advantages of ferrocement include tremendous strength, which theoretically increases with age due to slow curing; rigidity, with the ability to absorb heavy impact; fire resistance; low maintenance; and natural insulation against sound and temperature. The disadvantages are the difficulty of obtaining a fair hull due in part to sagging of the wire mesh under the weight of the mortar; susceptibility to abrasion, although new mortars such as Ferro-lite are said to overcome this problem; the difficulty of detecting and eliminating voids in the cement, which has contributed to a number of dangerously flawed home-built craft and a bad name for ferrocement in general; rust or galvanic corrosion within the metal framework; and excessive weight for small craft. Modern, lighter building techniques and materials may have reduced the smallest practical length of a seagoing cruiser to 40 feet or less. Indeed, the 35-foot ferrocement ketch *De Zeeuwse Stromen* sailed solo around the world nonstop, and she did so in the record time (since eclipsed) of 286 days.

Rust can be held in check by galvanizing, but one study of the problem reports significant galvanic action when galvanized and ungalvanized steels are mixed. An effective remedy is said to be the use of

Figure 2-14. *Pipe frames and longitudinal rods partially covered with wire mesh shown during the construction of a ferrocement boat.*

chromium trioxide (300 parts per million) in the mix water. To prevent possible unsightly rust streaks on the outside of the boat, mesh wiring ends should be on the inside of the hull. Some builders recommend welding to avoid the need for wire ties, but welding can exacerbate distortion.

Ferrocement has been touted as an inexpensive material well suited for home building, but more than a few backyards are home to distorted hulks left abandoned by frustrated builders. Unless you are exceptionally skilled and well informed, ferrocement building is best left to experienced professionals. If you do take it on, avoid slap-dash procedures and shortcuts such as the sometimes recommended use of chicken wire.

In conclusion, a boat owner must be certain his craft is suited in design and construction to her intended use, and avoid the temptation to use her for a purpose beyond that for which she is intended. But in addition, there must be a margin of safety for the unexpected, because one cannot always count on certainties where the sea is concerned.

Chapter 3
TYPES OF
SEAGOING CRAFT

What type of boat is the safest to take offshore? This question is the frequent subject of lively debates around the cabin table or yacht club bar. Typical choices range from a replica of Joshua Slocum's *Spray* to a conservative ocean racer, a heavy trawler-type powerboat, a double-ended Colin Archer Redningsskoite (sailing rescue boat), or even an unsinkable cruising multihull. The debaters can be grouped into three camps: the traditionalists, the modernists, and the moderates, whose ideas lie somewhere between the two extremes.

My own thinking belongs with the latter school. I believe that a monohulled, ballasted keel sailboat of moderate dimensions and proportions having good performance, a high range of stability, watertight integrity, and strong but not necessarily heavy construction is the safest boat to take to sea. Furthermore, I feel that a boat *specifically designed by a reputable naval architect for cruising offshore* is nearly always superior to a converted workboat such as an oyster dredger, fisherman, trawler, pilot vessel, or lifeboat, although it must be admitted that workboats can often be obtained at a low price and some have been converted satisfactorily. The design of a workboat or workboat derivative is influenced by the work she was made to perform, and she is given capabilities that usually detract from pure passagemaking.

It is often a mistake to judge a boat's seaworthiness by her record, especially for one particular passage. The success of a passage may hinge on good weather, good luck, or unusually good seamanship, rather than the inherent seaworthiness of the vessel. The Atlantic has been crossed by rafts, a rubber kayak, a canvas folding boat, an amphibious jeep, and two boats under six feet long, but few knowledgeable sailors would recommend such craft as the safest to take offshore.

Offshore Sailing Craft

Sailboat traditionalists prefer a heavy-displacement hull with a long keel, a deep forefoot, a generous beam, and perhaps a pointed stern for

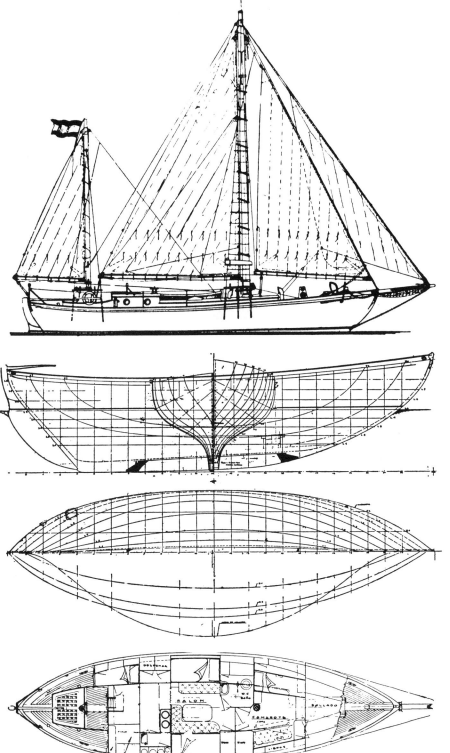

Figure 3-1. *Plans of the Gaucho, a Colin Archer Redningsskoite type, similar to Type A in Figure 3-2. She was built by Manuel Campos in Buenos Aires for Ernesto Uriburu, who made several notable ocean passages in her in the 1940s. Dimensions are: LOA, 50 feet; LWL, 42 feet; beam, 14 feet; draft, 7 feet, 5 inches; displacement, 28 tons; and sail area, 969 square feet.*

offshore work. Examples include the North Sea pilot cutters or Redningsskoites typical of designs by Colin Archer, or the so-called Tahiti or *Carol* ketches designed by John G. Hanna (see Figure 3-2 for the general type). Heavy double-enders have made many celebrated deep-water passages, which include the circumnavigations of Erling Tambs's *Teddy*, Al Petersen's *Stornoway*, Jean Gau's *Atom*, Tom Steel's *Adios*, J.Y.

Figure 3-2. *Offshore sailboat hull types.*

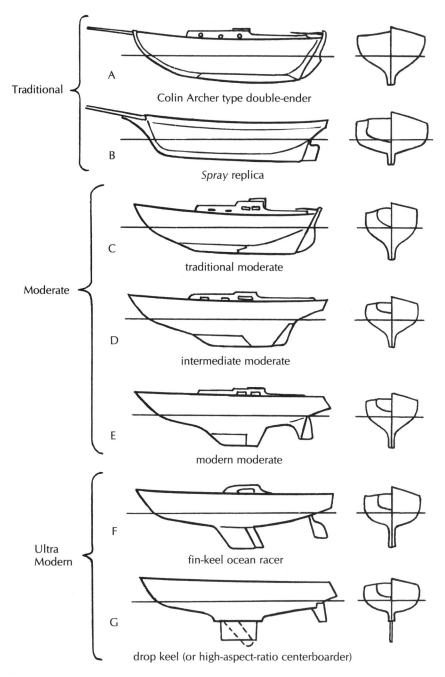

Traditional
A — Colin Archer type double-ender
B — *Spray* replica

Moderate
C — traditional moderate
D — intermediate moderate
E — modern moderate

Ultra Modern
F — fin-keel ocean racer
G — drop keel (or high-aspect-ratio centerboarder)

LeToumelin's *Kurun*, Vito Dumas's *Lehg II*, and Robin Knox Johnston's *Suhaili* (the latter three being quite similar to Colin Archer boats). These vessels are seakindly and able, but in boat design compromises are always necessary, and the heavy double-ender has weaknesses.

A decided drawback of this type is its poor to mediocre sailing performance, especially to windward and in light airs. Speed and weatherliness not only make a boat fun to sail, but they can be important for safety when one is trying to dodge a storm, make port in good time against a headwind, or claw off a lee shore in heavy weather. Then too, vessels with extremely long keels are slow to turn and subject to getting in irons when tacking. Smart maneuverability is becoming increasingly important on today's crowded waterways.

Though it was long argued otherwise, I think most designers now agree that the double-ender enjoys little if any special advantage when running off in a seaway. It has been said that a sharp stern will "part" a following sea, but the behavior of a vessel when running off will depend on her hull form forward as well as aft, her buttock lines and run, the distribution of her displacement, the shape of her ends, and the buoyancy of her bow and stern—whether the stern be pointed or square. There have been good and bad downwind performers with sharp sterns, with counters, and with transom sterns. It is true that a sharp stern will not slam as a long, flat counter will in certain conditions. Sufficient (but not excessive) buoyancy aft will encourage the stern to lift to a following sea. The designer of a double-ender must be especially careful to keep fullness aft, there being inherently less volume in a pointed (or sharp canoe-type) stern than in one that is square. The Colin Archer and Tahiti sterns are well rounded and thus have ample buoyancy. It is worth noting that the double-enders developed to cope with the short, steep seas of the Baltic have even more fullness above the waterline aft than the Colin Archer or Tahiti types. An example of a modern, smart-sailing boat with the rounded Baltic stern is the Robert Perry-designed Valiant, which has made many successful voyages, including several circumnavigations.

Whether or not its stern is sharp or square, a heavy, traditional hull typically carries generous beam and a deep forefoot. This combination can lead to problems when scudding (running off) in heavy weather if the entrance is fine, because the vessel may root (bury her bow and trip on her forefoot), and this might in turn cause her to pitchpole (turn end over end) or broach-to (turn uncontrollably beam-to the wind and seas).

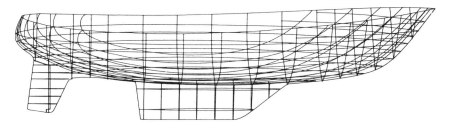

Figure 3-3. *The Valiant 40, designed by Robert Perry, shows the rounded Baltic stern in a modern hull. Her full sections aft produce plenty of buoyancy for following seas.*

Figure 3-4. *Plans of Joshua Slocum's* Spray, *the first boat to be sailed around the world singlehanded. The dotted lines in the sail plan show the rig changes made by Slocum in South America after crossing and recrossing the Atlantic. Her dimensions were: LOA, 36 feet, 9 inches; LWL, 32 feet, 1 inch; beam, 14 feet, 1 inch; draft, 4 feet, 1 inch; displacement, 16 tons; sail area (yawl rig), 1,161 square feet.*

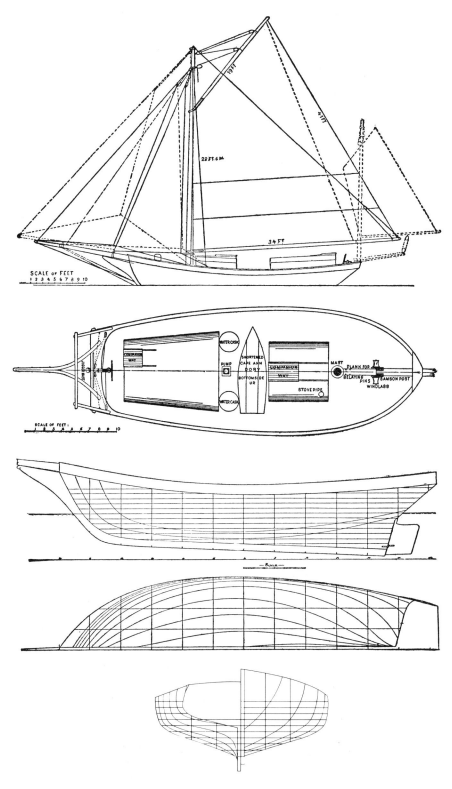

You will recall from Chapter 1 that broad beam has an adverse effect on a boat's stability range and resistance to capsizing. Roderick Stephens, Jr., experienced seaman and authority on yacht design, writes, "I presume the tendency to pitchpole is stimulated by excessive beam." Noted naval architect and design critic Robert G. Henry, Jr., elaborates by saying: "Given two boats of the same size and displacement, the one with the greater beam would have more displacement amidships and less in the ends. I think this loss of buoyancy in the bow tends to encourage rooting and possible pitchpoling. That is also why I like to have a fairly high prismatic coefficient in my designs, because a low prismatic is an indication that the midship section is too big compared to the other nine sections." (The prismatic coefficient is a measure of how the displacement is distributed longitudinally in a boat's underbody. A high coefficient, perhaps about .55 to .60, indicates abundant fullness in the ends.) Normally, the traditional double-ender has sufficient buoyancy in her ends, but it is worth noting that one of these vessels, the very beamy *Sandefjord*, pitchpoled while running before a blow in the mid-Atlantic in 1935. She survived but lost one crewmember and her mizzenmast.

For many traditionalists, Captain Slocum's *Spray* represents the ultimate in small boat seaworthiness. Slocum was the first solo circumnavigator, and his classic book, *Sailing Alone Around the World*, kindled the spirit of adventure in countless sailors and created a legion of *Spray* devotees. Many admirers of Slocum, including myself, have developed a real sentimental affection for the old *Spray*, which began her career as an oyster sloop decades before she rounded the world. Although this vessel

Figure 3-5. *The* Spray *steering herself on the wind with the jib trimmed in flat and the mainsheet eased just a bit. Her mizzen is not bent and her portable jibboom is run in. (Photo courtesy The Peabody Museum, Salem, Massachusetts)*

Figure 3-6. *The* Spray, *formerly* Sojourner, *a slightly enlarged (44-foot), ketch-rigged replica of Joshua Slocum's* Spray, *Type B in Figure 3-2.*

served her master well and had multiple virtues, we should not be blind to her faults. Her long keel and outboard rig (especially the long bowsprit) helped give her a remarkable balance that permitted self-steering, which is nearly essential for singlehanding. Her heavy displacement and great beam gave her high initial stability, roominess, and the ability to carry quantities of supplies without detracting from her performance. Despite her beam, she had ample buoyancy in her ends with a prismatic coefficient of .65. On the other hand, her rig was large, heavy, and less safe to handle than an inboard rig; she was a sluggard to windward; and she had a less-than-desirable range of stability. Latterday stability curves show that her maximum righting moment occurred at only about 35 degrees angle of heel, while positive stability was zero at 95 to 100 degrees. The ideal range extends at least to 140 degrees (see Chapter 1), at which angle the boat will right herself immediately. An offshore monohull sailboat should have positive recovery from a 120-degree knockdown *at the very minimum.*

The successful voyages of the *Spray* and her replicas are sometimes offered as evidence of extreme seaworthiness, but Slocum was a masterful seaman, and one of the replicas, the *Pandora*, did capsize (righting again when her masts snapped) in the South Atlantic shortly after rounding Cape Horn in 1911. Other craft with greater reserve stability have also capsized, and I do not mean to imply that the *Spray* is the worst type to take offshore. In my opinion, however, there are presently better and safer designs for bluewater sailing.

Vessels similar to the *Spray* or the double-enders carry little (and

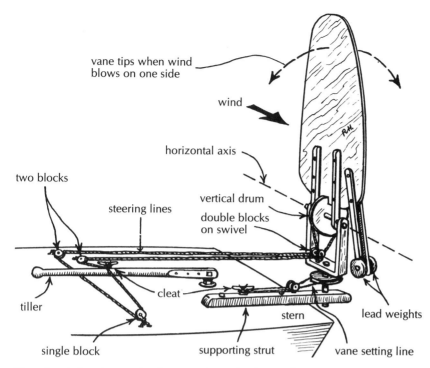

vane tips when wind blows on one side

wind

horizontal axis

two blocks

steering lines

vertical drum

double blocks on swivel

tiller

cleat

single block

supporting strut

stern

lead weights

vane setting line

Note: for clarity, the steering lines are shown leading to the side of the boat opposite the supporting strut, but in actual practice the steering lines would probably be led to the side on which the strut is mounted.

Figure 3-7. *A wind vane self-steerer with a horizontal axis.*

sometimes no) keel ballast, and they depend on their great beam, internal ballast, and heavy displacement for their stability. Many of these craft have made remarkable passages and weathered severe storms, but some have turned turtle. In addition to the *Pandora* and the Colin Archer-designed *Sandefjord*, the Tahiti double-enders *Adios* and *Atom* rolled over, and *Lehg II* capsized. Perhaps any other small craft would have done the same under similar conditions, but a greater range of stability and thus a greater margin of safety can be achieved with equally strong but less massive construction, the weight saved being consigned to outside keel ballast. This is perfectly possible with the technology, materials, and construction methods we have today. Such boats are now being produced in the form of fiberglass double-enders. There is a limit, however, since too much ballast would increase the metacentric height to the point of producing an excessively quick and uncomfortable rolling motion. As a rule of thumb, this tendency can be countered by limiting the beam to one-fourth the waterline length plus 3 feet.

Traditionalists feel that a long keel is necessary to facilitate self-steering. There was merit in this argument when self-steering had to be accomplished with sail trim alone, a near impossibility without the directional stability afforded by a long keel, but today, with the evolution of wind-vane steering (Figure 3-7) and power-efficient autopilots, it is possible to make most boats with short keels steer themselves on all

Figure 3-8. *Plans of the
Seawind-class ketch,
designed by Thomas C.
Gillmer, typical of Type C in
Figure 3-2. Her dimensions
are: LOA, 30 feet; LWL, 24
feet; beam, 9 feet, 5 inches;
draft, 4 feet, 3 inches; sail
area, 500 square feet.
(Courtesy Allied Boat Co.)*

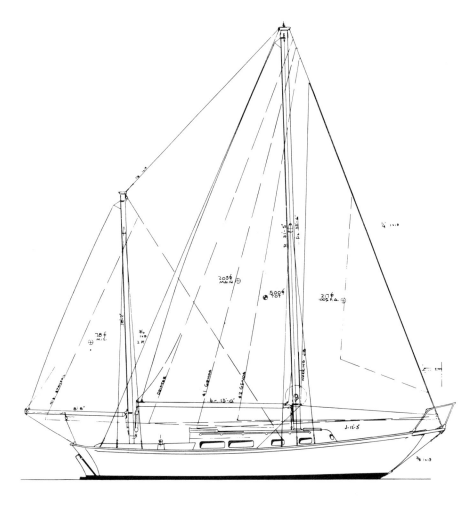

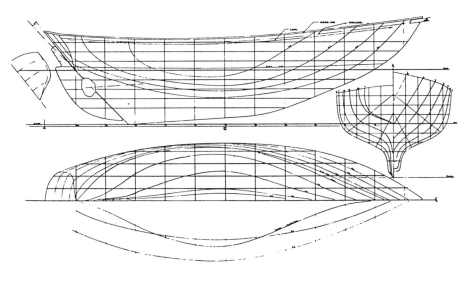

Figure 3-9. Seawind *ketch,
the* Ode, *on a close reach.
One of these 30-footers, the*
Apogee, *skippered by Alan
Eddy, is said to be the first
fiberglass boat to sail around
the world. Her robust
construction was sufficient to
withstand severe jostling
from a pod of whales at one
point during her
circumnavigation. (Courtesy
Mrs. Fred Thomas)*

points of sailing. In fact, the majority of singlehanded ocean racers produced today are so designed. A short, deep keel gives a boat more efficient lateral plane, which means greater hydrodynamic lift at moderate to fast speeds and therefore less tendency to make leeway; it also offers better maneuverability, the capacity to turn on the proverbial dime. In the cruising boat a short keel and cutaway forefoot lessen wetted surface drag and thus allow the use of a small, easy-to-handle rig. There is a point of diminishing returns, however, when directional stability becomes too sensitive and steering becomes difficult under unfavorable conditions, and a very short keel that is not excessively raked will require an undesirably deep draft and a nearly vertical leading edge subject to snagging underwater objects and shock loading when grounding. A moderately long keel allows easy hauling on a marine railway in remote cruising areas.

My choice would be D or E in Figure 3-2. Both boats have moderately short keels and hence reasonably low-wetted surfaces. Also, each keel is integral and is faired into the hull for maximum strength, leaving a hollow space above the keel ballast for tanks (effective additional ballast when full) and a sump to hold the bilge water (to prevent it from sloshing up under the bunks and cabin sole when heeled or in a seaway).

Offshore sailors seeking reasonable speed and performance to windward in a seakindly hull that can be balanced for self-steering without a wind vane might prefer type C (Figure 3-2). This type may use vane steering, but without it, her helm is reasonably steady, and usually she can be made to self-steer with sail combinations such as twin headsails (two similar-sized headsails boomed out on opposite sides with their sheets attached to the tiller). She is similar to the famous Laurent Giles-designed Vertue class. These small cruisers (or boats with similar lines) have probably made more extended offshore passages than any other small class boat. Some famous Vertues are: *Salmo, Speedwell of Hong Kong, Vertue XXXV, Icebird, Easy Vertue,* and *Cardinal Vertue,* the latter having been sailed around the world via Cape Horn by Bill Nance, an Australian. Also outstanding was the circumnavigation of South America via Cape Horn by the fiberglass Vertue *Sparrow,* sailed by Dan Hays with his father David exactly 20 years after Nance. The late circumnavigator and author Eric Hiscock considered the Vertue the "finest of all small cruisers," and his *Wanderer III* was a slightly larger version of a Vertue. I term Type C traditional-moderate.

Hull types F and G (Figure 3-2) are modern ocean racers of light displacement and low-wetted surface. They may be fast and close-winded, but in my opinion they are not the best type for extended offshore cruising. The extremely short keel can lead to steering difficulties while reaching or running in strong winds and confused following seas, even when the rudder is detached from the keel and moved aft. Behavior that is acceptable to an ocean racer with a large crew taking short tricks at the helm can be a serious problem for a shorthanded cruiser. Light displacement and hard, flat bilges are conducive to speed and high initial stability for sail-carrying ability, but this type of hull may have a quick, uncomfortable motion and will pound in head seas. Furthermore, it has a smaller roll moment of inertia than a heavier hull and, as pointed out in Chapter 1, may lack sufficient dynamic stability. If strongly built, such a boat will be seaworthy from the standpoint of constructional safety, but she is apt not to be seakindly or comfortable. An overly fatigued, seasick, or battered crew jeopardizes the overall safety of the vessel.

Another disadvantage of extremely light displacement for extended cruising is that the weight of stores for a full crew may seriously hamper performance. Moderately light displacement enhances buoyancy, however, and a light boat requires less sail area than a heavy one.

Hull type G represents the high-aspect-ratio, ballasted drop-keel boat

Figure 3-10. *The Classic 31, designed by Peter D. Van Dine, is representative of Type D in Figure 3-2. Dating from 1964, this boat has graceful lines. Her dimensions are: LOA, 31 feet; LWL, 22 feet, 4 inches; beam, 8 feet, 5 inches; draft, 4 feet 6 inches; sail area (of sloop), 393 square feet.*

Figure 3-11. *Plans of the*
Black Velvet II. *She was
designed by Ted Brewer as a
fast cruiser and is a fine
example of a Type E vessel
(Figure 3-2). Her dimensions
are: LOA, 43 feet, 2 inches;
LWL, 35 feet, 4 inches;
beam, 12 feet, 9 inches;
draft, 6 feet, 4 inches;
displacement, 12.4 tons; sail
area, 895 square feet.*

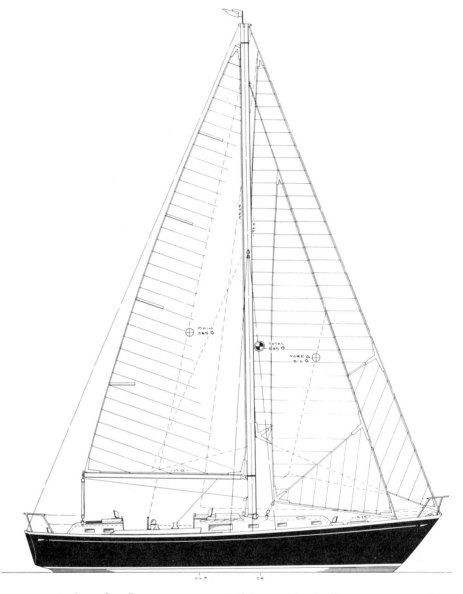

or centerboarder. In many respects this type is similar to some modern keel-centerboarders, the advantages and disadvantages of which are discussed in the section of Chapter 1 entitled "Designs for Open Waters." A drop-keel boat or centerboarder will yield to the seas when lying ahull and is not subject to tripping on a deep keel, but the ultimate stability of such a vessel concerns me. Before taking her to sea, consider having her stability at high angles of heel calculated by a naval architect; if the righting moments are questionable, it might be wise to keep the keel in its lowered position or to firmly secure added ballast deep within the bilge of a centerboarder. The stability range of many stock centerboarders can be obtained from USYRU (United States Yacht Racing Union). If the

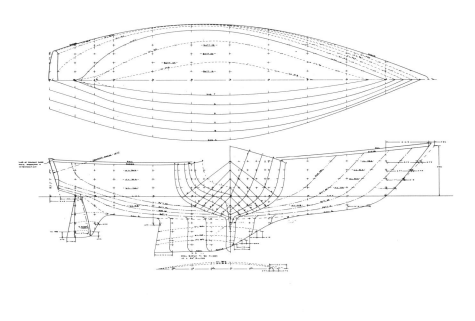

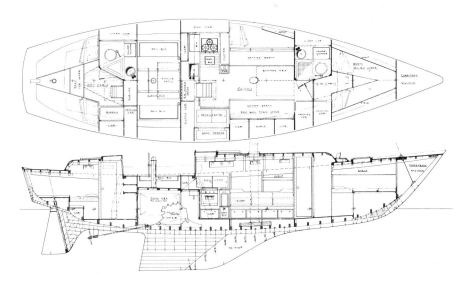

range is less than about 120 degrees, consider adding ballast for extensive voyaging.

A boat with a moderately short fin keel may have an advantage when lying ahull in that her keel will be stalled (not supplying lift for lateral resistance) when the boat is not forereaching, so that she will yield to beam seas and avoid tripping on her keel. In contrast, a long-keeled boat may have considerable lateral resistance even when she is not forereaching. This point will be dealt with in Chapter 12.

As previously alluded to, the modern trend toward low-wetted-surface, short keels has complicated steering. An offshore sailboat used

continued on pg. 62

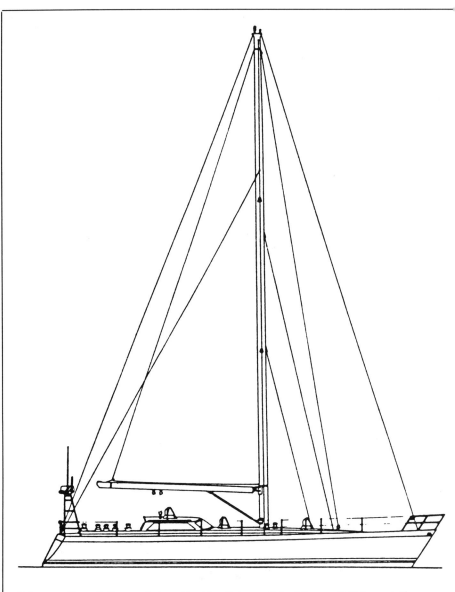

Figure 3-12. *Lines, sail plan, and deck layout of the* American Promise.

I have offered the opinion that hull type F in Figure 3-2 is not the best for ocean cruising. Tricky steering, the potential vulnerability of rudder and keel, an uncomfortable motion, and lack of dynamic stability often attend this hull shape in stock designs. Most of these problems can be overcome, however, and I present here three designs which have done or intend to do just that.

American Promise (Figure 3-12) is 60 feet long overall with a beam of 17 feet, 2 inches and a draft of 10 feet. Designed by Ted Hood for Dodge Morgan's record-setting nonstop solo circumnavigation, she is seaworthy, fast, and easy for a small crew to handle. The boat is

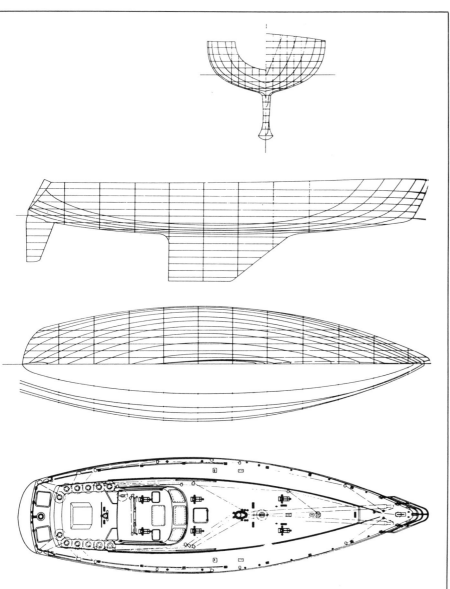

moderately light and cutter-rigged for efficiency on all points of sailing. *American Promise* is a high-tech boat with most systems redundant to allow backup capability for every type of gear failure. There is even an auxiliary rudder in a trunk that can be cranked down in the event the main spade rudder is damaged. The principal trade-offs are expense, the time and technical knowledge needed to service the copious gear, and her deep draft, which restricts cruising in shallow waters.

Figure 3-13 shows the *Sundeer*: LOA 67 feet; beam, 15 feet, 3 inches; draft, 6 feet, 2 inches. Based on Steve Dashew's *Deerfoot*

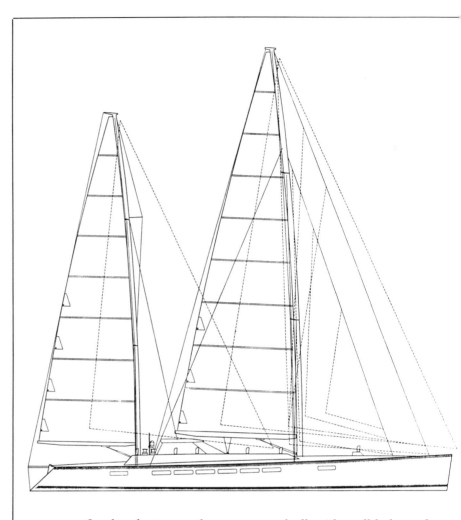

Figure 3-13. *The Dashew/Elvstrom – designed* Sundeer: *long and lean.*

concept, *Sundeer* features a long, narrow hull with well-balanced ends that will drive through head seas and keep a steady helm in most conditions even at fairly high angles of heel. She is capable of fast passages and handles exceedingly well under power. Her draft is reasonable for most cruising areas. Her narrow waterline beam compromises initial stability and room below somewhat, but the compromise is acceptable on a 67-foot boat with a small, easily shortened rig. Her low-aspect ketch rig achieves handiness and stiffness at moderate sacrifice to windward ability and performance under working sails in light airs. Although very comfortable and easily handled, she depends on complicated, expensive machinery and electrical gear. She'll be a fine cruiser if you like her looks and can afford her.

Holger Danske (Figure 3-14) is a 60-foot Class 1 BOC racer designed by Dave Gerr. This is a very specialized boat designed for

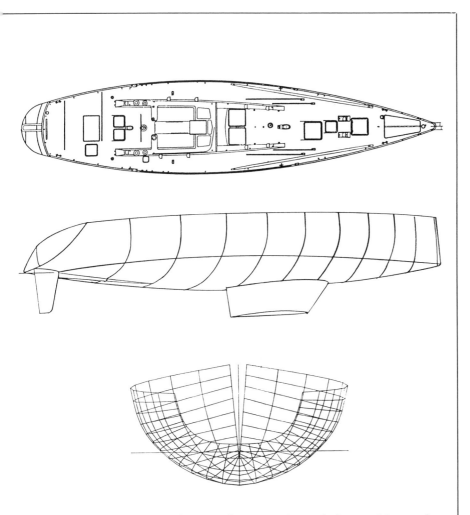

the specific purpose of succeeding in a 'round-the-world race for
singlehanders. Nevertheless, she has a number of features desirable for all seagoers, including the highest possible (180-degree)
range of stability to avoid capsizing, a small rig for easy handling,
the ability to beat to windward in heavy weather due in part to her
narrow beam (9 feet, 7 inches) and deep keel, and ample buoyancy
as a result of light displacement (7.5 tons). To obtain a light helm
with a large rudder at high speeds the rudder design was changed
from the skeg-hung version to a balanced spade, creating slightly
more drag. The rudder's position well forward of the stern will help
prevent ventilation from rollout when the boat is heeled, and the
trimming centerboard aft will help with directional stability at difficult times when running off. The helmsman's cockpit is rather
exposed, but there is a shelter cockpit offering fine protection at the
after end of the cabin trunk. The open stern affords quick cockpit

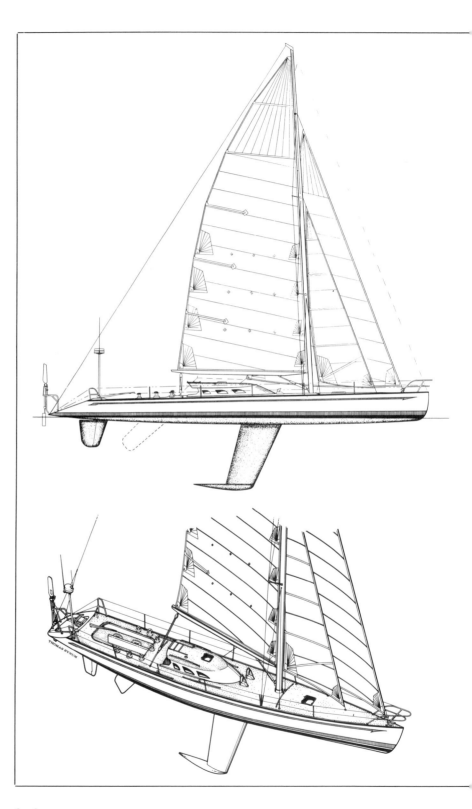

Figure 3-14. *The* Holger Danske, *designed for the BOC Round-the-World Race.*

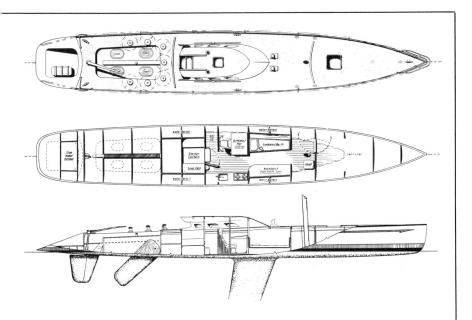

drainage but allows following seas to break aboard when running off at slow speeds in heavy weather. I would prefer that the crew's berth be farther aft near the boat's transverse (pitching) axis for less motion. The most obvious compromises rendering the boat impractical for a general-purpose cruiser are her deep draft (11$\frac{1}{2}$ feet), vulnerable keel, lack of accommodations, short rig and unfavorable sail area-to-wetted surface ratio (sacrificing performance in light airs), and the absence of an engine. Still, the *Holger Danske* will be extremely fast in a breeze and is about as safe as she can be made for her particular task, provided her wood/epoxy construction and keel/rudder engineering can be carried out according to expectations. The designer is fully aware of the stresses involved. The epoxy with which her hull is glued up, coated, and saturated is formulated by System Three Resins to cure properly at cold temperatures, which makes possible the choice of an inexpensive building site.

In sum, these three designs, well suited to their purposes, illustrate that a Type F profile can be combined with good balance, narrow to moderate beam, a modest, easily handled rig, and careful treatment of potentially vulnerable construction features to produce a fast and seaworthy offshore hull. These are, of necessity, big boats, and any such design will be a custom-built or at best a limited-production vessel. In other words, if you want a boat like one of these you must be able to afford it, which is why most of us oceangoing sailors will continue to find our boats among types D and E in Figure 3-2.

Figure 3-15. *Plans of the Noryema VII,* an ocean racer with a drop keel and outboard rudder, representative of Type G in Figure 3-8. She is from Dick Carter's board. Her dimensions are: LOA, 49 feet, 5 inches; LWL, 38 feet, 4 inches; beam, 13 feet, 8 inches; draft, 3 feet, 3 inches with keel and rudder raised, 8 feet, 2 inches with keel lowered; displacement, 14 tons; sail area, 958 square feet. (Yachting World)

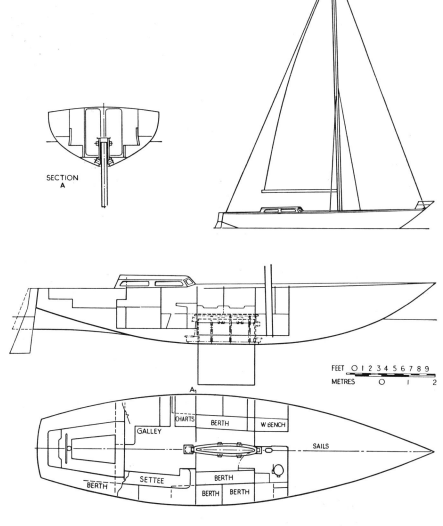

solely for cruising benefits from sufficient length of keel to permit hanging the rudder on the keel's trailing edge for maximum strength and protection. If the trailing edge of the keel is well forward of the after end of the waterline, however, the rudder must be detached from the keel and moved aft (as shown in E, F, and G in Figure 3-2) in order to lengthen the lever arm between the rudder's center of pressure and the boat's vertical turning axis. The freestanding spade (F and G in Figure 3-2) and the rudder attached to a skeg (E) are then the standard options. A spade rudder has its good points. It may be hydrofoil-shaped for great efficiency and also balanced (with its turning axis slightly abaft its leading edge) to let the water force assist in turning it. This allows use of a sensitive tiller even on a fairly large boat. A deep spade that is well placed and properly

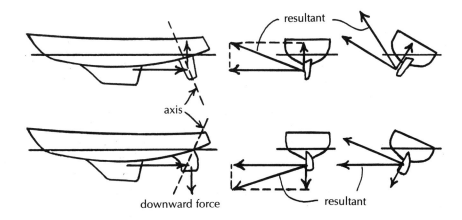

axis

downward force

resultant

resultant

Figure 3-16. *Raked rudder axes.*

raked can offer immediate response and very positive control when the helm is not hard over.

On the other hand, there are definitely some negative aspects of free-standing spades for cruising boats. An exposed rudder held only by its stock lacks the protection and support of a keel- or skeg-attached rudder, and it is more vulnerable to damage from grounding, flotsam, or even water forces in very bad conditions. As designer Dieter Empacher has written, "From the seaworthiness point of view, the stronger a rudder, the safer. Therefore a skeg-hung rudder is preferred over a spade rudder." Vulnerability can be reduced by extra-strong construction with exotic materials, but even these can fail, as demonstrated in the 1979 Fastnet Race when numerous rudders of carbon fiber disintegrated. Designer Karl Kirkman, chairman of the Cruising Club of America's Technical Committee, has written: "One of the greatest sources of trouble with high-strength composite materials, or 'exotics,' arises when a designer assumes for those materials properties derived from laboratory fabrication techniques, only to find that boatyard practice does not or cannot yield comparable results."

Another disadvantage of a balanced spade is that it will "grab" at times, and may cause the boat to spin rather than turn slowly should the helmsman release the tiller. Shorthanded, long-distance boats with spades may be more dependent on complicated self-steering devices, although this will vary in accordance with hull shape, length of keel, and other factors. Another consideration is that freestanding spades stall (lose their grip on the water) more easily than keel- or skeg-attached rudders, a characteristic that has contributed to the broaching or inadvertent rounding up of many a spinnaker-carrying racer when reaching. This problem is aggravated by an extremely short keel lacking a skeg; by positioning the rudder so far aft that it ventilates, sucking air down from the water surface; and especially by overly raking the rudder axis in the same direction as the leading edge of the keel, as shown in Figure 3-16. It is surprising how often one sees a spade rudder raked in this manner. Such a rake helps move the rudder's center of pressure aft for leverage, but when the boat is heeled and carries weather helm, the side force of the water on the rudder acts in an upward rather than a lateral direction.

Some spade rudders having little or no rake work well downwind when the boat is not heeled excessively and has good directional stability. Scott Allen, who helped his brother, Skip, sail a Cal 40 (a venerable class with a spade rudder) to victory in the downwind Honolulu Race in 1967, told me that the boat surfed under spinnaker for day after day, and there were never any steering problems even in strong winds. Naval architect Halsey Herreshoff attributes the Cal 40's steering control at least partially to the fact that "they have relatively long keels fore and aft, compared with the newest hot boats." The Cal 40's trapezoidal keel (not unlike E in Figure 3-2) is long at the top for directional stability but short at the bottom to reduce wetted surface; this shape also gives a high center of lateral resistance to lessen heeling, although it may not get the ballast as deep as a high-aspect-ratio fin.

Regardless of the effectiveness of this trapezoidal keel on ocean racers, however, for an offshore cruiser with a moderately short fin keel I would prefer a skeg aft, faired into the hull, and the rudder's entire leading edge attached to the skeg (see E, Figure 3-2). As mentioned, this arrangement not only delays stalling but also provides rudder protection and greater inherent strength than a freestanding spade. The skeg must be strongly made with a wide, sturdy base, and the hull should be reinforced above the base so that the skeg cannot be broken off or crack the hull.

An offshore monohull sailboat should possess the safety characteristics discussed in Chapter 1, including watertight integrity; self-bailing cockpit; adequate ballast, bilge pumps, and freeboard; proper piping and wiring; skidproof decks; sturdy handrails and toerails; an alternate exit hatch; unbreakable windows; and a raised companionway sill. In addition to these, a true seagoing boat should have moderate overhangs, a low and preferably rounded cabin trunk, small windows, large freeing ports if she has bulwarks, hatches and companionways located near the centerline, and preferably an inboard rig. The latter point will be discussed in Chapter 10, which deals with sails and rigging.

Overhangs should be moderate to dampen pitching and pounding, although slight overhangs offer reserve buoyancy when the ends are submerged in seas. Rod Stephens has written me in regard to the safest seagoing yacht, "Certainly the weight should be concentrated, which makes for a much drier boat reducing the amplitude of pitching."

Many modern racing cruisers and especially cruising racers have pronounced wedge-shaped hulls with very fine bows and broad, full afterbodies. This shape will knife through head seas, provide sail-carrying power, and encourage semiplaning of light, dinghy-type hulls, but it is seldom suitable for a seagoing cruiser. It produces an unbalanced hull that can develop bad steering characteristics including an intolerable weather helm and even complete loss of rudder control when the boat is well heeled, and it is vulnerable to rooting and possibly broaching-to

Figure 3-17. *A properly reinforced window and storm shutter of Plexiglas. (Rip Henderson photo)*

when running before steep, following seas. On the other hand, a completely symmetrical hull is undesirable because it lacks power, may roll rhythmically in following seas when the beam is narrow, and may hobbyhorse in head seas. A moderate, slightly wedge-shaped form with ample fullness aft and a fairly fine bow with sufficient flare and overhang for dryness and reserve buoyancy seems the best all-around compromise for offshore cruising.

A few bluewater sailors believe that the ideal offshore boat should be flush-decked, without any cabin trunk. I don't go this far, but I believe the cabin trunk should be as low as possible, rounded, and immensely strong. A trunk so designed affords the helmsman and those in the cockpit some protection against spray or seas breaking aboard, and its edge provides a convenient location for handrails to assist a crewmember moving along the deck. It also reduces negative (inverted) stability in the event of a capsize.

The large "picture" windows seen on many stock boats have no place offshore. Of course, as said before, glass should be unbreakable (safety glass, heavy acrylic, or preferably polycarbonate such as Tuffak or Lexan) and should be set in strong metal frames, but even so, the area should be small. The Offshore Rating Council recommends that windows with an area over two square feet be fitted with strong, rigid coverings (storm shutters). Other sponsors of ocean races require rigid covers for windows exceeding eight inches in height, regardless of area. Windows have been smashed not only by seas breaking aboard, but by impact with the water on the boat's lee side when she takes a sudden knockdown. An instructive example is the aforementioned case of Humphrey Barton in the *Vertue XXXV* (one window of which was considerably smaller than two square feet, by the way). In his book, Barton shows plans of a standard Vertue modified for "extended ocean cruising," with a lower cabin trunk and four small, round portholes on each side. Small ports may look old-fashioned, but they are sensible and have served well on such bluewater cruisers as Eric Hiscock's *Wanderer III*, Marcel Bardiaux's *Les 4 Vents*, Edward Allcard's *Sea Wanderer*, H.G. Hasler's *Jester*, Dr. Joseph Cunningham's *Icebird*, and many others.

Occasionally sailing cruisers have their companionways or hatches located off center, usually to solve some problem associated with the accommodation arrangements. For seagoing vessels, however, this practice can be dangerous, because a knockdown that submerges the rail nearest the off-center hatch could allow flooding or leakage through the hatchway. This happened to Captain John C. Voss when he rode out a typhoon in the 25-foot *Sea Queen* off Japan in 1912. The yawl heeled over and began shipping water through her companionway to such an extent that Voss was forced to wear ship onto the other tack in storm winds of nearly 100 miles an hour in order to keep his boat afloat. An especially dangerous practice is the use of nonwatertight spinnaker launching hatches on the bows of some racers. A ton-cup boat of my acquaintance took on considerable water through her spinnaker launchers during a heaving-down test.

Handicap rating rules have had and continue to have a tremendous influence on the design of offshore racing cruisers. This was not necessarily bad in the heyday of the CCA (Cruising Club of America) rule, when a yacht's rating was derived from a comparison of her measurements with those of a "base" or ideal boat, one that designers generally agreed was a reasonably sound, safe, and wholesome type. Unfortunately, the situation has now changed, and the IOR (International Offshore Rule) has produced boats that are far from ideal for ocean sailing. Some of these racers suffer from exceedingly light scantlings; overly wide beam amidships; a bow that is too low and fine with a deep, sharp knuckle under the cutwater that can lead to rooting; extremely chopped, retrousse sterns and even open transoms which lack reserve buoyancy and leave the cockpit vulnerable to following seas; daggerboards that detract from reserve stability or exceedingly short keels that can lead to steering problems and excessive leeway at low speeds (and even at high speeds when the boat is well heeled); vulnerable high-aspect-ratio skegs or spade rudders; and extremely tall and often flimsy rigs for offshore work. Rod Stephens once told me that many of the new boats were too wide and flat, while veteran sailor-designer Henry Scheel worried that the flat forward topsides of some of the new boats were susceptible to oil canning. In the second edition of this book I decried the IOR influence, saying: "Loss of life has resulted from the shortcomings of all-out racers taken to sea, and I think it is about time the rating rules are drastically modified to encourage seaworthy offshore boats."

Those words were written just before the infamous Fastnet Race in 1979, in which 15 sailors died, 77 boats suffered extreme knockdowns (masts deeply submerged) or capsizes, and 24 boats were abandoned. It would be wrong to blame this tragedy on poor yacht design alone, but some of the above-mentioned design deficiencies contributed in no small way to the problems encountered. A major culprit was indeed the IOR, which permitted racing in the most hostile offshore waters in small boats that were too light, too beamy, and too flat-bottomed, with high centers of gravity and vulnerable or improper (for severe storm conditions) keels, rudders, and rigs.

Now, changes are taking place—too slowly perhaps, but in the right direction toward the development of more wholesome offshore yachts. In America and even in Europe the IOR is gradually being replaced by the IMS (International Measurement System), which more equitably and scientifically handicaps yachts and encourages the design of dual-purpose boats (racing and cruising) that may be taken offshore with reasonable assurance of safety. The IMS is imperfect, and it may become less effective in producing seagoing boats as designers inevitably exploit the rating loopholes, but the rule is beginning to produce healthy effects on ocean racers. Hulls are not so distorted as a result of having their forms wrapped around optimal measurement points; light displacement is penalized; wetted surface is measured, obviating the need to skimp on rudder and keel area; moderate beam is encouraged; extremely light rigs are not allowed; and relatively sensible accommodations standards discourage the production of flimsy, skinned-out racing machines. There is even an ultimate stability requirement, although it is woefully inadequate. At present, IMS boats need a positive stability range to only 95 degrees, but in all probability this requirement will soon be extended to 105 degrees, and there is talk of an eventual extension to 120 degrees.

Offshore Multihull Sailboats

One of the most controversial subjects in the world of offshore cruising concerns the seaworthiness of sailing multihulls (catamarans, trimarans, proas, and the like). More and more of these craft are taking to the open sea, and many have made remarkably speedy and successful passages. Opinions of leading designers range from that of catamaran designer Roland Prout, who said, "I believe that a 45-foot catamaran is the safest possible craft, with few of the dangers of conventional ballasted boats," to the other extreme expressed by venerable monohull designer Olin Stephens, who has "no use for them [catamarans] at all as seagoing boats."

From the standpoint of safety, multihulls offer the following:

- Unballasted multihulls are (or can easily be made) unsinkable and can serve as a liferaft in the event of a capsize.
- There is almost no danger of accumulative or rhythmic rolling when sailing downwind.
- There is less danger of broaching-to.
- Thanks to the multihull's low angle of heel, there is less danger of losing crew overboard.

- The shallow draft of most multihulls allows beaching, which can allow the crew to escape from a serious lee-shore grounding.
- A multihull's speed enhances its chances of evading heavy weather.

Arguments against multihulls from the standpoint of safety include:

- *Most* multihulls have a *relatively low* range of static stability and are more susceptible to capsizing.
- They have enormous stability when upside down and lack the ability to self-right.
- Their great initial stability and inability to heel puts greater stress on the rig and does not allow the sails to spill wind.
- Most multihulls are extremely sensitive to weight, and overloading can be seriously detrimental to performance and even increase susceptibility to capsizing.
- Some multihulls are vulnerable to structural damage from forces tending to separate the hulls or amas (floats), or from stress generated by high speed combined with lightweight construction.
- Multihulls lack weatherliness, or the ability to claw away from a lee shore or quickly reach an upwind destination.

There are varying degrees of truth in these arguments both pro and con, but it is extremely difficult to generalize. Many of the multihull losses have resulted from the poor design and construction of home-built boats, from faulty seamanship, or from racing sailors driving over-rigged, lightly built boats too long and hard in heavy weather. Multihull designer Dick Newick has written, "Multihulls excel in high performance, which attracts those who want to win races; sometimes these speed demons don't have the discretion to know when to stop pushing their boats. Their disasters can be expensive lessons, showing us where the limits are, if we have the wits to learn."

It is perhaps necessary to take both the pro and con arguments with a grain of salt, for the critics as well as the enthusiastic proponents of multihulls often become emotionally involved and tend to overstate. Take, for instance, the claim that multihulls are safer because they aren't as apt to lose crew overboard. Since 1984, three of the most experienced, oceangoing multihull sailors—Rob James, Daniel Gillard, and Olivier Moussy—were lost overboard. It is true that knocked-down monohulls can and often have pitched their crew into the sea, but there are other security hazards for multihullers such as a jerky motion, sudden acceleration, and empty spaces between hulls. Every offshore boat needs pulpits, lifelines, jacklines, safety harnesses, and nets or barriers covering open spaces.

The claim by critics that multihulls can fall apart at sea is for the most part based on the experiences of those sailing home-built boats, far-out racers, or inexpensive stock designs that were never intended for offshore use. Nevertheless, it is true that the forces seeking to rip apart the hulls can be enormous, and high speeds increase stress on the hull and vulnerability to damage from collisions with flotsam or even sealife. Wing decks connecting hulls or amas must be substantial, but according to results of capsize tests by engineer Donald Jordan and the U.S. Coast Guard (see Chapter 12), the connecting members should not be entirely closed or airfoil shaped, as it is possible for wind forces to combine with wave forces to increase the possibility of a capsize. To guard against collisions at high speeds, authorities such as designer Chris White advocate collision bulkheads forward. These are especially important for a catamaran, which could capsize if one hull should be stove in and flooded.

It is difficult to compare the sailing behavior of a mono with a multi because of the differences among individual boats, but one might make a few generalizations, keeping in mind that there are plenty of exceptions. Multis have a far greater potential for speed, although many cruisers are slower than expected sailing upwind and in light airs. Speed can be a safety benefit at times, as when it becomes necessary to reach port in a hurry or to avoid a storm. The windward performance and tacking ability of many stock cruising multihulls leaves much to be desired, but weatherliness and smartness in stays can often be improved by deepening underwater appendages, concentrating weight amidships, and providing a solid anchor for the jibstay so that it can be carried taut. Multihull designers such as Andrew Simpson, Rudy Choy, and Dick Newick, to name a few, put some emphasis on windward ability, and many of their designs compare well with close-winded monohull racers. Even when a multihull cannot point very high it can often foot sufficiently fast for a respectable Vmg (velocity made good).

The Bruce number provides a quick means of evaluating a multihull's likely performance:

$$\text{Bruce number} = \frac{\sqrt{SA}}{\sqrt[3]{D}}$$

where SA is the working sail area (no overlap) in square feet and D is the displacement in pounds. In essence, then, the Bruce number is a simplified substitute for the sail area-to-displacement ratio, and 1.0 is generally considered the dividing line between sluggish and fast for monohulls in light airs. Many cruising multis have Bruce numbers of about 1.0 to 1.1, but according to Chris White anything less than 1.3 will feel sluggish in light air. On the other hand, a Bruce number over 1.6 in an offshore cruiser will require reefing most of the time, implying that the ideal range is perhaps 1.3 to 1.4.

It is true that many multihulls can run off with little risk of broaching and without suffering rhythmic or accumulative rolling. Designer Chris White writes, "Conditions that would have many monohulls broaching out of control, running great risk of being rolled over, will not even begin to trouble a well-designed multihull." Yet pioneering multihull designer Lock Crowther tells us that the broaching of some tris and even cats is not uncommon when they bury their lee bows. To help correct the problem he suggests increasing (but not excessively) float buoyancy and moving the mast aft. I should further point out that cruising monohulls sailed conservatively seldom suffer from serious rhythmic rolling and broaching. Such indignities usually result from running off too fast under excessive sail, especially when carrying a deeply cambered, oscillating spinnaker. Running with speed in horrendous weather is risky in any boat. This was the tactic used by designer/builder Walter Greene when he capsized the 60-foot trimaran *Gonzo* while crossing the Atlantic in 1982.

The characteristic of the offshore multihull that causes the greatest concern has to do with stability: a low range of positive static stability and inability to self-right. Actually, the range itself is less important than the rapid decline of righting moment after the windward hull (or central hull on a trimaran) leaves the water, plus the effect of aerodynamic and breaking-wave forces on wing decks. Multihull enthusiasts rightfully find comfort in the fact that an unballasted boat will not sink and therefore will provide the capsize victim with a crude liferaft, but as multihull designer/author Robert Harris admits, "Being capsized is a dangerous and miserable state in which to find yourself."

On the positive side, capsize is not at all likely on a well-designed multihull that is cautiously handled. Although multihulls have not been tested to the extent of monohulls for dynamic stability, Chris White and others claim that sizable multihulls, especially cats, have high roll moments of inertia, thus increasing their resistance to capsize from breaking waves. Furthermore, at low angles of heel most large multihulls have an enormous righting moment—up to 100,000 foot-pounds or more for a 40-footer—and this indicates high resistance to capsize from wind forces. On the other hand, a beamy multihull has tremendous bearing from her sizable waterplane area, causing high wave-slope response. Then too, overloading or an insufficiently buoyant leeward hull can cause rooting (digging in) and possible tripping, while lack of tenderness means that sheeted sails will not be depowered automatically. Bold enthusiasts should keep in mind that such eminent offshore sailors as Brian Cooke, Phil Weld, Philippe Jeantot, and Walter Greene have capsized large multihulls at sea.

There are means to help protect against multihull capsize, including those shown in Figure 3-18. The sponson illustrated, as used on the Newick-designed proa *Cheers*, is a flotation chamber protruding from the rail. A proa is similar to a catamaran but with its rig on one hull. If the ama is always kept to leeward (as is Newick's practice), a sponson is needed to prevent a capsize to windward. Other designers, such as Russell Brown, retain the sponson but keep the ama to windward, and long-time cruising multihull designer Jim Brown believes this configuration produces the safest of all multis—certainly the most resistant to capsize. Ballasted fins, as carried on the Michael Henderson-designed catamaran *Misty Miller* (Figure 3-18), are effective stabilizers but sacrifice some speed downwind and beachability. They may also increase the risk of

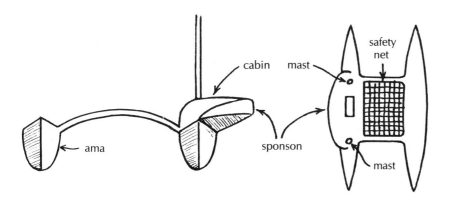

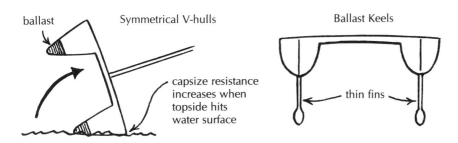

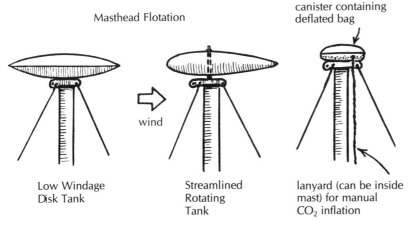

Figure 3-18. *Anticapsizing measures for multihulls. The advantages and drawbacks of each approach are discussed in the text.*

tripping, as can unballasted keels used for the sake of weatherliness. Flared V hulls as seen on the popular James Wharram-designed catamarans may combat capsizing at high angles of heel, especially if there is fixed ballast in the bilge, but performance will be compromised. Of course, any ballasted multihull should have flotation to prevent sinking and convert the overturned boat into an effective raft.

Another alternative is masthead flotation. A few designers still favor this, but more and more do not. Arguments against such flotation include excessive wind resistance and the possibility of the mast being broken by the float during a capsize in rough seas. Windage can be minimized by streamlining the float or using one that is inflatable, while mast and rigging can be strengthened to withstand all but the most severe stress from a float, though the effort to do so will further increase weight aloft unless exotic materials are used. It is certainly true that masthead flotation can be a great help against capsizing in relatively smooth water from sudden squalls or downbursts (see Chapter 8).

More obvious protection measures include automatic sheet releases and efficient sail-reduction systems. Sheet releases run the gamut from simple undersized cam cleats, to flip-up cleats held down with shock cord, to more sophisticated gadgetry controlled by mercury float switches set to release at a predetermined angle of heel. The main problem with mechanical release cleats is that they sometimes let go accidentally, as when the boat rolls and the boom jerks in a seaway.

Every multihull needs a speedy way to reduce sail. This can be accomplished with a well thought-out jiffy method or a variety of roller systems. Reefing is especially important on a multihull, because she cannot heel enough without risk of capsize to spill the wind from her sails. As a general rule for cautious cruising sailors, an offshore catamaran should not be heeled to the point where her windward hull will "fly" or leave the water, nor should a trimaran sail with her main hull in the air.

Design characteristics that help ensure against multihull capsizing are size, broad beam, small or open wing decks, and rigs of low aspect ratio. Size is important because, as it increases, so do the righting moment and the roll inertia. Several leading multihull associations require that participants in ocean races be at least 24 feet long overall. As mentioned earlier, Roland Prout feels that 45 feet or longer provides maximum safety for his catamarans. Chris White writes, "If a potential client walks in the door and tells me he wants a transoceanic cruising multihull, I will tell him that it ought to be 40 feet minimum." Lock Crowther agrees, after a particularly arduous race in Australia. Coastal and near-shore multis need not be as large.

Broad beam or wide spacing of the hulls increases the righting moment, and many of the most modern multihulls—especially racers that carry a lot of sail—epitomize this. There is a practical limit to beam, however. Apart from its disadvantages when docking and maneuvering, extremely wide spacing of the hulls can encourage pitchpoling in the worst weather. To minimize wind forces and the impact of breaking waves against the structures connecting the hulls, wing decks should be high above the water, as small as possible (commensurate with strength), open, and aerodynamically shaped to discourage lift. All openings between hulls should be fitted with safety nets.

For greatest security against capsizing, a seagoing multihull needs a reasonably short rig. Ocean-racing skippers sailing boats with extremely tall rigs and wing masts that cannot be shortened down in a blow are really pushing their luck. The 85-foot catamaran *Royale* capsized when she was overpowered by a tall, 700-square-foot wing mast that could not be reduced in area, and her skipper, Loic Caradec, was lost. The relatively short rigs on speedy Newick-designed trimarans prove that tall rigs are not always necessary for high performance.

Many safety-conscious authorities agree that a seagoing multihull should have a hatch in her bottom to allow access to supplies and shelter within the inverted boat in the event of a capsize. The boat should have ample flotation to make her float reasonably high, and the hatch should be far as possible above the water. Naturally, boats with heavy engines or those made of sinkable materials will need extra flotation. It is also advisable to install hand grips on the bottom and of course to have radio, flares, die markers, and other means of calling for help. Capsized trimaran sailor Tom Corkhill claimed that painting the bottom of his boat a bright air-sea rescue orange was a precaution that probably saved his life. It is best to have a means of righting a capsized multihull, such as by flooding compartments and later pumping them out, by using inflatable airbags, or both. This subject will be touched on in Chapter 6.

In an oceangoing multihull, strength must never be compromised for the sake of light displacement. State-of-the-art construction methods and materials need long testing in rugged weather before a boat is taken offshore. Consider not only the stress from high speed and the torque on hull connections, but also the strain imposed by rigging connected to a hull that lacks the ability to heel easily. The outer skin of a cored hull must be thick enough to withstand impact from flotsam, sealife, or even wave impact. The safest core is sufficiently ductile to absorb shock loading instead of transmitting it to the inner skin. One multihull authority even advocates a degree of flexibility in the attachment of hulls, but this could precipitate serious fatigue problems. As Dick Newick put it, "Beware the 'Befuddled Scientist' using fabulous figures for ultimate tensile strength, yield strength, or specific strength of whatever 'high tech' he is selling. All these one-time figures are provable in the lab but, alas, can often be proven meaningless by a reality of seagoing life: fatigue. Just as skippers and crews tire on long passages, materials in our vessels are also prone to fatigue after hundreds of thousands of cycles. They get tired and they break."

Watertightness is a feature that should probably get the same attention on a multihull as on a monohull. Cabin houses are often lacking in strength, companionways are sometimes excessively large and unprotected, and picture windows are too vulnerable. Designer Bob Harris has referred to excessive exposed window area on many trimarans of recent times as a "major malfeature." In his book *Racing and Cruising Trimarans* he decries "large unsupported areas of window glass, particularly forward," and adds, "In an effort to minimize weight, cabin trunks are normally thinner than is the usual practice; therefore the areas of fixed lights should be reduced." Even though a multihull is unsinkable, flooding can cause or contribute to a capsize.

As a final thought on monohulls versus multihulls for offshore work, I should add that while there is great merit in the often-heard argument

Figure 3-19. *This Atlantic 40 catamaran from designer Chris White exemplifies current thinking in the design of cruising multihulls. The slim hulls are easily driven by the comparatively modest sail plan, which uses a fully battened sail and a rotating mast to enhance sail shape at high speeds. The lightweight, thick-section, composite mast depends on three rigging wires to support it, reducing windage and weight aloft. The bridgedeck ends well back from the bows to reduce pitching, it is high above the water to reduce pounding, and it maintains a low, streamlined profile to reduce windage. Daggerboards protected by small ''bumper fins'' resist leeway. Boats of this type cruise reliably when carefully handled, with speeds in the 10- to 14-knot range—and bear little resemblance to the often-crude, sometimes dangerous specimens from the early days of multihulls. LOA, 40 feet, 6 inches; beam overall, 22 feet, 4 inches; beam at the waterline (each hull), 3 feet, 3 inches; draft (boards up), 2 feet, 6 inches; draft (boards down), 6 feet, 4 inches; sail area, 835 square feet; Bruce number, 1.40.*

that approbates the seaworthiness of the multihull because she cannot sink, one should not be misled into thinking that all sinkable boats are dangerous. A ballasted monohull will sink if she is filled with water, but she will not sink, no matter what happens, if she is kept watertight. She can capsize, turn turtle, or pitchpole, but she will remain afloat so long as her openings are closed and she is not holed or punctured. Furthermore, in the bottom-up position, a boat with modest beam is fairly unstable, tending to self-right. The safest possible boat would be a ballasted, self-righting monohull fitted with enough flotation to keep her

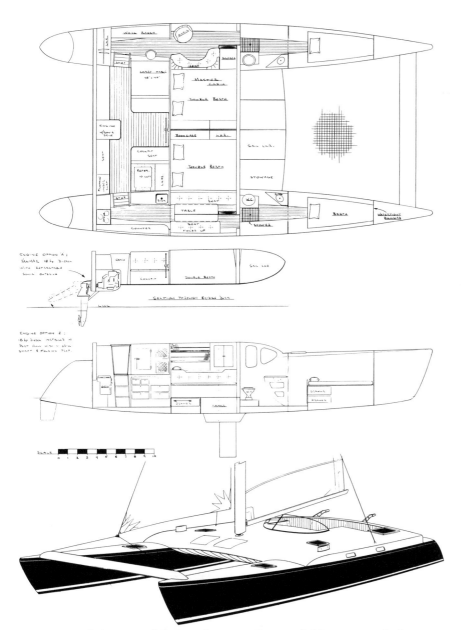

afloat even if she were filled with water. Boats of this type are being produced today, and undoubtedly more will feature flotation in the future. It should not be necessary, however, to buoy up a soundly designed and constructed monohull sailing boat when her decks and cabin are watertight and all of her openings can be absolutely, quickly, and conveniently closed. More will be said about multihulls and their handling in heavy weather in Chapter 12.

Bluewater cruising may offer the ideal means of escaping increasingly constricted, overpopulated, and polluted waters, but offshore ventures

Figure 3-20. *The plans of Robert P. Beebe's seagoing powerboat,* Passagemaker. *She is a heavy, extensively modified MFV type, with a round-bottomed hull of moderate speed. She has fairly deep draft and a single screw that is well protected by the keel. Her dimensions are: LOA, 50 feet; LWL, 46 feet; beam, 15 feet; draft, 5 feet, 4 inches; power, Ford 330 diesel; range, 3,300 miles at $7\frac{1}{2}$ knots on 1,200 gallons. (Courtesy Robert P. Beebe and* Motor Boating and Sailing*).*

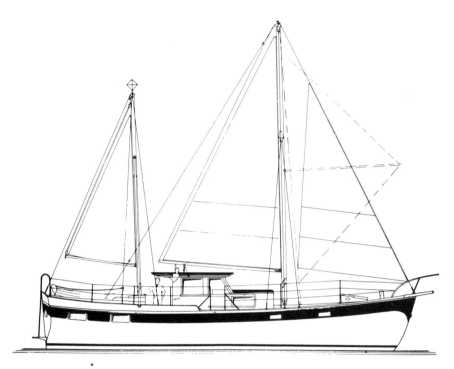

should never be attempted in vessels that are not entirely seaworthy. An unsuitable craft may make many successful passages, but sooner or later she will be caught out in heavy weather. In summary, I think the most important qualities of seaworthiness are strength, watertightness, ultimate stability, and either self-righting ability for a monohull or buoyancy for a multihull. Any sailor who goes to sea in a vessel lacking these qualities is either misinformed or deliberately thumbing his nose at fate. He won't get away with it forever.

Offshore Powerboats and Motor Sailers

Heavy power craft derived from commercial fishing boats have long been regarded as the safest kind of motorboat for extended passages offshore. These boats are deep-bodied, full-ended, and heavily built, with considerable beam and draft, short overhangs, ample sheer, and round bilges. Such a heavy-displacement, nonplaning hull cannot readily be pushed above a speed (in knots) of 1.34 times the square root of its waterline length (in feet) without a tremendous waste of power and the creation of a formidable wave system. Pleasure craft of this kind are often called MFV (Motor Fishing Vessel) yachts.

Although MFVs are suitable for continual offshore work, seagoing boats should not necessarily be slavish, exact imitations of fishermen, because of the considerable difference in purpose between a workboat and a pleasure craft. In an old but still interesting article (*Yachting World Annual*, 1964) on MFVs, British designer-author Douglas Phillips-Birt

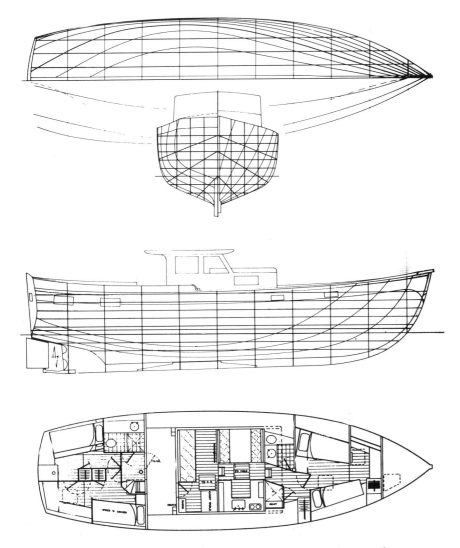

suggested slight variations on the fisherman design that might improve it for yachting purposes. Those modifications included somewhat lighter displacement, slightly finer ends, greater overhangs with some flare forward, and more freeboard amidships.

Robert P. Beebe's *Passagemaker* (Figure 3-20) is an offshore powerboat capable of extended voyaging. In his book *Voyaging Under Power*, Captain Beebe argued against calling his boat a modified MFV, but I use the term to connote a powerboat with a deep, full-bodied hull that cannot plane and that normally carries a steadying sail and has a single, relatively slow-turning screw ahead of a large rudder. This meaning is not in opposition to Phillips-Birt's definition of the type. In deference to the late Captain Beebe, I'll call *Passagemaker* an *extensively* modified MFV type.

A reasonably deep forefoot and deeply veed bow sections with rounded sections farther aft lessen pounding in head seas, but the

Figure 3-21. *The Passagemaker leaving Bermuda for Newport, R.I. She has made many ocean passages. Rolling is minimized with paravane, "flopper-stopper" stabilizers. (Norris D. Hoyt photo)*

designer of an MFV yacht has to keep the stern reasonably narrow to avoid excessive buoyancy aft, which might make the bow root (bury) in a following sea. As designer Bob Henry wrote me, "The powerboats that seem to perform well at sea are the round-bilge displacement type with a narrow stern to prevent broaching in a following sea. However, one needs the opposite for good performance in calm water—a broad stern to prevent squatting and a hard chine to induce planing. I really think seagoing powerboats are more of a compromise than seagoing sailboats." Another consideration is that narrowing the stern sections overmuch can encourage rolling in unfavorable seas.

A planing hull with a sharp V bow, a wide, flat stern, and hard chines is unsuitable for extended passages offshore not only because of difficult steering in rough following seas, but because steering may be difficult under any conditions at low speeds, when the submerged fine bow causes the boat to lose directional stability and small rudders fail to provide immediate response. Furthermore, in some sea conditions there may be pounding under the chines when the deadrise is flat. This type of hull can be dangerous in steep head seas when it lacks adequate flare and freeboard forward and has a ramped or sloping down foredeck.

One way to achieve planing speeds without great sacrifice to seaworthiness is to fit a deeply veed hull with longitudinal steps or riding strakes (Figure 3-22) and carry the V sections all the way aft to the transom. The result is the famous *Hunter* or *Moppie* type designed by Raymond Hunt and produced by Richard Bertram, which is used extensively in offshore races. Its hull has reasonably matched ends and gives a fairly soft ride without excessive pounding, although trim tabs are nearly always necessary, and sufficient beam should be carried aft to inhibit squatting. There is some sacrifice in speed and quickness to plane in smooth water as compared with a hull having less deadrise, and there is some loss of seakindliness as compared with an MFV displacement yacht.

Other compromise forms include the semiplaning, moderately deep V hull; the so-called cathedral hull; and the semiplaning round-bottomed form typified by the Maine lobsterboat. The latter has little deadrise but is rounded at the turn of the bilge. A common variation of the cathedral hull (deriving its name from catamaran and dihedral) is centrally veed in section but with a small underwater V-shaped sponson on each side (Figure 3-22). Although this form is subject to pounding, the sponsons afford good stability, and a certain amount of air-cushioning is provided in the tunnels between the sponsons and central hull. The moderately deep V hull is similar to the above-mentioned constant-deadrise offshore racing hull but with greater beam and displacement and less power. It has good resistance to rolling and can be pushed quite easily beyond hull speed (1.34 times the square root of

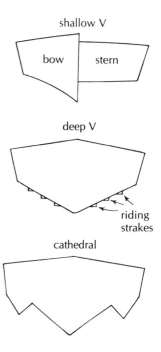

Figure 3-22. *Variations on the V hull.*

Figure 3-23. *Richard Bertram's* Lucky Moppie, *a nearly constant-deadrise, V-bottom, offshore racing powerboat designed to withstand severe pounding in a chop. (Roland Rose photo)*

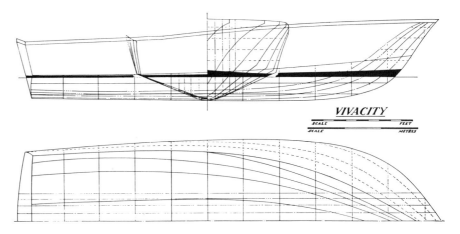

Figure 3-24. Vivacity, *a successful, nearly constant V design by Ray Hunt. The deadrise aft is 20 degrees, which proved a good compromise between seakeeping and planing ability.*

VIVACITY

waterline length) without excessive pounding. She concedes a minimal loss of seaworthiness to attain her semiplaning speeds. The legendary Bertram 31, with a nearly constant deadrise (23 degrees aft), exemplifies this hull type. Bertrams, Strikers, Blackfins, and other sportfishing models have been showing for years what a pounding a well-designed veed hull can take offshore, though not with anywhere near the crew comfort afforded by an MFV. These compromise configurations provide a good blend of speed and seaworthiness in moderate conditions, but their large exposed cockpits and limited ranges preclude transoceanic passages. For the worst conditions far offshore (where shelter cannot be reached), the deep, round-bilged, moderately heavy, modified MFV yacht affords greater comfort and safety than other motorboats. The MFV yacht also consumes little fuel and can carry large fuel tanks with no harm to its performance, so it permits a much greater range for passagemaking.

Offshore powerboats should share many characteristics with offshore sailboats, such as watertight integrity, unbreakable windows of minimal area, generous freeboard, reasonably low superstructures, liferails or bulwarks with large freeing ports, a low center of gravity (often assured with the use of inside ballast), and perhaps even some sail to mitigate rolling or to serve as emergency propulsion. Of course, offshore power craft and sailing craft have differences in safety requirements, but it is not so much that different characteristics are required as that some of the same characteristics need to be more extreme in sailing craft. For instance, a powerboat does not need as much reserve stability as a sailboat because the former is not subject to extreme knockdowns from wind pressure on a lofty rig. Also, a powerboat's windows can be larger than a sailboat's because they need not withstand the impact imposed by a beam-ends knockdown; nevertheless, glass area on any offshore boat should be kept reasonably small, windows and windshields should be strongly framed with adequate bracing, and the panes should be of safety glass, heavy Plexiglas, Perspex, or preferably polycarbonate.

Time and again, power craft have had their windows smashed by

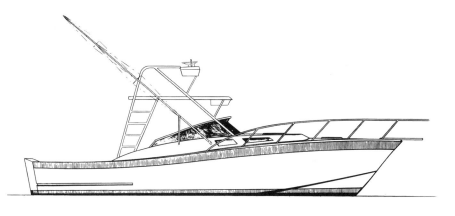

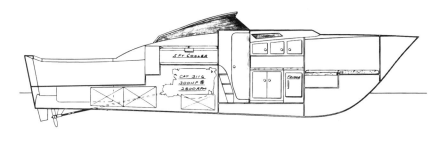

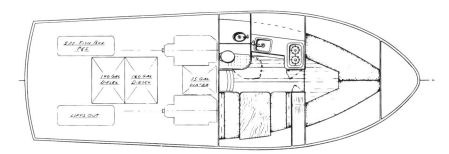

Figure 3-25. *The* Offshore 34, *a twin-engined offshore sportfisherman designed by Dave Gerr. With a fairly sharp entry and narrow beam (for its type) this boat can effectively drive into head seas. The moderately deep V sections aft with slight tunnel effect at the chines are a compromise to afford good stability with reasonable softness of ride at high speeds. Moderate buoyancy aft with larger-than-average rudders for twin screws enhances steering control at slow speeds and discourages broaching. Although the powderhorn sheer lowers the freeboard aft, it assures dryness forward when combined with ample flare and overhang. Other seagoing features include a low, well-rounded cabin trunk, small Lexan ports, centerline hatches, and a fast-draining cockpit. Despite its attributes for offshore use, the designer admits that boats of this type ''are not suited for rounding the Horn.''*

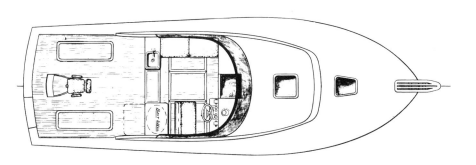

Figure 3-26. *Profile, deck, midsection, and construction plans of a Maine lobsterboat, this one a 36-footer designed for wood construction by Royal Lowell. A successful compromise between speed and seaworthiness, the Maine lobsterboat has proven itself in rough coastal waters. Although the angle of deadrise becomes increasingly flat aft to allow planing (when heavily powered), seakindliness is enhanced by moderately soft bilges and rounded chines. With its usual sweeping sheer, ample freeboard with some flare forward, and minimal areas of glass, the Maine lobsterboat can effectively drive into head seas. A modest afterdeck helps protect against following seas, but the cockpit is quite large and freeboard is low aft. These characteristics together with her relatively short cruising range limit her to coastal waters, where she excels as a yacht as well as a workboat.*

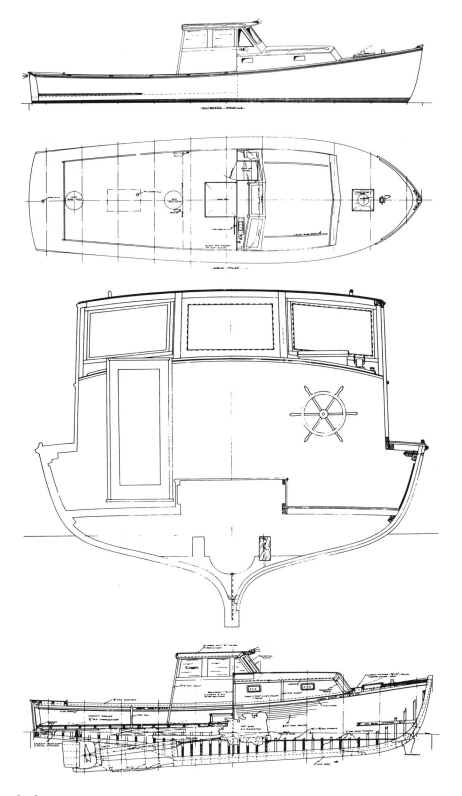

Figure 3-27. *A small offshore cruising powerboat. Notice her small portholes in the cabin trunk instead of the customary large glass windows and also the large freeing ports through her bulwarks. Her small, two-masted rig gives versatile sail combinations for the purposes of steadying, lying-to with the bow held up, or scudding. (Courtesy* National Fisherman *magazine)*

seas or heavy spray breaking aboard, and in more than a few cases the windows were of ordinary, single-thickness, breakable glass. Windows should be oval or rectangular with rounded corners to prevent stress concentrations, and allowance should be made for expansion of plastics. Offshore powerboat windshields are unavoidably vulnerable if the helmsman is to have a reasonably large area of glass ahead of him for good visibility. One supposedly effective method of preventing damage to windshields or pilothouse windows is to attach, when the seas are heavy, a fine-mesh wire screen mounted on a rigid frame in front of the windshield or window, about one inch away from the glass. The theory is that solid water striking the screen will be divided into tiny particles that will lack the power and velocity to break the glass. The Coast Guard sometimes specifies wire-inserted glass for vulnerable windows on passenger vessels.

Superstructures or deckhouses can be higher on power vessels than on sailing craft, but extreme height raises the center of gravity and presents a large area to the wind; this acts almost like a sail, producing a side force and consequent heeling if the boat is caught beam-to a squall. Deckhouses should be tremendously strong in all cases. Experienced yacht deliverer Peter Hayward has written concerning the seaworthiness of motor yachts, "The hull may be capable of surviving very heavy weather, but it is the tophamper and wheelhouses which may be a source of weakness." While generous freeboard in an offshore motorboat is desirable, excessive freeboard should be avoided for the same reasons that should prohibit high deckhouses and extremely lofty superstructures such as flying bridges and conning towers.

Although it is necessary to keep the center of gravity fairly low on a

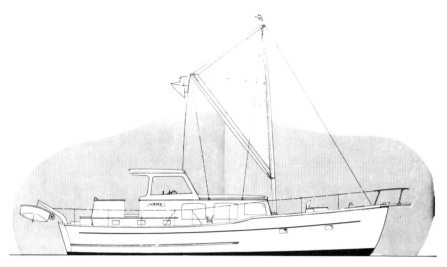

Figure 3-28. *An offshore powerboat with steadying sail. Notice how maximum sail area is kept high to avoid being blanketed in the troughs of ocean waves. I would prefer that the forward windows in the superstructure were considerably smaller. The dinghy in the stern davits should be brought aboard in heavy weather at sea. (Courtesy Palmer Service, Inc.)*

seagoing motorboat, she should not be excessively ballasted, as said earlier, because of the possibility of increasing the GM to the point of producing a violent rolling motion. However, MFV yachts usually need some inside ballast, primarily because they are often fitted with riding or steadying sails. As the noted designer of offshore powerboats, Edwin Monk, has stated, "The steadying sail should be used with a little caution, and the boat should be ballasted." Of course, the more sail the boat carries, the more ballast she will need.

Inside ballast should be securely fastened so that it cannot possibly shift. Many vessels have been lost through shifting ballast, but one of the most dramatic examples took place in 1867 when the small ketch *John T. Ford* capsized far off the coast of Ireland. Her ballast shifted in such a way that she could not be righted, and as a result three people drowned. The sole survivor was a man who was finally rescued after clinging to the bottom of the upturned boat for three days and four nights.

The center of gravity on a seagoing powerboat is usually kept low partly by the placement of water and fuel tanks deep in the bilge. Quite often the engine is placed low also, but care should be taken not to put it in harm's way should the bilge be flooded. On some offshore boats, ocean racers especially, the engine is placed right down in the keel, but in my opinion this practice is unsound. It makes servicing difficult, and oil or fumes may accumulate deep in the keel. Also, gasoline engines can suffer from wet ignition systems, and even diesels may be subject to severe damage if water gets sucked into the air intake. According to W.S. Amos, in an article written for the July, 1969, issue of *Yachting World*, a diesel engine drowned in this manner could actually "explode," as a result of a "hydraulic lock" in the combustion chamber, with such force that the hull as well as the engine might be damaged. Mr. Amos speculates that this kind of damage led to the loss of the 34-foot MFV *Mhairi Dhonn* when she foundered in Scottish waters during a gale in 1968.

Another factor that may have contributed to the loss of this fisherman, according to Mr. Amos, was the fact that the boat had very high bulwarks without properly designed clearing ports. He suggests that a heavy sea broke aboard, deep water lingered on deck when the narrow, slit-like clearing ports became clogged with ropes, nets, or fish, and this allowed water to leak through the hatches, which were not designed to withstand total immersion. Consequently, the engine sucked in more than enough water to cause the hydraulic lock which blew apart the engine and damaged the hull. Of course, high bulwarks with inadequate freeing ports can also contribute to a capsizing, as the free-surface liquid rushes to leeward when the vessel rolls. The lessons seem clear: Engines should not be placed where they can be drowned, air intakes must be high out of the bilge and protected, hatches should be watertight, and bulwarks must be low with ample, large ports, or else open stanchions and railings should be fitted.

Powerboats with a large fuel capacity should not have tanks that are extremely wide and flat, as the free-surface movement of the fuel in a partially filled tank when rolling produces sizable heeling that could contribute to a capsize. Tanks should be well baffled, of course, and the baffling should be designed with the intent of keeping the free-surface movement out of phase with the vessel's period of roll; otherwise a possibly dangerous rhythmic rolling could develop. When a vessel has many tanks, it is advisable to keep them topped and to use only one tank until it is nearly depleted in order to minimize free surface. Keel tanks should be used last of all because of their low placement, which increases stability, and their deep, narrow shape, which minimizes the effect of free surface. During a Pacific typhoon in 1944 three U.S. destroyers capsized and went down with practically all hands. There were a number of reasons for this tragedy, but one significant contributing factor was that all the lost vessels carried little if any water ballast, and they were adversely affected by free surface as well as insufficient ballasting.

Most MFV yachts are powered with diesel engines because of their fuel economy, reliability, and safety (diesel being a fuel that doesn't easily explode). Usually these boats have a single large, on-center propeller well protected by the keel. The MFV's relatively deep draft allows ample rudder depth and deep immersion of the propeller. One problem with a single-screw offshore motorboat lacking propulsion sail, however, is the possibility of engine failure. From this point of view, twin engines with twin screws are safer, but with such an arrangement propellers and shafts are usually more vulnerable to damage from driftwood or grounding and cannot be immersed as deeply as can a single screw. Also, a single engine normally has greater space surrounding it and is thus more accessible for servicing and maintenance. If the propeller is too shallow, it will race and lose power, both when the vessel is plunging into a head sea and when it is running before a high following sea. Some single-screw offshore yachts are equipped with standby power in the event the main engine breaks down. Quite often the secondary power is supplied

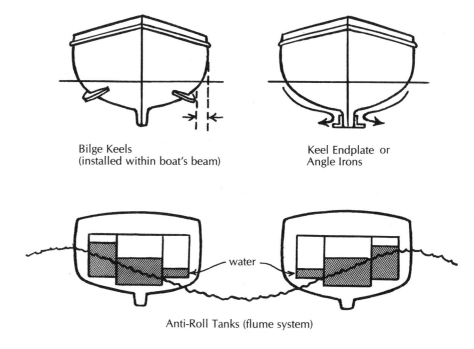

Bilge Keels
(installed within boat's beam)

Keel Endplate or
Angle Irons

water

Anti-Roll Tanks (flume system)

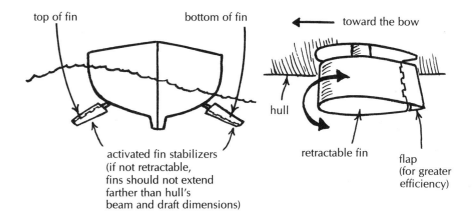

top of fin

bottom of fin

toward the bow

hull

activated fin stabilizers
(if not retractable,
fins should not extend
farther than hull's
beam and draft dimensions)

retractable fin

flap
(for greater
efficiency)

Figure 3-29. *Permanent powerboat stabilizers or antiroll devices. Figure 3-30 offers a more detailed look at fin stabilizers.*
Non-permanent stabilizers—paravanes or flopper-stoppers—are touched on in Chapter 13.

by the generator with a belt or chain linking it to the main shaft, or the generator may have its own shaft and small auxiliary propeller which might be located above the main prop, behind the keel deadwood and forward of the rudder. An interesting and still-relevant article on emergency engine propulsion, written by naval architect William Garden, appeared in the December, 1968, *Motor Boating* magazine. Of course, many seamen would prefer to rely on some sail for standby propulsion, but usually true powerboats cannot be made to sail to windward.

Perhaps the greatest drawback of the modified, round-bottomed MFV, apart from her slow speed, is her tendency to roll. Sails can help dampen rolling in beam seas, but if the boat has no sail, she will need

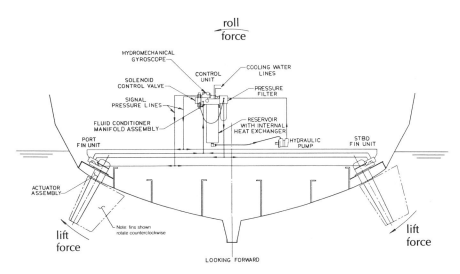

roll force

HYDROMECHANICAL GYROSCOPE
COOLING WATER LINES
CONTROL UNIT
SOLENOID CONTROL VALVE
PRESSURE FILTER
SIGNAL PRESSURE LINES
FLUID CONDITIONER MANIFOLD ASSEMBLY
RESERVOIR WITH INTERNAL HEAT EXCHANGER
PORT FIN UNIT
HYDRAULIC PUMP
STBD FIN UNIT
ACTUATOR ASSEMBLY
Note: fins shown rotate counterclockwise
lift force
lift force
LOOKING FORWARD

Figure 3-30. *This fin-stabilizing system works similarly to the ailerons on a plane. A gyroscope directs the fins to produce a counter-roll opposing the wave-induced roll. (Courtesy Naiad Stabilizers)*

some other form of roll damping, such as keel-end plates, bilge keels, or fin stabilizers (see Figure 3-29). The theory behind the end plates or angle irons is that they help stabilize the boat by blocking the flow of water from one side of the keel to the other when the boat rolls. This method is undoubtedly helpful, but to what extent is open to debate. Bilge keels are also helpful, but they should not extend very far forward because of the likelihood of emersion and pounding in head seas. Probably the most effective means of reducing the roll of a large vessel is with fin stabilizers. These are short hydrofoils projecting from each side of the hull underwater; first one, then the other is twisted mechanically to vary its angle of attack and thus cause an upward or downward force opposing the direction of roll (Figure 3-30). The twisting is controlled by sensing gyroscopes, and some systems allow the fins to retract or fold into the hull when they are not in use.

Fin stabilizers are not effective unless the vessel is moving ahead with considerable speed, but antirolling tanks can be effective regardless of speed. These are not usually very practical on a small boat because of her quick period of roll and the fact that transverse tanks take up valuable room. Such tanks are partially filled with water, and the free-surface flow is controlled with baffles so that it is out of phase with the period of roll. As the vessel rolls, the greatest amount of water is held temporarily in the high tank to produce a stabilizing effect (Figure 3-29). Some modern systems use tubes managed by vacuums and microprocessors to control the movement of fluid. There is even an antiroll system that moves a solid weight from side to side, but it is highly complex and expensive for its effectiveness. An effective temporary or removable antirolling method is the use of fisherman paravane stabilizers, which are often called "flopper-stoppers." These will be discussed briefly in Chapter 13, when we deal with powerboat management at sea. Incidentally, violent pitching can be alleviated when the vessel is designed with a bulbous bow.

When an MFV yacht is rigged with small steadying sails for roll

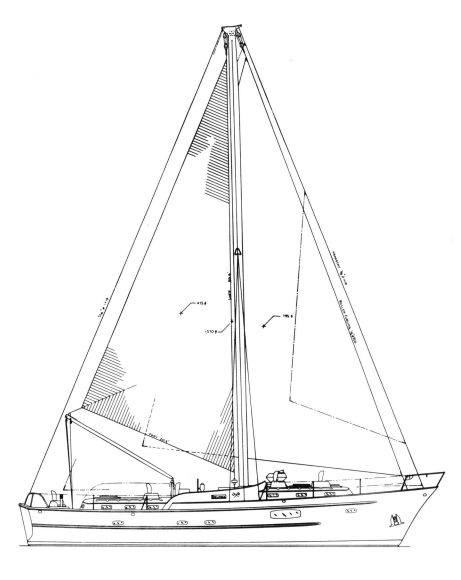

Figure 3-31. *Plans of the* Delfina, *an ocean-cruising motorsailer designed by MacLear and Harris. Her dimensions are: LOA, 52 feet, 4 inches; LWL, 45 feet, 10 inches; beam, 15 feet, 3 inches; draft, 5 feet, 9 inches; sail area, 1,270 square feet.*

damping, the sails may be used for emergency propulsion toward a destination that lies to leeward or across the wind. As mentioned earlier, however, powerboats seldom can make progress to windward under sail. To sail to windward, the vessel must have a fairly large, efficient rig and also ample lateral plane and draft to prevent leeway. A powerboat with such characteristics may be termed a motorsailer. Definitions of this type of vessel vary, but to my way of thinking, a powerboat with sails is not a motorsailer unless she can make at least some progress to windward, and usually this vessel is fairly close to the type known as a fifty-fifty, meaning that about half the propulsive power is allotted to the engine and the other half to sails.

Motorsailers have many advantages over powerboats for long-range

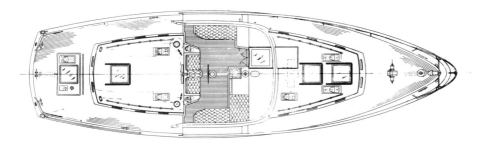

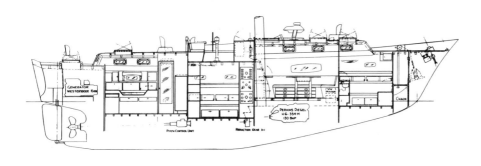

cruising and passagemaking. A reasonably efficient sail plan provides economy of fuel, roll damping, emergency propulsion, greater versatility for heavy weather management, and the alleviation of annoying engine noises, smells, and vibrations for lengthy periods of time. Compared with auxiliary sailboats, motorsailers provide more space for comfort, fuel capacity for long-range powering, the ability to escape the doldrums or lengthy calm spells, and the ability to make progress to windward under adverse conditions by using the engine and sails simultaneously. Their chief disadvantage is in poor sailing ability, especially in the fifty-fifty type. Personally, I would prefer the so-called seventy-thirty type, which is really a heavily powered sailboat. Such a vessel has a comparatively tall, efficient rig, with fairly deep draft and a relatively high ballast-

Figure 3-32. *The* Delfina *stepping along under sail and power. Both sails are roller furling. She has a three-bladed, 30-inch, controllable-pitch propeller driven by a 130-h.p. Perkins diesel. An adjustable propeller pitch is especially helpful when using the engine to increase the speed under sail. (Brian Manby photo)*

to-displacement ratio; at the same time, she has reasonable fuel capacity and a slow-turning engine directly driving a large two-bladed propeller, which can hide behind the keel deadwood to reduce drag under sail. Although not a racer, she should be a fairly smart sailer having sufficient engine power to escape calms and drive the vessel into strong winds and heavy seas.

Chapter 4
HULL INSPECTION
AND PREPARATION FOR
SEA

Before any extended passage, a boat should be thoroughly tried and tested in short shakedown cruises. "Bugs" should be eliminated before she ventures into exposed waters or leaves the vicinity of readily available help and repair facilities. Even if your boat is not new and you have used her in sheltered waters for many years, give her a thorough inspection before braving unprotected waters, especially if you contemplate a lengthy cruise. She must be well found and properly equipped for safe operation.

Choosing a Surveyor

Before buying a used boat or, in many cases, even a new one, it is highly advisable to have her surveyed. Also, I think it is a wise plan to have any boat, even a familiar one, inspected by a competent surveyor before she is taken on an extended offshore passage. Dependable surveyors, however, are not always easy to find. More than a few of those who hang out a shingle or advertise in the yellow pages of the telephone directory are not entirely competent. I know of several boat buyers who were badly misled by poor surveys that resulted in repair costs far beyond expectations. Then again, some quite competent and honest surveyors temper their reports slightly when they are hired by yacht brokers, insurance agencies, marina operators, or other professionals from whom future survey jobs are expected.

There is no sure way of picking a reliable surveyor, but the following suggestions might help. Select a surveyor who is a naval architect and marine engineer, or, alternatively, one with extensive yacht construction experience. Ideally, this experience will be supplemented by a lengthy apprenticeship in the survey business itself. It is perhaps reassuring to discover that the surveyor is a member of organizations such as the National Association of Marine Surveyors, the Marine Surveyors Bureau, or one of the classification societies mentioned in Chapter 2, but don't be misled by the display of a license, for presently only an occupational license is needed. Be cautious about selecting a surveyor who is recommended by the yacht broker from whom you are buying a boat. It is often safer to select a surveyor from one of several recommended by your local yacht service yard or a reputable, disinterested design firm. (On the other hand, a broker comes in contact with surveyors more often than a service yard manager does, and a reputable broker isn't likely to recommend a disreputable surveyor.) You can also ask knowledgeable boating friends who have had their boats professionally inspected. In the latter case ask to examine the surveyor's written report so that you can judge its thoroughness and perhaps glean clues to its competence. Be wary of stock reports with check-off lists. Good as well as bad qualities of the boat should be extensively written up, and specific defects warrant a description in reasonable detail. If you are not at all familiar with a prospective surveyor, ask for his credentials and references. Don't hunt for a bargain survey, and be suspicious if the surveyor is able to inspect your boat immediately; this may indicate he is not very busy, perhaps for good reason.

If the boat to be surveyed is some distance from a known, capable surveyor, it is often well worth paying his travel expenses. After all, the survey cost is usually a very small percentage of the total investment, and a thorough inspection may save money in the short run by exposing problems that warrant a decrease in the selling price, and in the long run by revealing a condition that can be cured before it gets out of hand. Some surveyors are touchy about being disturbed, followed, or peppered with questions while they are inspecting a boat. Certainly distractions should be minimized, but you have every right to quietly watch the survey and later to ask questions. After all, you are paying for the work. Expect a full and detailed written report, preferably in a letter as well as on a standard printed form.

The Hull

As a current or prospective boatowner, it is wise to learn all you can about hull inspection procedures, in order that you can spot a problem before it becomes serious and so that you can intelligently observe a survey and ask meaningful questions of the surveyor. On an extended cruise, especially offshore, an owner must often be entirely self-sufficient, and he must observe his vessel with an eagle eye and make continual inspections. Read all you can on the subject, ask questions of boatyard foremen and technicians, and ask opinions of respected "old hands." A word of warning, however, about advice from sailors with only slightly more experience than yourself: There are more than a few self-appointed experts, and free advice is sometimes worth exactly what it costs.

Before giving a new or used boat a detailed examination, the prospective buyer should give her an overall sizing-up. Observe her lines, rig, cabin house, accommodations, cockpit, brightwork, general appearance, state of upkeep, condition of equipment, and so forth. Observe the fairness of her topsides, and look at her trim to see if she is listed or floating down by the head or stern. If she is a fairly small boat, notice how much she heels when you step aboard at her rail, for this will give some indication of her initial stability. Bounce up and down while walking across the deck to test its sturdiness. Of course, all deck gear and mechanical devices should be looked over, although later all mechanical and electronic equipment should be carefully examined by a surveyor or marine technician. Take particular notice of the joinerwork, as this is indicative of the degree of care taken in the boat's entire construction. As designer-sailmaker Ted Hood has said, "The things you can see are an indication of the things you can't see." The mast and rigging should be very carefully examined later, but a glance up the sail track will often reveal an unwanted mast bend or permanent set. In short, don't discount a boat's first impression. It can tell a great deal. Needless to say, the boat's past history, designer, and builder should be known. Make every attempt to discuss the boat with the yard manager who serviced her, but don't expect him to be extremely critical if the seller is a regular customer. If the boat is a stock design, look for a review in a yachting periodical or talk to the owner of a sister boat. What you learn could put you well ahead of the game.

As for the thorough boat examination, a few tips follow: In a wooden boat, examine the bilges under the cabin sole, the floor timbers, keel, mast step, and especially the frame heels for rot, splits, corrosion, or insecurity. Look for marks, stains, blisters, and blemishes that indicate water leaks, especially around deck beams, under the head and icebox, at the stem, in the stern lazarette (near the horn timber particularly), under the rail, and along the sheer clamp and deck shelf. Blemishes in these areas hint at the possibility of rot in a wooden boat or corrosion in one of metal. Bulging or buckling of decks or other surfaces may indicate rust swelling on steel hulls. Look for dank-smelling, mildewed areas indicating lack of ventilation. These places are a possible source of rot in a wooden boat. Likewise, unfairness in the hull's exterior or areas of blistered, peeling paint or rust streaks could mean rot or wasted members or fastenings. These areas should be examined carefully and sounded (gently) with a small hammer. Most surveyors make maximum use of the hammer to detect wasting, rot, delamination, weak fastenings, voids, and so forth. When the hammer's tap produces a solid, hard ringing sound, it indicates a healthy condition, whereas a comparatively dull, dead thud could indicate deterioration. Competent surveyors prod no more than absolutely necessary with a knife or ice pick to detect soft wood, but some prodding will be needed on areas strongly suspected of rot. Sometimes, as when a boat is double planked, it may be advisable for the surveyor to drill a small test hole, with the permission of the owner, in order to examine the wood chips. If they are punky, powdery, or sour smelling, rot may well be present.

Boats should be carefully examined for strains. Signs of severe strain include cracked frames; hogged sheer or sagging ends; wide seams or splits in planking; slight shifting or movement of bulkheads, straps, or chainplates; irregularities in the topsides; sinking or movement of the cabin sole; separation of joints; slight changes in the hull's shape (comparing one side with the other); sinking or change in the crown of a cabintop, especially when the mast is deck-stepped; bent or sagging beams, posts, partners, step, and other members in way of the mast; and so forth. Cracks in the structural members of wooden boats may not be indicative of strains, but simply of the wood drying out during a long period of dry storage. In many cases, the wood will swell and lose the splits after the boat has been launched. Nevertheless, it does no good to leave a wooden boat out of her natural element for long periods of time. Seams in the topsides should be examined carefully. Very often a sailboat that does not leak a drop at anchor will make water seriously when heeled in a breeze, because caulking has not been renewed and the topsides have dried out and opened up in the hot sun. Such topsides should generally be painted white to minimize heat absorption. Wooden boats should also be examined for evidence of worms or other borers, especially at the bottom of the keel or inside the bottom of the centerboard trunk.

Fiberglass and ferrocement construction are far more difficult to inspect than wood, because strengths and weakness are concealed inside the material. In a ferrocement hull, look for cracks, pinholes, leaks, rust stains, and irregularities in the surface, and sound with a hammer for voids. Also, check the attachment of bulkheads, decks, and chainplates. Learn all you can about the boat's construction: where she was built, who designed her, and the exact method used. Most important, if she passes your inspection, hire a surveyor who has had experience with the material.

With fiberglass, learn what you can about the method of construction (whether it was hand lay-up or chopper gun, and the molding method), the character of the laminate (the number of layers of roving, for example), the laminate thickness, the core material if any, the method of stiffening and reinforcing the hull and deck, and the method of joining the deck to the hull. If you are the owner of a glass boat, save any sections cut out of the hull or deck, such as those cut out when through-hull fittings or ventilators are installed, in order that laminate thickness and construction can be judged or tested. Tapping with a hammer or even a coin can reveal air pockets or delaminations; sighting along the topsides or bottom of the hull can reveal hardspots (mentioned in Chapter 2) or areas that need stiffening; and applying pressure to certain areas, such as the deck, can reveal over-flexibility. Hammer sounding is especially important when there is extensive osmotic blistering, as this condition may indicate water in the laminate. A moisture detection meter can be a useful instrument in the hands of someone who knows how to interpret it. (Blister repair was discussed briefly in Chapter 2.) Look for delaminations at any exposed edges, chips in the gelcoat, and deep cracks at any sharp bends, especially at hard chines. Most gelcoat cracks do not penetrate into the laminate, unless perhaps they are concentrated and of a radial pattern that indicates stress. Fatigue cracks in the gelcoat, though not serious in themselves, might warn of a condition that could later crack the laminate. Look for these cracks around engine beds, under the bows of fast, V-bottomed powerboats, or around any hardspot or area that seems comparatively flexible. Such areas might need to be stiffened inside the hull with structural members reinforced with extra plies of laminate, or otherwise have the stress distributed over a larger area. Other areas subject to great stress, such as at fittings and chainplates, should be strengthened with extra-thick laminate in the manner suggested in Chapter 2.

Through-bolts and rivets should be carefully checked wherever possible, especially where the deck joins the hull. See that all nuts are tight on the bolts, as neglect in this area can cause vital fittings to shear off. In one case of my acquaintance, a stemhead strap sheared as a result of loose nuts, and the boat was dismasted. Check the keelbolt nuts periodically, and keep them snug. When the ballast is internal, listen for sounds of shifting in the keel when the boat is rolled. Some stock boats have chunks of ballast sealed, but not always properly bedded and secured, inside a fiberglass keel. Resin can be pumped in to improve the bedding.

Some surveyors shine a strong light through the hull when pigmentation in the gelcoat or interior finish allows transmission. This method of inspection can be helpful in detecting areas that are resin-rich (with too much resin) or resin-starved. The former condition may result in crazing of the resin, while the latter may lead to voids or delaminations. Laminate flaws revealed by light transmission usually show up in the form of irregular, spotty, or stained areas, but they are often difficult to interpret accurately and so should be left to the surveyor's experienced eye. General translucence is not usually considered harmful. In fact, sunlight shining through and visible from the inside of a hull may indicate a healthy unpigmented and unadulterated laminate rather than one of insufficient thickness, as is often supposed.

With any type of construction, the condition of the fastenings is of utmost importance, especially on boats of wood or other materials that are put together piecework. Fastenings should be inspected wherever possible by tapping them, looking for hairline cracks in paint around their plugs and cracking paint between the frames and planking, by scraping the heads of fastenings to look at their metal, and by looking for corrosion or rust stains. In suspicious areas where fastenings are concealed, wood plugs covering screws should be removed, and occasionally a few fastenings themselves might be taken out for careful examination. Most high-quality boats will have fastenings of a good bronze such as Everdur, copper rivets, or in some cases Monel. Be extremely wary of boats put together with uncoated ferrous fastenings or yellow brass screws. Look for erosion or deterioration of the wood surrounding a fastening. Tannic acid from improperly seasoned wood (especially oak) can attack the fastenings and cause subsequent decay in the nearby wood. Test the nuts on major bolts to see that they are not wasted and that the threads are not stripped. Washers should be amply large. Suspicious-looking keelbolts might have to be removed for examination, especially when a long offshore passage is planned. A fairly new method of inspecting keelbolts, using a portable X-ray machine, is now said to be practical and reasonably priced in major yachting centers.

Other nondestructive methods of inspecting metals for cracks, wasting, or hidden flaws include magnetic particle examination, which is limited to ferrous metals or those that can be magnetized, and in limited cases, eddy current analysis. The latter method uses an electric probe to create circular currents of electrons in the metal being tested. Even the smallest discontinuity will reduce current through the probe to reveal a flaw that might not be detected by any other means. More common tests include ultrasonic examination, whereby a piezoelectric transducer is applied to the suspect metal and the transmission of sound waves is measured and displayed on an ultrasonic gauge or occasionally on an oscilloscope. These methods can be utilized by corrosion engineering specialists, but the average yacht surveyor does not have the knowledge or equipment for such inspections; instead he will most often rely on dye-penetrant testing, which will generally suffice when an internal flaw extends to the surface. The metal is stained with a brightly colored liquid, which is then wiped off and made visible in way of the defect with the application of a developer. More will be said about this procedure in Chapter 10.

Galvanic and Stray-Current Corrosion

The metal fastenings, hull straps, chainplates, and particularly the underwater fittings (such as struts and propellers) of boats used on saltwater must be compatible, for the use of dissimilar metals can lead to galvanic corrosion. Boats with metal hulls are especially vulnerable. Figure 4-1 shows the galvanic series, a scale of metals listed in the order of their corrosion resistance. Fastenings and underwater metals should, if possible, be close together on the galvanic scale to minimize corrosion. For instance, copper, bronze, and Monel are close together on the list, but bronze and ferrous metals or bronze and aluminum are far apart, and their combinations may cause serious problems in saltwater.

Corrosion may show up in two related but slightly different forms: galvanic action, and stray-current corrosion (commonly but incorrectly referred to as electrolysis). The first results when two metals are immersed in, or even subjected to moisture from, an electrolyte solution (seawater). If the two metals are electrically connected inside the boat by the bonding system, wiring, or intervening metallic structures, a spontaneous low-tension current is generated along the pathway, which raises the voltage potential of the less noble metal (or anode) and lowers the potential of the more noble metal (cathode). The anode then exchanges

Metals and Alloys [1]	Corrosion-Potential Range in Volts [2]	
Magnesium and Magnesium Alloys	−1.60	to −1.63
Zinc	−0.98	to −1.03
Galvanized Steel or Galvanized Wrought Iron		NA
Aluminum Alloys	−0.76	to −1.00
Cadmium	−0.70	to −0.73
Mild Steel	−0.60	to −0.71
Wrought Iron	−0.60	to −0.71
Cast Iron	−0.60	to −0.71
13% Chromium Stainless Steel, Type 410 (active in still water)	−0.46	to −0.58
18/8 Stainless Steel, Type 304 (active in still water)	−0.46	to −0.58
Ni-Resist	−0.46	to −0.58
18.8, 3% Mo Stainless Steel, Type 316 (active in still water)	−0.43	to −0.54
Inconel (78% Ni, 14.5% Cr, 6% Fe) (active in still water)	−0.35	to −0.46
Aluminum Bronze (92% Cu, 8% Al)	−0.31	to −0.42
Naval Brass (60% Cu, 39% Zn)	−0.30	to −0.40
Yellow Brass (65% Cu, 35% Zn)	−0.30	to −0.40
Red Brass (85% Cu, 15% Zn)	−0.30	to −0.40
Muntz Metal (60% Cu, 40% Zn)	−0.30	to −0.40
Tin	−0.31	to −0.33
Copper	−0.30	to −0.57
50-50 Lead – Tin Solder	−0.28	to −0.37
Admiralty Brass (71% Cu, 28% Zn, 1% Sn)	−0.28	to −0.36
Aluminum Brass (76% Cu, 22% Zn, 2% Al)	−0.28	to −0.36
Manganese Bronze (58.5% Cu, 39% Zn, 1% Sn, 1% Fe, 0.3% MN)	−0.27	to −0.34
Silicone Bronze (96% Cu max, 0.80% Fe, 1.50% Zn, 2.00% Si, 0.75% MN, 1.60% Sn)	−0.26	to −0.29
Bronze, Composition G (88% Cu, 2% Zn, 10% Sn)	−0.24	to −0.31
Bronze, Comp. M (88% Cu, 3% Zn, 6.5% Sn, 1.5% Pb)	−0.24	to −0.31
13% Chromium Stainless Steel, Type 401 (passive)	−0.26	to −0.35
90% Cu – 10% Ni	−0.21	to −0.28
75% Cu – 20% Ni – 5% Zn	−0.19	to −0.25
Lead	−0.19	to −0.25
70% Cu – 30% Ni	−0.18	to −0.23
Inconel (78% Ni, 13.5% Cr, 6% Fe) (passive)	−0.14	to −0.17
Nickel 200	−0.10	to −0.20
18/8 Stainless Steel, Type 304 (passive)	−0.05	to −0.10
70% Ni – 30% Cu Monel 400, K-500	−0.04	to −0.14
18.8, 3% Mo Stainless Steel, Type 316 (passive)	−0.0	to −0.10
Titanium	−0.05	to +0.06
Hastelloy C	−0.03	to +0.08
Platinum	+0.19	to +0.25
Graphite	+0.20	to +0.30

anodic ← → cathodic
least noble ← → most noble

1. Each metal has a unique voltage potential.
2. Half-cell reference electrode, silver-silver chloride.

Figure 4-1. *The galvanic series.*

ions with the seawater in an effort to return to its natural voltage potential, corroding in the process.

In stray-current corrosion, the current is supplied by an outside source, such as the boat's battery, a ship-to-shore AC electrical cable, a poor electrical connection in a damp area of the boat, electrical leaks from on-board equipment to the ground system, or a haphazard ground system that uses undersize wire or grounds the positive rather than the negative sides of the electrical circuits. The currents generated can be orders of magnitude larger than those generated by galvanic corrosion, and can waste metal fittings in no time at all.

Galvanic corrosion may be prevented or minimized by using high-quality noble metals that are close together in the galvanic series for fastenings or underwater appendages; by isolating or insulating the metals whenever possible so that no current can flow through the metallic contact side of the circuit; by using sacrificial anode protectors, usually of zinc but occasionally of magnesium or aluminum; or by using an impressed current control system. The latter method passes a small electrical current from a battery or shore power into the water via a control anode, which converts the boat's metal appendages into cathodes (negative electrodes) that won't corrode. The installation of sacrificial zincs is

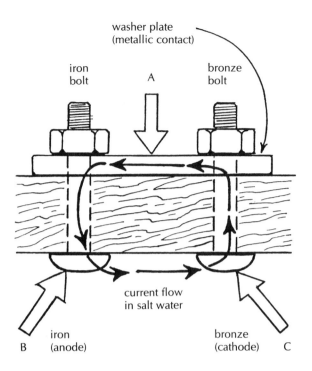

washer plate
(metallic contact)

iron
bolt

A

bronze
bolt

current flow
in salt water

iron
B   (anode)

bronze
(cathode)   C

Simple Corrective Measures

A - break connection (by using   C - replace either bolt with one
     separate washers)   made of metal that is closer
                                          on the galvanic scale to the
B - add sacrificial protectors   metal of the other bolt
     to anode

Figure 4-2. *Principle of the galvanic circuit.*

usually a simpler if sometimes less effective method of controlling galvanic corrosion. In this case, zinc blocks or collars, specially designed for the purpose, are secured to any appendages that can corrode, and the zinc, which is almost the least noble metal in the galvanic scale, corrodes instead of the appendage. The sacrificial metal decreases harmful corrosion by increasing the negative voltage of the metal being protected. Of course, zinc protectors have to be replaced periodically when they deteriorate. To be successful, one must deploy them in sufficient numbers and large enough size, yet avoid excessive use, which may cause hydrogen embrittlement in some metals. The zincs must be electrically connected to the appendages they are to protect, and they should not be painted. A steel or copper wire run through the center of the zinc helps assure electrical contact after the surface of the zinc has been used up, but there is no substitute for direct contact between the anode and the metal it is to protect.

Sacrificial anodes are especially important to protect brass alloys such as manganese bronze and naval or Tobin bronze, which will dezinc in

Figure 4-3. *Corrosion at the base of an aluminum mast may be caused by galvanic action between the heel casting and the spar. This heel was replaced by one of inert Micarta. (Rip Henderson photo)*

saltwater. Surveyors often sound the propeller with a metal hammer to test for dezincification, and they examine any brass alloy for a change in color from yellow to pink or copper-red. Incidentally, take care to use bottom paints whose metallic contents are compatible with the metals on the boat's bottom. Beware of using mercury antifouling paints especially. Figure 4-2 shows the principle of galvanic action.

The fundamental principle in avoiding stray-current corrosion is to keep both alternating and direct currents (AC and DC) inside their respective wires and ground the electrical system on its negative side. If wires or electrical connections should leak current, or cross-grounding should allow a flow of current from a ground plate to an appendage, for instance, serious corrosion might occur. Separate the AC and DC systems as completely as possible (ABYC tests show that stray direct currents are much more devastating to metals than stray alternating currents), which certainly means separate electrical panels for DC and AC distribution. Take particular care with the installation of radio telephones having their own external (immersed) ground plates, for, if the current is not properly confined in a two-wire system, the flow might run underwater between the radio's plate and the boat's battery ground, which is often by way of the propeller, shaft, and engine. Be sure that a well-qualified marine electrician has installed or inspected the radio and the entire wiring system. Another source of serious corrosion, and perhaps serious shock to a swimmer coming in contact with underwater metal appendages, is cross-grounding with shore current at marinas. At some dockside installations, incorrect positioning of the electric plug in its receptacle might cause a current flow from the hot side of the shore-line through the boat's ground system, through the water, and back to the shore. One means of avoiding cross-grounding is by using an isolation transformer capable of handling all current needs. A polarity indicator that has a warning light or buzzer may sometimes be used.

Theoretically, a boat connected to AC shore power via a ship-to-shore cable is grounded ashore through the ground prong in the shore power receptacle. Many boatowners feel it is therefore safe not to connect the ground return wire (i.e., the green or bare wire) from onboard AC appliances to the boat's engine block or other common ground point. By eliminating that connection, the boatowner prevents stray current leakage from the AC system to his boat's underwater hardware, with its attendant corrosion. This practice is *not* safe however, since it places total reliance for grounding on the shoreside connection, and a corroded terminal or some other discontinuity shoreside could pose a dangerous shock hazard to people on board or to swimmers. True, corrosion can be a problem, particularly when boats at the marina have different underwater metals, but the way to combat this is with an isolation transformer or an isolator. By means of a magnetic transfer of power from the shore to the boat side of the transformer, an isolation transformer eliminates the direct electrical connection between boat and shore. Alternatively, the boatowner can install an isolator either between the AC grounding circuit and the boat's common ground point or directly on the incoming shore-power ground connection. An isolator is a device that blocks the flow of low-voltage DC stray currents but will pass a strong current safely to ground in the event of a short in the AC system. Complete details on these subjects are offered in the ABYC Electrical Standards and in a first-rate treatment in *The Boatowner's Mechanical and Electrical Manual* by Nigel Calder (International Marine, 1990).

For additional protection against shocks from a ground fault—a failure in the onboard AC electrical circuit that allows current to flow from a hot wire to ground—the ABYC recommends the use of GFCIs (ground fault circuit interruptors) for AC receptacles in the galley, head, machinery spaces, and weather decks. One GFCI serving as the first receptacle from the breaker panel will protect all downstream receptacles on the same branch circuit as well as itself.

Wiring and Piping

Wiring can cause stray-current corrosion when it leaks current through inadequate insulation or moisture, or in some cases, through damp wood. Look for high-grade, stranded copper wire of ample size, protected by an impervious insulating cover, installed high out of the bilge, and secured with insulated clips. The electrical system should be protected by fuses or circuit breakers installed on the hot (ungrounded) side of the system, and terminal connections should be secured so that they cannot work loose from vibration. A master cut-off switch should be installed on the hot DC conductor as close as possible to the battery's positive terminal and accessible outside the engine compartment. Use of heavy wiring between battery terminals and a radiotelephone, including the ground plate wiring, will curb electrolysis between the ground plate and propeller caused by voltage drop through the wiring. Wiring should be installed so as to cause minimal compass deviation.

The storage batteries belong in a well-ventilated area, away from the engine fuel line fittings, filters, and tanks, in a well-secured, lead-lined box (or fiberglass-lined box on a small yacht) protected by a nonconductive cover, so that metal objects cannot fall on the terminals and cause sparks or a short circuit. Federal standards forbid the use of spring-loaded connectors on the battery terminals. Details for sound wiring are set forth by the U.S. Coast Guard and the National Fire Protection Association (Batterymarch Park, Quincy, Massachusetts) in the booklet No. 302 entitled *Fire Protection Standards for Motor Craft*. Another good guide is *Standards and Recommended Practices for Small Craft*, published by the ABYC.

The electrical bonding of sizable metal fittings within the hull to prevent corrosion is a controversial subject. Some surveyors advocate the practice because it will protect against electrolysis, but other authorities believe that wiring the fittings together is apt to cause galvanic corrosion, especially if the fittings are of highly dissimilar metals. Robert Kocher, technical editor of the *National Fisherman* magazine, has advised against bonding partly because the ground will bleed off the protective negative charge, and also because bonded bronze through-hull fittings can seriously soften a wooden hull in way of the fittings. If bonding is done, great care must be taken to inspect and renew zinc protectors. There is no question of the advisability of grounding for lightning and fire protection, and this important subject will be discussed in Chapter 6.

Properly installed and carefully inspected piping is no less important than proper wiring; it is obvious that a broken pipe can result in foundering. As mentioned in the last chapter, all through-hull pipes should be fitted with readily accessible valves, and these should be inspected periodically, lubricated, and kept in good operating condition. Shut-off valves of the seacock type—tapered plug valves that operate with lever handles—are preferable. An alternative, perhaps, is the ball cock, which operates in a similar manner as the seacock—that is, with a handle that turns 90 degrees. Some of the cheaper, non-flanged types used on inexpensive stock boats are undesirable, but I have read and heard good reports about the flanged ball cock called Sea Flange made by the Apollo Ball Valve division of Conbraco Industries (Box 125, Pageland, South Carolina). Many modern boats use rubber hoses such as Sureflex marine hose; these are metal-reinforced and resistant to fatigue (which is sometimes caused by engine vibration), but they should be *securely* attached to the through-hull fitting with proper stainless steel hose clamps (two clamps if possible). I know of a boat that sank because she was fitted with a stiff, inflexible PVC hose that could not be effectively squeezed onto its through-hull nipple by clamps. The hose simply slipped off the fitting. This was not an isolated occurrence. Beware of plastic through-hull fittings; some have been known to break, and hoses can slip off plastic nipples quite easily.

Plumbing fixtures such as pumps and the head should be installed so as to prevent back-siphoning; otherwise, a faulty or stuck check valve

Figure 4-4. *Some plumbing suggestions. **A**: anti-siphon vents. **B**: bilge pump installed in cockpit (not in seat locker). **C**: plug-type seacocks. **D**: sturdy, unbendable rod or preferably a diaphragm pump with a removable handle stowed or lashed nearby. **E**: pump discharge as high as possible, but below tumblehome to avoid staining topsides (may be in transom if discharge is not excessively long or crooked). **F**: strainer attached to end of intake hose. **G**: hose flexible to allow lifting to clear strainer. **H**: sink as close as possible to centerline. **I**: looped lines and sinks above highest normal angle of heel. **J**: easily accessible shut-off valve if sink is not on the centerline. **K**: sink discharge above LWL or at least one foot below LWL to avoid freezing. **L**: head W.C. above LWL. **M**: head outlet below LWL but abaft and higher than intake **N**.*

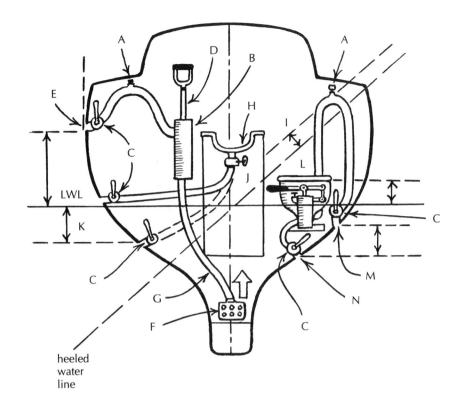

could allow the boat to flood and possibly sink. The discharge hose should be looped and vented with a siphon breaker as shown in Figure 4-4. Even if the head bowl is above the waterline, as it should be, a sailboat's discharge hose should have a high loop to prevent back-siphoning at large angles of heel. Beware of weak holding tanks and self-contained chemical toilets; several heavy-weather races have demonstrated their vulnerability to falling crew or gear and even to flexing hulls. Sinks are usually higher above the waterline, but they can admit water into a sailboat when she is heeled; thus they should be located as close as possible to the boat's centerline, and of course, their discharge lines must have a readily accessible shut-off valve. Some details are shown in Figure 4-4. Water tanks should be well secured and baffled to prevent violent sloshing in a seaway. A seagoing boat should have her water supply divided between several tanks in case one tank leaks or the water in it goes bad.

Inspect piping around the engine for fatigue cracks or leaks from vibration. Metal pipes subject to severe vibration should be fitted with short lengths of hose at connections to tanks, engines, etc. Inspect the propeller shaft for correct alignment; serious vibration and other troubles can result when the shaft and engine are out of line. Copper lines should be connected to the engine with flexible tubing. Where vibration is minimal, a slow bending, circular loop in a copper line may suffice, but some surveyors frown on this practice. If the engine is flexible-mounted to reduce noise or vibration, all connections between the hull

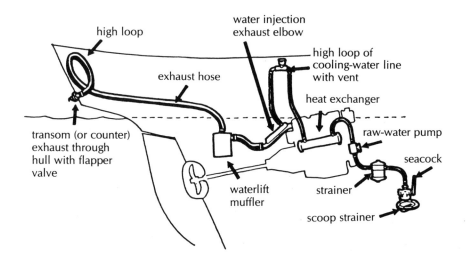

Figure 4-5. *A proper exhaust installation on an auxiliary sailboat. (From* What Shape Is She In: A Guide to the Surveying of Boats *by Allan Vaitses; International Marine, 1985)*

and engine must also be fully flexible. The stern tube area (where the shaft penetrates the hull) can be damaged by poor shaft alignment; by a broken, unbalanced propeller; or by one blade that fails to open on a folding propeller, which will cause violent vibration. (Incidentally, if a folding prop vibrates when the engine is first started, shift into reverse gear immediately to open its blades.) It is wise to release the shaft at the engine coupling and pull it out just enough to check for wear or shaft scoring at the bearings. Be sure the propeller is securely attached to the shaft.

The exhaust installation should be carefully inspected to see that sea-water or cooling water cannot run back into the engine manifold regardless of heeling or pitching. There should be a high loop in the aft end of the exhaust line to prevent water entry through the outlet, and a drain at the line's low point. In the commonly used waterlift muffler system with the engine below the waterline, the muffler's canister should be located well below the engine, and the exhaust cooling waterline needs a high loop with an anti-siphon vent (see Figure 4-5). It is most prudent to fit the exhaust outlet with a shut-off valve as a safeguard against water entry when the engine is not running in heavy weather. Powerboats do not have the same need for this valve as auxiliary sailboats, because they don't heel as much and because their engines are nearly always running in heavy weather. But a shut-off might be needed if the powerboat should drift or lie to a sea anchor with motor off.

Inspection of the engine should be left to a qualified mechanic, who will measure the compression and check for worn bearings, valve seatings, and so forth. A trial run can tell you a great deal. Easy starting, quietness, lack of vibration even at high RPMs, ability to idle down, sufficient oil pressure, smoke-free exhaust, etc. are favorable indications. Proper fuel tank installation, as well as engine room ventilation, will be discussed in Chapter 6.

Steering Gear and Centerboard

The steering system warrants thorough inspection. Check the rudder-head fitting for cracks or wear; keys in keyways for tightness of fit; steering cables for broken strands or play; cable sheaves for wear, security, and fair leading; the quadrant for cracks, looseness, or improper alignment; the rudderstock for signs of wear, corrosion, or warping; the rudder tube stuffing box for leakage, wear, or binding; the rudderstops to see that no jamming of the rudder or damage from being thrown hard over in heavy weather can occur; gears and bushings in worm gear or rack-and-pinion systems; and all seals if the steering is hydraulic. The rudder inspection is even more important. Check for excessive play or looseness; wear or cracks at the pintles and heel fitting; and delamination, blistering, cracking, or warping of the rudder blade. Inspect any visible rudder straps, drift bolts, and gudgeons on the keel or skeg. The tiller or steering wheel must be unquestionably strong, and on any sailboat there should be a practical means of attaching an emergency tiller. Large powerboats are seldom fitted with emergency tillers because of visibility problems and perhaps also because twin-screw boats can be steered with their throttles. Nevertheless, any offshore passagemaker needs thought concerning emergency steering. If the rudder stock cannot be extended to deck level where an emergency tiller can be attached, then perhaps a jury rudder can be rigged as suggested in Chapter 6. One can't be too careful in checking the steering gear, because rudder losses and other steering failures at sea are all too frequent.

Centerboard boats need periodic, thorough inspection of the pivot pin, pendant, cable sheaves, and all parts of the lifting mechanism. Look for signs of corrosion, wear, chafe, or fishhooks (wire snags) in the pendant, and see that all parts are well lubricated. Some authorities prefer centerboard pendants of synthetic rope to avoid corrosion, but this system needs an easy means of inspecting and replacing the pendant. Be alert to thumping of the board in its trunk. If it is excessive, you might shim the well. For reduced stress the lowered board should extend far up into the trunk, at least half its depth below the keel.

Inspection of the rig will be discussed in detail in Chapter 10.

Chapter 5
SAFETY EQUIPMENT AND OFFSHORE GEAR

In fitting out a boat for safe operation on any waters, give your first consideration to legal requirements. Federal requirements for recreational boats are set forth in the Coast Guard's pamphlet CG-290. Mandatory equipment includes such items as engine ventilation, backfire flame arrestors for carburetors, fire extinguishers, bells, whistles, personal flotation devices (PFDs), and navigation lights as stipulated by the Rules of the Road.

Appendix A contains equipment and standards recommended for power and sailboats by the Coast Guard Auxiliary. In many particulars these standards go beyond those of the Coast Guard. More comprehensive equipment lists for sailboats have been compiled by yacht racing organizations. Standard requirements for races are set forth by the Offshore Rating Council (ORC) in its Offshore Equipment Lists, reproduced in Appendix B. These lists, which are revised and updated periodically, vary according to the length and exposure of a race. Although not all the equipment and standards suggested by the ORC are required for cruising, the lists form a good basis for equipping any boat.

Listed equipment requirements are the *minimum* that should be carried on a vessel. Even lists as comprehensive as the ORC's do not include items that many experienced sailors would consider valuable or even essential. In the following paragraphs we will elaborate on some of the more important equipment recommended by the ORC, and then we will suggest a few additional items that don't appear on current ORC lists.

One of the most important pieces of equipment is the bilge pump. It is surprising to see the number of new boats that have either no permanent bilge pump or a faulty or inadequate installation. Pumps are not merely conveniences. In the event of a collision, grounding, knockdown, broken pipe, working of the hull in a seaway, or related emergencies, a means of clearing the bilge quickly could mean the difference between reaching port or foundering. Pumps should have ample capacity—at least 13 gallons per minute for small cruisers. Larger offshore boats need pumps of greater capacity, preferably 30 gallons per minute. Many boats

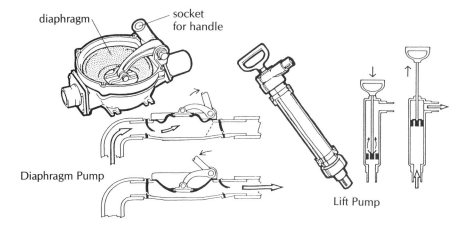

Figure 5-1. *Diaphragm and lift pumps. (Jim Sollers illustration from* Elements of Seamanship *by Roger Taylor, International Marine, 1986)*

diaphragm

socket for handle

Diaphragm Pump

Lift Pump

are fitted with small, cheap, plastic pumps of the plunger type, but most of these are unreliable in heavy weather partly because their flimsy plunger rods break or bend easily and their cylinders crack with rough use. Large-capacity navy-type plunger lift pumps made of brass are generally reliable, but even more highly recommended are diaphragm bilge pumps such as the Edson, Whale, and Titan brands. Small manual pumps of the diaphragm type can be obtained with double action, meaning that water is pumped when the handle moves in each direction; they can pump 30 gallons per minute with a hose of 1.5-inch diameter. Electric pumps are a great convenience but not always dependable, especially in heavy weather or emergency conditions when they are most apt to be needed. Centrifugal or impeller-type engine-driven pumps will remove large volumes of water with minimal crew effort so long as the engines can be started and kept running, although belts may slip when wet. The water pump on the boat's propulsion engine can be converted to an excellent bailer, as will be discussed in the next chapter under "Emergency Repairs."

It is not unusual to see a permanent bilge pump's discharge line connected to a cockpit scupper outlet below the waterline. This practice is dangerous, because check valves are not always reliable. A pump's discharge outlet should be as far as possible above the waterline to prevent back-siphoning, and on a sailboat that can submerge the outlet while heeling, the line should be looped and vented. Hoses should be of large diameter and noncollapsible, and the intake at the low point in the bilge should be fitted with an *accessible* strainer. All too often pumps become clogged with the trash and dirt that always seems to accumulate in the bilge. Another source of pump clogging is paper labels that peel off canned goods. If cans are kept in the bilge, their labels should be removed.

The recommended location for a permanent bilge pump is in or near the cockpit, but not inside a seat locker unless the locker is an integral part of the watertight cockpit. If it is necessary to open the lid of a seat locker to reach the pump, and the locker is open to the bilge, then the

very act of pumping during a knockdown or when the decks are awash may do more harm than good. It is wise to install another pump below in the cabin in case it becomes necessary to pump without going on deck, or to supplement the deck pump. In addition, carry a portable pump with a long, flexible hose that can be moved to various locations. Finally, keep a few buckets around for a real bailing emergency. Over the short term, at least, few pumps can equal the efficiency of one scared man with a bucket. I know of an ocean racer that nearly sank at sea as a result of a broken discharge pipe when the bilge pump clogged and no bucket could be found on board. The crew was forced to bail with a suitcase.

In the interest of watertight integrity, every sailboat should have sturdy companionway slides that can be locked in place. These are particularly important on a boat that has no bridge deck and a low companionway sill. Locks or latches are absolutely vital when the sides of the companionway angle away from the vertical, because a slide need only

Figure 5-2. *The importance of a self-draining cockpit is dramatized by this heavy-weather photograph. In addition, the lack of a lifeline in such a situation could easily result in the loss of the helmsman. (Norris D. Hoyt photo)*

Figure 5-3. *Fastnet storm slides ensure that the dropboard will remain locked in place. When the dropboard's handle is turned to the side (top), the board is locked at the side. When the handle is turned down (bottom), the board is locked at the top. (From* Sailing in Windy Weather *by Richard Henderson, International Marine, 1987)*

be lifted a slight amount before it will fall out. In Europe, offshore boats are now being fitted with Fastnet storm slides (see Figure 5-3), which better assure that the sliding hatch cover and dropboards remain well secured. When the handle is horizontal the latch extends out from the side, and when the handle is vertical the latch protrudes at the top edge, engaging the sliding hatch cover.

Details of lifeline installations are given in the appendix lists. Stanchions must be through-bolted, and the entire installation should be strong enough to withstand the weight of a heavy man thrown hard against the assembly. The ABYC proposes that the installation be capable of withstanding a "static" force of approximately 600 pounds. Beware of small, triangular stanchion bases whose corners can cut through the deck when a severe bending force is applied to the stanchion. Sailboats with outboard shrouds often pose a special problem where lifelines attach to a bow pulpit, because the foot of a low-cut jib will chafe on the upper lifeline or pulpit rail. The most practical solution to this problem with a minimal sacrifice to safety seems to be the installation of forward stanchions set slightly inboard of the pulpit in order to provide a narrow gateway for the passage of the jib's foot. Racing sailors concerned with the greatest possible aerodynamic efficiency will prefer the low-footed "decksweeper" jibs, but cruising sailors will normally carry a jib with its foot sufficiently high to clear the lifelines, which also affords much better visibility for the helmsman and catches less water.

No piece of permanent equipment is more important than an accurate, easy-to-read compass. The main steering compass should be mounted directly forward of the helmsman on the boat's centerline, or forward of the helmsman's sitting position, at a comfortable reading distance below his eye level but in a spot that is out of the way as much as possible so that the instrument will not be hit, stepped on, or bumped. Small cabin sailboats should usually have their compasses mounted behind small windows or domes in the bridge deck or after end of the cabin trunk. Larger sailboats with wheel steering will normally have their compasses mounted in binnacles atop a sturdy pedestal just forward of the helm. These pedestals cannot be made too strong, because heavy crewmembers often grab them for support or are sometimes thrown against them in a seaway. Some years ago a pedestal was torn from the cockpit sole of an ocean racer when it was entangled by the mainsheet during an all-standing jibe. A curved piperail over the binnacle might be installed to afford a convenient hand grip and guard against fouling of the mainsheet.

Great care must be taken to place the compass where deviation is minimal. Keep it away from ferrous metals and as far as possible (at least three feet is the rule of thumb) from electronic equipment. Electric wires should be distanced from the compass, but where they must be close, the wires should be run in twisted pairs (one lead twisted about the other) in order to help cancel out their magnetic fields. Keep portable gear that is electrical or of ferrous metal away from the compass. The

Figure 5-4. Fiddler's Green *after grounding off Pawley's Island, South Carolina, as a result of a photographic light meter being placed too near the compass. (W.H. Burney photo)*

yacht *Fiddler's Green,* owned by Dr. Edmund B. Kelly, was lost on a lee shore at night because someone inadvertently put down a photographic light meter too close to the binnacle. Remember that even a beer can placed next to the compass may cause deviation.

Compass errors from deviation can be minimized by adjustment with correcting magnets. These are often built into the compass and can be moved with adjusting screws. On sailboats, however, every effort should be made to minimize deviation in order that correcting magnets will not be needed, because they can cause errors when the boat heels. In most cases, for greatest accuracy, the compass should be corrected by a professional compass adjuster unless the skipper is experienced with such matters. Seldom can all errors be eliminated, given the sizable masses of iron (the engine or keel, for example) and electronic gear near the cockpit in most boats. Thus, most craft should carry "deviation cards" to record the compass errors on various headings. All compasses should be gim-balled, but sailboats require special gimballing that allows the card to remain horizontal and swing freely at large angles of heel. Don't use a powerboat compass on a monohull sailboat.

The modern fluxgate compass sidesteps the traditional concern with deviation and adverse effects from the boat's motion, but the fluxgate, which uses a magnetometer to sense position relative to the earth's magnetic field, is dependent on electrical power. Therefore, any boat venturing far offshore should carry a magnetic compass as a backup.

Navigation light requirements are specified in the Rules of the Road, under which all vessels operate. International Rule lighting is required on the high seas, and this same lighting is permissible on U.S. inland waters. In the interests of simplicity and uniformity it seems highly desirable that boats be equipped with international lighting, except in the rare instance where a state law might prohibit this. Sailboat lights are often obstructed by sails; therefore, it is advisable to carry the optional lights described in Rule 25(c). This rule allows a vessel under sail to carry, in addition to her normal red and green sidelights and sternlight, a 32-point red light over a 32-point green light at or near the top of the mast where they can best be seen. The latest version of the U.S. Inland Rules also gives a sailing vessel under 65.6 feet (20 meters) the option of carrying the sternlight and sidelights combined in a single multisector light at the masthead. If this is done, the red-over-green optional lights may not be used. In steamer lanes at night, it is prudent to carry a powerful flashlight that can be aimed at your sails when converging with a ship. The owner of a new boat, either sail or power, should be sure his boat's lighting meets legal requirements; believe it or not, some stock boats are fitted with improper lights.

The ORC equipment list once required a marine radio transceiver of at least 25 watts for sailboats racing long distances in unprotected waters. A powerful radiotelephone remains a wise investment for any vessel going offshore, but the range of radio signals does not depend only on the power of the set. In addition, it has to do with such matters as frequency, antenna length, time of day, proper grounding for single-side-band and ham radios, and antenna height. Maximum height is essential for VHF (very high frequency) radio, the range of which is essentially line-of-sight; the higher the elevation of the transmitting and receiving antennas, the greater the range. The average maximum communication distance is 10 to 15 miles between vessels and 20 to 30 miles between vessel and shore.

An offshore boat equipped for long-distance radio communications will have a VHF-FM radio and an SSB (single-sideband) set capable of receiving and transmitting on medium and high frequencies, usually up to 23 MHz. Medium frequency is needed for coastal operations beyond VHF range, normally 50 to 150 miles in the daytime. This frequency band from 2 to 3 MHz includes the international distress, urgency, and safety frequency, 2182 kHz. The distress signal transmitted over 2182 kHz is the spoken word "Mayday" ("m'aidez"—"help me" in French) or a two-tone warbling alarm similar to that used by some ambulances. The distress frequency for VHF-FM is Channel 16, 156.8 MHz. Before using a radiotelephone for nonemergency communications, listen on the distress frequency (156.8 MHz or 2182 kHz) to make sure it is not being used. Three-minute silent periods are maintained by the Coast Guard on 2182 kHz immediately after the hour and the half-hour. During these periods only distress or urgency calls may be made.

Short-range CB (Citizens' Band) radios operating on 27 MHz are used by some boats that stay close to shore. Channel 9 on CB has been designated an emergency channel.

For communications over very long distances, a single-sideband set should provide coverage of high-frequency (HF) marine bands. These bands normally extend up to 23 MHz, but an SSB set with a power output of, say, 150 watts may broaden the band to 30 MHz. Beware: Operating a powerful radio can discharge a boat's battery very rapidly.

Long-distance communications are made possible by skywaves reflecting from the ionosphere, high above the earth. Since the ionosphere comprises several ionized atmospheric layers generated by sunlight, range and clarity of transmission will depend on the time of day, season of the year, and sunspot activity. As a general rule, the more HF bands available, the better the opportunity for successful communication; the highest frequencies most often provide longer ranges. Daytime usually provides the most reliable long-range communications, but with medium frequency, long-distance skywave transmission is often possible at night.

A long antenna may be needed, especially for a reasonable range on medium frequency. Sailboats often have their permanent backstays insulated for this purpose, but then when the mast is lost, the radio is put out of action. It is now customary to carry a less efficient but more dependable loaded whip antenna mounted on the stern or, when the backstay is used, to carry a jury whip or about 50 feet of wire for a backup.

Given the possibility of radio failure or the need to transmit after abandoning ship, every offshore vessel should carry EPIRBs (emergency position-indicating radio beacons). These are small, lightweight, waterproof transmitters, usually with folding or telescoping antennas, that send out a distinctive alarm over a distress frequency. Class A and B EPIRBs broadcast distress signals on emergency frequencies 121.5 MHz and 243 MHz, and their signals can be received by overflying aircraft or SAR (search-and-rescue) satellites. Class C units operate on VHF channels 15 and 16. A second-generation, more expensive EPIRB, model 406, transmits to transponders on U.S. TIROS and Soviet satellites. If you have the funds, you can even be continually monitored by an Argos satellite. The newest EPIRBs are the mini B models, which are small enough to be carried in your pocket or on a life preserver. The longevity of batteries seldom meets advertised claims, so the EPIRB should be tested periodically. This may legally be done with a 121.5 MHz EPIRB if the test

Figure 5-5. *EPIRBs carried on the author's boat. The small one, a Narco, transmits distress signals on 121.5 and 243 MHz, while the larger one, a Callbuoy, will transmit voice as well as signal on 2182 kHz.*

lasts less than one minute and falls during the first five minutes of an hour. Use an FM radio tuned to 99.5 MHz. If there is no permanent radiotelephone aboard, it is a good idea to carry a VHF handheld transceiver and a portable unit such as the British-made Callbuoy or Safetylink, which transmits voice or a distress signal on 2182 kHz. An advantage of a portable unit, of course, is that it may be carried in a liferaft.

Speaking of portable safety equipment, none is more important than life preservers, or what the Coast Guard calls PFDs (personal flotation devices). The boatowner's first consideration must be to meet the letter of the law by carrying at least one Coast Guard-approved PFD for each person aboard. Federal regulations require that every boat under 16 feet in length be equipped with a type I, II, III, or IV PFD for each person on board. Larger craft need a type I, II, or III PFD, *plus* a type IV, for each person. The latter is a throwable device such as a ring buoy, horseshoe, or seat cushion. Types II and III, usually contoured vest or yoke designs, are fairly comfortable to wear but lack adequate buoyancy except in calm or nearly calm waters. A number of people have drowned while wearing these devices in rough seas. Type I has adequate flotation and will float the victim face upward, the trade-off being that it is bulky, cumbersome, and may seldom be worn.

Inflatable life preservers are usually more buoyant than noninflatables and allow more unrestricted movement when deflated, but they must be inspected and serviced periodically. Most convenient perhaps is the belt pack, such as the inflatable horseshoe buoy sold by Survival Technologies Group, although climbing into it may be difficult. Inflatables can be accredited by the Coast Guard provided that they are Type V PFDs (hybrid devices, normally vests, combining some inherent buoyancy with inflatable bladders), they incorporate some permanent flotation (normally in a hybrid vest form), the vessel is 40 feet long or smaller, and the PFD is worn rather than stowed away in a locker. Beware of cheap inflatables that can be worn on the wrist; their effectiveness is limited, and I've been told that one make can explode. Before purchasing any PFD, read the fine-print disclaimers on the device or its package.

Buoyant cushions may legally be used as type IV (throwable) PFDs provided they meet certain requirements as to buoyancy and construction and have their buoyancy material (kapok, for instance) sealed inside a vinyl bag. Even though such cushions meet Coast Guard requirements, however, they are inferior for lifesaving purposes as compared with life preservers designed for no other purpose. Nevertheless, cushions are usually handy, and when they are sufficiently long (at least 22 inches with handles at least 20 inches), they can be worn similarly to a life vest by inserting a leg through one handle strap and the opposite arm and shoulder or neck through the other; with the cushion covering his chest, the wearer floats face up (never wear a cushion on your back). Be sure the handles are securely attached. Seat cushions are nearly always readily available and can be tossed overboard in an instant, but do practice throwing them, because they tend to "sail" or veer off course in a wind. Some Coast Guard–approved wearable life preservers and buoyant vests have no straps that pass between the legs, but a recent fishing boat sinking shows that such straps are important to keep the preserver from riding up. Several unconscious crew drowned because their life jackets rode up and failed to keep their heads sufficiently high above the waves. Life preservers must be readily accessible from the bow as well as the stern, with jackets or vests distributed throughout the boat. Keep a ring buoy or horseshoe near the helmsman. Ring buoys should never be lashed in their holders, nor should they be attached to standing rigging that can render the buoys inaccessible in the event of a dismasting. At night, water lights should be attached to ring buoys, and at sea, 8-foot-high man-overboard poles, as described in the ORC lists, should be attached to them. Horseshoe-shaped buoys are usually prefer-able to closed rings because they are easier to don; they should be equipped with whistles, dye markers, and drogues or small sea anchors to lessen drift. An alternative to standard man-overboard poles is MOMs (Man Overboard Modules), developed and manufactured by Survival Technologies Group (101 16th Avenue South, St. Petersburg, Florida 33701). These are inflatable poles with a horseshoe buoy or one-man liferaft that can be quickly released from a pack hung on the stern pulpit or rail. Advantages are quickness of deployment and good visibility, but the equipment needs yearly servicing. Other man-overboard rescue gear, including the Lifesling, will be discussed in Chapter 7. In shark-infested waters, repellent is often recommended, but a more modern and effective means of protection is with the use of the Johnson shark screen, a durable, black plastic bag with buoyancy rings that can be unfolded from a small package to house and hide a man overboard. Aquatic Habitats in Apalachin, New York offers the Schneider Shark Belt, which uses a new type of repellent said to be effective. Water lights should be high-intensity, preferably the Xenon strobe types, sufficiently bright to be seen in fog or broad daylight. Life jackets should always be worn by non-swimmers, by young children, by water-skiers, and by adult swimmers in heavy weather or in other potentially hazardous con-ditions. Life preservers, jackets, and even cushions that will be used for life preservers should be bright yellow or international orange for maxi-mum visibility. Even brilliantly white preservers or life buoys can be diffi-cult to see amidst breaking seas. All lifesaving devices that are stowed in closed areas should be removed periodically for airing and inspection.

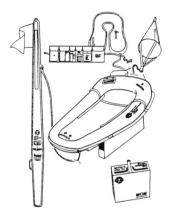

Figure 5-6. *The MOM VII Man Overboard Module. All gear, including the inflatable raft and man-overboard pole, is packed in the canister at the lower right. (Courtesy Survival Technologies Group)*

The necessity for liferafts will depend to a large extent on how the boat will be used, her condition and design, and the characteristics of her environs. Well-found boats with adequate flotation that stay close to shore in protected waters will not need a liferaft, but sinkable boats that sail at night and venture offshore or into foggy waters near rocky shoals or dangerous lee shores should carry a raft (or rafts) capable of taking off the entire crew. Of course, racing sailboats must meet the ORC raft requirements (Appendix B). The modern inflatable "rubber" (now neo-prene or urethane-coated nylon fabric) raft of proper design is consid-

Figure 5-7. *A canopy will greatly increase the odds for survival in a liferaft in heavy weather at sea, especially in cold waters. Note the boarding ladders on both rubber rafts. (Courtesy U.S. Coast Guard)*

ered far more suitable for lifesaving than conventional dinghies or even inflatable boats. Noninflatable liferafts of balsa or other lightweight, rigid materials are satisfactory when they have watertight bottoms and canopies to reduce the hazards of exposure, but they lack the buoyancy of gas-filled rubber rafts and they may be more subject to capsizing, while the deck space they require for stowage makes them impractical for most small craft. Dinghies can serve as lifeboats in some emergencies, such as an uncontrollable fire in fair weather, but in heavy weather they are vulnerable to serious damage and swamping. Inflatable liferafts provide great resistance to capsizing and damage (except from the blow of a sharp object), tremendous buoyancy, easy motion in seas, a large load capacity, and good protection for occupants when equipped with a canopy. They should be compartmented with at least two separate air chambers, and they should automatically inflate and eject from their cases. It is important that the manufacturer or a competent service depot inspect the raft periodically for corrosion of gas cylinders or valves; condensation or leakage of the container; and deterioration of the flares, lights, batteries, etc. The ORC requires inspection every two years, but England's Royal Ocean Racing Club (RORC) requires that this be done annually.

Stowage of inflatable rafts often presents a problem, because they must be instantly available yet strongly secured and protected against sun, prolonged water soakage, and physical damage. Ordinarily stowage should be on deck near the cockpit or a special stowage locker opening immediately to the deck and containing liferaft(s) only. The CCA has suggested that an ocean racing sailboat keep her raft in a well-secured pen-box (a square, topless container with low sides as shown in Figure 5-10) just forward of the companionway hatch. The bottom of the pen-box should be open and slightly raised off the deck with a slatted grating to support the raft and permit water to drain. Nowadays, however, the preferred arrangement is to pack the rafts in tightly sealed fiberglass canisters that are secured to stainless steel mounting cradles—possibly with rope lashings, which may be cut easily with a knife or released with pelican hooks or pull-pin shackles. Liferaft manufacturers offer special quick releases, including a hydrostatic release that can be operated manually or automatically by water pressure in the event a vessel sinks before anyone can reach the raft. On the new Navy 44s used at the U.S. Naval Academy, the raft is stowed under the bridge deck, and its canister can be slid aft into the open cockpit when it is needed. This arrangement offers a good compromise between protection and availability, though the raft cannot be hydrostatically released. A raft inflated on deck can easily be blown or washed away in heavy weather, so the stowed, deflated raft should have its painter well secured to the boat. When at sea, emergency equipment to be packed in the raft includes a sea anchor; an air horn; a whistle; a hand-operated pump and perhaps a spare cylinder of CO_2; flares (including smoke), dye marker, a strobe or flashlight, signal mirrors, and a EPIRB beacon; a bailer; a fishing kit; screw-type wooden plugs and a repair kit for punctures; a knife; a rescue quoit with line; a space blanket; two paddles; a first-aid kit with sunburn lotion, antibiotic, and pain killer in addition to standard items; emergency drinking water; and a few cans of food (pemmican is recommended). A solar still is available from Survival & Safety Designs (P.O. Box 562, Alameda, CA) or from Survival Technologies Group. A recently proven effective watermaker made by Recovery Engineering, Inc., of Minneapolis, Minnesota, is the Survivor 35, a hand-operated reverse-osmosis desalinator. Standard rafts may not include all this equipment, and it is important to compensate for deficiencies with an emergency grab bag containing what is lacking in the raft canister.

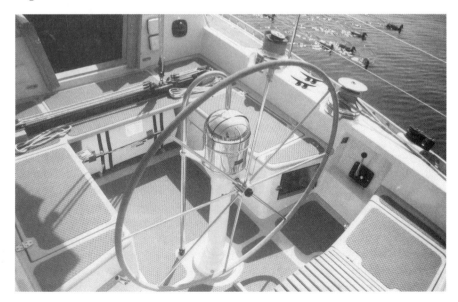

Figure 5-8. *Liferaft stowage under the bridge deck of a Navy 44. (Bill Brooks photo)*

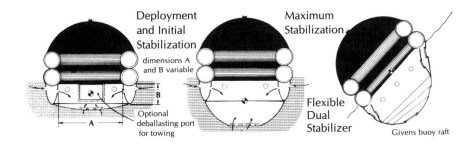

Figure 5-9. *This inflatable Givens liferaft has a huge water ballast bag and is the most stable type, but not the most mobile. (Courtesy Naval Institute Press)*

The choice of a liferaft involves a compromise between stability and locomotion. The most stable raft is the Givens type, which has a large, water-filled stability bag attached to its bottom, but this limits locomotion. The Givens raft may be deballasted, however, to allow towing and paddling. A very mobile raft is the Elliot Sea Jay, which is oblong-shaped and can be propelled by paddles or sail (downwind). Reasonable resistance to capsize is provided by four water pockets. Switlik may be converted to a sail-away configuration that uses one arch tube and part of the canopy for sail, and collapsing water pockets to allow limited sailing directly downwind. My own preference for warm waters is for some mobility even if it involves a minor compromise in stability.

Safety belts are essential on a seagoing sailboat, and at times could be just as valuable on an offshore powerboat. These belts are equipped with stout lanyards and heavy snaphooks that allow the wearer to attach himself to a handrail, bolted fitting, or some part of the rigging (not lifelines) so that he is able to work with both hands. In other words, when secured with a proper belt, a crewmember can temporarily disregard the old adage, "one hand for the ship and one hand for yourself." Most agree that the best safety belts are the harness type with shoulder straps. Offshore sailors should occasionally practice using them in daylight and fair weather so that their proper use will be instinctive under adverse conditions. A friend of mine, a good sailor, hooked his safety belt's lanyard to a shroud while preparing to lower a sail at night. The lanyard was shorter than he realized, and when he moved away from the shroud the line took up abruptly and jerked him off balance so that he fell to the deck. This kind of accident, which might seem amusing but could be serious, is best avoided with practice.

The lanyard should be secured to the safety harness with a snaphook so that the wearer can release himself easily if held underwater. Some cautious seamen advocate having two lanyards, so that the wearer can move about the boat without ever being unattached. One hook is clipped before the other is released. Jacklines—wire or, preferably, synthetic lines running fore and aft along the sidedecks—accomplish the same thing. The safety lanyard's snaphook simply slides along the jackline as the wearer moves forward or aft. Still another approach is the RVL (Ronstan-Viking-Latchway) system developed and sold by Ronstan Marine of Clearwater, Florida. A small cylindrical turnstile accepts the lanyard hook and slides on a heavy wire, deftly passing obstacles such as lifeline stanchions. Some flotation jackets have an integral safety harness with lanyards.

A radar reflector hoisted aloft greatly improves the chance that a boat will be spotted by radar-equipped ships in conditions of poor visibility. However, skippers should not be overconfident that they will be seen merely because their vessel carries a reflector. Visual and radar watches are sometimes lax on merchant ships, and heavy rain, high swells, or rough seas can hamper or obscure the signal reflected by a boat. Reflectors should be carried at night and in foggy weather, especially in steamer lanes, but even with a reflector, the small-boat skipper should assume that his reflection is not seen and give ships a wide berth whenever possible. Radar reflectors are generally most effective when they are prevented from swinging excessively, when they are hoisted as high as possible, and when they are as large as practical. Many makeshift reflectors, such as crumpled sheets of aluminum foil, are said to be nearly worthless, but homemade reflectors can be effective when made in conformity with standard models. The surfaces should be smooth metal or wire mesh and meet each other at right angles to form corners, so that if the radar signal is not reflected directly back to its source, it will return indirectly after bouncing from one surface of the reflector to another. Suspending the reflector from three points in the so-called rain-catch position, as illustrated in Figure 5-10, will provide optimum effectiveness. This position is only ideal, however, if the boat is not heeled. To mitigate the heeling problem, I rig my reflector from the backstay and angle it with a downhaul line led to either side of the boat depending on whether she is on the port or starboard tack. Plastic-enclosed reflectors, such as the Firdell Blipper, respond well to angles of heel up to 30 degrees, and they protect against chafe. It has been suggested that offshore sailboats in steamer lanes might improve their visibility on radar screens with large swatches of aluminized tape or cloth sewn into reinforced areas of the sails. To a large extent, however, the effectiveness of such an arrangement would depend on the angle of the sails to the direction of the radar signal. Flat-sided metal masts can be helpful in reflecting a signal, but in most cases only when the boat is not heeling.

Another aid to collision avoidance is the use of extremely bright Xenon strobelights mounted on the masthead or some other high point. These lights can be seen in fog, smoke, or haze, and they are allowed under the Rules of the Road as "flare-up lights," to be used in distress or when in need of assistance.

Distress signals are included in the Rules of the Road (see Appendix C). Equipment needed for International distress signals consists of a Very pistol with parachute flares; hand-held red flares and orange smoke flares; radio transmitter (already mentioned); dye marker; International code flags N and C; a square flag of International orange that may be waved from side to side or hoisted over or under a ball; the Canadian "Surface-to-Air" signal, consisting of a four-by-six-foot red-orange cloth with an 18-inch black square and an 18-inch black circle 18 inches apart on the longitudinal axis of the flag; a gun or firecrackers; and a loud, dependable horn. Freon horns are loud but not always dependable, because they may leak gas or become inoperable during cold weather. It is advisable to carry such a horn with spare cans of freon, but only to supplement a loud mouth horn or a hand-pumped bellows-type fog-horn. The national ensign flown upside down is a commonly recognized

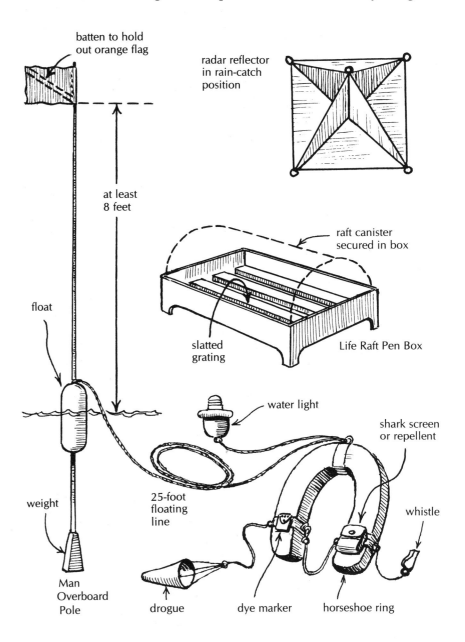

Figure 5-10. *Some safety equipment.*

batten to hold out orange flag

radar reflector in rain-catch position

at least 8 feet

float

raft canister secured in box

slatted grating

Life Raft Pen Box

water light

shark screen or repellent

weight

25-foot floating line

whistle

Man Overboard Pole

drogue

dye marker

horseshoe ring

distress signal, and a knotted flag is an ancient means of signifying distress.

Since 1981, U.S. boats have been required by law to carry visual distress signals. Day and night signaling devices are required on recreational boats 16 feet or longer, though the Coast Guard permits a number of options to satisfy minimum requirements. Perhaps the simplest legal combination consists of day/night pyrotechnics such as red meteors or flares, at least three being required. Many standard flares are ineffective and sometimes fail to work, so extras should be carried. As a general rule, pyrotechnic equipment labeled SOLAS (Safety of Life at Sea) is more reliable and superior in brightness and longevity. If you use hand-held flares, be aware that they can drip hot slag and possibly cause a fire or melt a hole in a liferaft. Hold the ignited flare overboard to leeward, and wear protective gloves. Coast Guard-approved pyrotechnics carry an expiration date. A device older than 42 months (from its date of manufacture) does not count toward minimum requirements.

In addition to its purpose-designed safety equipment, an offshore craft should carry essential tools, repair kits, and spare parts. A suitable wrench or a spare tiller might become as vital to the crew's welfare as the boat's lifelines. Basic tools for a seagoing boat include several sizes of screwdrivers, including one that can be used with a brace; brace and bits; hand drill with bits; adjustable, nonadjustable, needle nose, and Vise-Grip pliers; an assortment of wrenches (monkey, Stillson, crescent, end, socket, spark plug, etc.); hammer and hatchet; hacksaw and small wood saws; chisels; marlinespike; crowbar; tin snips; files; sandpaper; a small wood plane or surform; sheath knife; clamps; vise; wire cutter; bolt cutter; and a hand clamping tool for installing compression sleeves on wire cables.

Repair kits should include a complete sewing kit with assorted needles, thread, twine, beeswax, tape, cloth patches, etc. for mending sails, whipping lines, and combating chafe; an electrical kit with spare batteries, bulbs, fuses, electric tape, copper wire, etc.; a fiberglass kit (resin, catalyst, fiberglass cloth, tape, and roving); engine spare parts kit (gas engine: points, condenser, rotor, water pump seal, impeller with pin, distributor cap, ignition spray, generator belt, fuel pump diaphragm kit, coil, spark plugs, and lube oil; diesel engine: starting motor solenoid, primary fuel pump, fuel filters, injector feed lines, water pump impeller, belts, lube oil, hydraulic clutch fluid, possibly a spare injector or two, and an aerosol can of starting fluid [containing ether], a slight amount of which can be squirted into the air intake to help starting in an extreme emergency); a plumbing kit with spare parts for the head, extra hoses, hose clamps, a siphon hose, gaskets, nipples, packing, and tapered softwood plugs that may be driven into any through-hull fitting's orifice; leak repair kit (caulking cotton, bedding and seam compound, foam rubber, waterproof adhesives including underwater epoxy and Thiokol or silicone rubber, cup grease, putty, small sheets of plywood and soft metal); and a rigging repair kit (extra turnbuckles, toggles, clevis pins, cotter pins, sail slides, hanks, a grommet-making kit, bullseye clamps, shackles, a coil of flexible wire as long as the longest stay to replace broken rigging, binding wire, wire clamps, chain or metal straps for rigging extensions, and the hand clamping tool mentioned earlier).

Other spares for extended cruising would include an extra or emergency tiller, an extra rudderhead fitting, a spare spreader, spare battens, spare handles for winches and roller reefing, blocks, sail stops, lines of every size, an extra heavy anchor (perhaps a disassembled type for easy stowing), and plenty of extra sails, especially storm sails. Of course the

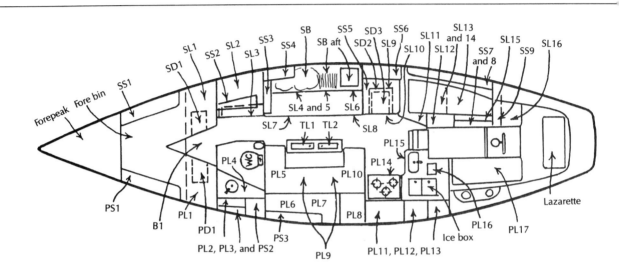

Figure 5-11. *A typical stowage plan.*

Forepeak - soft drinks; beer; spitfire jib; 13-pound Danforth anchor; light anchor line; life preservers; fresh vegetables (hung in net bags)

Fore bin - 35-pound CQR anchor; anchor rode and spare rode; 30-foot anchor chain, 150 feet of spare Dacron line (one-half inch); large tools (saws, surform, brace, rigging cutters, long threaded rod, large wrenches); handybilly; wedges and plugs; spare steering cable and clamps; hoses and clamps; pump for fuel tank; engine lube oil; spare log; extra wire cables (shroud and steering cable); rigging kit; emergency repair kit; beer; soft drinks

SS1 - flammables (solid stove primer, engine-starting booster); CRC lubricant; small Zenith radio; clothes

SD1 - camera and photo equipment

SL1 - canned goods (vegetables)

SL2 - (hanging locker) shore clothes, jackets, dry foul weather gear

SL3 - (in floor of hanging locker) largest wrench; wrecking bar; large channel pliers; short pieces of chain

SS2 - (above hanging locker) dark glasses and sunburn cream

SS3 - books; small radio

SS4 - short pieces of line; marlin; shock cord; extra sail stops

SL4 and 5 - clothes; personal items; games

SL6 - snack locker (crackers, cookies, candy bars, etc.)

spares should also include an assortment of nuts, bolts, screws, tacks, nails, and miscellaneous boat hardware that has not yet been mentioned, such as eyebolts, eye straps, cleats, sheet track slides, tangs, and so forth. On sailboats, ample chafe preventers such as baggy wrinkle, split rubber hoses, etc. should be carried. Spare parts for the stove might be considered more closely related to convenience than safety, but obviously these should be carried too when it is necessary for the vessel to be self-sufficient for considerable periods of time.

Other safety items not mentioned in the present ORC equipment lists

---

SL7 - safety belts; canned goods
SL8 - alcohol for stove; lamp oil; canned goods
SB - signal flags; flare kit; drifter; spinnaker
SB aft - navigation books and tables; chronometer; sextant
SD2 - cutlery; eating utensils; galley equipment
SD3 - small readily available tools and small fittings
SL9 - (chart desk) charts; documents; engine manual; etc.
SL10 - (under chart table) tool kit; mechanical kit; electrical kit; sail kit; Callbuoy;
    fire extinguisher
SS5 - hand-bearing compass and Narco beacon (on bulkhead)
SS6 - transoceanic radio and RDF (under); flashlight; books
SL11 - (in quarter berth step) ready locker (food for next meal)
SL12 - (foul weather locker) wet foul weather gear; shut-off valve for scuppers;
    life preservers
SL13 and 14 - canned fruit juices and milk; fathometer battery
SS7 and 8 - clothes
SL15 - spare freon and horn; bell; loud hailer
SS9 - blocks; roller reefing and winch handles
SL16 - sheets; guys; lead line; kerosene lights
Lazarette - shut-off valve for exhaust line; folding deck chair; fenders; dock lines;
    portable bilge pump; life preservers
PS1 - clothes
B1 - (bilge) speedometer transducer (through-hull fitting)
PL1 - canned meats
PD1 - sketching and writing materials; games; flashlight
PL2, PL3, and PS2 - toilet articles; towels; linen
PL4 - shut-off valve for wash basin; first aid kit; paper towels and toilet paper in large
    plastic bags
PS3 - clothes
PL5 - intake valve for head; egg cartons
PL6, PL7 - clothes
PL8 - dry goods (paper towels, plates, bags, etc.); extra binoculars
PL9 - canned goods in milk crates
TL1, TL2 - (in table) extra compass; gloves; matches; cards; flashlight; etc.
PL10 - alcohol tank and shut-off valve; funnels; spare kerosene stove
PL11, PL12, PL13 - dried food; plates; cups; glasses; coffee; tea; chocolate;
    seasonings, etc. (extra lamp chimney under locker bottom)
PL14 - (under stove) liquor
PL15 - bilge pump; scupper shut-off valve; cleaning supplies; spices on door
Ice box - fresh foods; pots and pans
PL16 - wine; liquors; bottled drinks
PL17 - battery box; buckets; oars; emergency rudder and stock; awning and poles;
    apples and other fresh vegetables (hung in net bags) storm slides; fuel oil
    measuring stick

---

but which many experienced sailors consider important include a bosun's chair for inspections or repairs aloft; a face mask for underwater inspections or repairs; a barometer; safety nets, especially at the bow to provide extra protection for the crew and prevent sails from washing overboard; a collision mat (to be described in Chapter 6); a sea anchor, useful especially to slow drift when near a lee shore; an easily accessible marine fuel line filter, or preferably twin filters, installed so that one can be removed without shutting off the engine; a jury rudder or emergency means of steering if the main rudder is damaged; weather cloths secured to the lifelines aft to help keep water out of the cockpit; a strong dodger to keep water out of the companionway, especially when the after end of the cabin house is raked forward; and binoculars for spotting distant channel marks and increasing visibility, especially at night. The ORC requires an adequate means to disconnect or sever standing rigging from the hull after a dismasting. Tools that might prove vital for this job are a hacksaw and *heavy-duty* rigging cutters. Other gear that can be useful in keeping crew on board or recovering persons overboard will be mentioned in Chapter 7.

A well-equipped boat will have a tremendous amount of gear distributed throughout her hull, necessitating a graphic stowage plan so that any member of the crew can locate a needed piece of equipment without having to search for it. Figure 5-11 shows the offshore stowage plan for *Kelpie*, our 37-foot sloop. In our coding, S stands for starboard and shelf, P for port, L for locker, D for drawer, T for table, and B for berth. The contents of each stowage area are listed, and the plan is posted near or stowed in the chart desk. I don't mean that such a plan should be followed literally—it is just an example.

A thorough coverage of first aid is beyond the scope of this book, and I am not a doctor. I strongly recommend that every offshore boat without a doctor on board carry a complete and detailed first-aid manual and the medical supplies suggested by the manual. Two highly regarded books are *First Aid Afloat*, written by Paul B. Sheldon, and *Advanced First Aid Afloat* by Peter F. Eastman. Both authors are seamen as well as physicians. Other recommended references are *Handy Medical Guide for Seafarers* by Dr. R.W. Scott, written especially for commercial fishermen; *Sailing and Yachting First Aid* by John Bergan (published by the United States Yacht Racing Union); *Dr. Cohen's Healthy Sailor Book* by M.M. Cohen, M.D.; *The Ship's Medicine Chest and Medical Aid at Sea*, published by the U.S. Department of Health and Human Services; and *Your Offshore Doctor* by M.H. Beilan, M.D. A useful list of medical supplies and drugs for offshore voyages is shown in Appendix H. The list was prepared for the Cruising Club of America by CCA fleet surgeon Dr. G.H.A. Clowes, Jr., and it is reprinted with the kind permission of Dr. Clowes.

There is much wisdom in the saying, "Be ready for the worst, and the best will take care of itself." This is a good slogan to keep firmly in mind when preparing for sea.

Chapter 6
VESSEL EMERGENCIES

Multihull sailor-designer James Wharram has written, "Sailing the sea is like playing a continuous game of chess, and the only way to be safe is to be several moves ahead." This simile is particularly apt for a discussion of emergencies afloat, for the odds definitely favor the sailor who anticipates a crisis and plans well in advance how to cope with it. Forethought should be given not only to rectification of possible emergencies, but also to preventive measures that will minimize the possibility of their occurrence.

Capsizing

On small, properly buoyant boats in warm, protected waters, capsizings are seldom dangerous, but in cold, rough waters, offshore or away from help, such an accident might very well be a serious emergency. Take extra precautions against capsizing when the boat lacks proper flotation, has a known tendency to turn turtle, is in unprotected or cold waters far from rescuers, is manned by an inexperienced crew, or is operating in conditions of poor visibility. Keep bilges dry; be careful not to overload (especially small, open boats); pay attention to weight distribution (for example, keep a heavy crew fairly far aft on a boat lacking adequate buoyancy forward in steep head seas, and don't allow the stern to squat excessively on a small outboard motorboat); shorten sail on capsizable or swampable sailboats; and add flotation (temporarily at least) to any sinkable boat. When reaching or maneuvering in a strong breeze in a sailboat having a nonballasted centerboard, keeping the board about halfway up reduces the length of the heeling arm (Figure 1-12), and may help avoid tripping on the board. Non-swimmers should don life vests or flotation jackets, especially in strong winds or rough seas that could break aboard and fill a boat lacking a self-draining cockpit.

Last minute actions to avoid capsizing include slacking sheets on sailboats (offshore multihulls should have automatic sheet releases); luffing up when sailing close-hauled, but bearing off when the apparent wind is definitely abaft the beam; shifting crew weight to the high side; keeping small power craft with open cockpits stern-to or bow-to dangerous seas; and slowing down in rough seas. Avoid shipping water or allowing heavy seas to break aboard; the water rushing to leeward can seriously endanger stability. A surprising number of small sailboats are not fitted with reefing gear; you need a handy means of reducing the mainsail with such arrangements as roller reefing, reef points, or the so-called jiffy reefing method (see Chapter 11).

Take the following steps after capsizing a small sailboat: (1) Climb over the windward side and station at least one crewmember on the centerboard to prevent the boat from turning turtle. (2) Check the crew to see that none is injured, missing, trapped under the sails, or tangled in a line. (3) Don life jackets if they are not already on and the boat cannot be righted immediately. (4) Secure a float such as life preservers or an empty plastic jug to the masthead to help prevent the boat from turning turtle. (Some boats with metal masts may have a strong tendency to turn bottom-side up when their masts become filled with water.) In attaching a temporary float, secure it to the halyard in such a way that it can be pulled down after the boat has been righted. (5) Retrieve any loose gear that may be floating out of the cockpit, and lash it to the boat. Locate and secure the bailing bucket and pump. (6) Lower sails, stop them to the booms or deck, and secure the outboard end of the boom to the boat near her centerline. (7) Try to anchor if the boat is drifting toward a lee shore or in rough seas and strong winds. (8) Put an extra crewmember (if available) on the centerboard and have the crew lean back (outboard) while holding onto the rail or a short line attached to the rail in order to right the boat. (9) Climb aboard over the stern or one side while a crewmember counterbalances the boat, and squat in the center of the cockpit after the boat has been righted. (10) Bail as rapidly as possible with a large bucket until the boat is sufficiently empty for the other crew to climb aboard and assist in bailing and general cleanup. In a very small boat with abundant, suitably placed flotation, when the weather is not too heavy, righting can often be accomplished quickly without even lowering sails. It is helpful when the boat can be turned bow to the wind. On the other hand, in severe weather in a fairly large boat, the righting procedure just listed may not work. In this case, the capsized victims must simply wait for outside assistance or for conditions to moderate to the point where self-rescue is possible. *Stay with the boat.* If she floats, she will afford support, and you will be more easily spotted by rescuers when you are with the boat. Victims are often drowned when tempted to swim for a "nearby" shore.

Overly zealous rescuers in boats under power are sometimes more harmful than helpful. Rescue boats often approach a capsized craft too soon, too closely, with too much speed, and from the wrong side. Normally the rescue boat should stand by well clear to leeward, because a high-sided powerboat to windward will drift down on and possibly damage the capsized boat or injure her crew. Unless the skipper of the capsized craft is inexperienced, incapacitated, or asks for instructions, he or she should be in charge of the operation and give instructions to the rescue boat. If any crewmember in the water is injured, fatigued, or seriously chilled, he must be rescued immediately, and possibly this could justify a downwind approach. Ordinarily, however, when there is no immediate urgency, the capsized boat should be approached cautiously from leeward, well to the side of any floating gear or lines, with the rescue boat's bow angled to the wind. A line can be thrown to the capsized crew and the rescue boat can be held or even pulled to windward when she is a small boat, or the capsize victims can be pulled to the rescue craft. The rescuer must see to it that his propeller is not turning (so those in the water will not be cut) by putting the gear in neutral or perhaps by cutting power. Care should be taken to keep crewmembers away from the prop and from where they could be crushed between the boats. The rescue crew should fend off and be careful not to damage the sails or mast of the capsized boat or foul floating lines in the prop. Although it is usually better to approach a capsized boat from leeward, an individual man in the water should nearly always be approached from the windward side. The specific problem of rescuing a man overboard will be discussed later in Chapter 7.

If all the crew of the capsized craft are fit and the situation is well in hand, it is usually best that the boat be righted before the rescue boat comes alongside. After the capsized boat is upright, she can be partially cleared of water by lifting her bow from aboard the rescue craft to let water flow out of the cockpit and over the stern. Further clearing with buckets or pumps then follows, or the swamped boat can be gently towed a short distance, which will make the water rush aft and flow over her transom or through transom bailers if she has them. A boat should never be towed in the capsized position, as this will almost certainly cause damage. Unless there is a substantial bitt on the bow of the capsized boat, the towline should be made fast around her mast and led through a chock near her stem. At least one person should remain aboard to steer her.

The most difficult boat to right is a multihull that has turned turtle. Due to her extreme beam and the fact that she normally lacks ballast, a multihull usually has far greater stability upside down than right side up. When outside assistance is available, a tow boat pulling laterally, at right angles to the multihull's longitudinal axis, can often right her. Once attached to the rail or to a bridle running between the bow and stern of the farther hull, the towline is run over the bottoms of the hulls and then made fast to the stern bitt or a cleat on the centerline of the tow boat. When the towing operation begins, the hulls will start to move sidewise, but the mast and sails sticking downward in the water will resist the movement. The rig's resistance combined with the pull on the far hull will create a powerful turning moment that should soon right the boat. In stubborn cases an anchor and gin pole might be used as illustrated in Figure 6-2. Proceed slowly, and if necessary put some crew weight on (or

Figure 6-1. *Lefthand
column (top to bottom):
''Centerboard sling''
recovery allows towing from
any direction but requires a
towline strain about equal to
the multihull's displacement
weight. Center column: This
bows-down somersault shows
that even poor towline
alignment succeeds,
indicating that tow-over
should work in difficult
conditions. Righthand
column: Bows-up recovery
begins with towing on a
single sternline. This is to
align the multihull with the
bridle for a directionally
stable rotation. Towing strain
equals about one-fourth the
multihull's displacement
when the ama bows are
flooded. Completed recovery
leaves the tow-over bridle
ready for towing the
re-righted craft at sea. (Tom
Crabb. From* The Case for
the Cruising Trimaran *by
Jim Brown, International
Marine Publishing
Company, 1979)*

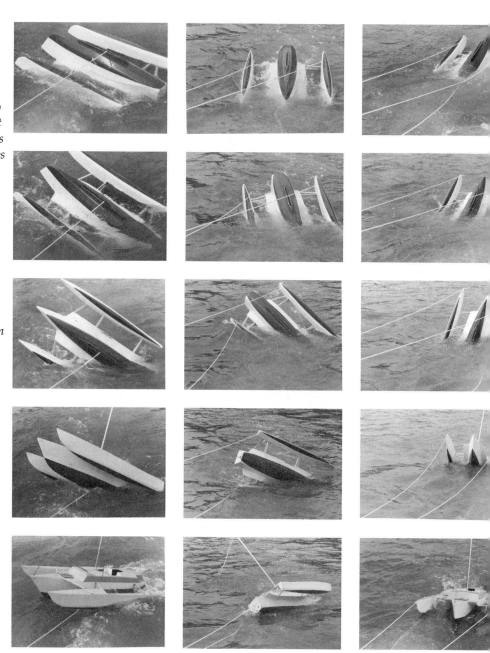

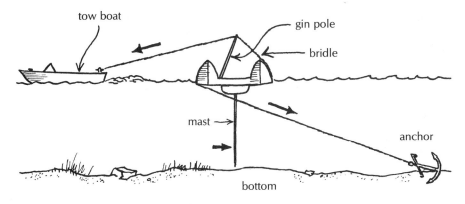

Figure 6-2. *One method of righting with a tow boat of limited power.*

flood) the near hull during the initial stages of the operation. Small multihulls are often righted by the longitudinal method, end over end. The sterns of an inverted Tornado catamaran, for instance, are submerged with crew weight while a tow boat pulls on a line attached to the bows and leading aft between the catamaran's hulls, thereby pulling the bows up over the sterns.

When no rescue boat is nearby, righting an upside-down multihull may be impossible unless the boat has special provisions for flooding and pumping her hulls. Figure 6-3 shows one solution, which requires specially installed hoses, valves, and a sizable pump. For such a system

Figure 6-3. *A multihull self-rescue possibility.*

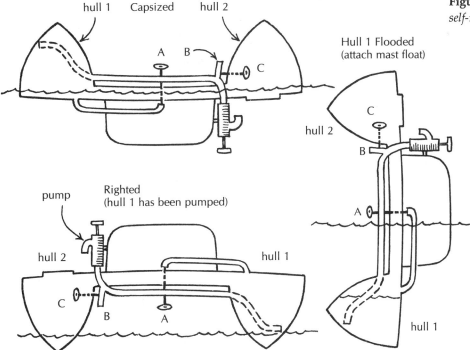

Figure 6-4. *In these four photos, Rob Wright demonstrates a modified "Ruiz system" self-rescue of his 21-foot Tremolino trimaran. (Jim Morse photos)*

to be effective, the boat must have at least some positive stability (tendency to right) at a 90-degree angle of heel. Positive stability for most multihulls ends (begins to become negative) between the heeling angles of 80 and 105 degrees, with the lower angles generally applying to unballasted catamarans. Shifting of ballast or heavy gear during a capsizing could seriously hamper a righting operation. All boats, multihulls especially, should have their ballast and heavy equipment secured to withstand a 180-degree turnover.

In Figure 6-3, after the multihull turns bottom side up, valve A is opened in order to flood hull 1 (hull 2 being fitted with flotation). Then plug B is pulled from the end of the vent line leading from that hull, because water will not fill it unless the air is allowed to escape. The flooding of hull 1 causes it to sink and the boat to turn on its side, bringing the

mast approximately horizontal and on or close to the water's surface. At this point a liferaft or float may be hauled with a halyard or floated to the masthead to protect against turning turtle again, or a folded buoyancy bag secured to the masthead is inflated manually or automatically with CO_2. To convert the air vent line into an intake hose for the powerful hand pump secured to the side of the deckhouse, shut valve C, which may be reached through a hatch in the deck of hull 2. The hose that allowed the flooding of hull 1 now becomes a vent pipe to let air into the hull as the water is pumped out. As the hull is pumped clear of water, a boat with positive stability to at least a 90-degree angle of heel should right herself, though it might be necessary to put some crew weight on the keel or centerboard of hull 2. Sails should be lowered. If the boat will not right herself even with crew on the centerboard, a method can be employed similar to one used by multihull designer/builder Walter Greene on his catamaran *Sebago*, whereby airbags are hauled or winched down to the submerged hull to lever the boat upright.

Successfully righting a boat in this fashion during a storm would be improbable at best. The crew must try to hang on to the multihull's bottom and survive until wind and seas abate. If the boat is fitted with a permanent masthead float that prevents her from turning turtle, additional temporary flotation such as a rubber raft should be attached to the masthead immediately after capsizing as a precaution against the permanent float breaking off, which is a distinct possibility in rough seas. The mast and rigging must have considerable strength to withstand very rough treatment until the storm abates.

End-over-end righting has also been proposed for offshore multihulls. At the first World Multihull Symposium held at Toronto, Ontario, in 1976, Carlos Ruiz used a catamaran model to demonstrate his method of self-rescue by longitudinal righting. Two spinnaker poles are rigged to the bottom of the capsized catamaran to form a bipod overhanging the bows, and a water bag is attached to the apex of the bipod. The bows are then flooded by releasing air from built-in bow chambers, and after the bows sink, the crew attaches a line to the apex of the bipod and attempts to hoist the water bag with a winch. This action will fail to hoist the bag, but it will cause the boat to stand on her head. The bipod pivots so that the sterns can rise and fall over the bows, thus bringing the boat to an upright position. The flooded chambers are then pumped out. Full details of the Ruiz system with pictures of his demonstration have been published in *The Symposium Book*. More recently, this system has been used effectively on full-sized multihulls; a demonstration by Rob Wright is shown in Figure 6-4.

Erroneous Navigation

If you would avoid faulty navigation, see first that your compass is reliable and easy to read. As mentioned in Chapter 5, care must be taken to keep magnetic objects away from the compass. Deviation can be caused by such items as winch handles, magnetic safety harnesses, steel-rimmed glasses, and even nickel plating on the binnacle. Also, check the compass accuracy after a close lightning strike.

Carry all the charts you will possibly need, and be sure they are up to date. Relying on old charts is dangerous, not only because aids to navigation are sometimes moved, renumbered, or changed in color (from black to green for example), but also because local variation (as printed in the chart's compass rose) changes with time. When the printing on a chart becomes indistinct or is obscured by folding or the erasures of pencil markings, the chart needs to be replaced. Don't try to get by with a chart of the wrong scale. You may need the detail of a large-scale harbor chart for entering an anchorage in poor visibility.

In addition to dividers, parallel rules, a hand-bearing compass, and

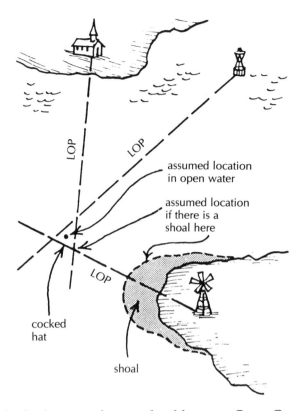

assumed location
in open water

assumed location
if there is a
shoal here

LOP

LOP

LOP

cocked
hat

shoal

Figure 6-5. *A fix from three lines of position.*

other standard piloting tools, you should carry a Coast Guard *Light List*, which gives details of local lighthouses, channel markers, and other navigational aids. Equally important are local tide and current tables and current charts, for a large percentage of boats that pile up do so because of failure to recognize or predict a current that pushes them off course. Currents sometimes behave erratically, so a vessel's position should always be checked with electronic and celestial navigation (as opposed to dead reckoning, which does not account for the current) when out of sight of land, and with visual bearings when operating close to shore. A depth sounder is valuable when making a landfall, approaching a coast, or finding one's way in fog. A handy feature is an alarm that can be set to sound off when the vessel reaches shallow water. When there is only one transducer on a sailing vessel's centerline, the calibrated depth must be adjusted as necessary for heeling error.

Total reliance on electronic navigation is dangerous. Loran and satellite navigation receivers are valuable tools and can be extremely accurate, but what if the power goes dead or the equipment malfunctions? Satnav, in particular, has an unenviable reputation for going on the blink at inconvenient times. Perhaps the Global Positioning System (GPS) will fulfill our wildest expectations when it comes fully on line over the next few years, bringing reliable, pinpoint satellite navigation to everyone's receivers. For now, though, the receivers remain very expensive, and nothing that depends on electric power at sea will ever be infallible.

Radio direction finding (RDF) is still useful in making a landfall, but this relatively old method of electronic navigation should never be considered a precise system; factors such as atmospherics, deviation, and distance from the transmitter all affect its accuracy. Electronics have their place, but a navigator should be skilled at dead reckoning and should know at least the basics of celestial navigation. As a passagemaker you should certainly have the ability to find your latitude and approximate longitude from a noon sight (altitude of the sun measured with the sextant at noon).

It is only common sense to err on the side of caution when using any system of navigation. If you take three bearings and the plotted LOPs (lines of position) do not meet exactly (they seldom do; as shown in Figure 6-5, a triangular "cocked hat" is formed by the LOPs), assume that you are on the intersection closest to the shoal you are trying to avoid. Keep constant track of where you are, and doublecheck the identification of all navigation aids. In a potentially hazardous situation, don't depend solely on one navigation aid, particularly one that floats, as it could be carried off station by ice or some other cause, and its light or sound device could be malfunctioning. For that matter, never depend entirely on one system of navigation, but have one or more backups for verification.

Running Aground

Despite the fact that careful navigation will nearly always avoid grounding, many of us at times become careless or overconfident, especially in our home waters, and "taking the ground" is a common mishap. Such an accident is seldom serious in sheltered waters when the bottom is soft and the boat is moving slowly, but grounding on rock, coral, or even hard sand or shell at high speed can be serious, especially in rough waters. Because of their comparatively deep draft, sailboats are subject to grounding more often than power craft, but the latter are more often vulnerable to rudder or propeller damage when contact with the bottom is made. As with any emergency afloat, rules cannot be given to cover every situation, but some general suggestions for action after grounding follow.

When under sail with the shoal on the lee bow, try to come about at once. If the helmsman reacts instantly when he feels contact with the bottom, he may be able to tack with the help of a backed jib. Tacking will usually head the boat toward deeper water and permit heeling, which will decrease draft and allow the boat, in most cases, to be blown away from the shoal. Modern sailboats with keels that are short fore and aft can be turned most easily. If the boat cannot be tacked immediately, lower all sail promptly. One of the most common mistakes in a sailboat grounding is failure to lower sail at once when the boat cannot be headed for deep water. The boat is consequently generally driven farther and farther ashore.

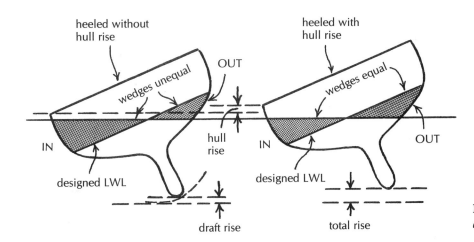

Figure 6-6. *Rise of hull and draft when heeled.*

Once sail is lowered or if the boat was run aground under power, try backing off on a reciprocal course under power or by kedging with an anchor when the boat has no engine. Kedging requires setting an anchor far astern (or ahead when trying to move forward) and then pulling the boat toward it. Backing by any means, however, should usually not be attempted unless the rudder and propeller are free. When the keel has considerable drag (i.e., when it is deeper aft than forward), it will pay to put crew weight on the bow. Every skipper should be thoroughly familiar with the underwater shape of his boat. If the boat does not back off immediately, study charts, take soundings from the dinghy, or dive underwater with a face mask to determine how the boat should head to find deep water. While this study is being made, it may be necessary to anchor in order that the boat not be driven harder aground. If the grounding was on rocks or a hard bottom, inspect for damage. Think twice about getting free if the hull is holed, because the boat might sink into deep water after she is extricated. When the boat is lodged in a soft bottom she might be pivoted so that she can be pulled off in the direction of least resistance toward the closest deep water. In the absence of a tow boat, the grounded vessel will probably be pivoted most easily by kedging off the bow (or stern in some instances) with an anchor laid out abeam. Anchors may be carried out in a dinghy or raft or in some cases by wading.

Heeling a grounded boat is advantageous for two reasons. First, it reduces draft. The second reason, not so obvious, is that the hull lifts slightly when heeled. This is explained in Figure 6-6. If we assume that in the fore-and-aft view of a hull the heeled waterline passes through the intersection of the centerline and the upright load waterline, then it can be seen that the immersed area, called the "in wedge," exceeds the volume of the emersed area, the "out wedge." In actuality, however, if there is no change in the boat's displacement, there must be equality between the in and out wedges; therefore the boat lifts or "rolls out" to create this equality.

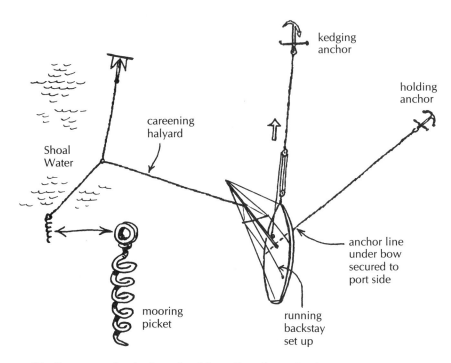

Figure 6-7. *Kedging off.*

Heeling may be induced with sails when the boat is positioned in such a way that she will blow away from rather than toward the shoal. Alternatively, hang weights from the boom ends and swing the booms out abeam to produce moderate heel. A dinghy filled with ballast, heavy gear, or even water hoisted to the end of the main boom with a tackle or the mainsheet can be effective. Of course, the dinghy might also be lifted by securing it to the boom end and then topping up the boom. For extreme heeling or careening it is usually necessary to set out abeam a large, heavy anchor, to which a masthead halyard is attached for the purpose of hauling the masthead down. Be careful about using the main halyard for this purpose; unless it is designed to take a lateral strain, it could jam or break its sheave. If the anchor will not hold, very shoal water might permit the use of mooring pickets. These twisted metal rods, illustrated in Figure 6-7, can be screwed into a soft bottom. Perhaps an anchor and a picket (or another anchor) spread far apart may be used as shown in the illustration. If the boat is heeling toward the shoal, it may very well be necessary to set out, in the direction away from the shoal, another anchor that will oppose the pull of the careening anchor or pickets in order to prevent the boat from being pulled farther aground after her keel breaks free. Notice in Figure 6-7 that the anchors are not set directly abeam but lead somewhat forward of the beam so that the boat can be pulled ahead, the forward pulling force being supplied by the kedge, a tow boat, or perhaps by the grounded vessel's own power. As the vessel moves ahead, slack must be taken in on the careening halyard and opposing anchor line. Anchors will have to be reset farther ahead if she is still not off.

When a boat grounds on a soft mud or clay bottom in calm water, very often she is held fast by the suction of her embedded keel. Frequently, this suction can be broken by rolling the boat. She might be sallied (rolled from side to side by shifting crew weight), or perhaps a rescue boat could be persuaded to power back and forth nearby to create waves.

If the grounded vessel is towed off, care must be taken to see that securing bitts or cleats are substantial and firmly bolted. Some authorities recommend taking a slight running start with the tow boat to jerk a grounded vessel free. This method can be effective, but it can also be *extremely dangerous*. Towlines are often elastic, especially those made of nylon, and if they break under great strain they can whiplash and seriously injure a crewmember. In one case a man was killed when the heavy towline cleat pulled off the deck and was catapulted by the springy line against his head. Everyone should stand well clear of a line under severe strain. It is usually safer to secure a towline around the base of a mast, but the lead chocks must be well fastened. In some cases it may be advisable to secure the towline to a bridle that passes entirely around the hull. Before being towed off, be sure to check the vessel's bilges to see that she is not badly holed. If she is impaled on a sharp rock or coral, her bottom might rip, and again, if she is badly holed, she might sink into deep water when she is pulled free. Develop a clear understanding with the towing boat as to how the operation will proceed. It is often preferable that both ends of the towline are secured with turns around the bitt or cleat in order that the line can be eased or cast off at any given moment from either end.

If your vessel grounds on sand (or other bottoms of loose consistency), take care when she uses her own power that quantities of sediment are not sucked into the engine's water intake. When she is heeled, be sure that the intake is submerged or the engine will overheat. Check also that the propeller is free to avoid damaging the blades.

Centerboard boats enjoy a great advantage in shoal waters, since the board hitting bottom provides a forceful warning of a grounding. It is often risky to sail among shoals with the board fully down, however, because it can be damaged or perhaps bent during a hard grounding when the boat is heeled. Daggerboards are far more susceptible to this kind of damage than are pivoted boards. It is generally safest to sail with the board partly housed when there is any possibility of grounding, and this is especially true with most metal or high-aspect-ratio centerboards.

Obviously, tide is a consideration when a vessel is grounded. Unless the grounding took place at high water, it may pay to wait until the water rises before attempting to free the boat. In areas of extreme tides, consider whether a keel boat will fall over on her side when the water recedes. Unless she can be shored up securely, it is usually best to let her heel progressively farther as the tide drops until she rests on the turn of her bilge. Padding in the form of cushions, coils of rope, and fenders under the bilge will protect against a hard bottom. If the boat is induced to remain upright, balanced on her keel, she could fall over and be seriously damaged, so don't attempt this unless she can be properly shored up or immobilized with a masthead halyard attached to an anchor, picket, or even a tree on a nearby shore.

Collisions

On today's increasingly crowded waterways, collisions are one of the most frequent forms of marine accidents. Small-boat collisions grow ever more serious in the extent of damage and personal injury because powerboats grow ever faster and increasingly are operated by inexperienced skippers. Occasionally, these skippers are exhibitionists wishing to demonstrate the speed of their craft, and some have been known to operate in crowded waters at speeds up to 100 knots. More than a few lethal accidents have been caused by loss of control at high speeds. The two principal causes of collisions are failure to keep a lookout and failure to obey the Rules of the Road. The importance of keeping a good lookout cannot be overemphasized, and the latter is the greatest single cause of collisions according to the U.S. Coast Guard. The Rules of the Road are seldom disobeyed deliberately, but usually through ignorance. It is more and more apparent that a shockingly large number of boat operators are not thoroughly familiar with the Rules of the Road. In many areas of the United States, mere children without knowledge of the rules or skill and judgment in boat handling are careening about at lethal speeds in high-powered motorboats. Furthermore, many motor manufacturers seem bent on increasing the horsepower of their products. Few of us want legislation enacted that would require the licensing of boat operators, but unless the collision rate decreases and novice boaters are made aware of their responsibilities, we may soon see the day when licenses are mandatory for boat operators just as they are for automobile drivers. In some states children 16 years old or younger are now required by law to pass a boating safety course before they may operate a state numbered or documented pleasureboat.

Lack of knowledge of the rules is not entirely due to irresponsibility or apathy on the part of boat operators; in more than a few instances, boaters are simply confused by the rules. This might be due in part to the fact that not long ago there were four different sets of rules in use on U.S. waters, and they didn't always agree. In fact, they were a confusing, sometimes contradictory patchwork of requirements. But in 1980 the various U.S. rules were unified under a new set of Inland Rules that now closely agrees with the International Rules.

A few points of confusion still remain for old-time skippers as well as less experienced operators who have not carefully read the new rules. A case in point involves right of way when a fishing vessel meets a sailboat. Rule 18 of the Inland (and International) Rules states that a sailing vessel shall keep out of the way of a vessel engaged in fishing. Prior to 1981, the term "engaged in fishing" included any vessel fishing with nets, lines,

Figure 6-8. *Coast Guard statistics show that most accidents and personal injuries result from collisions—with failure to keep a forward lookout being the major cause.*

or trawls, but now, Definition 3(d) in the Inland Rules states that the term "does not include a vessel fishing with trolling lines or other fishing apparatus which do not restrict maneuverability." Apparently, many sportfishermen who are trolling believe they have the right of way over a sailboat, yet the rules state otherwise.

Another source of confusion in densely populated boating areas is the use of whistle signals. The various Rules of the Road specify these signals, and they can be essential in converging situations to signify intent or agreement. The fact is, however, that most small-boat operators seldom use sound signals, and some boatmen never carry the horn where it is available for instant use. Whistle signals should always be answered, but there are some good arguments for using restraint in initiating whistle signals in certain situations. Take the case of a popular, narrow fairway which, on a typical Sunday in midsummer, is crowded with every variety of small craft coming and going. If all the boats were to blow their horns at the same time, the result might be chaotic. Furthermore, it is unfortunate but true that many novices might become confused and make unpredictable and possibly dangerous changes of course. Even Coast Guard vessels at certain times decline to initiate whistle signals to small boats for fear of causing confusion. A common-sense approach to the problem is to refrain from sounding the horn every time another boat heaves into view, and to use whistle signals only when responding to another boat that has initiated signals, when it seems advisable to let another boat know your intentions, when another boat's intentions are not obvious or are questionable, or when there is a definite risk of collision. The dilemma is that care must be taken not to let

Figure 6-9. *With the increasing traffic on today's waterways, it is vital that we have clearly written and uniform Rules of the Road that can be understood by all boaters. (Lee Troutner photo)*

failure to sound the proper signal contribute to a collision. When approaching another craft, it is advisable, whenever possible, to alter course early so that your intentions will be clear, even without sound signals, long before you come close.

In recent years, a number of small craft have been run down or nearly run down by steamers in certain areas where ship traffic is concentrated, such as in the English Channel. Often the reason is the overconfidence of boat operators that they can be seen and easily avoided by large ships. During many close calls and sometimes when collisions occur, the small boat involved is not seen at all, or else she is seen too late for evasive action by the large vessel. Remember that large ships moving at high speeds are very slow to turn or reduce speed. Bear in mind that small craft are often hard to see from ships even in fair weather, that lookouts and radar watches are sometimes lax on merchantmen (especially on automated ships that carry a reduced crew), that small-craft navigation lights are difficult to see (or impossible to see when blocked by sails), and that radar signals, even those returned by a lofty radar reflector, are often difficult to see or interpret in heavy weather. It is always safest to assume you are not seen by a larger vessel and keep well clear. At night or when visibility is poor, keep the radar reflector hoisted, and keep a loud horn, bright spotlight, and flares readily available to the helmsman. Converging steamers should be checked constantly with bearings and their courses estimated by noting the position of range and other navigation lights. Figure 6-10 plainly shows how the proximity of range lights

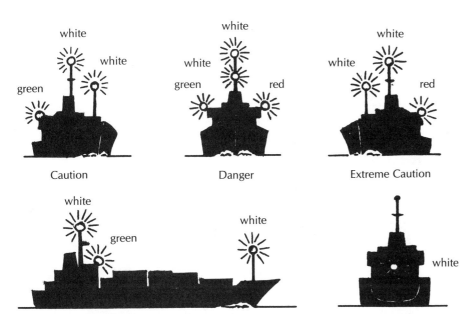

Caution   Danger   Extreme Caution

white   white   green   white

Figure 6-10. *Navigation lights for a power-driven vessel 164 feet or longer. Notice how the range lights, appearing closer together or farther apart, indicate the vessel's heading.*

(the upper white lights) indicates a potentially dangerous crossing situation even when the red and green lights aren't seen simultaneously. When close to a ship at night, it is wise to shine repeatedly a powerful light on your sails (or deckhouse on a powerboat) and also to aim the light beam directly, but very briefly, at the ship's bridge deck and pilothouse windows. A quick sweep of the bridge with a light will attract attention without blinding the helmsman. During a close crossing, take bearings repeatedly as the vessels converge. If the bearings do not markedly change, a collision is possible.

Another reason for keeping well clear of a large ship is to avoid close contact with her entrained wave system. Even when a boat is so far from a ship that there is little concern over the possibility of collision, the wave train of the large vessel moving at high speed can combine with wind waves to produce steep and perhaps dangerous seas. The Tumlare-type double-ended sloop *Cohoe* was pooped in 1950 by a sea which, in the opinion of her skipper, Adlard Coles, was made to break aboard by the wash of a passing ocean liner. More recently, a man was washed overboard (but recovered) from the deck of the schooner *America* (replica of the famous *America*) when she nosed into the wash of a large passenger ship making 18 knots during a moderately calm day on the Chesapeake Bay.

Small craft often collide with each other or with heavy flotsam such as floating timber through negligence in keeping a constant lookout. Motorboat operators must be sure that they have good visibility over the bow at planing speeds (see Chapter 1), and there must be at least two people aboard a boat towing waterskiers so that the helmsman is free to look ahead continually. Sailboats often present a problem of good visibility over a high cabintop. It is not sufficient that the helmsman have clear

Drinks	Body Weight in Pounds								
	100	120	140	160	180	200	220	240	
1	.04	.03	.03	.02	.02	.02	.02	.02	BE
2	.08	.06	.05	.05	.04	.04	.03	.03	CAREFUL
3	.11	.09	.08	.07	.06	.06	.05	.05	
4	.15	.12	.11	.09	.08	.08	.07	.06	OPERATION
5	.19	.16	.13	.12	.11	.09	.09	.08	IMPAIRED
6	.23	.19	.16	.14	.13	.11	.10	.09	
7	.26	.22	.19	.16	.15	.13	.12	.11	
8	.30	.25	.21	.19	.17	.15	.14	.13	DO NOT
9	.34	.28	.24	.21	.19	.17	.15	.14	OPERATE
10	.38	.31	.27	.23	.21	.19	.17	.16	

One drink is 1¼ oz. of 80 proof liquor, 12 oz. of beer, or 4 oz. of table wine.

Figure 6-12. *The effect of alcohol on boat operation. (Courtesy U.S. Coast Guard)*

Figure 6-11. *A moderately long tack pendant gives the best visibility without unduly compromising sail power.*

visibility forward when he is standing; his seat should be sufficiently high so that his view is unobstructed when he is sitting. Low-cut sails present a serious obstruction to the helmsman, especially the deck-sweeping Genoa jibs seen on most modern racing boats. Some of these sails have plastic windows, but these can seldom be made large enough to eliminate dangerous blind spots. I would like to see racing organizations ban decksweepers, because their slightly superior aerodynamic efficiency hardly seems worth the risk of collision. A jib cut with a reasonably high clew can make a world of difference to good visibility, and this can have a great bearing on safe sailing in crowded waters. Every sailing cruiser should have a selection of tack pendants to raise headsails off the deck.

Before closing this section, I should mention that excessive use of alcohol is a major cause of collisions and other boating accidents. Just as alcohol impairs the operation of an automobile, it follows that boat operation is likewise affected. The degree of impairment depends on such matters as the individual's metabolism and body weight, how much the drink is diluted, proof of the liquor, time between drinks, the amount of food recently consumed, fatigue, and exposure to heat; thus it is difficult to define precisely what is meant by excessive imbibing. Figure 6-12 provides a rough guide.

Emergency Repairs

Any skipper taking his boat offshore or away from readily available assistance and repair facilities is well advised to give considerable thought to the subject of emergency repairs. For maximum self-sufficiency, the vessel should be well equipped with tools, spare parts, and repair kits. These were discussed in Chapter 5. Some of the more common accidents requiring emergency repairs are rigging failures, hull damage that results in serious leaks, and rudder or steering gear failure.

Perhaps the most frequent failures offshore occur in the rigging of

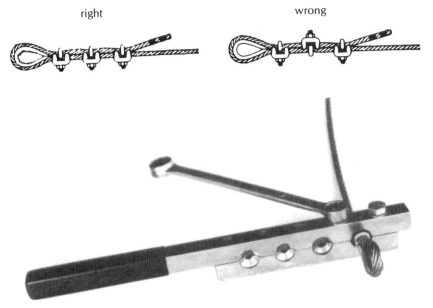

right   wrong

Figure 6-13. *The right and wrong ways to apply bulldog clips. (From* The Handbook for Riggers.*)*

Figure 6-14. *A compression sleeve being crimped onto a rigging wire with a Nicopress tool.*

sailboats, principally from breakage due to flaws, fatigue stress, or wear of metal linkage fittings. The reasons for such failures, as well as other aspects of rigging, will be discussed in Chapter 10. The discussion here will deal with emergency action and repair after the damage occurs.

The importance of continuous rigging inspections, especially at sea, cannot be overemphasized, because the failure of a single fitting could allow the whole rig to go by the board. Keep a watchful eye for worn threads on screw fittings; hairline cracks in turnbuckles, toggles, tangs, and especially swaged end terminals; loose nuts; missing or weak cotter pins; broken strands on standing rigging; and any bent or worn fitting that helps support the mast. Any fitting that shows signs of weakness should be replaced or reinforced at once. To minimize fatigue, be sure that all rigging components are in alignment (a straight line from chainplate to tang) and that there are toggles or at least universal movement at both ends of all shrouds and stays (see Chapter 10).

When a rigging weakness is spotted on one side or at one end of the vessel, she should immediately be put on the tack or point of sailing that minimizes stress on the weakened area until repairs can be made. For instance, if a crack appears in a starboard shroud turnbuckle, the vessel should be put on the port tack. Spares may not always be available, so improvisations may be necessary. Quite often a weak fitting can be reinforced with shackles or a short length of chain and shackles, or a stay with a broken strand may be strengthened by clamping a short length of wire beside the stay's weak area with bulldog clamps (Figure 6-13) or compression sleeves installed with a hand clamping tool, such as a Nicopress (Figure 6-14). Beware of using small screw shackles, however, because they are weak at the threads, and if cotter pins are used with shackles, be sure that the pins as well as the shackles are strong. Don't

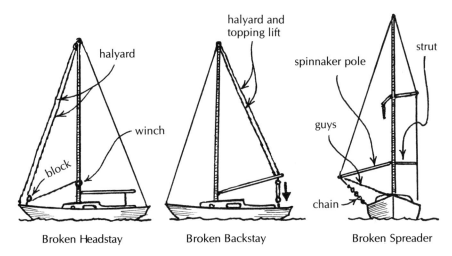

Figure 6-15. *Jury rigging hints.*

Broken Headstay   Broken Backstay   Broken Spreader

use compression sleeves on wire rope that has a hollow or crushable fiber core.

If a headstay or forestay should break, it is important to head off onto a dead run immediately to make the wind pressure act in a forward direction. If a headsail is still standing, delay lowering it until one or more halyards can be secured to the stemhead, bowsprit, or bitts or windlass (if far enough forward) in order that the mast be held forward. To direct as much pull forward as possible, rig both ends of a halyard forward (as shown in Figure 6-15), and then lead the hauling part aft to the halyard winch mounted on the mast. If a backstay breaks, luff up the boat head to wind while the mainsheet is strapped in tight to hold the mast back. It is usually a good idea to start the engine to hold the boat into the wind. When the boat is equipped with runners, these should of course be set up tight. The mainsail may be lowered if there is a stout topping lift against which the mainsheet can pull to exert a force aft. Later the main halyard can be shackled to the end of the boom to reinforce the topping lift (see Figure 6-15).

When a windward spreader or shroud breaks while the boat is heeled to a fresh breeze, it is very doubtful that the mast can be saved, but this might be possible if the helmsman can tack immediately. Develop the seamanlike habit of glancing at the leeward rigging and spreaders immediately before tacking to see that the shrouds or fittings are not hanging loosely. A sagging spreader end can often be pulled up from the deck as follows: Secure the end of a halyard to the shroud in question and, after a downhaul has been rigged, haul the halyard end aloft until it makes contact with the spreader. Put the hauling end of the halyard on a winch to force the spreader up. As mentioned in Chapter 5, a spare of the longest stay should be carried on an extensive passage offshore. This spare should be flexible 7 × 19 or 7 × 7 wire, so that it may be cut to any required length and eyes can be formed easily with clamps or sleeves to replace any broken shroud or stay. If an entire stay or shroud cannot be replaced, however, a short piece of wire rope can be clamped beside the break, provided there are sufficient clamps or compression sleeves (at least two or three) on both sides of the break. Broken spreaders may be fished together with splints and binding wire if there are no spares. Quite often the sea will be too rough to allow working aloft. In this case, a boom or spinnaker pole may be used temporarily as a long spreader close to the deck (see Figure 6-15). It really doesn't matter, from the standpoint of mast support, whether the spreader is short and high or long and low, if the angle between the mast and shroud remains about the same. The long spreader should be secured with guys so that it doesn't swing forward or aft, and, if possible, the inboard end of the pole should be secured against the mast (not merely hooked to the spinnaker pole track, which might be pushed off the mast by the strong lateral force). The outboard end of the pole should be securely lashed to the shroud, leaving the inboard end somewhat higher than the outboard end so that the angles between the pole and shroud above and below the pole are equalized. The shroud will have to be lengthened to accommodate the long spreader, possibly with a short length of chain as shown in Figure 6-15.

Unfortunately, dismastings are not uncommon. Although such accidents are usually frightening, they are seldom extremely dangerous. Crewmembers are seldom injured, because the rig normally falls overboard to leeward. The first action to take after a dismasting is to be sure that no one is injured or pinned under the fallen rig. Then the mast must be brought on board before it can puncture or otherwise damage the hull. If it cannot be lifted aboard and heavy seas are causing it to pound against the hull, it should be cut away before the boat is holed. A metal mast cut loose will generally sink, but it may be possible to tow one of wood on a very long line so that the spar cannot be thrown against the hull by the sea. Spars may need to be cut loose with heavy, preferably hydraulic, wire cutters, or even a hacksaw. An acquaintance of singlehander Jean Gau told me that after the *Atom* was dismasted off the coast of South Africa in February 1966, Gau lost his wire cutters overboard but was able to cut away the masts with a hacksaw blade held between his fingers. It is usually easier to cut through bronze turnbuckles than stainless steel rigging. Bolt cutters will not cut cleanly but will merely crush heavy 1×19 stainless steel wire, but some fittings such as pins or open-barreled turnbuckles might be broken with heavy bolt cutters. In most cases, of course, it will be easiest to remove the rigging pins after pulling or cutting away their cotters. Bringing the broken mast aboard will be quite a chore, but parbuckles fore and aft on the spar will facilitate the lifting operation. A parbuckle (rope lifting sling) is rigged by attaching one end of a line to the rail, passing the line under the spar, and bringing it back to the rail where it may be hauled on to raise the spar (see Figure 6-16). The hauling end of the line might be led through a block attached as high as possible on the stump of the broken mast, or to another mast on a two-master, to facilitate lifting. If friction of the mast against the hull prevents hoisting, then perhaps the parbuckle might be led outboard

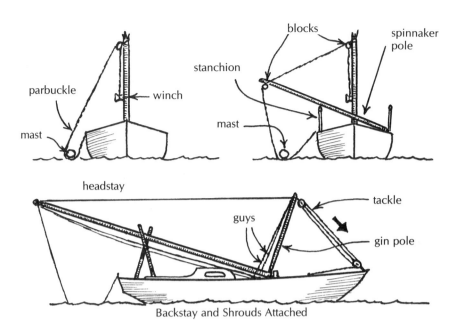

Figure 6-16. *Rig recovery techniques.*

Backstay and Shrouds Attached

through a block at the end of a pole or boom suspended over the lifelines as shown in the illustration.

After a dismasting, help may be summoned with distress signals—usually with flares, EPIRB, or a radiotelephone (if the antenna was not part of the rigging). If help is not forthcoming, the victims will have to proceed under power or devise a jury rig. When the weather moderates, the broken spar on deck (or the towed spar) may have to be used for a jury mast. It might be possible to lash the broken spar to its stump, which still remains stepped and vertical, but more than likely a short stump will have to be unstepped and the longest section of the fallen mast stepped in its stead. This will require squaring off a ragged break and shortening the stays. When the break occurs far aloft, it is often only necessary to remove the broken top or lash it securely to the standing part of the mast. In some cases, however, stays and shrouds will have to be attached to the mast just below the break. Even with only a short section of spar standing, a surprisingly efficient jury sail plan can be improvised. Very often small heavy-weather sails can be used on the shortened spars, or large sails can be hoisted by their tacks or clews in lieu of their heads. A sail can sometimes be made smaller simply by knotting one corner, normally the head. New fittings are readily secured to a wooden jury mast, but fastening to an aluminum spar may be a little more difficult. Stainless steel self-tapping screws or, possibly, U bolts such as the flexible OLO "U" bolt made by the Cal-June Corporation are good for jury use with aluminum.

Raising a jury mast requires ingenuity and reasonably calm weather. A tall mast section is often stepped most easily with the use of a gin pole as illustrated in Figure 6-16. A strong halyard or stay from the masthead is attached to the top of the gin pole on its after side, while a tackle used

Figure 6-17. *A 35-foot Ohlson yawl successfuly jury-rigged with only a mizzen mast.*

for hauling the mast up is attached to the top, forward side of the gin pole. Shrouds and guys must be rigged to prevent the pole and mast from swinging and falling over to one side. Strong heel ropes must be used to keep the heel of the mast from slipping forward. Before strain is taken on the tackle, the top of the mast should be lifted by hand (or with sheer legs) as high as possible so that the force applied will largely lift the mast rather than slide it forward. Sometimes a jury mast in the form of an A-frame can be made by fastening the ends of two spars together. Canadian John Hughes sailed over 4,000 miles and rounded Cape Horn under such a rig improvised from two spinnaker poles with their lower ends planted in rag-filled coffee cans. He depended on a cat's cradle of lines to keep the flimsy rig intact.

Less frequent but often far more serious than dismastings are hull punctures or major leaks. Hulls can be stove in from collisions with other vessels, grounding on rocks, or striking at high speed heavy flotsam such as driftwood; serious leaks can be caused by broken through-hull fittings or their pipes and hoses, seams that open up, stress cracks, broken fastenings, spewed caulking, and so forth. The first action to take after discovering that water is rising rapidly in the bilge is to slow down; on a sailboat, reduce sail quickly. Have crewmen start pumping or bailing immediately, and try to discover the source of the leak. Check the head and all through-hull fittings, and if a pipe or hose has broken or become detached from its nipple, shut off the seacocks at once. If there is no seacock, tape the hose or remove it and drive a tapered softwood plug into the orifice that penetrates the hull. It is a wise precaution to tie or otherwise secure a wooden plug right next to the hose and seacock it will service. When there is nothing wrong with the through-hull fittings, a careful search must be made for holes, cracks, or open seams. Check to see that the water didn't come through an open hatch or porthole or from a ruptured water tank. A broken cooling waterline, which can admit considerable water into the bilge when the engine is running, is a not-uncommon occurrence. If no one heard a loud thump from striking a floating or submerged object and the seas are rough, you might assume that a wooden boat has started her caulking or opened one or more seams, or a fiberglass boat has possibly developed cracks from being hard driven. Minor leaks may be in way of the chainplates, around the mast partners, through the deck, or through stuffing boxes. The latter are often sources of unexplained water in the bilge. Carry spare packing and by all means a wrench that will fit the packing nut. Three or four rings of packing are recommended, with the rings inserted so that their joints do not line up. Manila rope impregnated with grease has been suggested for emergency packing. Be sure to check the rudderstock stuffing box, which is often susceptible to leaking when the boat is pitching violently in heavy weather. In any case, slowing the boat and easing the motion and strain will help alleviate most such leaks. In searching for open seams or cracks, check the bow along the stem; at and below the chines forward; under transverse bulkheads, especially those forward; along the garboards, especially in way of the mast step; the counter, transom, and stern tube; the keel; and the hull-deck connection. Cracks or seams can be plugged with caulking cotton and seam compound; rags covered with cup grease can effectively plug large seams. I once kept afloat an ancient wooden boat with wide-open seams by smearing them with a mixture of cup grease and soft putty.

Leaks are far more easy to locate and plug when they are accessible. If possible, see that sections of the boat's ceiling can be removed and that lockers, all parts of the bilge, and closed spaces can be reached. A leak near the waterline on one side might be raised out of water by heeling or listing the boat, while a leak at the bow or stern might be minimized by changing the trim of the vessel. Even if the leak location cannot be raised into the air, reducing its underwater depth will lessen the hydraulic pressure and therefore the rate of flow.

It is important to empty the bilge as soon as possible. When this cannot be done with the pumps, try removing the engine's water intake line from its through-hull fitting (after its seacock has been closed, of course) and placing the hose in the bilge so that it will suck up the bilge water and remove it through the exhaust. This neat trick has been used successfully several times. Be sure that the bilge is free of any floating matter that could clog the engine's water pump. Cover the end of the intake hose with a screen or a can with puncture holes to act as a filter. Once the bilge is emptied, of course, the engine must be stopped or the intake hose reconnected to its fitting to avoid overheating.

Large holes through a hull below the waterline are challenging to plug. Sometimes all that can be done is to delay sinking until help can be summoned or the boat can be run into shallow water, when she is close to shore. If the hull is holed from grounding, don't be too hasty about freeing the boat, for she could later sink in deep water. When the bottom or topsides are stove in, and the hole is not too large, a temporary repair might be made from the inside by covering the fracture with grease and putty-covered rags, followed by a kapok cushion and then by a small sheet of plywood, all of which is pressed tightly against the hole with a shoring piece. The shore may be a pole or plank, one end of which is forced against the plywood patch while the other end is wedged against a vertical surface on the opposite side of the boat. A telescoping boat-hook or whisker pole might work. In a wooden boat, after the patch is forced tightly against the hole, a stringer can be nailed over the patch to ribs on either side of the hole. The cushion, which is used to fill in the hollow or curve of the bilge, may not be needed if the hole is in a flat section of the hull, and in some cases the plywood or possibly a sheet of lead or copper might be applied directly to the hull skin. In addition to the repair inside the hull, the hole might be covered from the outside with a collision mat. This is a rectangular, circular, or triangular piece of soft canvas (sometimes weighted with lead or chain) with lines attached to the corners so that the mat can be held in position over the hole with at least one line (a hogging line) passing under the hull. Depending on the size and location of the hole, you may want to slow it with a collision mat before tackling it from inside the hull. When enough crewmembers are available, pursue both avenues simultaneously. Slow and heel the boat for best advantage in raising the hole and securing the mat.

A true collision mat is thrummed on one side—i.e., short yarns are pulled through the cloth to give a rough texture to the side of the mat facing the hull to discourage slipping. Water pressure will tend to force the mat against and into the hole. If possible, when the hole is partially above or near the waterline, wood battens should be nailed over the canvas to help hold it in place.

Holes in metal or fiberglass hulls present a problem in that patches cannot be nailed on. Planks or pieces of plywood might be screwed with self-tapping screws to fiberglass or metal boats in some cases, while wood wedges or plugs wrapped in rags smeared with grease or tallow might be driven into small holes in a metal hull. Before a patch is applied, its underside should be thickly covered with soft putty and grease or bedding compound, and the patch will have to be held or wedged in place with shores while the screw holes are drilled. Of course, a collision mat or even a piece of soft blanket (perhaps smeared with grease) covering the hole from the outside will be most helpful. Cracks or seams might be filled underwater with the flexible compounds used to caulk swimming pools, such as Permanent Sealer or Hypalon. Some holes might be plugged with underwater epoxy, or even concrete, preferably applied from outside the hull. Underwater epoxies such as Syntho-Glass, sold by Survival Technologies Group, can be formed into a ball to plug a hole or wrapped around a damaged pipe. An authority on boat salvage, Captain C.M. Crichton, has written that concrete prepared with soda can be used successfully to plug holes. For the fastest

Figure 6-18. *Jury steering possibilities.*

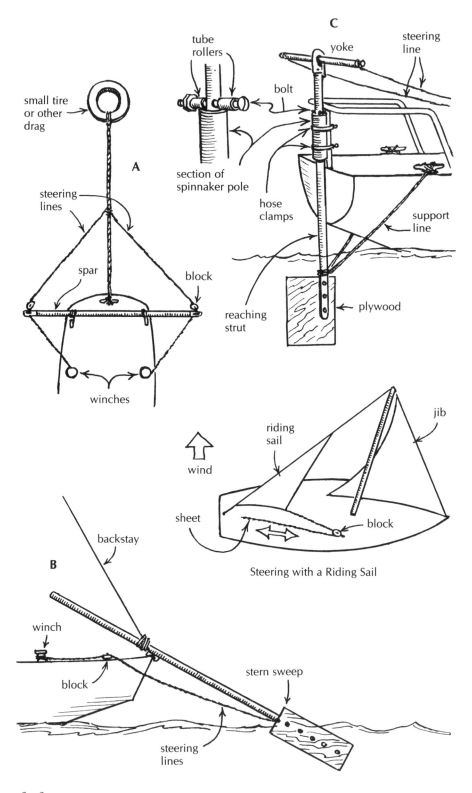

small tire
or other
drag

A

steering
lines

spar

block

winches

C

tube
rollers

yoke

steering
line

bolt

section of
spinnaker pole

hose
clamps

support
line

reaching
strut

plywood

wind

riding
sail

jib

sheet

block

Steering with a Riding Sail

backstay

B

winch

block

stern sweep

steering
lines

setting, Crichton recommends a mixture of half cement and half soda, which he says will harden underwater in half a minute. He warns, however, that the mixture will not be strong. Another trick is to hang a bag of sawdust over a small hole or split in an attempt to plug it from the outside while repairs are made inside. A bag made from coarse cloth or a fine net will emit grains of sawdust, which will be sucked into the hole or crack and hopefully clog it. The sawdust will be encouraged to escape through the bag if it is prodded with a boathook. Incidentally, a readily available material that can clog a small hole or crack is hair.

Of course, holes or damage above the waterline—to the hull, deck, or cabin trunk—will be much easier to repair, but ample tools and patching materials should be carried. Your emergency equipment should include a few sheets of plywood, lead, and copper, perhaps stowed out of the way under bunks. Emergency planking, splints, or shores might be obtained from doors, tables, bunk boards, boom crutches, spinnaker poles, oars, dinghy seats, and so forth. Sails and awnings make good emergency patches for holes in the deck or cabin trunk, but a large cloth patch should be braced with a wood framework, and battens should be nailed over the cloth to hold it in place.

Recommended tools were listed in Chapter 5.

Marine-Tex plastic metal and Devcon, a semiflexible epoxy developed specifically for underwater repairs, are both recommended for patching metal pipes and valves as well as hull cracks. Both are available in packaged repair kits. Waterproof tapes can also be used to great advantage on pipes or hoses. A handy fiberglass repair kit intended for pipe and tank repair is Bond-Aid, sold by Survival Technologies.

Let us now turn to steering casualties. The rigors of distance sailing and especially racing offshore impose tremendous strains on the entire steering mechanism of a sailboat. As suggested earlier, an extra tiller and rudderhead fitting should be carried, and in some cases, on an extended passage, it is wise to carry a preassembled jury rudder. An emergency outboard rudder might be hung quite easily on gudgeons premounted on the transom of a boat having a plumb stern. Other kinds of jury rudders are suggested in Figure 6-18. System A depends on the shifting of a drag, towed astern, from one side of the boat to the other with the use of a steering bridle attached with rolling hitches to the towline. The farther to one side or the other the drag can be moved, the more effective it will be; hence it will help to lead each end of the bridle through blocks at the ends of a spar lashed across the stern and extending outboard on each side as illustrated. The drag must be capable of exerting considerable force, or the system will not be effective. Perhaps a small weighted motor scooter tire or a very small drogue would supply about the right amount of drag for an easily turned medium-sized boat.

System B is a simple stern sweep, nothing more than a crude steering oar. Although you might be able to steer by pushing the inboard end of the sweep from side to side, it is doubtful you could generate sufficient leverage to turn a vessel of any size; thus steering lines will undoubtedly have to be attached near the blade. These lines may be led to each quarter and then to sheet winches on either side of the boat. A sweep can be attached to the boat with shackles or stout lashings around the permanent backstay fitting as illustrated; a more sophisticated solution would be to attach the sweep's end to a spinnaker pole fitting secured to the stern rail. This was the system used aboard Clayton Ewing's yawl *Dyna* when she sailed 980 miles without a rudder during the Transatlantic Race in 1963. *Dyna*'s stern sweep was attached to her boomkin with a bell fitting. If the sweep is attached to the backstay, be sure there are rigging toggles to prevent repeated bending of the backstay turnbuckles, which could cause metal fatigue.

The third jury rudder illustrated is similar to the one used by Wallace Stenhouse's sloop *Aura II* when she sailed 1,800 miles without the use of her rudder during the 1968 Transatlantic Race. This rig consists of a vertical rudderstock (made from a spinnaker guy reaching strut in *Aura*'s case) turning inside a section cut from a hollow aluminum spinnaker pole, which is secured to the stern pulpit with steel hose clamps. The rudder is turned with steering lines attached to a yoke at the top of the rudderstock. In *Aura*'s case, the yoke was a boathook run through the strut's inboard-end fitting, where it was secured with bolts. The illustration suggests a method of preventing the stock from dropping through its casing (the hollow pole section), which consists of inserting a bolt through the stock just above the casing. Both ends of the bolt protrude slightly and are covered with short sections of metal tubing that roll against the top of the casing, thereby minimizing friction of the bolt ends bearing on the casing.

I use a variation of the *Aura II* method on my boat, as illustrated in Figure 6-19. The rig requires a specially made rudderstock, which fits through a pipe that is clamped and lashed to the stern pulpit. The bottom of the stock is bent aft for proper leverage and bolted to the engine compartment door, which doubles as the emergency rudder blade. Notice that the steering lines from the crossbar on the stock are led to a drum on the steering wheel.

The least effective emergency rudder rig illustrated is steering with a drag, but few jury steering rigs of any kind are really efficient, so it is extremely important that the crippled boat be well balanced under a suitable combination of sails. In many cases sailboats, especially those with divided rigs, can be steered with sails alone, simply by trimming and slacking sheets. Twin headsails boomed out on each side are often effective when running. Sometimes a jib boomed out to windward can be carried with a reefed mainsail when well off the wind. When reaching, a staysail trimmed flat but sheeted to weather will help hold the bow off when the boat tends to round up into the wind. It is difficult to steer a reaching sloop with her sails alone, but one possible method is suggested in Figure 6-18. A large jib supplies the power and holds the bow off, while a small riding sail set on the backstay acts as a steering sail. Trimming the sheet of the riding sail will cause the boat to luff, while

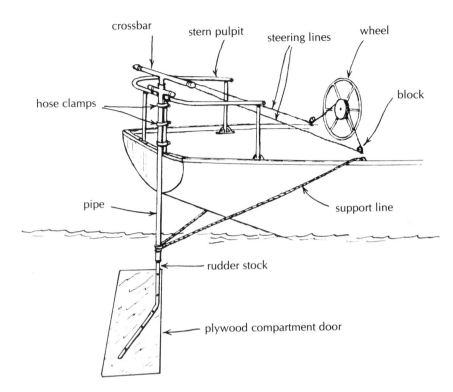

crossbar · stern pulpit · steering lines · wheel · block · hose clamps · pipe · support line · rudder stock · plywood compartment door

Figure 6-19. *The author's jury rudder uses an engine-access door for a blade.*

slacking the sheet will let her fall off provided the boat has a lee helm under jib alone. If the boat has insufficient lee helm, a non-overlapping jib could be used, or perhaps a drag could be rigged to leeward. There are all kinds of alternatives, and the best method of emergency steering can only be found with experimentation. Such experimentation is well worth the effort before a steering casualty occurs.

The jury rudder systems illustrated in Figure 6-18 may also be used on many single-screw powerboats. With small planing boats particular attention must be paid to distribution of crew weight. At slow speed, many planing boats with fine bows need weight aft to keep the bow high for the best steering control. With twin-screw boats, steering nearly always can be controlled with the throttles. When a turn to starboard is required, the port screw is given more speed than the starboard screw, and vice versa.

When you are steering with a jury system, vessels nearby should be warned of your lack of maneuverability. The International Code flag D (Delta) signifies, "Keep clear of me; I am maneuvering with difficulty."

Fire and Lightning

Coast Guard statistics on boating accidents show that almost every year fires and explosions are the leading cause of property damage and are second only to collision in causing personal injuries afloat. Improper installation, inadequate ventilation, and carelessness in the handling of

Figure 6-20A.
*Recommended fuel tank fill and ventilation practices. **A:** cowl ventilators, intake higher. **B:** ducts sufficiently far apart for thorough purging. **C:** blower location. **D:** fill pipe connected to deck plate. **E:** flexible hose with stainless steel clamps. **F:** jumper wire for grounding. **G:** tank grounded. **H:** deck scupper at low point to discharge fumes or spilled gas. **I:** air vent outside coaming securely attached and protected and with swan neck facing aft (powerboat vent may go through upper topsides if there is a high loop in the line). **J:** removable flame screen. **K:** Coast Guard once recommended fill pipe extend to bottom of tank in well to form liquid seal. **L:** tank baffle. **M:** baffle's distance to end of tank not over 30 inches. **N:** secure holding straps insulated from tank. **O:** shut-off valve. **P:** fuel line at top of tank.*

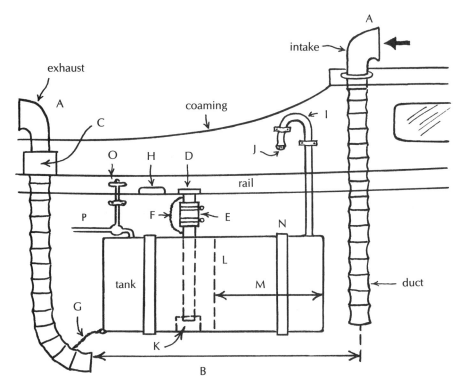

gasoline engines, liquefied petroleum (LP) gas, and alcohol stoves or their fuel systems account for most of the accidents. Minimum federal requirements for prevention of fires and explosions (specifically, ventilation, backfire flame control, and fire extinguishers) are found in the Coast Guard pamphlet entitled *Federal Requirements for Recreational Boats*, and required standards for electrical and fuel systems are outlined in the Coast Guard's Boating Safety Circulars and the book *Rules and Regulations for Recreational Boats*, published by the American Boat and Yacht Council. Further details on fire protection are found in the ABYC book *Standards and Recommended Practices for Small Craft* and the National Fire Protection Association booklet *Fire Protection Standards for Motor Craft*. The best protection is afforded by having a boat inspected or surveyed to see that she conforms in every way to the highest standards of the Coast Guard, the ABYC, or the NFPA on volatile fuel systems, electric wiring, and fire fighting equipment. Supplement this by learning all you can about the causes of fires and explosions.

Many boaters seem insufficiently impressed with the potential shipboard hazards of gasoline. Perhaps this results from the casual way the fuel is handled on shore, around filling stations and automobiles. It should be remembered, however, that gasoline on a boat presents an entirely different safety problem, not only because self-sufficiency is a vital factor when afloat but because the hull of a decked boat is a natural catchment for gas fumes. It is the fumes and not the gasoline itself that are explosive, and since fumes are heavier than air, they will sink to the

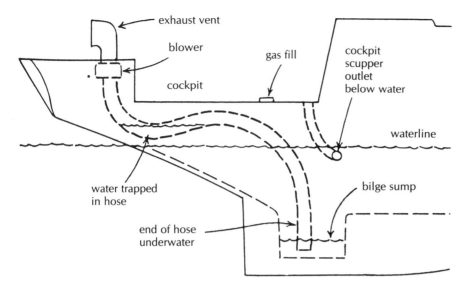

Figure 6-20B. *Possible causes of trapped gasoline fumes.*

bottom of any closed receptacle such as a hull. A Coast Guard pamphlet once warned that one cup of gasoline can produce enough fumes to equal the explosive force of fifteen sticks of dynamite. Although this statement has been called an exaggeration by some authorities, there is no question that the explosive potential is tremendous. The message seems clear: First, don't let any fumes escape inside a boat, and second, if they do escape, remove them as quickly as possible with a good ventilating system. In addition, prevent ignition of possible fumes with safe electric wiring and the careful use of matches or lighters, and take care when creating sparks from spark testing or jump starting with a screwdriver. Diesel fuel is relatively safe because it doesn't have the explosive potential of gasoline, but it still can be a fire hazard if the bilge or other parts of the engine compartment are allowed to become saturated with oil.

To prevent fumes from escaping inside the hull, the essential consideration is the resistance to leakage and reliability of the tanks and fuel lines. The entire fuel system must be tight, from the top of the fill pipe to the engine carburetor. Approved practices and standards for the fuel system in brief form are as follows:

- The tops of all fill pipes should be securely attached to deck plates, which ought to be located outboard of cockpit coamings at a point where any fumes or spillage of gas will go overboard. If the gasoline fill is on the cockpit sole, the scupper outlets should be above the waterline so that fumes can escape (see Figure 6-20B).

- Fill pipes should, if possible, be straight, and if there is any flexibility in the hull (there usually is), which allows a slight movement between the deck plate and tank, a section of flexible hose should be used near the top of the fill pipe. This section must be securely fastened to the fill pipe with noncorrosive screw-type clamps at least 1/2 inch wide, and the hose should be located where it can be easily inspected. The Coast Guard formerly recommended that a fill pipe extend to the bottom of its tank, where it will terminate inside a well to form a liquid seal so that the tank cannot be exploded from an ignited fill pipe (see Figure 6-20A).

- Fuel tank vents should also be outboard of the cockpit coamings, where fumes can escape into the open air. A vent anywhere inside the hull is extremely dangerous. The ABYC and NFPA recommend that the vent pipe have a minimum inside diameter of $9/16$ inch and that vent outlets be fitted with removable flame screens as protection against flash-back from an outside source of ignition. The top of a vent pipe should have a loop or swan neck bent aft in such a way that it cannot admit rain or seawater.

- Fuel tanks must be securely fastened to withstand continuous motion and a beam-ends knockdown or even a capsizing, but gasoline tanks in particular must not be integral with the hull. NFPA and ABYC standards recommend that the tanks have no openings or fittings in the bottom, sides, or ends and that they have permanent labels giving the manufacturer's name, date of manufacture, capacity, construction material and thickness, intended fuel, and maximum test pressure. A tank must be capable of withstanding a pressure of at least three pounds per square inch without leaking. Recommended tank materials are Monel (nickel-copper), aluminum, fire-retardant fiberglass (approved by the Underwriter's Laboratories), and galvanized steel (but not internally galvanized when the fuel is diesel oil). Fuel tanks made of terneplate (a sheet steel coated with lead and tin) are now prohibited by the Coast Guard. Tanks of stainless steel are not always recommended due to the possibility of galvanic or shielding corrosion and fatigue stress. Rounded tanks are preferable, and they should have a reasonable amount of air circulation on all exterior surfaces. Baffles are extremely important to give strength and to restrict the surging of fuel inside the tank. The NFPA allows brazed construction, but be wary of low-heat solders. I have vivid memories of a copper tank's soldered seam bursting open and spilling gas in the bilge while I was sailing a small yawl during a rough night offshore. The all-welded tank is far safer than one that is soldered or riveted. The Coast Guard has specific fuel tank testing and labeling requirements that may be found in the USCG Boating Safety Circulars, the *Code of Federal Regulations*, or the ABYC book *Rules and Regulations for Recreational Boats*. Some fuel tank installation and ventilation details are shown in Figure 6-20A.

- Fuel-distribution metal tubing for gasoline engines should be seamless annealed copper, nickel-copper, or copper-nickel with a minimum wall thickness of .032 inch, according to the recommendations of the ABYC (the Coast Guard allows .029-inch thickness). The tubing must be well supported and protected as much as possible against vibration. Securing clips or straps should be resistant to corrosion and of a design that cannot cut or abrade the fuel line. Flexible tubing should separate a fuel line secured to the hull from that part of the line secured to the engine, but the flexible tubing should be the heavy-duty, USCG Type A1 hose (Types A2, B1, and B2 are allowed in certain cases). Hoses for alcohol-blended gasoline should be marked J1527. The Coast Guard requires that the fuel line from the tank to carburetor "must either be above the level of the tank top or have an anti-siphon device or an electrically operated fuel stop valve—(I) at the tank withdrawal fitting; or (II) installed so the line from the fuel tank is above the top of the tank." Metal fuel lines must be insulated if they are near the top of a battery.

- A fuel-line shut-off valve should be installed close to the tank, and another should be located near the engine. They must be firmly secured and supported independent of the tubing. The tank valve should be operable from outside the engine compartment, perhaps with a reach rod. Packless valves should be used, and shut and open positions must be plainly marked or designated with positive stops at both positions.

- Gas line filters must be readily accessible and independently supported. As with any component of the fuel system, filters should be made and approved for marine use. It can be dangerous to use an automobile-type filter on a boat. The bowl should be of noncorrosive metal and large enough to trap at least a pint of water. For maximum safety, glass bowl strainers are generally not recommended. Marine filters should be designed for top servicing because drains at the bottom could leak. The Coast Guard now requires the testing of filters, strainers, and gaskets to assure against leakage. Gaskets must be unsplit rings.

- The carburetor must be fitted with a backfire flame arrestor secured to the air intake in accordance with federal requirements, and carburetors need drip collectors of adequate capacity, which return all drips and overflow to the engine intake manifold.

- Electrical grounding of the fuel system is extremely important to prevent a buildup of static electricity that could cause a spark. Any nonmetallic flexible hoses in the line must be bridged with heavy (at least No. 8) copper wire. Sparks due to static electricity can result from a number of activities, such as the filling of a gasoline tank, friction caused by a boat working in a seaway, or even the running of water through a hose. Thus it is advisable to bond and ground all metal fittings that could produce a spark anywhere that fumes could accumulate. Some essential safety points in connection with electric wiring and the battery were discussed in Chapter 4. It is well to emphasize that all electrical devices should be approved for motor craft use; wiring should be well insulated and of adequate size to prevent voltage drops and overheating; each circuit should be fused or fitted with non-self-resetting circuit breakers (the Coast Guard specifies that a circuit breaker or fuse be within 72 inches of the battery measured along the conductor unless the circuit has a switch that disconnects the battery); and only sparkproof switches located as high as possible above the bilge should be used (don't use a knife-type switch in a low position or anywhere fumes could possibly accumulate). Electrical components of the engine should be as sparkproof as possible. Spark plugs, for example, need caps or shields to prevent arcing. It is not unusual to see sailboat batteries in the bilge, but this is a potentially dangerous practice not only because of the possible accumulation of explosive fumes but because seawater and charged batteries can form deadly chlorine gas.

Batteries have an explosive potential of their own when they lack ventilation. In fact, I was once aboard a boat whose batteries blew up. A tightly covered battery box can trap hydrogen gas generated by a lead-acid battery, which could be detonated by a spark. Replace any battery with a bad cell or cracked casing. Battery boxes must be covered to prevent the accidental dropping of tools on the terminals, but the lid should have airholes, and the entire battery compartment should be reasonably ventilated. Batteries must be well secured. The Coast Guard prohibits movement of more than one inch in any direction when a pulling force of 90 pounds or twice the weight of the battery is applied.

- Engine and fuel tank compartment ventilation is set forth in Coast Guard Pamphlet No. 395 and in *Rules and Regulations for Recreational Boats*. Some general rules on the subject are as follows: There should be one or more intake ventilator ducts with cowls (or the equivalent) bringing air into the engine compartment, and one or more exhaust ventilators with ducts. The NFPA recommends two intake and two exhaust ventilators with ducts. The exhaust ducts must lead from the lower portion of the bilge and the intake ducts lead at least midway to the bilge below the carburetor intake. Ducts are generally made of noncollapsible flexible hose, and they must be routed clear of and protected from contact with hot engine surfaces. The NFPA recommends a minimum duct sectional area of one square inch per foot of beam. Although not required for diesel power, the Coast Guard now requires that each compartment in a boat with a permanently installed gasoline engine having a cranking motor must be ventilated with an exhaust blower. Certainly a bilge blower is a real safety feature, but it should be a sparkproof marine type located as high as possible above the bilge in an exhaust duct. It is essential that the bottom of an exhaust duct go to the lowest point in the bilge, but it must be kept above the normal level of bilge water, and ducts should be installed without dips that could catch rainwater, which might blow into the cowls. Figure 6-20 shows how water blockage can prevent the dis-

Figure 6-21. *Coast Guard statistics on boating accidents show that fire and explosions are the leading cause of property damage. Improper fueling is often the culprit.*

sipation of fumes and render the blower ineffective. Although the forward cowls usually face forward and are the intake vents, in some cases (if both ducts are sufficiently low in the bilge), when a boat is at anchor, the circulation of air below might be improved by turning the forward vents aft and the aft vents forward, so that air below will flow from aft forward. On sailboats in rough weather when the engine is not running, ventilators should be removed and their openings closed for the sake of watertightness, but every effort should be made to keep air circulating below as well as possible. In the final analysis, of course, watertight integrity is more vital than ventilation. Thus it is important, especially in powerboats, that engine room vents be positioned where they will be protected from water coming aboard in rough water.

Carelessness in fueling is probably the greatest cause of explosion and fire. A list of precautions follows: Take on fuel during daylight whenever possible; be sure the boat is securely made fast; find out how much fuel is needed and check the condition of the vent line (see that it is not loose or clogged); close openings into the cabin through which fumes might enter; turn off switches and shut down motors, engines, or any devices that could cause sparks; don't smoke, strike matches, or light stoves while fueling; keep the fuel hose nozzle firmly in contact with the fill pipe to avoid the possibility of a spark from static electricity; do not run fuel into a tank so fast that it spills or overflows; after fueling, wipe up all spills; if the fill pipe is in the bottom of the cockpit, fan out the fumes before opening the companionway slide and see that cockpit scuppers are above the waterline so that fumes can escape; open all hatches and ports and let the boat air out for at least five minutes before turning on switches or striking matches; and run the blower for at least four minutes, sniffing the bilge and blower outlet for fumes to be sure that all gasoline odors have disappeared, before starting the engine. Boats have exploded after powering some distance away from the fuel dock, because the fumes were too rich to explode before getting under-way. Introducing more air to the engine compartment created the explosive mixture. This fact should impress us with the necessity of removing *all* fumes before starting the engine. When the gas tanks are aft, it is usually advisable to take on fuel with the bow headed into the wind, so that fumes are blown away from the cabin.

A few final thoughts relating to engines and fires: Be sure there is ample insulation between a hot exhaust pipe and any wooden member of the hull; be sure that exhaust system support straps are resistant to heat; see that the drip pan under the engine is of ample size and deep enough not to overflow on a heeled sailboat; keep the bilges and engine compartment clean and free of oil or grease. Many people do not realize that, although the explosive hazards of oils are much less than those of gasoline, diesel fuel can be explosive under certain conditions of fume concentration, and of course, risk of fire is present whenever flammable fuels are carried.

The greatest source of boat fires other than the engine and its fuel system is the galley stove. Traditionally, alcohol has been considered the safest fuel for cooking stoves, but there have been numerous galley fires from pressurized alcohol, mainly as a result of careless handling or improper stove design and installation. The safety advantages of alcohol as a fuel are that it will not readily explode and its flame can be extinguished with water. Although the use of water on alcohol fires is recommended by the ABYC and NFPA, my own experiments have shown that a small amount of water that is insufficient to extinguish the fire completely could float it to a potentially dangerous location, such as an oily bilge, where ignition could take place after a brief period of smoldering. My feeling is that unless a considerable quantity of water is used, an alcohol fire should be smothered with dry chemical, carbon dioxide, or perhaps a wet towel. Soda or flour can smother such a fire effectively, but great care must be taken when using any dry powder not to splash the flaming liquid.One man warned me that flour might explode, but I spent several hours pouring flour on alcohol fires, and nothing happened except that the fires were extinguished. Of course, water is a lot easier to clean up than any powder, especially those in dry chemical extinguishers.

Fires from alcohol stoves are generally caused by flare-ups, spillage of fuel, leaks in the fuel line, failure to watch a stove after it is lighted, and improper location of the fuel tank and its shut-off valve. To avoid these possible dangers, it is necessary to have a basic understanding of how the stove works. Alcohol is fed from its storage tank by gravity or air pressure to a "primed" or preheated section of tubing, where it is vaporized by the heat. The vapor then passes through perforations at the burner where it is ignited to give a hot, almost colorless and odorless flame. Flare-ups are usually caused by incomplete priming or failure to heat adequately the tubing near the burner where vaporization takes place, so that raw alcohol passes into the burner and bursts into a high flame when it is ignited with a match or lighter. Actually, these flare-ups need not be dangerous if the burner's valve is shut immediately, if the stove operator keeps clear, and if there are no hanging towels or curtains over the stove that can catch fire. With the valve shut, the blaze should soon die down. If not, let the pressure off the fuel tank, or, if the feed is by gravity, shut the fuel line shut-off valve. Remember that water will extinguish an alcohol fire, but a considerable quantity should be used. It is always advisable to have a large pot or bucket of water handy when lighting the stove in case a flare-up should get out of hand. After extinguishing a fire (with water, especially) don't immediately leave the boat, because re-ignition could occur from smoldering.

Other sources of stove fires include fuel spillages when filling the tank and overflow from the priming cups. The latter must be sufficiently deep to hold enough alcohol for adequate heating of vaporization chambers without danger of overflow even in rough weather. Also, there must be a large, deep, removable metal drip pan under the stove to catch any spilled alcohol. This pan should be thoroughly clean and dry of fuel before the priming cup is lighted. Be sure that there are no leaks in the fuel line. Tighten all threaded connections and see that the line is properly gasketed.

Once the stove is burning, it should be continually watched to see that all flames are burning properly. If an unwatched burner flame should happen to go out due to temporary clogging of the burner by sediment, a sudden draft, a pot boiling over, or some other cause, then raw alcohol could accumulate where it might be ignited by the hot burner and cause a flare-up. When a burner goes out, it might be relighted immediately (while there is sufficient heat for vaporization), but if it cannot be relighted at once it should be turned off. It will be necessary to reprime after allowing the burner to cool down. Although alcohol will not readily explode, it can do so when a high concentration of vapor is exposed to heat above 689 degrees Fahrenheit (whether the heat is an open flame or not). Don't fill an alcohol stove fuel tank anywhere near a burner unless the burner has been turned off and allowed to cool thoroughly.

More than one boat has caught fire because a stove flare-up made the fuel tank shut-off valve inaccessible. Despite contrary recommendations by the ABYC, many boats are equipped with shut-off valves that can only be operated by reaching across the stove. Valves should not only be accessible, but they should be capable of being closed with one turn, and the open and shut positions should be clearly marked. It is also wise to clearly mark the open and shut positions of all burner controls.

The latest trend in alcohol stoves is the unpressurized type, which produces flame from canisters filled with nonflammable wadding that must be saturated with alcohol. This type avoids some of the problems associated with pressure stoves, but there can be difficulties with refueling. Beware of overflowing the canister and of refilling before the canister has thoroughly cooled. Several people have been seriously burned from the ignition of alcohol vapors over the stove immediately after refueling.

Kerosene stoves are relatively safe, but they require a fire extinguisher (rather than merely water) to put out a flare-up that is out of control. (Regardless of the fuel, a fire extinguisher should always be mounted near the galley.) The ABYC does not recommend wick-type burners because their performance may be adversely affected by the boat's motion. All accepted standards warn against the use of gasoline for stove fuel aboard boats. With any kind of stove, the woodwork around it, especially overhead, should be well protected with sheet metal over insulation. It is important to keep all stoves clean, because accumulations of grease from cooking can be highly flammable.

Many boats are fitted with liquefied petroleum (LP) gas stoves (or other appliances) because of their convenience in not needing to be primed. These appliances can be extremely dangerous if they are not properly installed and carefully handled. They should be given the same respect as a gasoline engine and its fuel system, because LP gas and gasoline vapors have the same dangerous characteristics: Both are heavier than air, and both are potentially explosive. In some respects, LP gas, which includes propane and butane, may be even more hazardous than gasoline, because it is easily diffused and difficult to dispel by overhead ventilation. Furthermore, it is relatively odorless, but the law now requires that an odorant be added to commercially available gas to facilitate leak detection.

Despite its explosive potential and the fact that it has been banned by the Coast Guard on vessels carrying passengers for hire, LP gas is now considered safe when installed and used as follows: Gas cylinders must be carried where any possible leakage of gas will escape well clear of the boat's interior. This means that the cylinders should be stowed on deck in a well-ventilated box or in a vaporproof, ventilated locker fitted with a drain at the bottom that leads overboard. Be sure the outlet for the drain is sufficiently high above the waterline that it will not be submerged by the stern wave or when heeling, and never stow gear in the cylinder locker that could clog the drain. The plumbing can be copper tubing with flexible hose ends, but all flexible high-pressure hose meeting the highest burn-through standards and well protected against chafe is preferred. There should be an electrically operated solenoid shut-off valve in the cylinder locker, with its switch and warning light located in the galley. The valve should be the type that automatically closes in the event of a power failure. LP gas systems need a pressure gauge to facilitate periodic checking for leaks. The pressure should be read with the main shut-off valve and the cylinder valve open, while the appliance valves are shut. If the pressure remains constant for 10 minutes after the cylinder valve is shut, there are no leaks. If the pressure drops, the application of soapy water to all connections is an effective means of locating the leak. Further protection can be obtained from thermocouple heat sensors at the burners and a gas-detecting "sniffer," which sounds an alarm and shuts off the fuel if there is a gas leak into the bilge.

A few rules for safe operation of LP gas stoves (or other gas appliances) are as follows:

- Always keep the cylinder valve shut unless the appliance is actually in use. Be sure that the valve is shut in any emergency.
- See that the appliance valves are shut before the cylinder valve is turned on.
- When lighting the stove, apply the lighted match (or lighter) to the burner *before* its valve is opened.
- Watch the stove while it is being used to see that the flame does not go out. If it should go out (from a sudden draft, a pot boiling over, etc.), shut the valve immediately.
- In order to ensure that minimal gas will remain in the fuel line, shut the cylinder valve first and allow the fuel to burn out of the line before shutting the appliance valves.
- Test for leaks at least every two weeks.
- See that the entire system is installed in accordance with NFPA standards (set forth in Booklet No. 302).
- Never use a flame to look for leaks.
- Be sure flexible fuel lines near the stove are *fireproof* (not fire-resistant), as a stovetop fire could burn through the line and cause a serious explosion.

Although compressed natural gas (CNG) is often hard to obtain, it is becoming increasingly popular because it is lighter than air, and, unlike LPG, will not sink into the bilge. This characteristic is a very desirable safety advantage, but nevertheless CNG is highly explosive and fumes should be vented out of the boat's interior. Gas lockers need vents at their tops, and care must be taken to see that no rising fumes can be trapped under an overhead.

Other main causes of fires on boats are from solid-fuel heaters, overheated electric wiring, spontaneous combustion, and smoking in bunks. The latter should never be permitted. Heaters burning wood, coal, or charcoal must be surrounded by insulation. They should preferably be on hollow tile bases or legs and have a proper stack to prevent spark emission and back draft. Careful measures should be taken to see that the fuel cannot spill out in a seaway, and the heater should never be left for long periods unwatched. Open fireplaces need screens to assure that sparks will not be emitted. Electric wiring has already been discussed. As said earlier, major safety considerations are proper fusing, wire size, and insulation. Spontaneous combustion can result when oily rags are stowed in an airtight space, perhaps in a paint locker or, in the old days, an oilskin locker. Do not stow foul-weather suits in airtight spaces if they are genuine oilskins. Be sure that all lockers are ventilated, and do not keep old paint rags.

Three elements are necessary to support a fire: high temperature, oxygen, and fuel. Fire-fighting techniques are concerned with eliminating one or more of these elements. The temperature can be lowered with water or other cooling agents; oxygen can be removed or partially eliminated by smothering with a blanket, salt, soda, foam, by keeping hatches closed, etc.; and the fuel can be cut off by shutting fuel tank valves or cutting away the burning material. Fires are generally classified into three categories according to the material afire and the recommended method of containing and extinguishing it. Class A fires are those in ordinary, solid combustible materials such as wood, cloth, and paper. These are usually most easily extinguished by cooling (or quenching) with water or solutions containing large amounts of water. Class B fires are those in flammable oils, grease, petroleum products, etc., and should be extinguished by smothering and by shutting off the fuel supply when possible. Throwing water on this type of fire might spread it, because burning gasoline and oils float. Class C fires are those in electrical equipment. Water should not be used to fight Class C fires because of the danger of shock or even electrocution where high voltages are involved. This type of fire is best fought with a nonconductive extinguishing medium that smothers the flames. It is important to cut off electrical switches and deenergize the affected circuit during a Class C fire.

Extinguishers approved by the Coast Guard include foam, carbon dioxide (CO_2), dry chemical, and Halon. These are all B-type extinguishers (mainly for class B fires), and size requirements are specified in the Coast Guard publication, *Federal Requirements for Recreational Boats*. Dry chemical extinguishers use a powder contained under pressure, such as sodium bicarbonate (baking soda) or potassium bicarbonate ("purple K") combined with certain additives. Approved extinguishers of this type have a gauge to indicate whether or not the unit has adequate pressure for effective operation. Dry chemicals smother flames and will extinguish C as well as B fires. A multipurpose type, basically ammonium phosphate, will even work against class A fires, but water or foam is usually much more effective against A fires of considerable size. Foam consists mainly of water and therefore should not be used on C fires, but it is effective against A as well as B fires even on vertical and overhead surfaces. CO_2 is an oxygen-depriving, smothering gas. Indeed, humans should not breathe it more than momentarily in tightly enclosed spaces. It can be used on any class of fire but should be followed with water on a class A fire to prevent reignition of smoldering embers. CO_2 is especially effective against low fires, in the bilge for example, because the gas is heavier than air and will sink down and blanket the fire. The ABYC recommends that a portable CO_2 extinguisher be used in the vicinity of the galley. Large boats often have built-in CO_2 systems that are automatic or manually operable from the bridge or helmsman's position. As a matter of fact, permanent CO_2 systems are a very good idea on some small boats with inaccessible engine compartments. A relatively new and very effective extinguisher is Halon, a Freon gas, which works almost instantaneously by inhibiting the chemical reaction of oxygen with fuel and

breaking down the chain reaction that keeps a fire going. It is most effective in closed areas, as it dissipates rapidly and is easily dispersed by the wind. Halon 1301 (bromotrifluoromethane) is used occasionally in portable extinguishers but more often for fixed manual and automatic systems, and it is minimally toxic. Exposure to a seven percent (by volume) concentration for up to five minutes is considered safe. I was told by sellers of Halon that Halon 1211 (bromochlorodifluoromethane), which is used mostly for portable extinguishers, is more toxic, and one should avoid breathing its fumes in a closed compartment over prolonged periods. Halon 104 (little used on boats) is even more toxic. The Coast Guard advises that personnel should be evacuated from closed compartments prior to the release of Halons.

Be sure to keep extinguishers where they will be readily available and most likely needed, in or near such areas as the galley, the engine compartment, and the steering position. Inspect them periodically to see that they are in top working order, but do not test by opening the extinguisher's valve, because this might partially deplete the contents or allow pressure to leak out. Rather, examine the pressure gauge, look at safety pins and wires, or weigh the extinguishers. Follow maintenance instructions or have extinguishers checked by qualified authorities such as a competent chandler, the manufacturer, or the Coast Guard. Do not use extinguishers that are not recommended—such as carbon tetrachloride or chlorobromomethane (CBM)—because they can give off a poisonous and potentially lethal gas.

Some general rules for fighting fires are as follows:

- With an LP gas fire, shut cylinder valves immediately.
- With Class B fires, shut fuel supply valves at once.
- With Class C fires, turn off electrical switches to deenergize the affected system.
- With Class A and alcohol fires, use water. A draw bucket can be a most effective fire-fighting tool.
- When underway, reduce the speed of the boat and turn her so that the wind blows the fire in the direction of least flammability or

vulnerability. If the fire were in the bow, for example, the boat should be headed off with her stern to the wind. Above all, the boat should be headed so that flames are blown away from fuel tanks or other vulnerable areas.

- With any fire, keep calm but act at once. The longer a fire is allowed to blaze, the more the temperature will increase and the more difficult the extinguishing operation will be. Bring all available extinguishers to bear immediately.

- Small fires might be smothered before they get started with anything available, such as a cushion, dish towel, blanket, salt, baking soda, etc.

- Consider throwing the blazing object overboard. In some cases this might involve chopping away the burning material; thus, an ax or hatchet can be valuable.

- A fireproof glove could be handy not only for gripping hot pots in the galley, but for throwing a flaming object overboard, beating out a small fire, or shutting hot valves that are surrounded by flames. Be sure you are well protected with clothing when fighting a fire.

- Remember that even though water should not be used on Class B and C fires, it might be used effectively to cool adjacent areas to help prevent the fire from spreading. Electrical equipment can be wet down when it is deenergized, and shock hazards from the 12-volt systems of most small pleasure craft are minimal.

- Make every attempt to reduce drafts. They fan the flames and supply oxygen. Whenever possible, shut doors, vents, portholes, and hatches. An open hatch directly above a fire can be particularly harmful, because it will act like a chimney. Don't introduce oxygen too soon after a fire has been extinguished.

- Learn how to remove and operate a fire extinguisher before facing a fire. In most cases, direct the extinguishing agent at the base of the flame in a back-and-forth sweeping motion.

- Do not remain in a closed compartment where CO_2 or Halon has been squirted.

- Call for help from the Coast Guard or others early, because power may have to be shut down or the fire might otherwise destroy your ability to communicate by radio.

- Consider launching a liferaft early if there is danger of an explosion.

- Clean up thoroughly after using dry chemicals, as their residue is extremely corrosive and damaging, especially to electrical installations.

Lightning is not only a fire and explosion hazard, but it can cause lethal injury and can puncture or otherwise damage a hull. Boats are not struck very often, but the danger exists, and some form of protection is needed except perhaps in certain cases when the boat has a metal hull. The main principle behind lightning protection is the provision of a low-resistance path from the point where the lightning bolt strikes to the ground. In addition, grounding bleeds off and thus helps prevent a buildup of static electricity in vulnerable parts of a boat, which might possibly encourage a lightning strike. In most cases, lightning will strike the boat's highest point: the masthead of a sailboat or the top of a tall antenna on a radiotelephone-equipped powerboat. For adequate protection of a nonmetallic boat, the high point must be connected with a reasonably straight, low-resistance conductor to a groundplate or perhaps a metal keel. The grounded mast or antenna will nearly always divert to itself direct lightning strikes that might otherwise fall within a cone-shaped area (called the protective cone), the apex of which is the top of the conductor and the base of which is a circle on the water having a radius of about twice the conductor's height (see Figure 6-23). For maximum safety, the conductor's top (masthead or antenna tip) must be sufficiently high that every part of the boat lies within the protective cone.

Details for lightning protection systems are given by the ABYC and NFPA. Some of the main points are as follows: The entire conducting circuit, from high point to ground, should be equivalent in conductivity to No. 8 or larger copper cable running as straight as possible. Large metal objects anywhere near the conductor should be bonded to it to prevent side flashes. The top of the conductor should terminate in a point and protrude at least six inches above the mast. This is especially important when there is an electronic wind indicator or anemometer at the masthead. A powerboat with a radiotelephone can be protected if the antenna is not spirally wrapped and is provided with a transmitting lightning arrester or a means of direct grounding with a switch arrangement prior to an electrical storm. There is at least one switch made for this purpose that operates automatically, with the antenna being connected indirectly to ground when the radiotelephone is turned off. I am told that some ham radio operators use a spark plug as a lightning arrester, and some use a neon bulb rigged between the hot side of the antenna and ground to bleed off static charges. One can see, in the proximity of an electrical storm, the bulb light up and bleed off as the antenna charge is drained. Antennas with loading coils need a bypass gap or shunt (jumper) in order that the entire aerial height can be utilized for lightning protection; otherwise the apex of the protective cone should be considered as being located just below the coil (see Figure 6-23).

Although many boats are grounded to through-hull fittings, the ABYC recommends that the groundplate for lightning protection be no less than one foot square. Only recently, I heard of a boat that nearly sank because a lightning strike blew out a bonded through-hull fitting. In some cases the backstay can be grounded to the propeller shaft, but the bearings may be destroyed by a strike. A boat with a metal hull is already grounded, provided the wire standing rigging and metal mast

Figure 6-23. *Lightning protection. Note: For masts over 50 feet above the water, the ABYC now considers the protective zone to lie between two semicircular arcs positioned forward and abaft the mast in such a way that the arcs pass through the masthead and are tangent to the water's surface.*

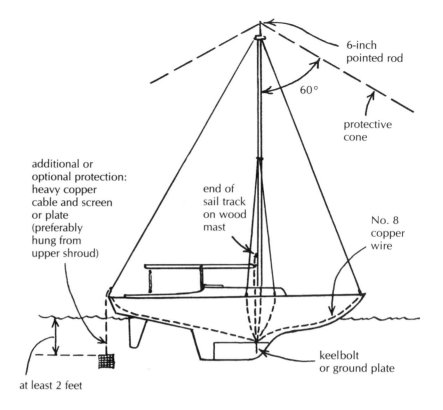

6-inch pointed rod

60°

protective cone

No. 8 copper wire

additional or optional protection: heavy copper cable and screen or plate (preferably hung from upper shroud)

end of sail track on wood mast

keelbolt or ground plate

at least 2 feet

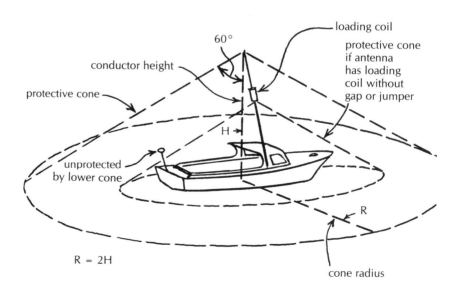

60°

loading coil

protective cone if antenna has loading coil without gap or jumper

conductor height

protective cone

H

unprotected by lower cone

R

R = 2H

cone radius

(or the track on a wooden mast) are well bonded to the hull. On non-metal sailboats with external ballast keels, the conductor can run from the base of the mast or sail track to the nearest keelbolt under the mast step (see Figure 6-23). If the boat has internal keel ballast, the conductor can be connected to the propeller shaft if it does not have a nonconductive flexible coupling, but this arrangement is inferior to a proper groundplate. Stays and especially upper shrouds should be grounded, as well as any large metal objects that protrude above the deckhouse. In the absence of a proper lightning ground system, a heavy copper cable clamped to a masthead stay or shroud and dangled overboard provides some protection. A screen or large copper plate attached to the underwater end of the cable should increase its effectiveness. This temporary rig should prove most effective when connected to a leeward upward shroud, since a lightning bolt seeks the most direct, straight-line route to ground. For a small outboard motorboat, the Coast Guard has suggested lightning protection in the form of a temporary mast connected to the outboard. The jury mast might be a long, telescoping boathook, and it should make metal-to-metal contact with the motor. A transom-mounted outboard would require that the crew sit fairly far aft to be under the protective cone.

During a thunderstorm, the crew should go below if possible and should avoid contact with rigging or any large metal objects. Avoid touching and especially bridging objects connected to the conductive system or other metal fittings that might be struck by lightning. For instance, the helmsman exposes himself to danger when he grips a stanchion and a metal wheel simultaneously. Wet sails make good conductors, so if possible they should be lowered and furled prior to a bad electrical storm.

In this chapter the most common emergencies affecting the vessel itself have been discussed. Other crises that affect the crew more directly will be dealt with in the next chapter.

Chapter 7
CREW SECURITY AND WELFARE

Shaping Up to Ship Out

Many emergencies involving the crew or vessel can be avoided by preliminary and ongoing physical and mental preparation. Before embarking on an offshore passage, you ought to be in good physical shape, properly garbed, and psychologically prepared. Try to follow a regular routine of moderate exercise several weeks or more before the voyage to firm up flabby muscles, improve your lungs, increase endurance, possibly build up resistance to certain disorders, reduce fatigue, and simply to feel better. Pay particular attention to arms, legs, and stomach muscles, as these are used a great deal to maintain security and balance in rough seas. Be sure that you have no medical problems, or if you have, see that the skipper, ship's doctor, or medical specialist knows about them.

Personal equipment includes warm clothing, foul weather gear that is truly waterproof but easy to don and doff, skidproof shoes and boots, a wide-brimmed or long-billed hat that will stay on, proper sunglasses, tightly woven but lightweight clothing to protect against sunburn, and by all means a motion-sickness medicine that works for you. When purchasing foul weather gear, forget about style. Choose bright orange or yellow, not those blue or white suits that blend so nicely with the water. For warmth, wear numerous garment layers, which provide plenty of air spaces for insulation and at the same time allow flexibility in movement and the ability to peel or add layers as temperature and wind dictate. Natural fabrics are normally superior to synthetics for undergarments that will not be exposed to solid water. In cold weather there is nothing like a woolen watch cap. For severe conditions, consider an exposure suit, some of which are less bulky than one might expect and provide flotation as well as excellent protection against hypothermia. Be sure the soles of your deck shoes and boots are not worn down, because, when they are, they can be treacherously slippery on a wet surface. As for going about the deck barefoot, forget it! Incidentally, you should carry a pocketknife with a spike and/or shackle opener.

If you are well garbed, you not only will be more comfortable and better protected, you will maximize your efficiency and improve your morale and hence your general state of mind. A healthy mental attitude encourages good judgment and sound seamanship. Minds under stress can make costly, careless mistakes, lose concentration, and even hallucinate at sea. Don't leave shore with the expectation that you can escape from your problems: They may only grow worse under stress offshore. Be sure you are well rested before getting underway, and get all the sleep possible during the passage, because fatigue leads to mental lapses. Deep fatigue has also been responsible, or partly so, for dangerous hallucinations, the kind that cause the helm to be abandoned when it shouldn't be or the sailor to walk overboard on his way to some imaginary haven such as the local tavern. Fears can be alleviated with preliminary preparation. Read and learn from others, practice your navigation and seamanship ahead of time, and prepare for a voyage well in advance of your scheduled departure. Few pressures cause more stress than rushing to meet a deadline. Plan on a departure date about three months ahead of the time when you actually have to leave.

Hypothermia

In most safety-at-sea symposia nowadays there is a discussion of hypothermia. As a result of more than a few deaths of commercial fishermen and yachtsmen who have fallen overboard or capsized in small boats, we have become painfully aware that seafarers can die from exposure to the cold. Such exposure is much more likely when a person is wet, especially if he is immersed, but hypothermia, a dangerous loss of heat from the core of the body, is possible even when a crewmember is dry in cold weather. As a matter of fact, the weather need not be extremely cold to cause this condition if the victim is not well protected with clothing and is exposed to temperatures lower than his skin temperature over a long period of time.

Hypothermia is defined as a condition in which the core temperature of the body drops below 95 degrees Fahrenheit. In the early stages of this affliction, the victim's skin will pale, he will lose manual dexterity, and, unless perhaps he is exercising with some degree of vigor, he will shiver uncontrollably. In later stages he will become confused, disoriented, and amnesic, and shivering will be replaced by muscular rigidity and stiffness of movement when the core temperature drops below about 89.6 degrees Fahrenheit. A further drop leads to semiconsciousness, then unconsciousness, shallow and irregular breathing, a slower heart rate, and eventually a deep coma, extreme rigidity, and possibly cardiac arrest.

During the early stages, hypothermia is easily reversible. Very often, merely removing wet clothes and replacing them with ample dry, warm clothing or closely wrapped blankets will suffice. Warm beverages can be helpful, but avoid caffeine, alcohol, and milk. Frank Tulloch, an experienced sailor/doctor specializing in emergency medicine, suggests giving

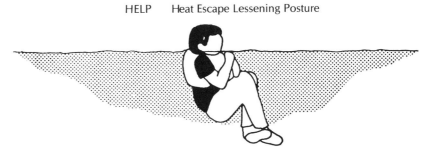

Figure 7-1. *Heat escape lessening posture (HELP). (Reprinted, by permission, from Robert S. Pratt,* Hypothermia: The Chill That Need Not Kill, *American College of Surgeons Bulletin (Chicago, October 1980))*

the conscious victim warm water, bouillon, or decaffeinated tea. He thinks warm Gatorade might be perfect if you are sure it will not produce nausea and possible vomiting. Contact with a warm body in a sleeping bag or under blankets is also an effective warming method and has been used for hundreds of years by the Eskimos.

Treating severe hypothermia is not so easy, especially on a boat offshore. Indeed, controversy lingers concerning aspects of rewarming therapy, but doctors generally agree that the body core should be warmed before the periphery (exterior). Warming the surface or extremities first can cause "core temperature afterdrop," a temporary decrease in temperature deep within the body when the central circulation receives blood that has been cooled at the periphery. As Dr. Michael M. Cohen, author of *Dr. Cohen's Healthy Sailor Book*, puts it, the victim should be warmed from the inside out, not from the outside in. The sudden introduction of colder blood to the body core could cause cardiac arrhythmia or arrest.

Warming the core may be difficult on a small boat at sea. It has been suggested that the victim's torso (groin, armpits, abdomen, and neck) be warmed with heating pads or warm wet towels, or the body can be immersed in a tub of water heated between 105 and 110 degrees Fahrenheit. If the boat has a tub and the latter treatment is attempted, be sure the victim's arms and legs are kept out of the water. Do not massage the body surface, as this could cause core afterdrop. For an unconscious victim, Dr. Tulloch suggests an enema using a 0.9 percent solution of warm saltwater. According to Tulloch, the medical equipment on every offshore vessel venturing into cold regions should include an enema bag and a low-reading rectal thermometer. The critical core temperature is about 86 degrees Fahrenheit or below, when breathing and pulse may be undetectable. Even if the victim appears dead, don't be too quick to abandon rewarming; a medical rule proclaims, "No one is dead unless he is warm and dead." Cohen warns against beginning CPR (cardiopulmonary resuscitation) before there is definitely no pulse or breathing, because CPR can precipitate cardiac arrhythmia or arrest.

The best defense against hypothermia is plenty of warm clothing (including a cap) and staying dry. If you should happen to fall overboard, swim and exercise as little as possible and assume a body attitude that conserves heat. The most effective attitude is the one referred to as HELP (heat escape lessening posture), a near fetal position with the legs crossed below the knees and drawn up to protect the groin. Some authorities say that the arms should be held close to the sides with the hands squeezing the PFD closed (when the victim is wearing one, as he should be) and drawing it close to the body. Others recommend that the arms be wrapped around the drawn-up knees. When more than one person is in the water, they should usually huddle together to lessen loss of heat. Keep heads as high as possible out of the water. From the standpoint of avoiding hypothermia, do not use the older drownproofing technique whereby the victim floats with his head periodically submerged, as it has been found that immersing the head quickly depletes body warmth.

Man Overboard

When proper precautions are taken there is but minimal risk that a crewmember will fall overboard, but complacency and overconfidence in one's surefootedness lead to carelessness. Typical causes of lost crew include failure to abide by the nautical dictum, "one hand for the ship and one for yourself"; failure to use a safety harness; failure to kneel while working on the foredeck in a seaway; lack of caution when moving along the side deck in heavy weather; failure to watch one's feet to avoid tripping over fittings or slipping on loose sails or wet brightwork; and the use of unnecessary acrobatics (when handling racing sails or furling the mizzen on a yawl, for example). More than a few male drowning victims have been recovered with their flies unzipped; the head is a safer place to relieve one's bladder than the leeward shrouds or after deck. It might also be added that a boatowner's failure to install pulpits and lifelines of adequate height (above knee level) has contributed to falls over the side. As said earlier, lifelines must be at least 24 inches but preferably 27 inches or higher above the deck. There should be ample grabrails along the cabin house, and in some cases, usually on larger offshore boats, curved piperails should be installed near the mainmast and the helm, just forward of the binnacle perhaps. Keep in mind that a boat's motion in a seaway can be extremely irregular, and even the wake of a powerboat passing close aboard can cause a crewmember to lose his or her balance. Surprisingly, a few of the most experienced offshore sailors refuse to wear safety harnesses even in the heaviest weather, calling them a serious encumbrance, but you can't argue with the logic that the only sure way to prevent a drowning is to keep the crew on board. Practice using your harness and its encumbrance will be minimal.

Immediate Action

When a crewmember is seen falling overboard, the observer shouts, "Man overboard to port [or starboard]" as loud as he can to alert the rest of the crew, while simultaneously reaching for the nearest life preserver to throw near and, if possible, just to windward of the victim. The nearest crew to a ring buoy with drogue and a man-overboard pole or MOM

(Chapter 5) should immediately deploy these, and another crewmember, often the one who first observes the accident, should keep his or her eyes on the victim or man-overboard pole (when the victim is not visible) or waterlight at night. It is extremely important that one crewmember devote his undivided attention to the victim's location. He should rivet his gaze on the man (or woman), the equipment near him, or the spot where he was last seen before disappearing behind the wavetops, meanwhile pointing to him. In the confusion of rapid maneuvering, it is all too easy to lose track of the exact direction in which the victim lies, and in rough water it is difficult to spot the man again, even when he is not far away. When the vessel is under power, the helmsman puts the gear into neutral and turns the stern away from the victim to avoid cutting him with the propeller, and then maneuvers into a recovery position.

Returning Under Sail

The method of returning to a person overboard will depend to some extent on the point of sailing and the sails being carried. A basic principle is to stay close to the victim and return as quickly as possible. In former times, the standard rule was to jibe around unless sails or complicated gear prevented doing so immediately, and the fast jibe still has its place in good weather (or even bad if tacking is difficult) when the boat is simply rigged and has ample crew to handle sheets and grab the victim. But the return method now favored by the U.S. Naval Academy and espoused by American safety symposia is the so-called quick-stop, whereby the boat is immediately luffed up and then tacked. Figure 7-2 shows the recommended quick-stop procedure when the boat is beating or close reaching, and it also diagrams the technique for quick-stopping when sailing downwind with a spinnaker set.

Notice that the close-hauled boat is promptly turned into the wind and tacked with her jibsheet remaining cleated, the sail being left aback to rapidly reduce speed. Before all way is lost, however, the boat is headed downwind with her mainsail centered, and the jib is dropped. When the victim is well abaft the beam, the boat is jibed, rounded up, and headed just to windward of the victim. The engine may be used to help in maneuvering alongside, but be sure there are no lines overboard that might foul the prop, and put the gear in neutral when close to the victim to avoid cutting him. In most cases, the boat should be brought to windward of the victim and slowed with the engine in reverse or the mainsail pushed or pulled up to windward so that it is aback. A line is thrown to the person overboard and he is secured to the boat until he can be hauled aboard.

If a crewmember falls overboard while the boat is headed downwind with the spinnaker set, the pole is promptly eased forward and the boat is headed up into the wind. After the sail breaks (flaps), it is lowered to the foredeck, the mainsail is trimmed in, and the boat is tacked. She is headed off a bit to gain headway, then luffed close to windward of the victim.

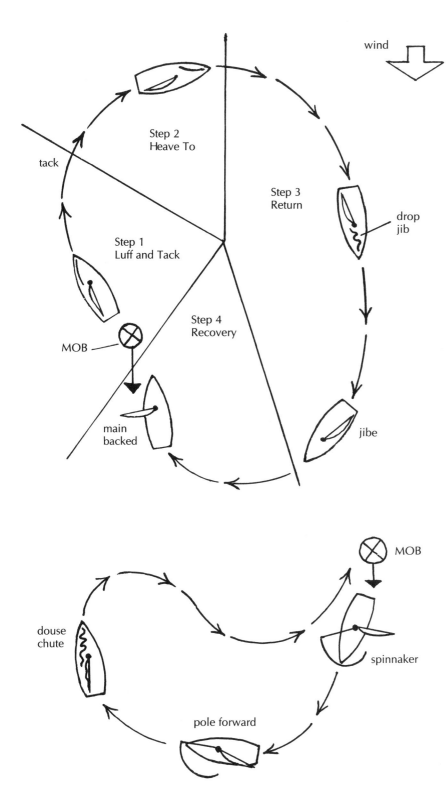

wind

Figure 7-2. *Quick-stop methods, based on U.S. Naval Academy techniques, showing the maneuvering sequence from an initial close-hauled course and from a broad reach with the spinnaker set.*

Step 2
Heave To

tack

Step 3
Return

Step 1
Luff and Tack

drop jib

MOB

Step 4
Recovery

main backed

jibe

MOB

douse chute

spinnaker

pole forward

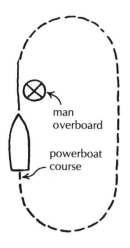

Figure 7-3. *The racetrack turn.*

Another method of returning formerly endorsed by some sailing schools, especially in England, is the "reach-tack-reach," whereby the vessel sails away from the victim on a beam reach, momentarily bears off, and then tacks, returning on a reciprocal course. Well before reaching the victim, the boat should be headed off and then up so that sails can be luffed to kill speed. I understand that the reach-tack-reach method was still favored over quick-stopping at a recent Yachtmaster Instructors conference in England, but it was also recognized that the most effective plan is the one most often practiced. My own preference is for a method such as fast jibing or quick-stopping that keeps the boat close to the victim so that he can be reached promptly and will always be in sight.

Returning Under Power

On a maneuverable powerboat in clear weather, a simple rudder-hard-over turn is the quickest way to return to a man overboard. As said before, the boat should be turned toward the side from which the man fell to swing the propeller away from him, and, on a single-screw boat, the propeller should be stopped temporarily. On a twin-screw boat, the engine nearest the side from which the man fell is stopped, and when clear of the man, the other engine is given full (or almost full) power to turn the boat in the quickest possible time. When the turn is half or more completed, the engine nearest the center of the turning circle might be reversed to tighten the turn further if this seems advisable. When fairly close to windward of the victim, the engines should momentarily be backed to kill headway and then stopped. Throw a line to the victim while the boat drifts down to him. For a more certain recovery, throw a long, floating line with a buoy on its end, then circle the victim; he will be able to grab the line much as a fallen waterskier retrieves his towrope. We'll speak more of this later under the discussion of the Life Sling system. Another return is the "racetrack" turn, which consists of an initial 180-degree turn toward the side from which the man fell, followed by a short run on a straight course reciprocal to the original course, followed by another 180-degree turn and another straight course on the original heading until the victim is reached. This maneuver, which makes a course configuration similar to a racetrack (see Figure 7-3), assures that the man will be inside the boat's turning circle and allows a straight final approach to the victim.

A recommended powerboat return in poor visibility is the maneuver that the Navy calls the Williamson turn (see Figure 7-4). This turn is also used if it is not known exactly when the crewmember fell overboard. Turn the vessel toward the side from which the man fell (or probably fell) until she is approximately 60 degrees from her original heading, and then shift the rudder to turn the vessel the opposite way, continuing the turn until she is back on her original track on the reciprocal heading. Although the method does not allow a quick recovery, it is advantageous in limited visibility because it brings the vessel back on her original track,

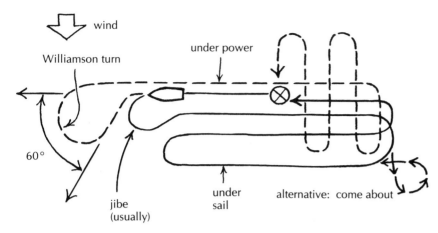

Figure 7-4. *Systematic search patterns under power and sail.*

and immediately after this turn has been completed, the skipper can be assured that the victim will be somewhere ahead, not astern. The 60-degree initial turn is by no means a hard and fast rule, and for a small, maneuverable boat the angle might be considerably less. The turning characteristics of the boat should have been determined through commonly used maneuvers or prior experimentation.

A victim will drift well to leeward if the vessel is slow to return, but this drift will almost always be less than the leeway of the searching craft, such as small cruising sailboats being luffed along slowly or high-sided, shoal-draft powerboats with wind and sea on the beam. When the boat is returning to the victim's position from a fair distance at a normal speed, the net difference between the man's drift and the boat's leeway may be very little, but in many cases a boat that makes significant leeway will end up to leeward of the victim. Current will not affect the situation, unless, of course, the victim and boat are in different conditions of direction or velocity of flow.

A large ship that loses a man overboard will generally commence backing when well clear of the victim, and when way is lost, lower a small boat. Indeed, theoretically at least, a small powerboat can back up to the person overboard in calm waters, but great care must be taken not to cut him with the prop. You must not approach stern first unless there is sufficient sternway to coast up to the victim from some distance away with the engine stopped or, if you can be sure the prop is not turning, with the gear in neutral.

Search Patterns

If a person should disappear overboard at night, in fog, or in other conditions of poor visibility, the helmsman should note his compass course and the probable time of the accident, because it may be necessary to calculate a return course. When the vessel has Loran in operation, her position should be stored as a waypoint in the Loran set. While the boat is readied to tack or jibe, the helmsman should hold a steady course. It is important that one capable crewmember be assigned the job of navigation. He must keep track of the time, speed of the boat, leeway, and course changes.

If the victim has not been spotted by the time the boat returns to the estimated position at which the accident occurred, the boat should continue sailing or motoring on a course reciprocal to the heading at the time of the accident until there is not the slightest possibility that the location has not yet been reached. (If the boat must beat back to the victim she should beat to a location about dead to windward of his estimated position. A boat with auxiliary power may save time and minimize navigational errors by using her motor to return on a direct reciprocal course.) When the skipper and navigator agree that they have gone past the victim on the return course, they should double back in a back-and-forth parallel search pattern, the parallel courses extending about equal distances on either side of the victim's estimated position and the tracks being no farther apart than double the range at which the man could be spotted, taking into account visibility and wave height. Search patterns are illustrated in Figure 7-4, with sailboat courses shown by solid lines and powerboat courses shown with dashed lines. Notice that a sailboat must reach back and forth when searching. Obviously she does not enjoy the advantage of a boat under power in being able to head directly into the wind. The sailboat may go well to windward of the victim's estimated position and then search downwind, but that would entail jibing many times; thus it might be better to start the search pattern well to leeward of the victim's estimated position in moderate weather and work to windward, tacking at each turn, as shown in the illustration, provided the boat will tack easily. Another advantage in searching to leeward of the victim is that his shouts will be more easily heard. In very heavy weather, however, it may be difficult or impossible to work the vessel to windward.

Reboarding

Getting the victim back on board can be difficult when the boat has high freeboard, particularly if the victim is exhausted or injured. More than a few people have been lost after the vessel has been brought alongside because they could not be helped aboard quickly enough. The first step in recovery is to throw the victim a line. This might be accomplished from some distance with a heaving line in a weighted sock (Survival Technologies sells such a device); a conventional line with a loop in its end might be used when closer. The Safety Line Plus, consisting of an eight-inch floating ball of latex attached to a 50-foot length of floating line, is a fairly new heaving device. The ball is heavy enough to be thrown a good distance, even against a fresh wind, yet it provides the victim some buoyancy. As soon as he grabs the heaving line, the victim should be pulled alongside the vessel and secured there while systems are rigged to help him back on board. Boarding assists might include a ladder, lifting tackle, parbuckle, scramble net, or a halyard led to a powerful winch.

Figure 7-5. *A scramble net.*
(Courtesy Cecil Barclay)

Rigid ladders are helpful in calm weather, but in rough seas they may fall off and even cause injury. Some authorities feel that the frequently seen, permanent fold-down stern ladders can be a hazard because the victim might be speared or hit on the head with the transom when the boat is pitching violently. Occasionally, rolled-up rope ladders are lashed to the side rail, pulpit, or lifelines and held closed with "rotten twine" that can easily be broken with a pulldown line. The so-called stirrup-type rope ladder, similar to the Jacob's ladder used on large ships, is recommended.

Some English sailors as well as the Royal Navy and National Lifeboat Institute prefer the scramble net, a kind of miniature cargo net hung over the side. This greatly facilitates helping a person on board, as other crew-members can climb down the net to lend assistance. The scramble net fouls quite easily, and it must be neatly stowed to avoid entanglements. Several practical suggestions have been made by the distributor of Neptune Nets in Diss, Norfolk, England: The net should be secured with red corner lashings (for easy identification) along the rail to strong points such as stanchion bases, and then thrown over the upper lifelines. The overboard edge of the net should be weighted (with shackles perhaps) to make it sink quickly to a depth of two or three feet below the surface. Two lines are attached to the lower corners so that the net can be used as

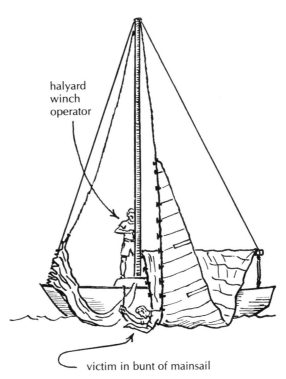

halyard
winch
operator

victim in bunt of mainsail

Figure 7-6. *A shorthanded rescue using the mainsail as a parbuckle.*

a parbuckle (a sling with one end fixed and the other lifted to hoist or roll an object on board) when the victim is injured.

Sails too can be used as parbuckles, and indeed I read of one man who was saved by this method, but usually the victim needs to help himself to some extent. Otherwise, it may be impossible to scoop him up in the bunt of the sail, and he may slide out when lifting commences. At one time the U.S. Naval Academy endorsed a method whereby the clew and tack of an unhanked jib are shackled to a halyard, and the head is tended aft from the cockpit. The bight of the sail's foot is lowered overboard and used as a scoop to pick up the victim, and he is hoisted with the halyard.

There is probably greater merit in lifting a person aboard using a sling and tackle or halyard on a powerful winch. The sling might be one specifically designed for man-overboard recovery as shown in Figure 7-8, or it might be a simple loop in the end of a line that is slipped under the victim's arms. Exhausted people have even been helped aboard with lines tied to their belts or life jackets. A rather handy device is made with a bowline on a bight (see Figure 7-7). One loop fits under the victim's arms and the other under his seat or bent legs. It is safer to lift a person in the sitting rather than the vertical position when the water is cold and his blood thin. To form the bowline on a bight, double the line back onto itself and tie as illustrated. A lifting tackle might be hooked to the end of a halyard or to the main boom. Quite often a boom vang can be used, or even the mainsheet tackle if its lower end can be released quickly. One boat I know of has her mainsheet tackle secured to its traveler with a

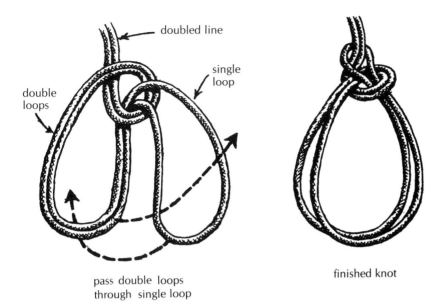

doubled line

single loop

double loops

pass double loops through single loop

finished knot

Figure 7-7. *Bowline on the bight.*

snapshackle so that it can be disconnected immediately for use as a lifting hoist. The boom may need to be controlled with guys, especially in rough seas.

An injured victim may need assistance from another man in the water. Needless to say, this second person should be well buoyed and tethered to the boat. A scramble net, inflatable dinghy, liferaft, or MOM might be used—even a rigid dinghy in calm weather. Tethered by a long painter, a partly inflated dinghy carried on the cabintop can quickly be thrown over either side, and it allows easier boarding. When the victim is light and can be lifted by his or her arms, a neat trick is for the lifter to cross his arms before grabbing the victim's hands. Then, as the lifter hoists, the victim can be turned around so that he can sit on the rail. Dropping the lifelines is helpful, so they should be secured with pelican hooks or preferably lashings that can be cut with a pocketknife.

Shorthanded Rescue Systems

Recovering a man or woman overboard becomes much more difficult when the boat is sailing shorthanded. Consider the following realistic scenario: A man sailing in breezy weather with his inexperienced wife goes forward to change jibs. He loses his balance while lowering sail on the bow and tumbles overboard. The wife performs admirably and manages to maneuver the boat back to her husband, but the process is slow, and she struggles in vain to get him back on board. In the cold water her husband soon succumbs to exhaustion, hypothermia, and the effects of swallowing water, and tragically slips beneath the surface. True experiences such as this have inspired at least one group of yachtsmen to expend a lot of thought on shorthanded recovery. Two of the best solutions to the problem seem to be the Lifesling system, developed by the

Figure 7-8. *The Lifesling.*

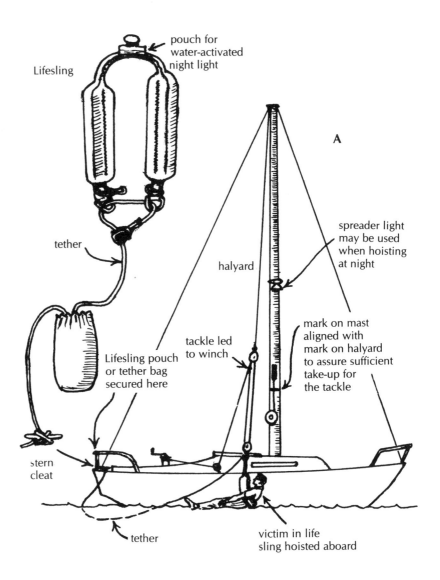

Sailing Foundation of Seattle, Washington, and the Jon Buoy, developed in England.

Currently touted at the major safety-at-sea symposia in America, the Lifesling is a buoyant, flexible horsecollar (similar to a helicopter sling) attached to the boat by a buoyant polypropylene tether 150 feet or more long. The sling is carried in a bag designed for quick release, hung on the stern pulpit. Its tether is faked (not coiled) and packed in a pouch that allows automatic deployment caused by the drag of the towed sling. When a person falls overboard, a PFD is thrown over, the sling is deployed, and the boat is luffed head to wind. The jib goes aback, and the boat goes about. She then bears off and proceeds to circle the victim under sail or power. This encircling wraps him with the tether and

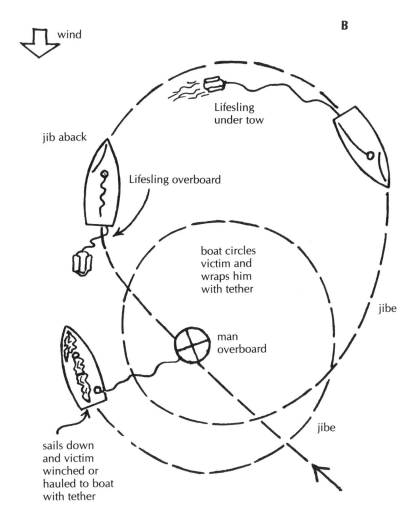

wind

B

Lifesling
under tow

jib aback

Lifesling overboard

boat circles
victim and
wraps him
with tether

jibe

man
overboard

jibe

sails down
and victim
winched or
hauled to boat
with tether

allows him to grab the sling. As he gets into the sling (placing it under his arms), sail is promptly lowered. The victim is then hauled or winched alongside where he can be lifted aboard with a tackle, winch, or both. The Seattle Sailing Foundation, which has practiced the method extensively, recommends hoisting the victim with a tackle suspended from the main halyard and then led to a large sheet winch as illustrated (Figure 7-8). The halyard should be premarked, perhaps, with tape to show when its end is 10 to 15 feet above the deck in order to allow ample take-up of the tackle. A self-tailing winch is highly desirable, and if it is large enough, a tackle may not be needed.

A substitute for a Lifesling is a horseshoe buoy tied to the end of a long floating line, but this lacks a proper lifting sling. One highly praised

Figure 7-9. *The Jon Buoy in operation. (Courtesy Transaqua Technology Ltd.)*

variation on this theme is Speedymat, a European system (sold in America) that carries 330 feet of line wound up on a reel attached to the stern pulpit. For lifting the victim aboard, Speedymat sells a rescue seat with tackle hoist. The suggestion has even been made that a buoyant throwball on a heaving line, such as the aforementioned Safety Line Plus, is a superior substitute for a Lifesling, but the ball system has only 50 feet of line and lacks a sling, and one should not always count on an initially successful throw. Another alternative is the combination of a floating heaving line and the inflatable SEAID, a throwable horseshoe (sold by Survival Technologies), that inflates automatically after hitting the water, but remember that inflatables require regular servicing.

The Jon Buoy, a man-overboard inflatable liferaft with integral lifting sling, is deployed either manually or by radio signal. This concept was conceived by British multihull ocean racer Peter Phillips after four of his friends (on four separate occasions) were lost overboard. The device is made by Transaqua Technology Limited of Callington, Cornwall, but I am told it will soon be sold in the U.S.A. Unique features of the system include the radio release and alarm, a means of stabilizing and preventing drift, and the built-in lifting sling.

The radio-activated Jon Buoy requires that each crewmember wear an armband transmitter. If he or she should fall overboard, the transmitter is activated automatically upon immersion and sends out a signal, instantly releasing the deflated raft, which is carried in a container hung on the stern pulpit. After hitting the water the Jon Buoy inflates and pushes down a cone-shaped keel that fills with water, stabilizing the raft and acting as a sea anchor to inhibit drift. The victim swims to the nearby raft, climbs aboard, and seats himself on the floor, which doubles as a lifting sling. Once alongside the vessel, the person in the sling is lifted out with a tackle or halyard, as with the Lifesling system. The raft is not difficult to board because it is low, has boarding assists, and is stabilized by the keel. About the only disadvantage of the Jon Buoy, apart from the need for periodic servicing, is its cost, approximately $1,800 for the most elaborate system with radio release and alarm.

The Wlochovski system of rescue made by Predica (in France) is similar. This system is triggered by the victim with a personal ultrasonic transmitter that sends a signal to a ceramic receiver mounted on the boat's bottom. The signal activates an electric motor, capable of overriding an autopilot, and turns the boat into the wind. At the same time a stern-mounted container releases 300 feet of floating line, a drogue, inflatable MOB pole, and raft. Manufactured in 1989 for several participants in the Globe Challenge, a round-the-world race for singlehanders, the Wlochovski system was not yet available commercially in early 1990, but it is expected to be marketed worldwide and will probably sell at a price comparable with that of the Jon Buoy.

The first priority in a man-overboard situation is getting flotation to the victim if he is not wearing a PFD or float coat. No matter what kind of rescue gear is aboard the boat, a life preserver should be thrown or dropped immediately. If buoyancy cannot be placed near the victim or he cannot be reached with a heaving line, the boat should be turned as quickly as possible for the primary purpose of providing flotation. Perhaps he cannot be brought aboard immediately and another pass must be made; thus, you trade some promptness of rescue for assured flotation. It is impossible to give hard and fast advice with respect to this tradeoff, because much depends on the state of the sea, water and air temperatures, the physical condition of the victim and his ability as a swimmer, and even how he is garbed (is he wearing large seaboots, for example, that could fill with water?). Nevertheless, except perhaps when the water is very cold, I think it is more important to furnish the person overboard with buoyancy, because it normally takes much longer to die from hypothermia than it does from drowning.

Advice for the Man Overboard

If you are the unfortunate one, here is some commonsense advice:

- Call out in a loud voice when you realize you are going over the side, but shut your mouth before hitting the water and cover your nose with one hand.

- When attached to the boat with a safety line, try to body plane with your face above the water. If you can't get your face into the air, release your safety line by unsnapping it or cutting it with your pocketknife.

- Try not to panic. Remember that you may not be able to see the boat even if she is fairly close, because your eyes are so close to the water surface.

- Swim toward a nearby buoy or man-overboard pole but do so slowly to prevent exhaustion and conserve body heat. If the floating buoy has a drogue, you should be able to reach it without undue loss of energy or heat.

- Use your whistle and pocket strobe if you have them, but don't waste energy by shouting.

- If the water is cold assume the HELP (heat-conserving) position. Don't kick off your boots and foul weather clothing unless they are really dragging you down. Often the air trapped in the clothing will afford some buoyancy.

- When the vessel returns, be ready to receive a retrieval line. Fasten it to your belt or harness or put the line's loop under your arms. Listen for instructions from the boat.

Further Comments

Notify Coast Guard and other boats in the vicinity by radio or other signals when the person overboard cannot be picked up promptly. The International Code signal for "man overboard" is the letter O (Oscar), which may be made with the O flag or any other method of signaling. When the victim is properly buoyed and the water is not cold, he or she can last longer than one might expect, so don't give up hope if he can't be found after a lengthy period of searching. The keys to a successful rescue are planning and practice. From time to time, try recovering an object thrown overboard. Coconuts make good practice objects, as they are close to the size of a human head and they do not drift as rapidly as, say, a life preserver or seat cushion. Familiarize yourself with your boat's turning and handling characteristics, and practice using your man-overboard gear. Try hoisting or otherwise assisting a swimmer to reboard your boat using tackles, halyards, ladders, nets, rafts, or other gear you have on board. Practice throwing buoys and heaving lines. Above all, develop the habit of using your safety harness so that this kind of accident will be extremely unlikely.

Shipboard Accidents

Whenever you board a boat, you enter a relatively accident-prone environment and at the same time remove yourself to a greater or lesser extent from medical facilities. Medical treatment and first aid are beyond the scope of this book, but a complete medical kit should be on board. Appendix H contains a list of medical supplies and drugs suggested by Dr. George H.A. Clowes, Jr., former fleet surgeon for the Cruising Club of America. It is important to carry a detailed first-aid manual written by a doctor, preferably one who is an experienced boatman. Several such manuals were identified in Chapter 5. This section will be limited to a list of causes and suggestions for prevention of common shipboard accidents that can result in personal injury. These hazards should always be pointed out to inexperienced crewmembers, who might not foresee them.

Falls

Most of the common causes of falls on deck were discussed in the man-overboard section, but it is worth repeating that slippery surfaces should be kept to an absolute minimum. It is inadvisable to varnish surfaces on which a person will walk. An unavoidably slippery surface should have strips of abrasive cloth glued to it; decks must be made skidproof with molded-in rough patterns, abrasive paint, the use of raw teak, or glued-on panels such as Treadmaster, and, as said earlier, there should be ample handrails both in the cabin and topside. Beware of leaving tangles of lines or loose sails lying on deck. Synthetic sails are especially slippery, and should be bunched together and tightly stopped when it is necessary to leave them on the foredeck. When moving along the deck of a heeled sailboat, favor the windward side. In heavy weather, never work with both hands simultaneously unless you are secured to the boat with a line or safety harness. Companionway ladders often cause serious falls. It is essential that ladders or steps be skidproofed, provided with hand grips, and well secured. You should nearly always face a ladder when using it; descending into a cabin with your back toward the steps can be dangerous when there is any motion. When furling the mainsail, close the sliding companionway hatch to ensure that no one will step through the opening.

Burns

A major source of burns on a boat is the galley stove. Cooking in a seaway, especially when the boat is heeled, should be done with caution. For heavy-weather cooking, it is essential that the stove have gimbals (with the turning axis running fore and aft) and an adequately high rail to prevent pots from sliding off. Pots should be deep and have wide, flat bottoms; they should fit the stove properly, with clamps to hold them securely in heavy weather, and they should never be overfilled. The cabin sole in way of the galley must be skidproof, and it is important that the cook be provided with a safety harness to allow working with both hands. The belt should completely enclose the cook so that he or she will not be thrown into or away from the stove. In heavy weather a waterproof apron and long pants are recommended, as these will protect legs if hot liquids are spilled. (Incidentally, the small, bulkhead-mounted, single-burner Sterno stove, which is gimbaled both fore-and-aft and athwartships, is handy and relatively safe in rough weather.) It is also desirable, whenever possible, that the dining table be gimbaled, but at least it should be provided with fiddles. In fact, all counters or working surfaces in the galley should have fiddles higher than those found on most stock boats.

A frequent cause of burns and falls below deck is the wakes of speeding powerboats that pass close aboard. It is almost criminal the way some powerboat operators fail to consider the effect of their wakes on other craft, especially on those at anchor that cannot maneuver to meet the waves bow or stern on. Waves caused by a speeding boat, especially one of heavy displacement, can be more dangerous than the seas normally encountered offshore, because people on a craft being rolled by a wake are often caught unaware. A wave-making boat should give any vulnerable craft a reasonably wide berth and slow down. The helmsman of the boat about to be rolled, or anyone on deck, should warn everyone on board, especially those below and the cook, that waves are coming. In some cases, when a planing boat will make smaller waves by going fast and when there is no speed limit or risk in going fast, it may be advisable for the wavemaker to speed up. After all, the important consideration is to minimize the size of the wake.

Injuries from Lines

There is tremendous energy locked inside a line under great strain, and this energy can suddenly escape with dangerous consequences if the line slips, breaks, or pulls its fitting loose. As said earlier, no one should stand directly behind a towline under strain, especially one made of a semi-elastic material such as nylon, because its parting could cause a dangerous whiplash. Also, it can be dangerous to snub abruptly a line

Figure 7-10. *As well he should, this midshipman looks apprehensively at the block that, in the event of failure, could injure his leg. He should be abaft the winch and facing forward where he can watch the jib and where his leg will not be in the bight of the sheet. (Courtesy U.S. Navy)*

under great strain. Snubbing should usually be done by surging the line with a turn or two around the cleat or bitt so that strain is put on the line gradually to minimize shock loading. Lines must be properly coiled to prevent kinking, which will weaken them. Some injuries occur when a crewmember tries to clear snarls, jammed knots, or jams on cleats while the line is under strain. Strain should be taken off the fouled line (usually with another line), and only proven, accepted knots such as the bowline, square knot, half hitches, sheet bend, rolling hitch, and towboat hitch should be used. Bear in mind that even accepted knots can seriously weaken a line. For instance, the well-respected bowline can reduce the strength of a line by nearly 50 percent. Halyards of slippery synthetic rope should usually be hitched on their cleats to assure that they will stay cleated. Be wary, however, of hitching the rare line made of vegetable fiber (manila, sisal) when speed of release is important, because the line may swell and jam when it gets wet. Never stand in a coil or in the bight of a line under strain. When a fitting is under stress from the pull of a line, always consider the direction in which the fitting will travel if it should let go, and stay well clear of its predicted path. Rope burns on hands can be avoided by handling a line under strain with a turn around a cleat or winch, and by using open-fingered sailing gloves.

Be especially careful with braided lines; they are smooth, and the smaller sizes are often difficult to grip firmly.

Winch Injuries

A number of serious accidents have resulted from sheet or halyard winch failures or improper handling of winches. Although the design and construction of winches have improved greatly in recent years, there are still occasional failures in brake mechanisms, pawls, and springs, especially in some of the cheaper makes. One reason for ineffective operation of the pawls is lack of proper lubrication. Such failures can allow a winch under strain to "run away," or spin inadvertently. The principal danger of a run-away winch is that its handle can strike someone. In some cases, usually on halyard winches without handle locks or with defective locks, handles can actually be thrown a considerable distance. Another potential danger in handling winches is catching one's fingers under the turns of line or wire on the winch. Allowing the rope to slip off the winch may also cause injuries if, for example, the mishap drops a boom on someone's head. In a similar vein, the self-tailing apparatus on self-tailing winches should never be used in place of cleats for lines that have a great deal of load on them, such as spinnaker guys. It is too easy for the line to pull inadvertently out of the jamming mechanism.

Some safety suggestions for handling winches are as follows: Keep your head well clear of a winch handle; grip the handle firmly when operating a winch; whenever possible, use winch handles that lock in place; remove winch handles when they are not in use; consider the use of winch wheels (special wheel handles) instead of conventional handles on reel halyard winches; don't oil the brake band of a reel winch; consider the use of an adjustable, toggle-and-screw-pin brake (such as the kind made by Barient) so that the load on a winch can be eased gradually; be sure the reel winch's screw-pin brake is *on* when hoisting the mainsail, and remove the handle before lowering; keep your fingers away from the "swallow" of a winch (the point where the line feeds onto the winch) when cranking in and especially when slacking off a line; keep tension on the fall (end) of the line when taking a turn of line off a winch if the line's standing part is under great strain; be careful (on halyard winches especially) to keep the fall of the line nearly at a right angle to the winch axis, or slant it toward the base of the winch, in order that the line cannot slip off the end of the winch; make sure when clearing an override or line tangled on a winch that the strain on the standing part is taken by another line; and be extremely cautious in handling winches while wearing full-fingered gloves, because a glove can lodge between the turns of line on a winch and perhaps draw a finger under a turn. (Open-fingered sailing gloves alleviate this concern.) Don't wear jewelry while handling winches or any gear on a boat.

Sailhandling Injuries

In heavy weather, sails are often difficult to manage, and poor handling

Figure 7-11. *Winch wheels are cumbersome, but they provide protection against being struck by the handle of a reel winch. Wheels are probably not necessary on the newest winches, which have brakes that can be eased gradually, and allow hoisting with the brake on. (Rip Henderson photo)*

can result in minor or sometimes serious injuries. The spinnaker frequently causes trouble in a fresh breeze. Failure to keep the sail blanketed and failure to keep a turn of halyard or sheet on a winch when hoisting or lowering the sail can cause bad rope burns on the hands. Spinnakers should be handed by one leech only in order that they will spill their wind. When hauled in by both leeches simultaneously, the sail will fill and take charge, possibly causing falls, rope burns, and other injuries. Crewmembers working on the foredeck should avoid standing under the spinnaker pole while it is raised or lowered, and the man tending the topping lift must be careful to see that no one is under the pole. More than a few foredeck men have been "beaned" with spinnaker poles. A more serious injury can result from being hit on the head with the main boom during a jibe. It is essential that the helmsman give all crewmembers ample warning of an imminent jibe in order that they may duck their heads and brace themselves when the off-center boom swings over. Sailing by the lee should be avoided, but if it is necessary, a preventer should be rigged from the boom's end to some point forward to guard against an inadvertent, all-standing jibe. In fact, a preventer or off-center boom vang should be rigged whenever sailing substantially off the wind, as waves can cause one to lose control and inadvertently jibe. When handing flogging sails, keep out of the way of fittings such as hanks and shackles. Muzzle the flapping sail and stop it immediately as it is being lowered in a strong breeze. It is usually a good idea to tie the working jib or staysail sheets to their clews with bowlines in order to eliminate hard, heavy shackles that could hit crewmembers in the head. Avoid the use of heavy steel "D" rings at the clews of headsails. Whenever possible, lower or hoist a sail in the lee of a sail that is already hoisted. On cruising boats, permanently rigged lazyjacks keep the sail under better control and thus minimize possible risks of injury or falling overboard when taking in sail during a blow. A short strop attached to the backstay is no substitute for a proper boom topping lift. A strong lift running from the boom's end to the masthead, controllable from the deck, is far handier and safer. Such a rig will permit lowering sail with the boom broad off in an emergency.

Mooring and Anchoring Injuries

Poor landings at slips, docks, or alongside other boats are an occasional source of injuries. Hernias or crushed feet or hands can result from trying to fend off a heavy vessel that is moving too fast. Risk of these accidents can be minimized with practice in boat handling, by carrying an adequate crew, and by judicious use of fenders. As previously stated, inexperienced crewmembers should be instructed with regard to possible dangers they might not foresee. Backs are sometimes injured when heavy anchors are weighed, and even a light anchor is difficult to break out when it is deeply buried in the bottom. When the anchor line is at a short stay, nearly straight up and down, the vessel should be propelled with power or sail to break the anchor loose in order to spare the human back. If the anchor is very heavy, consider bringing it on board with a windlass and tackle. There is a wide variety of windlasses to choose from—manual, electric, or hydraulic—and plow-type anchors stow easily on stemhead rollers. Light anchors can be hauled by hand using proper technique to minimize strain on the back. Instead of keeping your legs straight and bending your back when hauling in or up on the rode, alternately bend and straighten your legs and keep your back straight. In other words, lift as much as possible with your legs instead of your back. In letting out scope, keep adequate turns on the bitt or samson post to prevent the anchor line or chain from running away. Never grab a runaway line, or especially chain, close to the chock, hawsehole, or bitt, because your hand could be mangled. The bitter end of the rode should always be made fast to avoid losing the anchor, but lash the bitter end with a line so that it can be cut in an emergency.

Working Aloft

Although one seldom hears of a person falling from a mast, this kind of accident does happen on rare occasions. I once saw a man fall from aloft and hit the deck, and the sight is not easy to forget. It is hardly ever prudent to climb a mast hand over hand while a vessel is underway. Unless the mast is equipped with a ladder or steps or the shrouds have ratlines, you should nearly always be hauled aloft in a proper bosun's chair. People who have never been aloft in a seaway seldom realize how much a boat's motion is magnified at the masthead. Hanging on when aloft can be difficult even when the boat's rolling seems mild at deck level. It is important, therefore, that a crewmember in a bosun's chair be secured to the mast to keep him from swinging, and he should be lashed into the chair so that he cannot fall even if unconscious. While being hauled aloft in a seaway, of course, he must grip the rigging tightly, but in addition, there should be a downhaul line made fast to the chair's bottom and tended by a crewmember on deck, who prevents the chair from swinging by keeping the line taut. Normally two crew work the winch that pulls the chair aloft, and they must follow the orders of either the occupant of the chair or the downhaul tender, who should be looking up the mast continuously. Once the crewmember in the chair is where he wants to be, the brake must be fastened in such a way that it cannot be tripped accidentally, or the halyard must be hitched securely on a substantial cleat. Avoid the use of a reel winch for a bosun's chair if possible, but when this is unavoidable, see that the crew in the chair secures himself aloft with a safety line in case the winch brake should happen to slip. No one should stand under a man working aloft in case a tool is dropped accidentally. Lower slowly and smoothly, with a turn or two of the halyard around the winch or with two people *firmly* holding the handle of a reel winch. Before going aloft in the bosun's chair, be sure that the halyard and its block and shackle are adequately strong. Boats with fractional rigs benefit from an extra masthead halyard or a strong topping lift capable of supporting a man in a chair in the event the main halyard cannot be used.

Carbon Monoxide

Asphyxiation from carbon monoxide occurs on boats more often than most people would suppose. As most automobile drivers know, carbon monoxide is a colorless, almost entirely odorless (unless mixed with exhaust fumes) gas emitted from gasoline and diesel engines. Death can be caused by breathing heavy concentrations of the gas. Dangerous concentrations usually result from a leaking exhaust system inside an enclosed space, such as a cabin or engine compartment that lacks adequate ventilation. Death has even been caused by exhaust fumes blown into the outlet for the drain of a head sink. To safeguard against asphyxiation, check the exhaust line carefully for broken gaskets, holes from rust, etc., and ventilate the cabin as much as possible (without jeopardy to safety in heavy weather) when the engine is running. The Coast Guard has issued a warning about the danger from a backdraft of carbon monoxide-laden air sucked into the cabin of a boat powered with a gasoline engine. Heating stoves also can admit dangerous concentrations of carbon monoxide into a tightly closed cabin. Be sure to ventilate when using any kind of stove, even if it has a Charlie Noble (smokepipe).

Seamanship is a broad, rather nebulous term, but its essence is the ability to anticipate and thus avoid trouble. A thoroughly competent seaman should not have a great deal to fear from emergencies, because he or she not only plans how to cope with them, but takes all possible measures to ensure that they will never happen in the first place.

Chapter 8
WEATHER AND WAVES

Despite high-speed computer analysis of weather, observations from satellites, and the continuous availability of accurate forecasts, heavy weather surprises numerous small craft each year. Exposure to adverse weather is a serious threat to the safety of boatmen and their craft. We can best avoid heavy weather or reduce its effects to a minimum by listening to official forecasts and learning the basics of weather behavior. This knowledge provides a basis for judging when to leave port, when to return, the best course to avoid heavy weather, the proper route and time of year for a safe passage, when to prepare for a blow, and to a large extent, how to handle the vessel during a storm.

The Basis of Weather

A detailed study of weather is beyond the scope of this book, but a non-technical summary of the principles of weather behavior should be helpful to readers seeking greater familiarity with the subject.

The general wind circulation of the earth consists of polar easterlies at the top and bottom of the globe, westerlies in the middle latitudes (between 30 and 60 degrees, approximately) and easterly trade winds on either side of the equator (northeast trades north of the equator and southeast trades to the south). Between the westerlies and the trade winds are calm belts called the horse latitudes, and another calm belt called the doldrums divides the north and south trade wind systems at the equator. The earth's wind system is driven by temperature differences and the globe's rotation. In the northern hemisphere, hot air at the equator rises and flows northward. Some of this air cools and sinks at the horse latitudes, where a mound of high pressure girdles the earth (see Figure 8-1). The sinking air splits as it descends over the high-pressure mound—part sliding southward back toward the equator to form the northeast trade winds and part flowing north to form the prevailing westerlies. Air that does not sink at the horse latitudes moves on at high altitudes to the poles, where it sinks and then moves southwest-

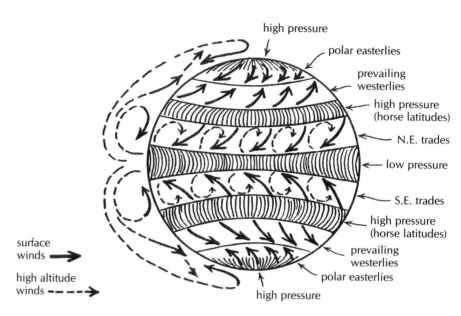

high pressure
polar easterlies
prevailing westerlies
high pressure (horse latitudes)
N.E. trades
low pressure
S.E. trades
high pressure (horse latitudes)
prevailing westerlies
polar easterlies
high pressure

surface winds ➡️

high altitude winds ➖ ➖ ➡️

Figure 8-1. *Simplified global winds.*

ward as the polar easterlies. The wind systems of both hemispheres are given their east and west directions by the Coriolis effect, the deflection of a moving body to the right in the northern hemisphere and to the left in the southern hemisphere due to the earth's rotation on its axis. Weather moves in the same direction as the global wind systems, so storms in the middle latitudes generally come from the west. Tropical storms, such as hurricanes or typhoons (originating in the low latitudes), travel along trade wind routes until they move northward into the prevailing westerlies, at which time, they generally curve to the eastward.

The preceding description of the global winds is simplified and generalized. In actuality, there is a complex, irregular pattern of swirling winds around areas of high and low pressure scattered through the globe, resulting principally from seasonal temperature changes and differences in heating between the oceans and landmasses. High-pressure cells, called anticyclones or simply highs, are mounds of concentrated air. Low-pressure cells, called cyclones, lows, or depressions, are troughs or hollows in the atmosphere. Winds flow out of a high toward and into the center of a low, and the Coriolis force turns the wind so that it swirls in a clockwise direction around a high but counterclockwise around a low in the northern hemisphere. Swirling occurs in the opposite direction in the southern hemisphere. Good weather is associated with highs, and stormy weather, with lows. When air masses of different temperatures (and moisture content) collide and do not readily mix, a weather front forms. A cold front forms when the cold mass advances against the warm air, and a warm front forms when the warm air advances and overrides the cold mass. Bad weather is usually associated with all fronts, but cold fronts may bring violent (although relatively brief) storms with strong winds as the cold mass plows under the warm air and throws it abruptly aloft. A low is often formed along the front between two adjacent air masses when their motions are opposed and

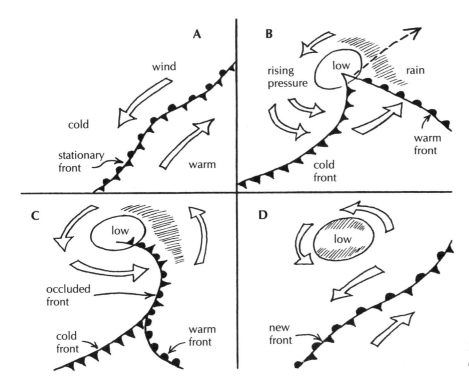

Figure 8-2. *Development of an extratropical low.*

friction causes a wave or bending of the frontal line into a V shape (see Figure 8-2). In the northern hemisphere, this wave moves in an easterly or northeasterly direction in the region of prevailing westerlies, and the low forms at or just ahead of the crest with a warm front to the east and a cold front to the west. Cold air to the north of the low swings around the wave crest in a counterclockwise direction and pushes the cold front around so that it chases the warm front. The faster-moving cold front eventually overtakes the warm front to form an occlusion, at which time the cool air ahead of the warm front and the cold air behind the cold front meet and force the warm air upward. This briefly describes the birth and action of the typical extratropical cyclone found in the middle latitudes. The sequence is illustrated in Figure 8-2.

Storms

High-pressure cells can occasionally generate storm-force winds, but storms are normally associated with depressions and their cyclonic winds. In general, there are four kinds of storms: thunderstorms, tornadoes, extratropical cyclones, and tropical cyclones. In recent years, our meteorological vocabulary has broadened to include the frightening terms "microbursts" and "weather bombs." These violent storms have always existed, but they are newly named and recognized. They will be discussed separately at the end of this section.

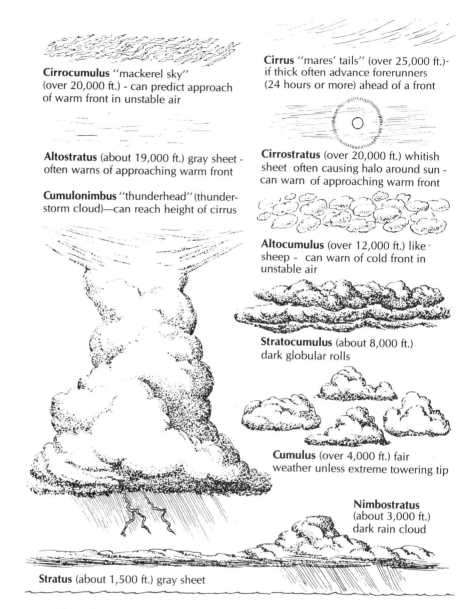

Cirrocumulus "mackerel sky" (over 20,000 ft.) - can predict approach of warm front in unstable air

Cirrus "mares' tails" (over 25,000 ft.)- if thick often advance forerunners (24 hours or more) ahead of a front

Altostratus (about 19,000 ft.) gray sheet - often warns of approaching warm front

Cirrostratus (over 20,000 ft.) whitish sheet often causing halo around sun - can warn of approaching warm front

Cumulonimbus "thunderhead" (thunderstorm cloud)—can reach height of cirrus

Altocumulus (over 12,000 ft.) like sheep - can warn of cold front in unstable air

Stratocumulus (about 8,000 ft.) dark globular rolls

Cumulus (over 4,000 ft.) fair weather unless extreme towering tip

Nimbostratus (about 3,000 ft.) dark rain cloud

Stratus (about 1,500 ft.) gray sheet

Figure 8-3. *Clouds. (From Hand, Reef & Steer, by Richard Henderson. Courtesy Contemporary Books, Inc.)*

Although there are usually turbulent vortices inside a thunderstorm, the principal internal wind forces are violent vertical currents. The two types of thunderstorms are air-mass and frontal. The latter is normally the most violent, especially when a fast-moving cold front meets an extremely warm, moist air mass. Thunderstorms may occur at intervals along the entire front and form what is called a squall line. Cold air burrowing low and throwing the warm air aloft will cause towering, ominous-looking cumulonimbus clouds (see Figure 8-3). Passage of the front will normally produce strong veering winds (shifting clockwise, perhaps from southwest to northwest). Some particularly violent squall

Figure 8-4. *A cumulonimbus, thunderstorm cloud. (Courtesy U.S. Navy)*

lines are preceded by long, dark, low "roll clouds," as air ahead of the front is sucked up into the storm's center. Following this initial breeze toward the storm, there will be a strong outflow of cold air that can cause severe knockdowns, blow out sails, and inflict other damage on an unprepared boat.

An air-mass thunderstorm is generally less violent. Although it also develops the cumulonimbus cloud, it is not associated with a front but originates from an isolated thermal, or updraft, of hot air that rises into relatively cold air aloft. This type of storm may be gusty and produce lightning, rain, and possibly hail, but it is usually short-lived, and weather conditions will probably return to those that existed before the storm.

Sailors are warned of thunderstorms principally by the appearance of the sky (and also by static on the radio). When cumulus clouds in the west (in middle latitudes) show marked vertical development during the afternoon of a hot, muggy day, the boatman should be especially watchful for thunderheads (cumulonimbus clouds). When a towering cumulus turns dark at the base and flares out in an anvil shape at the top, it marks a mature thunderstorm. Meteorologists warn us, however, not to put too much stock in the anvil top, as this can occur when the storm cell is past its prime and is in a milder stage of dissipation. The coastwise sailor can be forewarned of frontal storms by studying late weather maps when they are available and by listening to radio weather reports. Numerous stations along the United States seaboard transmit continuous weather forecasts (updated every two hours) over such stations as VHF/FM 162.55, 162.40, or 163.275 MHz.

Tornadoes are concentrated whirlpools of air that twist around a center of very low pressure. Normally cyclonic, these violent storms are extremely dangerous ashore because of winds that often exceed 300 miles per hour and because their low pressure, which is almost a vacuum, can cause buildings to explode. Tornadoes are rare and are usually not as dangerous at sea unless they are associated with a hurricane or typhoon. When one of these storms moves over the water, it likely will turn into a waterspout, and mitigated temperature contrasts will mollify the wind's intensity. Tornadoes are normally a product of extremely unstable cold-front activities and are often found in America's Midwest, especially the Mississippi Valley. When the weather bureau considers that conditions favor the formation of tornadoes, it broadcasts warnings or watches. In the rare case of a boat encountering a waterspout at sea, evasive action can usually avoid direct contact. The spout funnel is visible a long way off, its forward speed is relatively slow, and its destructive force is concentrated into a small area so that a boat with power stands a good chance of dodging it. Make all normal heavy-weather preparations, but pay particular attention to stopping sails thoroughly and lashing loose gear to the deck or cabintop because of the violent updraft within the storm's vortex. There are many mysteries and superstitions connected with waterspouts. One myth is that firing a gun at a spout will break it up. Perhaps there is some scientific basis to a large gun's concussion being able to break the partial vacuum and cause the column of water to collapse, but the efficacy of such a method seems very doubtful. At any rate, it is comforting to know that the greatest part of a typical spout is composed not of solid water but of sprayed mist. According to meteorologist George H.T. Kimble, solid water at the spout's base is seldom much higher than ten feet. Keep in mind, however, that a tornado or even a small twister can produce exceedingly strong local winds that can knock a sailboat flat.

Extratropical cyclones were described earlier, but it should be added here that low pressure (a falling barometer) will probably precede the depression and warm front. After passage of this front but before occlusion, there should be a brief period of fair weather with higher pressure, but the fast-moving, more violent cold front will not be far behind. Thus the sailor should look for even heavier weather after passage of the first front. Winds will veer as each front passes over. Advance warning of the approaching warm front may come from high-altitude, wispy "mares' tails" (cirrus clouds), which gradually thicken to partially fill the sky. As the front approaches, the sky may become covered with cirrostratus, which give it a white, hazy look and sometimes cause a halo around the sun. The next clouds filling in from the west could be fibrous gray altostratus if the air aloft is vertically stable (with little vertical movement), followed by low, dark nimbostratus rain clouds. In vertically unstable air, cirrocumulus, the small fish-scale clouds of the "mackerel sky," may make an early appearance, and they may be followed by bands of altocumulus (small, puffy clouds looking like herds of sheep) and still later by stratocumulus (darker globular clouds). Rain and squalls may come from low nimbostratus or, in very unstable conditions, thunderstorms from cumulonimbus. Clouds in advance of the cold front will probably be bands of altocumulus, and soon afterward towering thunderheads will appear. When violent weather is predicted, the prudent skipper will either seek shelter and anchor, normally behind a west or northwest shore, or head offshore to get all possible sea room. Sail should be short-ened or furled, and other heavy-weather preparations made. Bad weather from the cold front should not last long, no more than a few hours normally. With passage of the front, the barometer should rise rap-idly, and on many occasions the wind will blow harder for a short while even though the sky is clearing. An old weather adage warns, "Quick rise after low portends a stronger blow."

Extratropical cyclones frequently form in the fall when cold fronts from the north push south and meet moist, warm air over the ocean. A particularly dangerous spot is eastward of Cape Hatteras, where the Gulf Stream pushes warm water northward close to shore. This "Devil's Elbow" is only part of a much wider area of potentially dangerous weather known as the "Deadly Triangle," the boundaries of which run roughly from New York to Bermuda, to the Virgin Islands, and to the tip of Florida (see Figure 8-5). This general area, often the meeting place of tropic and arctic air masses, can very quickly generate storms that might escape the immediate notice of weathermen ashore, who pay closer attention to approaching weather from the west. The Deadly Triangle is subject not only to sudden gales in the fall and winter but to hurricanes in the summer. The safest time to venture off shore in these waters is in the late spring and early summer, but some fair-weather passages from south of Cape Hatteras to the West Indies have been made in late Octo-ber and early November.

A lot of publicity has been given to these waters, which are nearly always referred to as the "Bermuda Triangle." A number of sensational articles and books have attempted to explain the disappearance of ves-sels and planes in the area with such far-out fantasies as entrapment of the victims in time-space warps or hijackings by UFOs. Careful and sen-sible investigations indicate that the vast majority of disappearances are really the result of severe weather, although a few boats in recent times may have been pirated for drug smuggling. Surprisingly, the sensational writings usually describe the north side of the triangle as running from Bermuda to the tip of Florida, but this excludes the dangerous waters off Cape Hatteras.

The most dangerous and widely destructive storms are tropical cyclones. Known as hurricanes in the Atlantic, as typhoons in some parts of the Pacific, and simply as cyclones in the Indian Ocean, these storms are revolving lows, similar in many respects to extratropical cyclones. Those originating in the tropics are far more intense, however, and they are not frontal in that air-mass temperature differences are not involved. They often move more slowly, and they are quite symmetrical, with a calm "eye" at the center of rotation. Tropical cyclones are born near (but not on) the equator, usually in the intertropical convergence

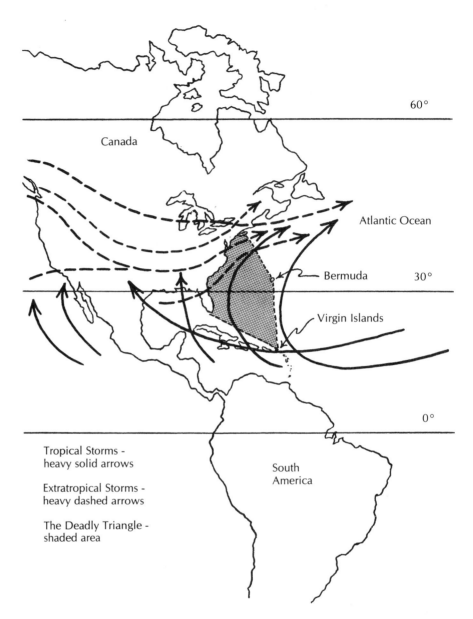

Canada

Atlantic Ocean

60°

Bermuda 30°

Virgin Islands

0°

South
America

Tropical Storms -
heavy solid arrows

Extratropical Storms -
heavy dashed arrows

The Deadly Triangle -
shaded area

Figure 8-5. *Typical storm tracks affecting U.S. weather.*

zone where the southeast trade winds converge with the northeast trades. Just as an extratropical cyclone can be formed when two winds oppose each other on either side of a front, the two trades may oppose each other when they are acted on by the Coriolis force and start a whirlpool of air. Under the right conditions of temperature, moisture, and pressure, this whirlpool develops into a severe cyclone. Another factor that frequently influences the formation of tropical storms is the presence of an easterly wave, a trough of low pressure crossing the easterly trade wind flow. Tropical cyclones follow somewhat predictable paths that generally run from their point of origin toward the west until they

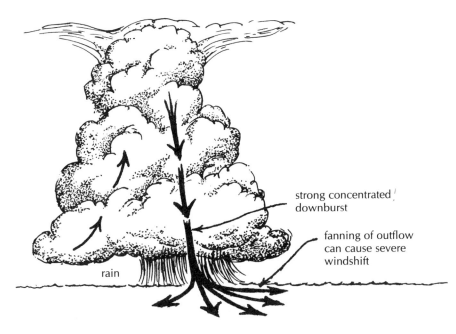

Figure 8-6. *A microburst. The thunderhead is not always present.*

strong concentrated downburst

fanning of outflow can cause severe windshift

rain

curve northward (in the northern hemisphere) and strike the prevailing westerlies, at which time they frequently recurve toward the east (see Figure 8-5). These storms are seasonal partly because they are most likely to occur when the intertropical convergence zone moves sufficiently far from the equator, following the seasonal declination of the sun, to be affected by the Coriolis force. Tropical cyclones occur most often in the late summer or early fall of their hemisphere. Indeed, West Indian hurricanes, which affect the East and Gulf coasts of the United States, occur between early June and late October, with their greatest frequency in September. A hurricane warning rhyme for the West Indies goes: "June, too soon; July, stand by; August, look out you must; September, remember; October, all over." Bear in mind, however, that hurricane season is not entirely over until the end of October, and there have even been a few of these storms in November.

The principal danger of microbursts and bombs lies in the rapidity of their development, sometimes with little if any warning. A microburst, or concentrated downburst, is a type of wind shear evident in a very strong downdraft and outflow when the falling air makes contact with the ground. Very often the sinking blast is accompanied by a column of rain or virga (high-altitude rain that mostly evaporates before reaching the ground).

Microbursts are most threatening to aircraft that are landing or taking off, but they can also be hazardous to sailing vessels. Indeed, it is now believed that microbursts sank the tall ships *Albatross, Marquis, Pride of Baltimore,* and *Calida.* All in excess of 100 feet in overall length, these vessels were historic replicas, at least partially square-rigged. Many unmodified tall ships built prior to the new regulations mentioned in Chapter 1

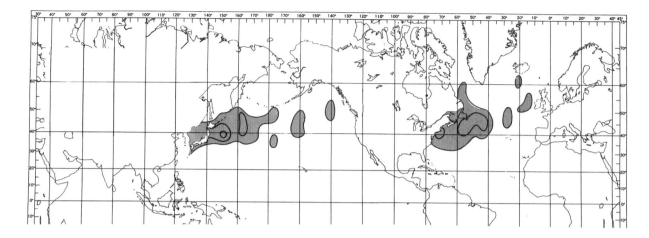

Figure 8-7. *Approximate geographical areas of weather bomb occurrences in the Atlantic and Pacific basins in 1978-79. (After Sanders and Gyakum; from* Heavy Weather Guide, *2nd Edition, by William Kotsch and Richard Henderson, Naval Institute Press, 1984)*

are particularly vulnerable to downbursts because of their low ranges of stability, susceptibility to downflooding, insufficiently secured ballast, lack of watertight compartments, and inability to reduce sail quickly. The outflow from a burst is not only high in velocity, sometimes as much as 100 knots or more, but it will often fan out and cause a sudden windshift that strikes the vessel on her beam and knocks her flat.

There is no sure way to spot an imminent microburst (unless perhaps the vessel is fitted with Doppler radar), because the phenomenon occurs occasionally in quite clear weather. In fact, some of the devastating "white squalls" of former times were probably downbursts out of cloudless skies. Nevertheless, there are warning signs. In most cases, microbursts are linked to overcast, unsettled weather and associated with weather fronts or land-sea breeze situations. Very often there will be thunderheads or altocumulus clouds in the sky. Frequently (but not always) a burst will fall from a thunderhead, although only one in a hundred or more thunderstorms will produce such extreme wind shear. One apparent clue is a column of rain or virga, although this is not always visible. Occasionally, the victim of a downburst will describe the wind as coming from a hole in the clouds.

About the best defense against a microburst is to stay alert during the above-described conditions, shorten sail early, batten down, and see that no openings lead below other than on the boat's centerline. Fortunately, downbursts don't last long. Their duration is seldom more than 15 minutes, and the most severe wind shear lasts only about two to four minutes. The blast will not have time to build up extremely dangerous waves. Keep your eyes open and be ready to drop all sail within 30 seconds to avoid a knockdown. As the jazz musician said to the pedestrian who stepped in front of his car: "Man, it's either C sharp or B flat."

In contrast, weather bombs last much longer, cover a broader area, and can build a vicious sea. A bomb is an extratropical cyclone that deepens with explosive rapidity. It is defined as a deepening low in which the pressure falls at least one millibar per hour for 24 hours. Most often developing within or just north of the warm waters of the Gulf Stream in the Atlantic or the Kuroshio current in the Pacific, bombs usually occur during the colder seasons. Occasionally, however, they form during the warm months.

One infamous summer bomb was the 1979 Fastnet storm. This particular disturbance developed from a secondary low near Nova Scotia, and it took about three days to cross the Atlantic to the coast of Ireland, where it deepened explosively. The track of the bomb became somewhat erratic as a result of what meteorologists call a Fujiwhara effect, whereby the two lows (the primary, then relatively weak, and the bomb) rotate about a point between them. Its devastation was attributed primarily to extremely severe seas produced by shifting Force 10 winds and possibly steepened further by shoaling bottom contours in the vicinity of land.

The best defense against a bomb is to stay away from the areas of warm current during the colder seasons, and to watch carefully for barometric pressure changes. Bearing in mind the dangerous seas produced by bombs, make sure you have a watertight boat with a great range of positive stability. Monitor weather reports religiously whenever there is a chance of bomb development.

Waves

The principal danger of heavy weather is not normally from the wind itself but from the seas produced by the wind. Although concentrated cyclones and sudden squalls can be extremely violent, their winds need not jeopardize a well-found vessel unless she is caught unaware. The real threat to her safety arises when a lengthy blow builds up heavy seas.

The size and character of wind-induced waves depend on the velocity of the wind, the duration of the blow from a constant direction, the wind shifts during the blow, the fetch or distance of open water over which the wind blows, the direction and strength of current, and the depth of water. For small craft, wave size is usually of less importance than the character of the waves. Dangerous seas are those that are short, steep, breaking, and chaotic, no matter what their size. Strong winds blowing for a lengthy period over a long fetch of deep water produce high but long seas that usually are not dangerous. In shoal water or with the current flowing against the wind, the seas shorten, become steeper, and break more frequently. When the wind shifts in such a way that waves move across each other from two or more directions, the seas can become extremely chaotic.

First let us consider deep-water waves, which are usually defined as wind waves in water whose depth is greater than half the wave length. Off soundings and in areas of little or no current, the three factors that influence wave size are wind velocity, duration of that wind from a constant direction, and fetch. At sea, the fetch is not necessarily the distance from a windward shore, but rather the distance from the wind's point of origin, perhaps at the edge of a storm. Without the limiting factors of

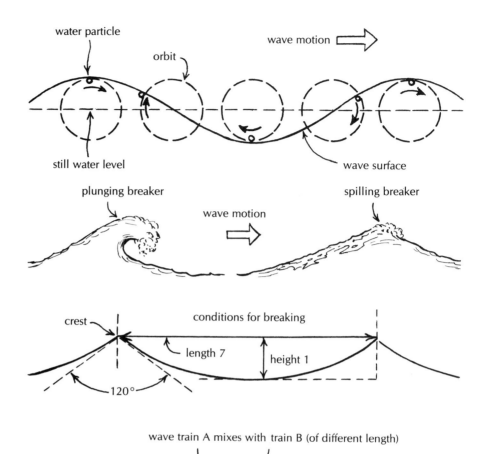

water particle

orbit

wave motion

still water level

wave surface

plunging breaker

spilling breaker

wave motion

crest

conditions for breaking

length 7

height 1

120°

wave train A mixes with train B (of different length)

to produce a wave pattern similar to C

Figure 8-8. *Waves and wave patterns.*

fetch and duration, waves in very strong gales can be enormously high. Such waves are called "fully developed." Fortunately for mariners, this stage of development is seldom reached in the higher wind velocities because waves are nearly always limited to some extent by fetch or duration, even in mid-ocean, and the stronger the wind, the greater the distance and time needed for a sea to reach its full height. Oceanographic tables tell us that fully developed sea heights can only be attained when a 10-knot wind blows for 2.4 hours over a 10-mile fetch; a 20-knot wind blows for 10 hours over a 75-mile fetch; a 30-knot wind blows for 23 hours over a 280-mile fetch; a 40-knot wind blows for 42 hours over a 710-

Figure 8-9. *The way it looks just before being struck by a breaking sea off Cape Horn. (Warwick M. Tompkins photo)*

mile fetch; or a 50-knot wind blows for 69 hours over a 1,420-mile fetch. These statistics make it easy to understand why so few monstrous waves are reported from reliable sources. Outside the high latitudes of the South Pacific or the South China Sea during the monsoons, very few places provide sufficient fetch and duration for a 40-knot wind to produce fully developed seas.

Comprehensive weather reports usually predict the wind strength, direction, and duration, and when the fetch can be estimated (by judging one's distance from a windward shore or storm, for instance), the height to which seas will build can often be predicted with reasonable accuracy. Oceanographic studies have produced tables and graphs that show the combined effects of fetch and duration on wave size in all strengths of wind. One such wave forecast graph is illustrated in Appendix G. It shows the height and period (the time it takes for one wave length to pass a given point) of deep-water waves for wind speeds between 10 and 100 knots over fetch lengths between 1 and 1,000 miles with durations up to 100 hours. Notice that wave height does not increase significantly after 30 hours in the lower wind speeds (under 35 knots approximately), and also, in still lower wind speeds, a fetch of greater than 200 miles will not have much effect. In using the graph, bear in mind that the more limiting of the two factors, fetch or duration, governs wave height. A 20-knot wind blowing over a 200-mile fetch can produce a wave 8 feet high, but if that wind has only been blowing for 7 hours, the wave will only be about 2.5 feet high. On the other hand, if the 20-knot wind blows for 30 hours, the wave could be about 8.5 feet

Figure 8-10. *A plunging breaker in the Gulf Stream. (Jan Hahn photo)*

high, but with a fetch of only 10 miles the wave would be slightly less than 3 feet high.

Wave forecast graphs are highly generalized, and the heights of individual seas vary considerably. These irregularities are largely due to waves coming from different directions and crossing each other at angles, as when a new sea runs over an old swell or when wave trains (groups or systems of related waves moving at approximately half the speed of the individual waves) mix. When one train mixes with another of a different wave length or period, some waves are reinforced while others are interfered with. The result, an irregular pattern similar to that shown in Figure 8-8, explains why there is some basis for the seaman's ancient belief that every seventh or eleventh wave will be extra high. Although there is really no invariable magic number for outstandingly high or low waves, their appearance may come at regular intervals (perhaps after the seventh, ninth, eleventh, thirteenth, or some other wave). Indeed, it is usually possible and advisable to pick a "smooth" (after the passing of an especially high wave or group of heavy seas) in which to perform a difficult heavy-weather maneuver such as tacking or wearing ship. In similar conditions of wind, fetch, and current, shallow-water waves are generally far more dangerous than those in deep water. Although waves off soundings can build to enormous height and normally move at higher velocities than those in shoal water, wave speed is not as important as the forward movement of individual water particles. In other words, what really matters is whether or not the sea is breaking and its manner of breaking. In his book *Safety in Small Craft*, D.A. Rayner explained it neatly when he compared a wave's movement to a mouse running along under a rug. No matter how fast the mouse runs, the rug's motion is simply up and down. Of course, the movement of water particles in a non-breaking wave is not strictly up and down, but circular (as shown in Figure 8-8), with the particles at the crest moving forward (in the direction of the wave's advance) and the particles in the trough moving backward. After completing an orbit, each particle returns (almost) to its initial position. Actually, wind-induced surface drift moves

Sea Sense

Figure 8-11. *Harvey Conover shown at the helm of his newly built centerboard yawl Revonoc, which was lost with all hands in the Straits of Florida in 1958. Revonoc was caught between a high pressure system to the north and an intense low to the south. When the winds of each system met, they reinforced each other to produce a sudden northeast gale with gusts up to 70 knots, which opposed the strong flow of the Gulf Stream, producing an untenable condition for the ocean racer and her experienced crew. (Morris Rosenfeld photo)*

Figure 8-12. *This dinghy with the small gash in her starboard side was the only trace found of the missing Revonoc. (Courtesy U.S. Coast Guard)*

the particles slightly downwind, but drastic forward transport occurs only when the particles tear away from their orbits as the wave breaks, and this helps explain why breaking seas can be dangerous.

As a deep-water wave moves into shallow water, it not only steepens, but the particles' orbits become more elliptical. Although the wave speed decreases, the horizontal particle speed becomes faster. Theoretically, a wave is likely to break when its crest angle becomes less than 120 degrees or its height exceeds one-seventh its length, as illustrated in Figure 8-8. The two general types of breakers are plungers and spillers, the latter having a more concave back and a crest that breaks gradually and continuously (see Figure 8-8). A plunger, which falls suddenly and violently, is nearly always more dangerous. While both kinds are found near shore and at sea, deep-water breakers are usually the spilling type. Bear in mind, however, that a wave is considered to be in shallow water when it begins to "feel" bottom, and this occurs when the water shoals to less than half the wave length. Given sufficient wave length, it is perfectly possible to encounter shallow-water waves at sea. As Willard Bascom pointed out in his book *Waves and Beaches*, a wave at the edge of the continental shelf in 600 feet of water with a period of 16 seconds is a shallow-water wave, for it would have a length of over 1,300 feet:

$$T^2 = L \div 5.12$$

where T is the period in seconds, and L is the length in feet.

In determining a proper storm strategy, therefore, you must know your position with respect to shore or shoals on which you could run aground, and consider the effect of water depth on the character of the seas in your location. Always move toward or stay in the deepest water possible when expecting a lengthy blow, unless you can reach a protected harbor before the blow begins.

Dangerous seas can also be caused by a current flowing against the wind. Major offshore currents are well known, and their basic tracks are marked on pilot charts, but they meander considerably. These currents are potentially dangerous because they can "breed" bad weather by bringing warm water into a cool area of the ocean and because they often produce short, steep, breaking waves when their flow opposes a strong wind over a lengthy period of time. The Gulf Stream is extremely troublesome to small craft off the southeast coast of the United States, especially off Cape Hatteras. Many boats, even large ones, have been lost during fall and winter gales in this area. As mentioned, these disappearances account for some of the so-called mysteries of the Bermuda Triangle.

It is not always easy to tell when you are in the main flow of an offshore or coastal current because of its frequent meandering. Useful signs include changes in the color of the water, the character of the waves, the water temperature, and sometimes flotsam from some remote location near the current's point of origin. The Gulf Stream, for example, is generally a deeper blue, has a considerably warmer temperature, and often has steeper waves than the surrounding ocean. A thermometer for measuring water temperatures can be a useful piece of equipment on an offshore boat.

Chapter 9
GENERAL STORM STRATEGY

S ailors cannot always outwit Mother Nature, but they can often avoid her wrath or defend against it. Later chapters will deal with boat handling and seamanship in storms, but here I will express a few thoughts on the basic principles of evading and preparing for the hard chance at sea, along the coast, and in port.

Planning for Storm Avoidance

To begin with, an offshore voyage should be designed to follow the safest route at the most favorable time of the year. It makes fundamentally good sense to avoid the regions of tropical storms during their dangerous seasons, and to cruise offshore in higher latitudes (above the areas most frequented by hurricanes and typhoons) only during the warmer months, when gale-producing depressions are at a minimum.

Start your planning with a study of the oceanic pilot charts, which show for each month of the year the average percentage of gales and calms, wind directions and strengths, fog, current direction and strength, mean atmospheric pressure, and storm tracks, as well as other information unrelated to the weather. Published in the United States by the Defense Mapping Agency Hydrographic Center, the pilot charts are based on the observations by mariners since the mid 19th century. They don't prognosticate (my wife calls them "fabulous fiction"), but they do allow a skipper to play the odds. Other important sources of weather information are the *Sailing Directions* (published by the National Ocean Survey) and British Admiralty Pilots, the British Admiralty publication *Ocean Passages for the World*, offshore passage guides such as *The Atlantic Crossing Guide* by Philip Allen (International Marine, 1990) and *World Cruising Routes* by Jimmy Cornell (International Marine, 1987), and *Worldwide Marine Weather Broadcasts* (published by the U.S. Department of Commerce). For the Atlantic Ocean, the information contained in the *Sailing Directions* and Admiralty Pilots is presented in summary fashion along with a complete set of pilot charts in the *Atlantic Pilot Atlas*, edited by James Clarke (International Marine, 1989).

Evading the Worst of an Extratropical Low

As compared with tropical lows, the heavy weather associated with extratropical lows may be more difficult to avoid because the latter are easily formed, sometimes with little warning. Unlike the former, they are almost always accompanied by weather fronts extending long distances from the storm center. Nevertheless, when you can predict with reasonable accuracy the track of an extratropical depression, you can change your vessel's course to evade the worst weather. In attempting to predict the path of a low, bear in mind that even though the entire weather pattern is influenced by steering currents, such as meandering jet streams aloft, storm systems in the middle latitudes generally move in an easterly or more northeasterly direction (in the northern hemisphere). Quite often they will form and track along a cold front. You can get information on weather movement from radio weather forecasts such as the hourly high seas reports on WWV and WWVH or VHF-FM transmissions (ranging from 162.4-162.55 MHz) when close to shore. Weather facsimile equipment can be invaluable.

As an example of the decision-making involved in storm-avoidance strategy, let us suppose that our vessel is in the middle North Atlantic headed west, and an extratropical low is approaching us. If we are due east of the storm or south of east, it might be best to head in a southerly direction because of the northerly component of the storm's probable track. On the other hand, if we are north of the projected storm track, a northerly course may earn us more favorable wind and seas in the northern sector of the counterclockwise-turning depression. That course might also enable us to avoid any severe disturbances from the typical double fronts, or at least the trailing cold front extending in a southwesterly direction from the low. Other possible hazards in the southern sector include squalls and a wind shift in the trough that sometimes follows the passage of the cold front. More serious is the possible formation of a secondary low in the southern sector, particularly when there is a second build-up of pressure along the cold front a long distance from the primary low.

Clues to a storm's movement also come from observations of the sky, wind direction, the barometer, and even waves. A significant storm will send out waves in a concentric pattern, just as ripples emanate from a stone dropped in water. The highest waves move ahead, in the direction the storm is traveling, and give warning from a great many miles away. The direction of the advance swell suggests the location of the storm's center at the time of generation.

Another early sign of approaching bad weather is high-altitude clouds. As mentioned in the last chapter, the sequence of clouds filling in from the west (in the middle latitudes) begins with the "mackerel sky" and "mares' tails" that "make tall ships carry small sails." An important clue as to whether or not you are in the path of a low comes from what meteorologist Alan Watts calls the crossed-winds rules. Observe the movement of the upper clouds (cirrus) and compare it with the move-

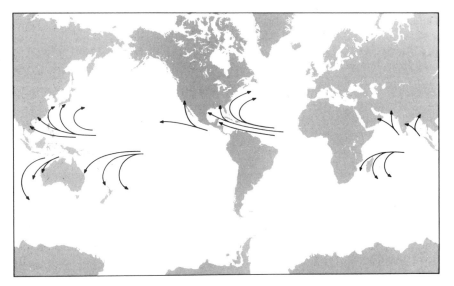

Figure 9-1. *Worldwide principal tracks of severe tropical cyclones (hurricanes and typhoons), greatly simplified. (From* Heavy Weather Guide, *2nd Ed., by William Kotsch and Richard Henderson, Naval Institute Press, 1984)*

ment of lower clouds, such as cumulus or stratocumulus. If the upper clouds come from the left while you stand with your back to the surface wind, you can expect a depression. If the upper clouds come from the right, the weather will usually improve. Upper and lower winds blowing in opposite but parallel directions indicate that the vessel is north of the low. When the upper and lower winds blow from the same direction and you are in the warm sector of the depression, you can assume that the vessel is south of the low-pressure center and should be prepared for the passage of a cold front. The directions in these rules apply only to the northern hemisphere, because cyclones and anticyclones rotate the opposite way in the southern hemisphere.

Observations of the surface winds together with periodic barometer readings also provide important information. According to Buys Ballot's Law, when an observer in the northern hemisphere faces the wind, the center of low pressure is about ten points or 112 degrees to his right. If the wind veers (shifts clockwise), the low is headed to the north of your position. If it backs (shifts counterclockwise), the low is headed south of you. An increasing wind of steady direction with a falling barometer indicates that the storm is headed directly toward you. Don't forget that a quick rise of the glass after passage of the low's associated cold front can produce very strong winds.

Tropical Storm Strategy

The offshore voyager's primary weather concern should be avoiding hurricanes and other tropical storms, because their full fury is always dangerous, even life-threatening. These storms are most likely during the late summer and early fall of their hemisphere, but in the western North Pacific typhoons have occurred during every month of the year. Note also that El Nino, the periodic warm current off the South American

Pacific coast, can alter the usual pattern of storms. Figure 9-1 shows in a greatly simplified way the principal tracks of tropical cyclones throughout the world. The black arrows illustrate the storms' points of origin not far from the equator, their westerly movements toward the poles, and the frequent recurvatures as explained in the last chapter.

Although hurricane predictions are fairly accurate now and warnings are generally adequate, the careful offshore sailor avoids extended passages offshore in areas subject to hurricanes during the dangerous months. If he is caught at sea in the path of a tropical cyclone, he must avoid the storm center and maneuver his craft to the sectors of least intensity. His course of action should be based on "the law of storms," devised in the last century by Henry Piddington and later endorsed by authorities on navigation and seamanship.

The basic principles expressed in the law of storms are as follows: The revolving circular hurricane has a "dangerous" and a "navigable" semicircle. In the northern hemisphere, the right side of the circle is the dangerous one because the forward movement of the storm's center reinforces the strength of the whirling winds. In the navigable semicircle on the left-hand side, the center's forward movement is subtracted from the spiraling wind velocity (see Figure 9-2). A fairly accurate means of determining your vessel's position with respect to a storm center is by careful and constant observations of the wind. In accordance with the law of Buys Ballot, a veering wind indicates that you are in the right-hand semicircle; if the wind backs, you are in the left semicircle. A constant (nonshifting) wind indicates that you are on the storm track, either directly ahead of (rising wind, falling barometer) or behind (falling wind, rising glass) the center. You may also periodically obtain a hurricane's position from radio weather bulletins, but there is often a considerable time lag between an observation of the storm and the report of its position.

Once you establish your boat's position relative to the hurricane, you may put her on the course that will best avoid the dangerous sectors. Standard accepted rules advise that a sailing vessel in the front quadrant of the dangerous semicircle should sail close-hauled or heave to on the starboard tack so that she will proceed (with speed if possible) away from the storm center. A vessel directly in the center's path should run on starboard tack with the wind on the starboard quarter, and likewise if she is in front of the navigable semicircle. Powerboats should follow the same general courses, but it may be necessary in very heavy seas for them to keep their bows or sterns facing the waves (more will be said of this in Chapter 13). When it becomes necessary for a sailboat to heave to, the standard rule of thumb is to do so on the tack that allows the shifting wind to draw aft. A modern fore-and-aft-rigged boat in the left front quadrant should run off under bare poles or storm jib on the starboard tack, allowing the wind to draw forward, in order to move as far as possible from the storm center. This tactic requires a boat that behaves well in quartering seas. The principal reason for avoiding the center is that winds reach maximum velocity near the center, and in the "eye," a rela-

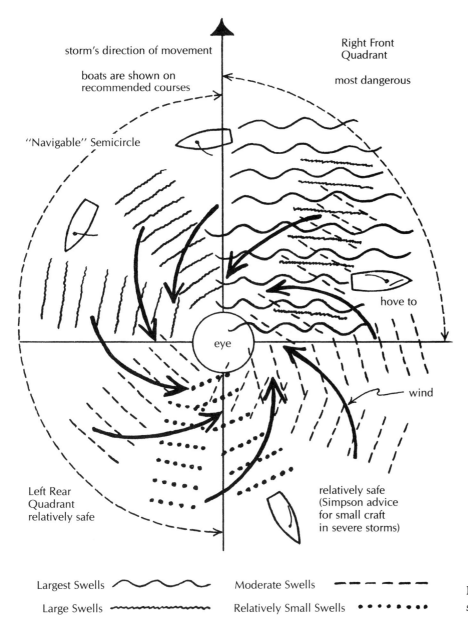

storm's direction of movement

boats are shown on
recommended courses

Right Front
Quadrant

most dangerous

"Navigable" Semicircle

eye

hove to

wind

Left Rear
Quadrant
relatively safe

relatively safe
(Simpson advice
for small craft
in severe storms)

Largest Swells ⌇⌇⌇⌇ Moderate Swells — — — — — **Figure 9-2.** *Tropical storm*
Large Swells ～～～～～ Relatively Small Swells • • • • • • *strategy.*

tively small area of about 4 to 30 miles in diameter at the center of rotation, the wind is so calm that it does not flatten or give order to the seas.
Indeed, vessels have sustained severe damage from rolling in the eyes of
hurricanes, where the waves can become huge, confused pyramids generated by seas converging from all directions.

In determining your proper heading away from a storm, consider
your vessel's behavior. When the boat is taking too great a beating or she
risks capsizing, she might have to be slowed or held end-to the seas.

Figure 9-3. *This dramatic photograph of the eye of Hurricane Gracie was taken from a ''hurricane hunter'' plane tracking the storm in September, 1959. (Courtesy U.S. Navy)*

Swells in a hurricane or typhoon generally come from a different direction than that of the wind (as much as 90 to 100 degrees different). If the vessel's course away from the storm puts dangerous seas on her beam, you might have to change her heading. Management of the vessel will be discussed in later chapters.

Although standard advice set forth in the law of storms is generally accepted as sound even today, it was originally intended for ships and large square-rigged vessels. One concern that probably lacks the same significance for the modern fore-and-aft-rigged boat was the danger of being caught aback by the suddenly shifting winds in a hurricane. Furthermore, advice intended for ships does not necessarily apply in all cases to small craft, so slight modifications of the rules may be necessary for small boats. In fact, one of the most experienced hurricane observers, Robert H. Simpson, believes that in many instances a boat will fare better in the rear quadrant of the dangerous semicircle than in the navigable semicircle. Simpson's advice should not be dismissed lightly, for he was chief of the National Hurricane Warning Center in Miami, a top-ranking meteorologist and formerly an associate director of the U.S. Weather Bureau. He also is an experienced yachtsman, owner of a stock racing/cruising sailboat, and has flown through hundreds of hurricanes. In an article in *Rudder* magazine (July, 1968), Simpson agreed with the standard advice to run from the center on the left side in small storms, but he

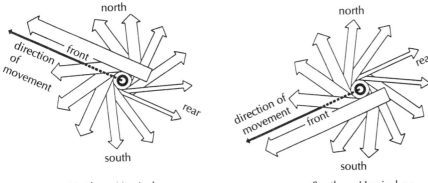

Northern Hemisphere	Southern Hemisphere

maintained that in large storms seas are more tenable for a small boat in the right rear quadrant. In this location, the waves are long, less confused, and flattened by the high winds. However, Simpson definitely agreed that the right front quadrant is the most dangerous sector of all, because this area has the combination of steep, confused seas with the highest winds, swells of the greatest magnitude, and in some cases, even tornadoes. Also, the wind in this quadrant tends to blow a vessel toward the storm center. Keep in mind that we have been discussing tropical cyclones in the northern hemisphere. Storms of this type rotate the opposite way in the southern hemisphere, and their dangerous semicircles are to the left of the storm track.

Warning signs of an approaching hurricane (other than from radio broadcasts) include a long, heavy swell preceding the storm, then sometimes "precursor lines" or bands of cumulonimbus clouds and thunderstorms perhaps a day ahead of the hurricane, then a gradually falling barometer. When the swell direction changes clockwise in the northern hemisphere (as the observer faces the storm), the center should pass from left to right, and vice versa when the change is counterclockwise. Next come clouds directly associated with the hurricane, which are normally like the cloud sequence preceding a warm front. These are cirrus, cirrostratus, and altostratus, perhaps mixed with some altocumulus. Movement of the high-altitude clouds and the swells may give a good indication of the hurricane's location and the direction in which it is advancing. As the storm draws near, clouds thicken, the barometer continues to fall, and the wind becomes gusty. Near the times of sunset or sunrise, the sky may develop a sickly greenish-yellow appearance. A heavy black wall of storm clouds, nimbostratus, surrounds the center of the storm.

As a final thought on hurricanes, a frequent mistake, made especially by people ashore, is to think that the storm has ended when the storm's eye passes. Quite often when the wind calms down and blue sky shows above, people rush out of houses, unshutter windows, replace lawn furniture, or move boats away from their hurricane berths. Soon afterward, when the eye has passed, the wind suddenly returns with its former strength but from the opposite direction. This is often the time when

Figure 9-4. Schematic diagrams of the swells generated by intense tropical cyclones in each hemisphere. Arrows indicate the direction of movement of the swells. The width of the arrows indicates the relative height of the swells. (From Heavy Weather Guide, *2nd Ed., by William Kotsch and Richard Henderson, Naval Institute Press, 1984)*

Figure 9-5. *The seas produced by winds of over 100 knots, from Hurricane Carol. This picture was taken from a Navy hurricane hunter aircraft just before it entered the eye of the storm. (Courtesy U.S. Navy)*

unnecessary damage and personal injuries occur. It is best to wait an hour or so after the weather has cleared before letting down your defenses.

Consideration in Coastal Waters

What has been said about the avoidance of storms at sea also applies to coastal waters, but there are other considerations when the vessel is close to shore. Avoiding a lee shore should be the main concern. Be sure you keep far away from land onto which the wind is likely to blow during the heaviest weather. This requires careful monitoring of weather reports together with a basic understanding of cyclonic circulation and how the wind shifts during frontal passages.

When close to shore, you will have to decide whether or not to seek shelter. This decision will depend on the storm's distance away, its rate of movement, the speed of your boat, and the availability of harbors. You may find some degree of protection under a windward shore when channels are well marked, but beware of trying for a harbor on a lee shore unless you are certain there is ample time before heavy weather arrives. Sometimes a strong sea breeze (blowing toward shore) opposing the steering currents will block an isolated thunderstorm that forms over the land, and this could buy you more time. When foul weather seems imminent, however, the safest policy is to obtain sea room as quickly as possible. In an offshore sailboat, take the tack that carries you away from land so that you can heave to or employ some other tactic as discussed in Chapter 12.

Obtaining sea room may also be desirable when it takes you into deep water or away from a coastal current. Shoals not only present the threat of grounding, but they can cause dangerous breaking seas. Strong currents, too, can cause a vicious sea, especially when the wind opposes the flow.

Preparing for a Storm at Sea

Although weather forecasts have improved in recent years, storm prediction is still far from an exact science. Even when the forecast seems favorable, the prudent seaman will prepare for a fast-developing low that might track with unexpected speed in an unpredicted direction. He will be constantly alert for signs of stormy weather, such as increasing seas and wind, threatening sky, a falling glass, distant thunder, and static on the radio.

In preparing for heavy weather at sea, one of the first actions should be taking a motion sickness medicine, since most such drugs take time to act. Dr. Michael Martin Cohen, author of *Dr. Cohen's Healthy Sailor Book*, says that Dramamine requires at least two hours before there is *any* anti-motion sickness effect. Even scopolamine, which acts more quickly, requires at least two to four hours if it is administered through the skin in the form of adhesive transdermal disks. It is important to treat any crew subject to seasickness well in advance of heavy weather, because severe affliction can cause total incapacitation and dangerous dehydration.

Other preparations for bad weather include inspection of the bilge, gear, and fittings; closing all deck openings; placing all needed gear so it will be readily available; securely lashing down all loose equipment that will be needed on deck; taking below all gear not needed on deck; carefully stowing all loose gear below; and donning foul-weather clothing, life jackets, and safety harnesses. All seacocks should be shut, except those on cockpit drains and deck scuppers. If there is no valve on the engine exhaust and the engine is not running, close the outlet with a tapered wood plug. Ventilators should be removed and replaced with screw plates, and this holds true even for Dorade trap types if extremely heavy weather is expected. Slides should be inserted and locked in the after end of the companionway, and the sliding hatch should be kept shut during the storm except when entering or leaving the cabin. All hatches and ports must be securely dogged. See that the bilge pumps are working and that the bilge is reasonably dry and clear of wood chips, paper labels from canned goods, or anything else that could clog the pumps. The radar reflector should be hoisted with a downhaul rigged from its bottom to hold it steady, and at night, a powerful waterproof flashlight, a foghorn, and flares should be readily available from the cockpit. The navigator should determine the boat's position before the arrival of heavy weather. It is often a good idea to rig lines for hand grips across or around the cockpit when the motion becomes violent. See that storm sails are bent or handy and that extra sheets, tackles, anchor (when near shore) or sea anchor, drags (which might be needed to slow speed) and properly coiled anchor rodes or warps are available. Take great care in stowing gear so that it cannot break loose and become dangerous projectiles. Pay special attention to heavy equipment such as extra batteries, tools, or anchors to make sure that they will not shift and fall against seacock handles, wires, pipes, or tanks. See that all lifesaving equipment is accessible and in working order.

Security in Port

Desirable, if not essential, ingredients for a harbor offering protection from storms include the following:

- A surrounding shore that affords a good lee in the direction from which the wind will blow.
- A harbor shaped in such a way that heavy seas or refracted waves cannot enter.
- A shoreline or seawall that is sufficiently high to be above the storm surge.
- When the vessel will be anchored, good holding ground and sufficient swinging room with ample scope.
- If the boat is docked, a substantial pier in good shape with proper pilings, cleats, and chafing gear.
- A "soft" shore or at least minimal rocks, piers, boats or other obstructions that could damage the boat if anchors drag.

The ideal harbor should offer some degree of protection on all sides, but especially on the sides from which the winds are expected. The wind will seldom swing entirely around the compass, but it may shift through a semicircular arc. Remember that in the northern hemisphere, a veering wind indicates you are in the right-hand semicircle of a tropical storm, whereas a backing wind indicates you are in the left-hand semicircle.

You want to be protected from swells and cross seas within a harbor. Swells taken on the beam will cause the vessel to roll, heave, and seriously chafe her gear. In finding a location where the waves are relatively calm, one should study the chart carefully and be aware of wave refraction and reflection. The latter occurs when waves bounce off a vertical object such as a seawall or bulkhead, causing a steep chop as the primary waves are opposed by those that are reflected. The refraction, or bending, of wave lines occurs when seas roll past a point, peninsula, or island. The wave lines bend around the land as friction decreases their forward speed in the relatively shallow water near shore. A cross chop can occur in the lee of a small island when wave lines bend around each side and meet at an angle to leeward.

For vessels in port, the most serious aspect of a tropical cyclone is usually the storm surge or extremely high tides. A forerunner rise in tide can be caused by advance swells, but the rapid rise of water in the surge results from a combination of wind pressure and falling atmospheric pressure. In the northern hemisphere, the surge usually occurs just to

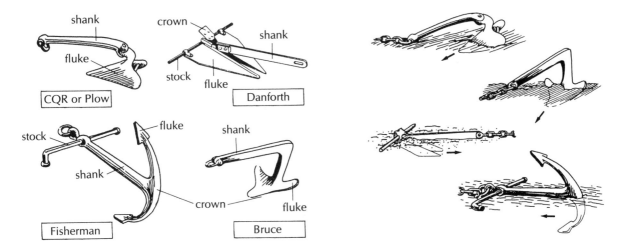

the right of the storm center. A hurricane hole should be as far as possible from the main body of water. The protecting shore must be generously high above the storm tide level, and docklines or anchor rodes should be long enough to allow for the rise of water.

An anchored boat has advantages over one tied to a dock—she will swing to the wind, thereby reducing windage, and she has no dock against which to pound or chafe. Safe anchoring requires a good-holding bottom, plenty of open space for swinging room, and ample scope. If there is any choice, anchors should be dropped behind a stand of new trees rather than old ones, which are more apt to blow over and drift down on the boat. Hard sand and sticky clay are the best bottoms. Anchors may wedge securely in rocks, but a severe wind shift can cause them to slip, bend, or break.

There is no universal agreement as to what type of anchor gives the greatest security. Favorites among the non-permanent anchors include the Herreshoff yachtsman, the Danforth fluke and plow, the Bruce, and the C.Q.R. plow. The disadvantages of any yachtsman or fisherman type are its small fluke area and the one fluke that sticks up and can foul the rode if the boat circles it. The Herreshoff type is probably least susceptible to this problem. The genuine C.Q.R. has often been praised, but it can easily drag in soft mud. Good deep-burying anchors are the Bruce and especially the Danforth Hi-Tensil Deepset fluke, but these may be very difficult to recover after the storm. Regarding these two anchors, impartial tests have shown the Bruce to be stronger but perhaps less reliable in holding power unless deeply buried. A standard method of lifting out a buried anchor is to shorten scope until the anchor line is vertical while all crew are on the bow, then move the crew aft and use the engine, waves, or both to break out the hook. I am told that the Deepset is more easily broken out under power by backing down rather than going ahead when the rode is at short scope. A problem with any Danforth fluke-type anchor is susceptibility to jamming from shells, weed, or

Figure 9-6. *Anchor types and their holding characteristics. (From* Anchoring *by Brian Fagan, International Marine, 1986)*

garbage on the bottom when the anchor has to reset itself after a wind shift. A deeply buried Deepset, however, may hold without resetting. For a permanent mooring, it's hard to beat a large, heavy mushroom anchor that is completely buried, but it may take a long time to sink far into the bottom.

Multiple anchors decrease the risk of dragging, and some systems also minimize extreme yawing. The latter problem can be alleviated with the so-called hammerlock moor, utilizing a second anchor put out at short scope and out of tandem with the primary anchor. The Houston Yacht Club, which has had considerable experience with the full force of hurricanes, recommends the so-called Galveston Bay anchoring system described in their booklet, *The HYC Hurricane Preparedness Plan*. This system requires two 45-pound Bruce anchors or a C.Q.R. and a Bruce set on 100 to 150 feet of 5/16-inch chain attached to 300 feet of 3/4-inch nylon rode. A 50-to-100-pound mushroom anchor is shackled to the chain where it joins the line. As an alternative, the HYC recommends setting two anchors out of tandem at a narrow angle (less than 45 degrees), although another system endorses a 60-degree angle. Still another multiple-anchor system suggested by the U.S. Coast Guard uses three anchors set 120 degrees apart, with the three rodes joined by a swivel to a single, heavy anchor line. This method is supposed to be effective where swinging room is limited, but swivels should be extra heavy, as I have known them to break.

With any anchoring system, a primary concern is chafing of the rode. Chain leaders prevent chafe on the seabed and chock, and a bridle or extra attachment line at the bow chocks provides a back-up if one line chafes through. You must have durable chafe guards. The Houston Yacht Club recommends neoprene hose chafing gear, and for a 3/4-inch anchor or mooring line they suggest a length of 2-inch hose over a length of 1-inch hose whipped or sewn to the line. The chafing gear should be long enough to extend from the bow chock under and around the stem when the boat yaws wildly, and there should be another guard at the bobstay if the vessel has one. An all-chain rode bypasses the chafing problem, but it will stretch taut and may cause damage or possibly jerk out the anchors. Nylon is the best material for a rode because of its elasticity and ability to minimize shock loading. If an all-chain rode is used, hook a piece of heavy nylon line to the chain forward of the bow, then lead it through the chock and all the way aft for maximum ability to stretch. The chain rode should have sufficient slack to allow the nylon to take the strain and introduce some elasticity into the system. Rubber snubbers holding slack in the chain are another alternative.

If the boat will be made fast to a pier, the mooring lines should be doubled or tripled, and they should be as long as possible to allow for the expected rise in tide. When possible, carry the lines across finger piers to distant pilings (see Figure 9-7), but be ever mindful of chafe. Docklines should be set out on both sides of the boat in order to hold her away from the pier. If there are no pilings to which the lines can be secured, anchors will be needed on the side without pilings. Unless the boat is tied away from the pier, the storm tide might lift her above low pilings, possibly impaling her. Rig plenty of fenders, especially on the side of the boat nearest the pier. Old tires are effective and normally readily available. Be sure that all cleats are well bolted and that the pull of a cleated line runs in the direction of the cleat's axis, rather than at a right angle to it. If you question the strength of a cleat, use a back-up such as the boat's mast or a piling. Don't forget that a piling to which a dockline is secured must be tall enough to prevent the line from slipping off with the rise of tide. If in doubt, rig tie-downs or nail down the line. You can't pay too much attention to chafe protection, especially where docklines are led through chocks. Rig ample springlines to hold the boat as steady as possible.

Whether the boat is anchored or docked, she should be stripped of loose gear and anything that will cause windage. Remove sails, weather cloths, dinghies, roller jibs, dodgers, extra halyards, and even ventilators. In some cases, however, when the boat is at anchor with a crew on board, Dorade vents can be left intact and storm sails might be left bent, provided they are tightly furled and thoroughly stopped. If a tornado is possible, leave open a "breathing vent" (protected opening) so that the air pressure inside the vessel can equalize quickly with the extremely low pressure at the heart of the tornado. Extreme differences of atmospheric pressure have caused buildings to explode.

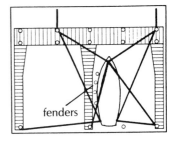

Figure 9-7. *Hurricane dockline configuration suggested by the U.S. Coast Guard. (From the* Proceedings of the Marine Safety Council*)*

Figure 9-8. *Damage caused by Hurricane Carol in 1954. Note how hurricane tides can impale a boat on pilings when she parts her lines or is not properly tied off from a pier on her windward side. (Peter Hicks photo)*

Chapter 10
SAFE RIGS

Despite occasional claims that the rigs on stock boats are adequately strong, I have found that the opposite is often true. During one long-distance race on the Chesapeake Bay, six boats were dismasted in winds whose gusts didn't exceed 25 knots. This doesn't count the rash of gear failures on boats that were not dismasted. Usually the rigging and fittings are simply too light to cope with the stresses of sailing in prolonged rugged conditions, in part due to the present fetish for reducing weight aloft. It is true that extra weight aloft can reduce a boat's initial stability far more than many people realize, but safety should come before every other consideration, especially on an offshore boat. Not only should the mast, rigging, and fittings be adequately strong for normal heavy weather, a considerable margin of safety should be allowed for unexpected stresses.

Common faults in the rigging on stock boats include the following:

- Fittings that are too light and too small.
- Use of closed-barrel turnbuckles with locknuts.
- Extensive use of cast metal fittings, especially those of aluminum, which may have hidden flaws.
- Chainplates and tangs that are misaligned with their shrouds or stays.
- Unsafe brakes on some reel winches.
- Winch pawls and springs of inadequate strength.
- Sheaves of insufficient diameter.
- Cleats oriented incorrectly to the direction of their lines' pull.
- Fittings that are not through-bolted, bolts that are too close together, or inadequate backing plates.
- Fittings of unsuitable materials such as unreinforced plastics.
- Lack of permanent slide stops at the ends of tracks, or inadequate stops.

- Sail tracks that are inadequately fastened for heavy weather.
- Mast or headsail-foil grooves that allow the luff's bolt rope to escape when sail is lowered.
- Blocks of the wrong design or construction for their intended purpose.
- Lack of fairleads or separators for halyards running through masthead sheaves.
- Mast tangs improperly bent, placed, or fastened.
- Mast sections that are too small, or walls that are too thin.
- Failure to use compression tubes inside a mast where there is pressure against the mast wall.
- Untapered filler pieces creating hard spots in hollow wooden masts.
- Standing rigging that is too light.
- Spreaders that are too short, creating a less-than-adequate shroud angle.
- Weak spreader sockets.
- A single lower shroud or some other shroud arrangement that allows excessive fore-and-aft movement of the middle of the mast.
- Inadequate stay support between the upper spreaders and the masthead.
- Lack of toggles on shrouds or, worse yet, on stays.
- Inadequate staying arrangements on mizzenmasts.
- Use of hinged or loosely attached spreaders on offshore boats.
- Too many holes drilled in a mast at one height.
- Use of improperly swaged end terminals on shrouds and stays.
- Roller reefing gear and goosenecks that are too small or of weak construction.
- Booms that are not tapered for roller reefing.
- Jiffy reefing gear insufficiently rugged for prolonged use at sea.
- Booms that are too long, creating a hazard of tripping on a wave or fouling on the backstay.
- Stays or shrouds made of nonflexible wire cable bent into eyes.
- Installation of relatively weak insulators on a stay in order to use it for a radio antenna.
- Lack of proper boom topping lifts or boom crutches.
- A mainsheet cleat that is out of reach of the helmsman.
- Use of shackles in standing rigging instead of toggles designed for heavy loads.
- Lack of stops or hoist limiting marks on halyards.

- Improper cottering or use of circular "ring-dings."
- Excessive use of rod rigging on offshore cruisers.
- Lack of bushings and spacers where fittings are connected, resulting in play and point loading.
- Use of continuous rod rigging in way of spreaders.
- Use of hook-on T-terminals aloft on large offshore boats.

Standing Rigging and Related Fittings

Fittings are often the weak links in a rig. The noted British author/designer Douglas Phillips-Birt has written that "the capital weakness" of the modern Bermuda rig "is its ultimate dependence upon many small metal parts." Turnbuckles, toggles, tangs, terminal eyes or jaws, and other essential hardware must be carefully selected and inspected for cracks or flaws. Fittings should be forged, extruded, or machined from bar stock to ensure that there are no internal voids or flaws, as are sometimes found in cast fittings. Rigging toggles are essential on offshore boats to supply universal joints between stays or shrouds and their attachment to the hull. These joints are especially important on stays, which are subject to lateral as well as fore-and-aft movements caused by a seaway, the side force of jibs or spinnaker poles against forestays, and the side force of riding sails or topping-lift strops against permanent backstays. Without toggles, the jaws or threaded portions of fittings can work and fatigue. Furthermore, it is a good idea to lubricate the toggles on headstays and backstays because they are often set up so tight (to prevent a large catenary in the jib luff) that the joints are reluctant to move. Despite the extra weight aloft, it is best to have toggles at the top as well as the bottom of the headstay and backstay (if a riding sail will be set on the stay). All shrouds need toggles at their lower ends.

Turnbuckles must be extra strong because they are held together by screw threads, where failures often occur. Ample lengths of shank should be screwed into the barrel at the top and bottom of a turnbuckle, and closed-barrel turnbuckles are dangerous precisely because it is impossible to see how much shank is screwed into the barrel. Use cotter pins to ensure that turnbuckles will not come unscrewed. Locknuts should be avoided because they work loose, and if they are set up extremely tight the threads are additionally stressed. Keep threads lubricated, especially those on turnbuckles that are frequently adjusted, and take care not to bend the barrel of an open turnbuckle by sticking a lever through to turn it forcibly. Although one frequently sees screw shackles used for linkages in standing rigging, this practice can be dangerous. It is safer to use threadless, toggle-type clevis pins with strong, heavy cotter keys. Be sure that cotters are not fatigued from frequent bending and that they are the same material as their pins (normally stainless steel or bronze), because galvanic corrosion can weaken the keys. As a matter of fact, this corrosion can even occur aloft, where the fitting is out of range of normal saltwater spray. When fittings of dissimilar metal are attached to aluminum masts, they should be isolated with plastic tape, silicone, neoprene, or some other barrier material. It is generally considered acceptable, however, to use stainless steel screws on an alloy mast, partly because the area of the more noble metal (stainless steel) is relatively very small. Top-quality stainless steel fittings have greater tensile strength than those of bronze, though the latter material is satisfactory when the fitting is of sufficient size. Steel turnbuckles sometimes bind and can almost weld their threads when under great stress. Any turnbuckle should be replaced immediately upon detection of galled or peeling threads. One simple test for appraising the strength of a stainless steel fitting (not wire) uses a magnet held in contact with the fitting. When there is a definite attraction between the metal and the magnet, the fitting should be viewed with suspicion. It could be dangerously weakened from bending or stressing or may not be a superior (300 series) stainless steel.

Standing rigging is generally composed of stainless steel cable of the 1 × 19 construction (one strand made of 19 wires), which is strong and has minimal stretch but is also nonflexible and difficult to splice. In fact, the vast majority of shrouds and stays made of 1 × 19 wire have swaged end eyes or jaws, eyes being preferable. These terminal fittings, which are squeezed onto the wire under high pressure, have a holding strength of up to 100 percent of the wire strength when the swaging is done properly. Swages do let go, however, and I have seen old and even brand-new rigging with minute longitudinal cracks in the terminal fittings. Swaged fittings should be carefully examined periodically with a magnifying glass. One recommended method of inspection is with the use of a dye penetrant and developer such as Spotcheck (made by the Magnaflux Corporation), which readily sinks into hairline cracks and makes them visible. There is also a fluorescent penetrant (Ardrox), which is visible under ultraviolet light. Less effective is a mixture of liquid detergent (the penetrant) and Mercurochrome (the stain). After the solution is applied, wipe it off and examine the fitting with a magnifying glass. Suspect fittings should be rejected, as they could cause the loss of the mast. One recommended method of protecting swaged connections from corrosive-stress cracking is with the use of fish oil or, preferably, Rustoleum 7769 Rusty Metal Primer. The oil, or the primer thinned with Rustoleum thinner, is applied to the wire at the top of the swaged fitting in such a way that the protective coating works down into the socket opening between the wire and the inside of the fitting. Some experienced sailors advocate sealing the top of a swaged terminal with silicone or plug cock grease where the wire enters the fitting. Even with this kind of preparation, though, regular inspections are necessary, and it is also important to check the cable itself to see that no wire strands are broken where they enter the socket.

Since failures in swaged fittings do occur (although not very often in nontropical waters when the fitting is properly swaged and periodically

Figure 10-1. *Standing rigging.*

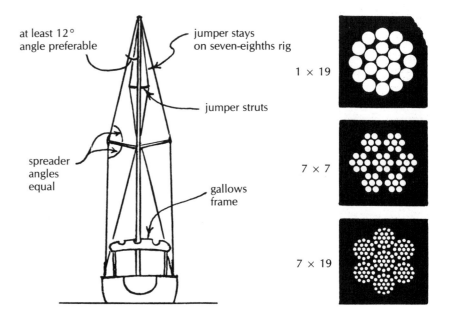

at least 12° angle preferable

jumper stays on seven-eighths rig

jumper struts

spreader angles equal

gallows frame

1 × 19

7 × 7

7 × 19

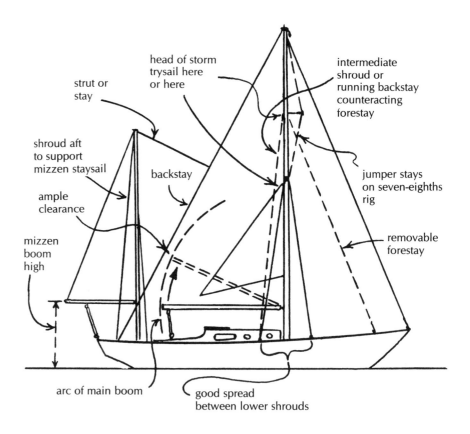

head of storm trysail here or here

intermediate shroud or running backstay counteracting forestay

strut or stay

shroud aft to support mizzen staysail

backstay

jumper stays on seven-eighths rig

ample clearance

removable forestay

mizzen boom high

arc of main boom

good spread between lower shrouds

inspected), some offshore cruising sailors prefer to substitute flexible cable that can be bent into eyes and spliced. Flexible rigging is not as strong and has more stretch than 1×19 wire, and a splice only gives up to 80 percent of the cable's strength. Small amounts of stretch can be tolerated on a cruiser, however, and a well-spliced eye over a large, solid thimble may instill more confidence because it will seldom let go suddenly. Captain John Illingworth, a noted authority on rigging, specified wire of 7×7 construction (seven strands of seven wires each) with spliced ends for the yawl *Lively Lady*, which Sir Alec Rose sailed around the world singlehanded in 1967-68. A couple of splices failed during the voyage. Several experienced offshore sailors with whom I have talked prefer 1×19 wire with removable terminals that have swage inserts, such as the Norseman or Sta-Lok fittings, because these can be renewed easily and their installation is simple and almost foolproof. A few ocean-racing skippers have their rigging hardware X-rayed for hidden defects, a troublesome procedure but prudent when extensive offshore work is anticipated. If the keel bolts are to be X-rayed (see Chapter 4), perhaps vital fittings could be done at the same time. In some cases, fittings might be examined by ultrasonics or another method mentioned in Chapter 4. When fittings are not cast and are of top quality and ample size, dye-penetrant testing should suffice.

Some stock boats have standing rigging a size too small for offshore sailing. A simple formula for determining the right size is:

$$Pt = \frac{RM_{30} \times 1.5}{beam}$$

where Pt is the load in pounds on the transverse rigging (shrouds) and RM_{30} is the righting moment at a heeling angle of 30 degrees. Half-beam is measured from the boat's centerline at the mast to the upper shroud's chainplate. RM can be obtained from the boat's rating certificate or that of a sister boat. (If the certificate gives righting moments for one or two degrees heel, RM_{30} can be extrapolated.) After you find Pt, multiply it by 2.5 for a minimal safety factor. The result is the maximum shroud loading, which you then multiply by a percentage for each shroud as shown in Figure 10-2. Having found the load for a shroud, obtain its breaking strength from a rigging catalog (or use the figures listed in Figure 10-2). Your rigging should be sufficiently large to equal or surpass the calculated loads. If your boat does not have a rating certificate, you can determine her righting moment by a simple inclining test, which can be done by a naval architect or yourself (see my book *Understanding Rigs & Rigging* for a simplified method). Headstays and backstays should have breaking strengths at least equal to the upper shrouds.

All interconnected parts in the rigging system should be reasonably matched in strength, although forked-end fittings that are subject to fatigue stress and those that rely on interlocking threads should be extra-strong. For example, if forged bronze turnbuckles are used, a 1/4-inch stainless steel cable having a breaking strength of 8,200 pounds needs a

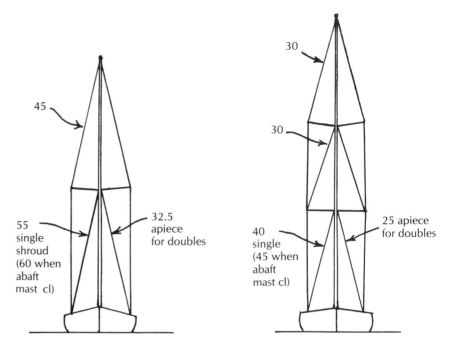

Figure 10-2. *Percentages of the maximum shroud load allotted to each shroud, and the breaking strength of 1×19 wire.*

Breaking Strength of 1 × 19 s.s. Wire

Diameter (inches)	Load (pounds)
1/8	2100
5/32	3300
3/16	4700
7/32	6300
1/4	8200
7/32	10300
5/16	12500
3/8	17500
7/16	23400
1/2	29700
5/8	46800
3/4	59700

1/2-inch turnbuckle with a tensile strength of at least 10,300 pounds. The working load should not exceed 40 percent of the tensile strength.

The use of solid rod rigging on an offshore cruiser is still controversial. A rod allows minimal stretch, but if it fails from stress corrosion, the mast may go by the board, whereas the breaking of one wire in a 1 × 19 cable still leaves 18 wires for support. Furthermore, solid rigging seems to have a greater likelihood of fatigue failure in the terminal fittings than does 1 × 19 cable. With rod rigging on a seagoer, use fatigue-indicating fittings with "warning pieces," such as the stemball fittings made by Navtec. These indicate the potential of rigging failure. After a rash of rod headstay failures in ocean races, the safety record has improved recently with the use of Nitronic 50 stainless steel and MP 35N cobalt alloy. Most authorities agree that the initial (at-anchor) tension put on a rod headstay before getting underway should be very much lower than the tension given a cable stay. Recommended tensions for precipitation-hardened stainless steel rod are from 15 to 20 percent of its breaking strength. It is generally thought that it is safe to tension 1 × 19 stainless steel wire to about 33 percent of its breaking strength. Rod rigging certainly has its place in around-the-buoys racing, but for greater safety in ocean racing I prefer stays of low-stretch Dyform 1 × 19, which has at least some stretch and therefore the ability to absorb unanticipated loads before it fails. Furthermore, this stretchability imposes less strain on the mast and hull in rugged conditions.

About the same could be said for the modern slotted headstay systems, which accept a jib's luff rope in a groove. Some makes have proven reliable, but others have failed or been damaged in heavy weather.

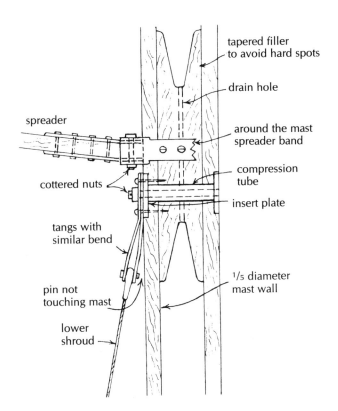

Labels in figure:
- tapered filler to avoid hard spots
- drain hole
- spreader
- around the mast spreader band
- cottered nuts
- compression tube
- insert plate
- tangs with similar bend
- pin not touching mast
- 1/5 diameter mast wall
- lower shroud

Figure 10-3. *Alternative methods of coping with spreader thrust and overtightened tang nuts.*

Although systems with more than one groove greatly expedite sail changes, they do not hold a jib's luff to the foil when the sail is lowered. As Rod Stephens has written, "These schemes (slotted headstays) are of interest to competitive sailors but are not recommended for cruising, primarily because a sail that is lowered is immediately disconnected. . . ." If I were to carry a slotted foil offshore, I'd prefer (for peace of mind) a type that fits around an existing headstay so that there is a back-up in the event of failure. Also, I might look into the possibility of using slugs fastened to the bolt rope so that the sail can remain attached by its luff when it is lowered. There are now at least two makes of roller jibs, Famet and Superfurl, that use this kind of system. A sail that is unattached can easily go overboard and be difficult to retrieve.

Aluminum masts on some stock boats are very light and thin-walled. These masts must be properly rigged and tuned, and they need compression tubes. Wood masts need tapered filler pieces where there is pressure from spreaders or tang bolts (see Figure 10-3). Such masts should be kept straight at sea, and the rigging should be positioned and set up sufficiently tight to prevent excessive mast movement and hold the mast in column, yet not so tight as to induce compression bends. I have seen slack rigging permit an out-of-column mast to collapse in a seaway without breaking a stay, shroud, or fitting. A pair of lower shrouds on each side of the mast is the safest arrangement, with sufficient spread between the forward and after lowers to hold the middle steady in a seaway. On masthead-rigged boats with a lot of distance between the upper spreaders and the masthead, a removable forestay with counteracting after-intermediate shrouds or running backstays (shown by dashed lines in Figure 10-1) may be necessary to prevent excessive fore-and-aft movement. The forestay may also counteract the pull of a reefed main or the head of a tall storm trysail. Seven-eighths-rigged boats may carry jumper stays and struts to control the bending and movement of the upper mast, but struts interfere with a masthead jib. Any system may be satisfactory as long as it holds the mast straight and reasonably steady. The simplest plan that can do the job adequately is usually the most desirable.

Yawls and ketches sometimes lack adequate mizzen support forward because of the difficulty of rigging a mizzen forestay that will not be fouled by the main boom. One solution is a jumper stay running from the mainmast's head to the mizzenmast head or a strut or wire from the mizzen's masthead to a point approximately halfway up the main backstay, as shown in Figure 10-1. The trouble with any rigging connection between masts is that if the mainmast goes by the board, it will probably carry away the mizzen.

Shrouds and stays should be properly tensioned. Headstays and backstays are often set up tighter than they should be for the greatest safety offshore. As a general rule, upper shrouds should be carried tighter than intermediates, and intermediates should be tighter than lowers, because the longer shrouds have more stretch and usually pass over spreaders. Several boats have lost the tops of their masts because their intermediates were tighter than they should have been.

Stays (and boom vangs) are often tensioned with hydraulic cylinders on modern ocean racers, but these devices seem unnecessary for cruisers. Hydraulics can leak fluid or otherwise fail, and there is a great temptation to overtension, which can impose severe stress on the rigging, chainplates, and hull. When there are several hydraulic adjusters, they should not be combined in a single system that would render all of them inoperable if the system fails. The latest racing rules legislate against the risky practice of adjusting hydraulics on both the headstay and backstay.

Another modern trend is the extra-flat trimming of genoa jibs. Sheeting angles (angles the chord of the sail makes with the centerline of the boat) have moved inboard from about 12 degrees to 8 degrees or less, and shrouds have been moved inboard and spreaders have been shortened to make possible such small sheeting angles. In my opinion, this practice can be dangerous on offshore boats because it reduces the angle between the upper shrouds and the mast. When this angle becomes smaller than 12 degrees, shroud loading increases considerably (Figure 10-4). Many of the newer boats have shroud angles of 11 degrees, and a few of the more recent boats have as little as $7^1/2$ degrees, thus creating an unnecessary risk.

Though one often sees boats with horizontal spreaders, they should nearly always be cocked up slightly so that the angles between the

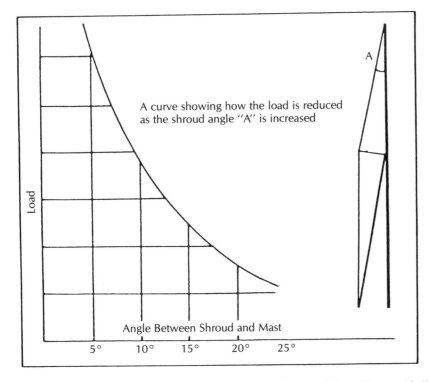

Figure 10-4. *Shroud loading.*

shroud and spreader above and below are exactly equal (see Figure 10-1). Otherwise, compression on the spreader will be out of column and the tip may slip. Wooden spreader tips should have metal ferrules to prevent splitting, and they should be securely lashed or clamped to the shrouds and then wrapped with felt or fitted with rollers to prevent chafe on the genoa jib. Don't use boat tape, which can cause chafe. The number of failures of aluminum spreader sockets indicates the desirability of stainless steel as the material for these important fittings.

Tangs and mast tracks should be securely fastened, but don't put too many fastenings at the same mast height. Not long ago I examined a broken aluminum mast that had nine holes drilled through its wall not more than a few inches apart in the vertical direction. The break ran from hole to hole around the mast circumference. It is especially important to stagger large holes such as halyard exits. All tangs and chainplates must align properly with the rigging, as misalignment can cause fatigue cracking. Mast tracks sometimes pull away from the mast, and so should be bolted in the areas of greatest stress. An especially important area is that adjacent to the head of a fully hoisted storm trysail.

Mast tracks, tangs, pins, sheaves, and all fittings aloft need careful inspection before you take your vessel offshore. The following are indications of weaknesses that could lead to failures: tangs with drilled holes having elongated oval shapes; masthead tangs that have sunk even slightly into the mast; poorly seated screws indicating possible slippage of the tang; bolts showing evidence of bending or wearing; eye splices with wire snags or enlarged eyes; worn lips on halyard sheaves; spreader fittings or tangs that show even a slight shifting of position; masthead cranes that are bent or slightly crushed; spreaders with considerable play or looseness at their inboard ends; and so forth. Beware of hook-on T-terminals that can fatigue or work loose on the lee side, and make sure that twin tang plates are equally bent (see Figure 10-3). All cotter pins should be carefully examined for crystallization or corrosion, vertical bolts should have their heads up, and nuts should be locked by peening or with cotters. All mast fittings should be examined for hairline cracks, weak weldments, distortion, wear, or serious corrosion.

Running Rigging and Related Fittings

The best materials for running rigging are polyester (or polyester with Kevlar core) line and 7 × 19 (seven strands, each made from 19 wires) flexible stainless steel wire rope. Called Dacron in the United States and Terylene in England, polyester is generally used for sheets, and the wire is used for halyards because of its low stretch and windage characteristics. The newest low-stretch fiber halyards are perfectly satisfactory for cruising boats, but wire is still best to minimize stretch on a racer. A reel halyard winch, which has a friction brake to stop rotation, allows the halyard to be composed entirely of wire. When non-reel ratchet winches are used, however, the wire halyard has a rope tail that can be cleated easily and coiled. The rope tail is joined to the wire either with two eye splices or with a wire-to-rope tail splice. Although tail splices are commonly used, I think they can be risky when reefing because the combined weight of sail and boom is supported by the relatively weak wire-to-rope splice. I was once on board a boat that lost her internal main halyard when the tail splice let go. Although a well-made tail splice is very strong, one cannot always be sure it is well made. From the standpoint of reefing, reel winches are better, though you can also rig a head pendant to extend the length of the halyard so that its wire part will go around the winch a few times when the sail is reefed, thus avoiding excessive strain on the tail splice.

If you use wire halyards, be sure the associated blocks and sheaves are proper. Standard blocks on stock boats are not always adequate in construction and design. A common failing is the use of non-swiveling blocks. When the line or wire running through the sheave changes direction and pulls somewhat laterally, it presses against the shell of the block, possibly breaking the shell or the edge of the sheave, chafing a line, or causing a wire to jam between the sheave and the shell. A sometimes satisfactory substitute for a swivel is the addition of an extra shackle to the fitting from which the block hangs. Be sure the block is large enough for its line, especially when using natural-fiber rope that can swell when wet. Blocks for wire should have deeply grooved sheaves and minimal space between sheaves and shells to lessen the possibility of a jam. Side-by-side sheaves mounted in the masthead should have metal separators between them, or else fairleads to prevent one halyard from jumping its sheave and jamming the other. There is hardly a worse feeling than attempting to lower a sail in a squall only to discover that its halyard is jammed aloft. If the halyard has very forcibly been pulled between the sheave and shell, quite often the block must be disassembled to remove the wire. A halyard can also jam when the shackle at its end is pulled into the sheave, but this problem can be avoided if the halyard is marked with a serving of wire or twine that can be aligned with a mark placed at eye level on the mast. Sheaves or winches intended for wire must be of sufficient diameter. A rule of thumb is that for 7×19 wire, the sheave or drum diameter should be at least 20 times the diameter of the wire rope. Otherwise, the wire will be weakened, and it may develop sharp snags or "fishhooks" and eventually break.

Fittings are sometimes made of unsuitable materials on stock boats. For instance, I have seen Tufnol blocks without metal straps connecting the sheave pins to the eyes by which the blocks are hung. Small cruising boats are sometimes fitted with genoa jib leads made of nylon, and sail slides are sometimes secured with nylon shackles. These fittings frequently carry away in heavy weather. (Incidentally, plastics that are not black can deteriorate from prolonged exposure to the sun.) Weak or improperly secured fittings are not just annoying; they can lead to serious injuries. In my sailing area, a young man was killed when a block let go and hit him in the head. Turning blocks have to be extra strong and well secured, because when a line enters a block and then reverses its direction, the strain on the block is doubled. If the pull on the line leading to the block is 500 pounds, the line also pulls with a strain of 500 pounds after it leaves the block, which puts a total load of 1,000 pounds on the fitting. Beware of turning blocks and other heavily loaded fittings that are made of cast aluminum.

Figure 10-5. *One unbroken winch pawl and two broken ones, which show where they usually break. Be sure that all assembly screws are tight, and carry spare pawls and springs similar to the one shown above. (Rip Henderson photo)*

Winches can be dangerous to handle. In fact, crewmembers have been "beaned"—and seriously injured—by runaway winch handles. Some of these injuries could have been avoided with careful seamanship, but in most cases the accidents were a result of broken pawls, pawl springs, or faulty brakes. Very often pawls or springs bind because of gummy grease, resulting from faulty maintenance or lack of adequate cleaning and routine lubrication. Avoiding cheap, unfamiliar equipment will help, but even the most costly winches fail occasionally. On a pair of new, expensive sheet winches made by a well-known firm, two pawls and three springs broke within a year after I purchased them. Brake handles on reel winches should be fitted with locks so that they cannot be accidentally tripped. The safest brake is the toggle-and-screw-pin type that allows the gradual easing of friction. Hoist sail with the brake on, and remove the winch handle when lowering.

Roller reefing mechanisms for mainsails are not so common as they once were, but those still found on new and used stock boats are often undersized. They should be sturdily made and fitted with a large flange to prevent the sail from sliding forward at the tack and getting tangled in the mechanism. Although booms are seldom tapered for roller reefing, I think they should have a larger diameter aft than forward; otherwise the after end will droop when a deep reef is rolled in. The gooseneck should also be very strong, and its track should be bolted to the mast, especially if the boat carries a vang that secures at the base of the mast. Such a vang will impart a powerful lateral thrust against the gooseneck and track when the boom is broad off.

Jiffy reefing gear often lacks the strength for prolonged use in heavy weather on extended offshore passages. Cheek blocks should be heavy and securely fastened, and there should be ample reinforcement at the reef grommets.

It is not at all unusual to see a main boom so long that it can strike the permanent backstay during a goosewing or flying jibe, which can occur if the mainsheet is not bowsed down sufficiently when wearing ship or during an inadvertent "all-standing" jibe. When this happens, the outboard end of the boom rides up and moves closer to the backstay. If the boom strikes the stay, it could break the stay or boom, strain the transom, pull out the chainplate, or cause a knockdown in heavy weather. Be sure the vertical arc made by raising the end of the main boom is well clear of the backstay, as shown in Figure 10-1.

A pet peeve of mine is the lack of proper main-boom topping lifts on stock boats. Standard practice is a short wire strop secured by means of a compression sleeve to the permanent backstay to hold up the main boom while the boat is at anchor. Quite often a weak snaphook at the end of the strop facilitates clipping the strop to the boom. Failure of the snaphook, which lacks the strength of a pin shackle, could allow the boom to fall on a crewmember's head. A major difficulty with the strop lift is encountered when lowering or raising the sail in a fresh breeze. The boom must either be held up by hand, a difficult and possibly dangerous task in heavy weather, or it is necessary to leave the strop attached to the boom while the sail is hoisted or lowered, in which case the boat is subjected to a possible knockdown unless she is held exactly head to wind. If the sail is going up or down while the boat is underway, it may be very nearly impossible to hold her head into the eye of the wind without auxiliary power, and there is always the possibility of a sudden wind shift, not uncommon in gusty northwesters in certain areas. A proper topping lift, adjustable at the mast, can be used to top up the boom when running off in heavy seas; to facilitate raising, lowering, and reefing the sail; and as an emergency halyard. In addition, I think boats should be provided with a boom crutch to support the boom when sail has been lowered. An offshore cruiser should have a sturdy gallows frame with boom positions on both sides, as well as amidships.

Cleats are often incorrectly mounted. Each should be placed so its longitudinal axis is angled slightly away from the direction of pull of the cleated line. If a cleated line under tension runs exactly along its cleat axis, it is liable to jam and be difficult to free in a hurry. A common mistake in mounting headsail sheet cleats is to place them in exactly the

Sea Sense

same position on one side of the boat as on the other. This symmetrical placement is seldom correct because sheet winches usually turn clockwise on both sides of the boat, and this means that a sheet will lead off the outboard side of the winch to starboard and the inboard side of the winch to port.

In many cases on stock boats, the mainsheet cleat is out of reach of the helmsman. Such an arrangement is not advisable, because there are times when the helmsman might have to release the sheet in a hurry. This is especially true when the boat is sailed shorthanded.

The Offshore Rig

Some 50 years ago, many seamen felt that the marconi rig, with its tall, intricately stayed mast, was unsafe to take offshore. In fact there are still a few non-racing sailors who think the gaff rig is the most suitable one for bluewater cruising. By and large, however, the marconi or Bermudian rig, as it is sometimes called, is almost universally accepted as the superior system for spreading sail, even at sea. Both rigs have their good and bad points, but most sailors agree that there are many more advantages to the marconi system. A gaff rig keeps the mast low when sail is down, and the rigging is simpler. There is often no need for spreaders, a great area of sail can be spread with a relatively low center of effort (geometric center of the sail, where the wind's force can be considered concentrated), and gaff sails may have less area blanketed in the troughs of waves at sea. The marconi rig, on the other hand, avoids a heavy movable spar aloft, which detracts from the gaff rig's stability and creates chafe; it more successfully avoids excessive sail twist and is more efficient to windward because of its long leading edge and high aspect ratio; more sail can be carried aloft (without the use of topsails) for effective light-weather sailing; there is little need for long booms that interfere with backstays, are subject to tripping, and move the center of effort outboard when reaching; and for a given sail area, the rig can be more inboard or compact longitudinally, allowing greater safety for the crew during sail handling.

An outboard rig, or one that is extended longitudinally, requires a bowsprit and perhaps a boomkin, and when sail is lowered in heavy weather, it is usually necessary for crew to be stationed on these spars, which are nearly always less secure than skidproof decks protected with adequate rails, pulpits, and lifelines. Although a bowsprit provides versatility in rig balance and a convenient place to cat an anchor, it has many disadvantages. Not only does it normally add to the risk of losing a man overboard, it supplies less structural support for a headstay than when the stay is attached to the vessel's stemhead. Furthermore, the anchor rode often chafes on the bobstay. If a bowsprit is necessary to balance the rig, it should be short, broad, and flat with toerails, lifelines, and a pulpit if possible. The bobstay must be tremendously strong, perhaps a solid

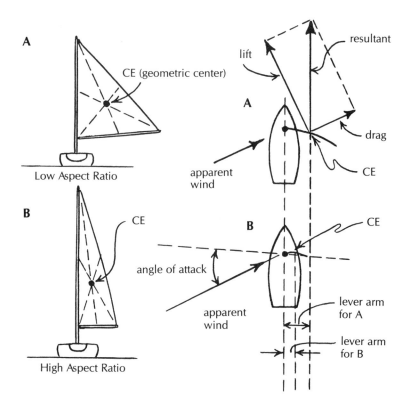

Figure 10-6. *Center of effort and balance. The true center of effort (center of pressure) is often slightly ahead of the geometric center.*

rod type, and the anchor chocks or rollers should be mounted at the outboard end of the sprit to avoid anchor-rode chafe.

A reasonably short boom for a given mast height produces a high-aspect-ratio sail (one that is tall and narrow). This sail shape not only has a high lift-to-drag ratio and great efficiency to windward, it normally permits easier handling and reefing. Although the aerodynamic advantages of a high-aspect sail are less apparent when sailing off the wind, the tall configuration has merit even on a broad reach. In the first place, lift (rather than drag) can be utilized when bearing away from the wind much longer than most sailors realize. It pays, in terms of speed and efficiency, to trim the sail so that it makes a small angle to the wind (a low angle of attack, roughly 30 degrees) so that the sail will produce optimum lift, even when the apparent wind is abaft the beam (see Figure 10-6). A definite advantage of a fairly high-aspect sail when reaching is that the center of effort (CE) of the sail is farther inboard as compared with low-aspect sail with a long boom. The farther outboard the CE is located, the greater the lever arm between the CE and the boat's vertical turning axis, and hence the greater the boat's weather helm or her tendency to round up into the wind. This point is illustrated in Figure 10-6. On the other hand, there may be some advantage in having the CE of the mainsail fairly far outboard when running so that it can balance a sail such as the spinnaker that is poled out on the boat's opposite side. Another, more obvious advantage of a short boom is that it is less subject

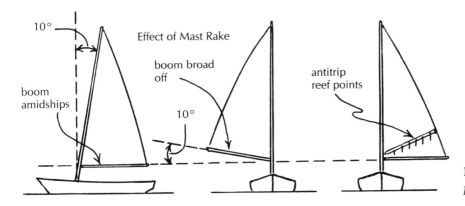

Figure 10-7. *Antitripping precautions.*

to tripping or dipping its end in the sea when the boat rolls while sailing downwind. Furthermore, a tall mast slows a boat's roll and increases her resistance to capsize from waves taken on the beam. Despite my enthusiasm for high-aspect-ratio rigs, I don't favor too much of a good thing. Some racing rigs have grown so tall that initial stability and control are adversely affected. A luff-height-to-foot-length ratio of $2\frac{1}{2}$ or 3 to 1, as shown in Figure 10-8, seems about right for the type of boat illustrated, assuming that she is reasonably stiff.

To ensure that the boom will not trip in the water, the seagoing cruiser can carry a slight or moderate mast rake aft. If the sail is cut so that the boom is horizontal when the sheet is trimmed flat (with the boom on the boat's centerline), the end of the boom will rise when the sheet is slacked off. This effect is exaggerated in Figure 10-7. Notice that if the tack angle is to remain constant, the angle of mast rake (angle between the mast and a vertical, 10 degrees in the example) will equal the angle of boom rise (the angle between a horizontal and the boom) when it is broad off. Another consideration relating to mast rake is how it affects the boat's balance. Ordinarily a rake aft increases a boat's weather helm, but since a short main boom on a single-masted boat decreases weather helm, theoretically there should not be a great deal of difference in the effect on helm balance between a vertical mast with long boom and a raked mast with short boom. Another, more minor benefit of moderate rake for a seagoing boat is that it helps concentrate weight amidships, which will slightly improve her pitching motion.

Divided rigs are necessary on large vessels so that individual sails can be small enough for easy management. At the present time, the most popular divided rigs are yawls and ketches. For offshore cruising, the ketch rig offers the advantage of having the smallest mainsail for a given amount of sail area. The schooner rig provides still another means of dividing sail area, but this rig is far less popular today than it once was, in part because the short foremast doesn't permit the setting of extremely large headsails for beating in light airs and parachute spinnakers for running. Then too, when hard on the wind, the schooner's powerful mainsail is backwinded to some extent by her forward sails, and her

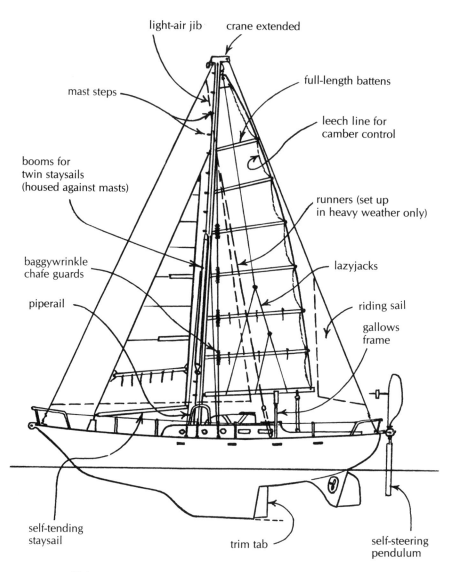

Figure 10-8. *A mannerly offshore cruising cutter.*

light-air jib   crane extended

full-length battens

mast steps

leech line for camber control

booms for twin staysails (housed against masts)

runners (set up in heavy weather only)

baggywrinkle chafe guards

lazyjacks

piperail

riding sail

gallows frame

self-tending staysail

trim tab

self-steering pendulum

narrow gaff foresail twists into a relatively inefficient shape for windward work, although use of a gaff vang will alleviate this problem. The three-masted schooner rig provides a balanced plan for very large vessels. On small boats, however, when the largest sail is not too large to be easily handled, I think there are many advantages in a single-masted rig. Although a two- or three-masted rig keeps the total center of effort low in heavy weather at sea, the CE should not be so low that the sails become blanketed in the troughs of seas. Captains of square-riggers realized this, and they often hove to under topsails rather than lower courses. A single-masted boat can carry a tall storm trysail or a Swedish mainsail (a tall, narrow, small mainsail for windward efficiency in heavy weather), which will reduce heeling but will keep enough sail area aloft to help damp rolling and avoid excessive blanketing from the seas.

An advantage of the modern sloop, and especially the cutter, is that the rig can be concentrated amidships. The cutter rig allows efficient use of a small mainsail, and with the mast near the point of maximum beam, there is a wide base for efficient staying and a relatively stable platform for crew safety when handling sails. The sloop or cutter enables a more continual use of a proper slot between sails for aerodynamic efficiency, even in heavy weather, and the mast weight amidships helps alleviate harmful pitching.

Figure 10-8 illustrates a seagoing cutter rig with many advantages for offshore cruising. Notice that the mast is stepped well aft, it carries a small mainsail, and it has a moderate rake that lifts the boom when it is broad off and further concentrates weight amidships to lessen pitching in a seaway. Her foretriangle gives a large area for versatile headsail combinations, and the forestaysail is sufficiently far aft for reasonably good helm balance under that sail alone if it becomes necessary to drop the mainsail during a real blow. Running backstays, not ordinarily needed, may be set up to reduce mast whip in heavy head seas. The staysail with a boom and traveler is self-tending, and its stay is far enough aft to permit fairly easy tacking of large, masthead jibs. A roller jib might be used, but I'm not in favor of a roller staysail because of the difficulty in controlling and tensioning the luff. Twin booms are shown housed against the mast. Their upper ends are lowered to hold out twin headsails for safe and comfortable running in fresh winds, an arrangement permitting easy self steering with the wind astern. The tiny riding sail shown in the illustration may be used to help hold the boat's head up when lying ahull. When reaching or sailing close-hauled, the wind vane and pendulum take over the automatic steering. Notice that in addition to the main rudder and the pendulum, which controls the main rudder, there is a keel trim tab with its heel well raised (to prevent damage from groundings). The tab serves as an emergency spare rudder and may be adjusted to control helm balance when reaching. Also, there are times when it might be turned in the opposite direction from which the rudder is turned to act as a brake in heavy weather.

Balance and proper sail concentration are easier to maintain as you reduce the cutter rig's sail area. Another point in favor of concentrating shortened sail amidships, rather than at each end of the boat, is that a heavy sea breaking over the side and striking the foot of a sail will not unduly affect the boat's directional stability. Solid water hitting a sail at the bow or stern will turn the boat, especially if she has a short keel. This happened when the 40-foot yawl *Puffin* broached and suffered severe damage while running before a strong wind in the Mediterranean Sea in 1966. A following sea broke against her mizzen and, in the opinion of her owner, Edward R. Greef, greatly contributed to the turning moment that caused the broach. If a midships sail blows out or its sheet parts, the wind won't weathercock the boat. When running off, sail should usually be concentrated somewhat forward of amidships to alleviate broaching tendencies. I would be wary of carrying considerable sail far forward,

Figure 10-9. *One of the U.S. Naval Academy's 44-foot Luders yawls shortened down with small genoa jib and reefed main. Note the jib's foot is well raised so that it will not scoop up seas. (Courtesy U.S. Navy)*

however, partly because the downward component of sail pressure at that location would tend to bury the bow. This could move the center of lateral resistance forward, which encourages rooting and broaching.

Although yawls and ketches have the advantage of being able to drop the mainsail to reduce sail during a sudden squall, progress to windward under jib and mizzen alone is usually poor, and it is not always the safest policy to sail for lengthy periods in steep head seas with no sail set in the area normally occupied by the hoisted mainsail. One reason for this is that almost any sail (storm trysail, Swedish mainsail, or reefed mainsail) secured to the mast will help hold the mast steady and alleviate excessive fore-and-aft pumping. It is not good to consign a heavy load to the mast-head only, especially in choppy waters. More than a few masthead rigs under heavy compression have gone by the board soon after the main-sail was lowered (but not replaced by a smaller sail) in rough seas.

The full-length battens shown in Figure 10-8 are now allowed with limitations by major handicap racing rules, and they have several advan-tages for cruisers. In addition to supporting a substantial roach for a more efficient sail shape, the long battens allow complete and variable draft or camber control. The deeper a batten is inserted into its pocket, either manually or by adjusting tension on a leech line, the greater the sail's camber at the batten's location. The latest method of adjusting ten-sion (and thus camber) on a full-length batten is with a threaded screw device attached to the sail's luff at the forward end of the batten. This avoids a protrusion at the after end, which can snag on the topping lift or backstay. In a strong breeze, the battens are kept straight to minimize

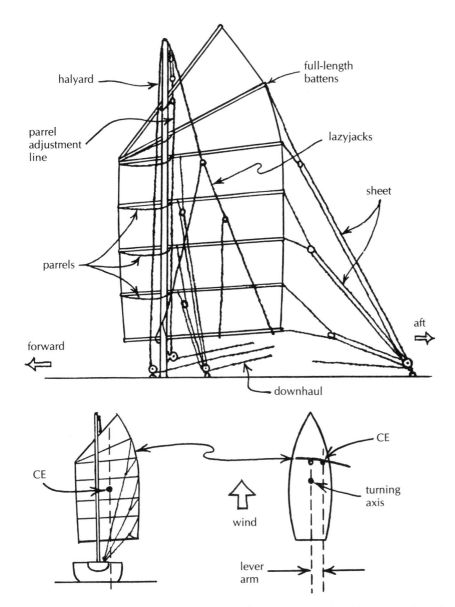

full-length battens

halyard

parrel adjustment line

lazyjacks

sheet

parrels

aft

forward

downhaul

CE

CE

turning axis

wind

lever arm

Figure 10-10. *A modified Chinese lug rig.*

camber. Long battens also minimize luffing from headsail backwind and permit the use of a narrow slot between the mainsail and an overlapping jib for greater efficiency.

Another advantage of long battens is that they will hold a sail steady in a breeze and let it "sleep" to a great extent, even when headed into the wind. This lessens damage from flapping. In addition, when the battens are properly placed and adjusted they can simplify reefing. Lazyjacks (as shown in Figure 10-8) contain the sail as it is lowered, and the battens neatly stack on top of each other. Reef points in the middle of the sail are not needed except perhaps in the heaviest weather. A patented system of this kind is the Stackpack offered by Doyle Sailmakers, which features

Figure 10-11. Jester, *a modified 25-foot Folkboat with a modern Chinese lug rig. Her skipper, H.G. Hasler, is shown in the hatchway where he can hoist, trim, reef, or hand the sail without moving from his station. With this rig Jester completed 13 transatlantic crossings. (Courtesy Eileen Ramsay)*

an integral sailcover pouch. Battens should be made of fairly stiff plastic, fiberglass, or moderately heavy wood strips covered with glass cloth to guard against risk of breakage. This full-length-battened, jib-headed mainsail has some of the virtues of a Chinese lugsail but retains most of the advantages of the conventional marconi sail.

The Chinese lug rig, shown in Figure 10-10, has special advantages in ease of handling for singlehanded cruisers, but it also has decided drawbacks when speed or windward performance is a major consideration. The rig, though ancient, was modernized in the late 1950s by offshore innovator Colonel H.G. Hasler. Among its advantages, sail twist can be controlled by the multiple sheets; the sail can be hoisted, handed, or reefed easily by one man from a central control position near the helm when reaching or running; and there is minimal compression on the mast and few metal parts that can break as compared with the marconi rig. Like any full-length-battened sail, strain on the Chinese lugsail is more evenly distributed, and violent flogging is avoided in a strong breeze. The modern lugsail is reefed with the four lines shown in Figure 10-10. First the halyard is slacked, which drops the lower battens to the boom, then the sheet and downhaul are tightened to pull snug and secure the lowered battens at each end. Finally the parrel line is adjusted to bring the yard in the proper fore-and-aft position.

A fairly recent vogue is the so-called cat ketch, which really goes back to the two-masted sharpie (or periauger) rig. The rig was publicized by the stock Freedom 40 class (see Figure 10-13). Although thin shroudless masts can break, and indeed this was considered a safety factor to pre-

Figure 10-12. *R.M. Ellison's* Ilala, *a two-masted Chinese lug-rigged singlehanded ocean racer. Note the details of her running rigging and the lack of standing rigging for mast support. (Courtesy Eileen Ramsey)*

vent capsizing on working sharpies, a large-sectioned stayless and shroudless mast with considerable taper has great resistance to breakage because of the lack of compression caused by standing rigging. The drawback of such a mast is that it can bend and whip considerably in a seaway. The shroudless and stayless *Ilala* (Figure 10-12) lost her mast from whipping, and I understand that the Freedom 40s need backstays to hold the mast steady when heading into a chop under engine power. Many of the latest freestanding masts are made from carbon fiber, and the claim is that they are up to 83 percent stiffer than those of aluminum. This helps to solve the whipping problem, but still the mast should be limber enough to bend off slightly in a breeze to help depower the sail.

A major consideration with any rig is the mitigation of chafe. At sea, when a vessel is constantly rolling and pitching, chafe is an insidious foe eroding the sails and rigging. With a mainsail or mizzen, especially one with full-length battens, you have to protect the sails where they lie against the shrouds when the boom is broad off. Vulnerable areas of a sail may be protected with baggy wrinkle or other chafing gear on the shrouds (see Figure 10-8). Spreader tips should be fitted with rollers or soft padding. Sails can be protected with reinforcing patches at vulnerable spots, and it is often wise to have vulnerable seams glued as well as sewn. Topping lifts must be kept clear of leeches, and spinnaker halyards must be rigged so that they do not chafe on stays. All lines subject to chafe should be fitted with proper fairleads, and whenever chafing cannot be avoided, the lines should be protected with chafe guards.

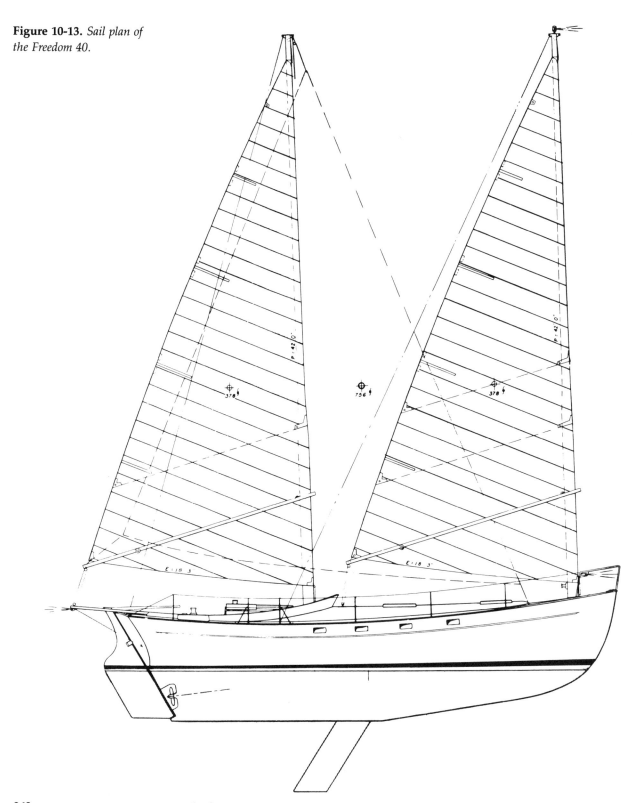

Figure 10-13. *Sail plan of the Freedom 40.*

Figure 10-14. *Although* Lady Pepperell *pitchpoled in the Southern Indian Ocean in 1983 during the BOC Challenge Race, her carbon fiber masts remained intact. (Courtesy West Point Pepperell)*

Figure 10-15. *For long passages, it is advisable to provide sails with chafing strips. In the mainsail illustrated, the nearly vertical strip protects the sail from the after lower shroud, while the horizontal strip prevents chafe from the spreaders. (Rip Henderson photo)*

Chapter 11
SAILING IN A BLOW

The question of when to shorten sail is not usually a very difficult one to answer on a cruising boat that is not concerned with maximum speed every moment, but on a racer, it often demands some agonizing soul-searching on the part of the skipper. He must consider the strength and behavior of his boat; her sails, rigging, fittings, and equipment; the weather conditions; the character of the seas; the number and quality of the crew; and the competence of the helmsmen. The decision to reduce sail is easier to make when the boat is beating or reaching in a steady wind, because if she is heeled beyond her optimum sailing angle, she will slow down. Usually the mainsail can be reefed with little or no loss of boat speed during the operation, especially if the boat has jiffy reefing. The optimum angle of heel can be determined without too much difficulty if the boat is fitted with an inclinometer and a speedometer, and even without these instruments, an experienced seaman can usually feel when his boat is not doing her best. A wind that

Figure 11-1. *One of the hazards of carrying a spinnaker in too much wind. This knockdown to windward might have been averted by trimming the sheet and sailing higher. This is a 5.5 meter. (Roger Smith photo)*

Figure 11-2. *In the heat of competition, when the wind pipes up, many skippers are tempted to carry parachute spinnakers when a single-luff spinnaker, half-winder, boomed-out jib, or twin headsails would give much better control and perhaps as much or more speed made good. (Morris Rosenfeld photo)*

constantly varies in strength often creates a problem. In this case, some skippers carry sail suitable for the average wind strength, or even the lulls when puffs are not too frequent. While this policy may produce a greater average boat speed, it might be hazardous under certain circumstances. Any skipper who matches his sail to the lower wind velocities should be as sure as possible that the hardest puffs will only slow the boat and not expose her to danger. Safety must be the first consideration, whether racing or cruising.

The real problem of deciding when to reduce sail comes when racing downwind in heavy air and seas with the spinnaker set, and especially when reaching. On almost any race course in heavy weather, spinnaker-carrying boats careening out of control, knocking down, and broaching to are a common sight, especially those craft with high-aspect-ratio fins and freestanding spade rudders that are raked aft considerably (see Chapter 3). Such a sight might indicate an alarming lack of seamanship, but competitive racing sailors are frequently enticed into carrying a big spinnaker despite the risk of damage, because the sail provides such tremendous power. The problem is well recognized, and race committees have even tried limiting the weight of spinnaker cloth so that the sails will blow out before the boat is endangered. This response has not been entirely successful, partly because of the differences in stress on a small spinnaker as compared with a large one of the same weight. Heavy-weight "storm spinnakers" with little camber and narrow shoulders have been allowed, and these are a safer design for heavy weather. They permit spinnaker sailing in winds stronger than those in which the normal, full, high-shouldered chute can be carried in safety, but even a storm chute has its limits. After a certain velocity of wind, boat control will become very difficult.

Spinnaker knockdowns are of two types, those that heel the boat to windward and those that heel her to leeward. The former is the most spectacular and frightening but usually easier to control. If the boat rolls to windward while running off, the helmsman luffs up to bring the wind more on the beam, the spinnaker sheet is flattened, and in some cases the pole is guyed forward. The leeward knockdown is often more difficult to avoid, especially when the wind is on the beam. At the first sign of a possible knockdown to leeward, the helmsman should bear off and the sheet should be eased. A major problem with the parachute (double-luff) spinnaker on a broad to beam reach is that the after leech curves around to such an extent that the after half of the sail exerts its drive laterally, causing a strong heeling moment. Some knowledgeable sailors feel that the old-fashioned single-luff spinnaker, which is somewhat like a parachute spinnaker cut in half, is a more sensible rig in strong winds when frequent jibing is not necessary. Certainly it is more snug, and its shape helps avoid the leeward heeling force. Another approach to the problem is the half-winder spinnaker, devised by British sailmaker Jeremy Howard-Williams and described in his book *Sails*. The half-winder has good points, in theory at least. It is similar in shape to a conventional double-luff chute, but its after half is porous so that it lets a certain amount of air flow through the sail (see Figure 11-3), thereby eliminating a great deal of harmful side force. Ventilation of the after half might be accomplished with porous cloth, mesh, or ventilating holes, but, as Howard-Williams points out, too much airflow through the sail will probably lead to premature collapsing.

The latest spinnaker-type sail, intended for easy handling on a cruiser, is the so-called flasher. It is carried without a spinnaker pole, usually has a radial head, and is cut asymmetrically, with the luff slightly longer than the leech. The tack is hooked to the headstay in such a way that it can slide up and down for optimal shaping of the sail in various conditions. Although the flasher is quite easy to handle and works well on a reach, it is less satisfactory on a run and does not eliminate the problem of the headstay wrap (when the sail winds itself around the stay). Furthermore, it is more difficult to hand than a headsail hanked to a stay.

More often than not, the most seamanlike rig for running off in a fresh breeze is the twin-headsail rig, or simply the mainsail and a jib "wung out" on the spinnaker pole; when it really comes on to blow, these sails may produce more speed than any kind of spinnaker. A boomed-out jib can usually be set quite easily by rigging the spinnaker pole to windward as though for the spinnaker, clipping the outboard end of the pole onto the windward jibsheet, then outhauling (with the windward sheet) the jib's clew to the end of the pole. A pole lift should be rigged in order to keep the outboard end of the pole high so that it will not dip into the sea when the boat rolls.

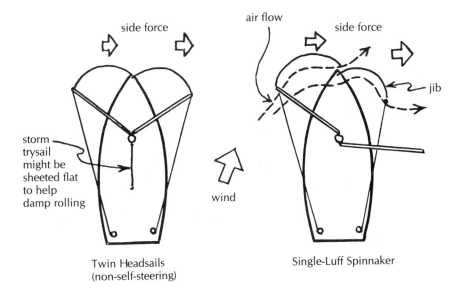

storm trysail might be sheeted flat to help damp rolling

Twin Headsails
(non-self-steering)

Single-Luff Spinnaker

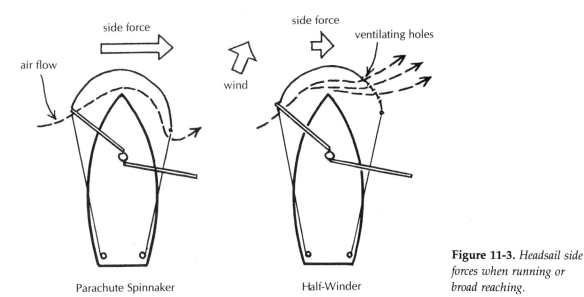

Parachute Spinnaker

Half-Winder

Figure 11-3. *Headsail side forces when running or broad reaching.*

In deciding when to change from spinnaker to boomed-out jib or twin headsails, a foremost consideration is the quality of helmsmanship. A skilled helmsman will anticipate waves and puffs and will not over-steer when the boat yaws or rolls. Leeward knockdowns can often be averted if the helmsman bears off on the leading edge of a puff. If he hesitates even for a moment, the rudder might stall and lose its bite on the water. This is especially true with spade rudders, which normally respond well when the boat is run off at once and not allowed to heel a

Figure 11-4. *The flasher, an asymmetrical poleless spinnaker produced by Ulmer-Kolius. (Courtesy Jack Quinn)*

great deal. After a racer takes her first spinnaker knockdown, the skipper should try to determine the cause. If poor helmsmanship contributed, greater attentiveness in steering or perhaps a new, more experienced helmsman is required. If the boat takes a second knockdown, a change to a heavy-weather spinnaker or boomed-out jib is certainly advisable, especially if weather and sea conditions are worsening. At sea, repeated knockdowns should not be allowed. Even when the hull and crew are sound and all vulnerable deck openings are closed, repeated spinnaker knockdowns impose tremendous stress on the rig. Not only is there danger of ripping sails and breaking booms, but the shock of a collapsed chute suddenly refilling with wind can put a dangerous load on the backstay and its fittings, not to mention the mast.

When a knockdown seems possible, a man should be standing by to slack the main boom vang instantly as the boat heels down. There is no quicker way to break a boom than to dip its end into a sea while its middle is bowsed down with a vang. As a matter of fact, when the mast is not raked aft considerably, offshore boats should have their mainsails fitted with antitripping reef points (see Figure 10-7) or simply a flattening reef grommet and earing on the lower leech in order to raise the outboard end of the boom. In a very fresh following breeze, lower the main and run under twin headsails alone, or, if rolling is severe, carry a storm trysail sheeted flat amidships (in addition to the twins) to help damp the motion.

Figure 11-5. *Broken booms are often caused by overly taut boom vangs, especially when the boom trips on a sea. (Morris Rosenfeld photo)*

It is easier to determine the proper time to reduce sail when the wind is on or forward of the beam. This judgment should largely be based on the vessel's angle of heel, but you must consider as well how the hull, rig, and crew are withstanding the strains of the heavy weather. If the boat is slamming violently into the seas, solid water is running over the decks, the cockpit is being filled, the mast is whipping excessively, the leeward rigging is overly slack, gear is breaking down under the strain, or the crew is exhausted and seasick, then the time has come to shorten sail, perhaps drastically.

Normally, the first steps in shortening sail are to set a smaller head-sail, reef the mainsail, and, on a modern yawl, lower the mizzen. When beating, however, don't lower the mizzen too soon as it will help prevent the bow from being knocked to leeward by the seas. A modern racing sloop with roller or jiffy reefing might reduce her main and keep up her large genoa jib on a short windward leg, but on a long beat at sea, it is usually better to change to a smaller genoa or a double-headed rig with staysail and jib topsail. A heavy-weather jib should have a short tack pendant to raise its foot well clear of the deck; otherwise it might scoop up seas. If the foot has a roach, it might be fitted with a grommet at its lowest point so that it can be lifted with a halyard or piece of shock cord fastened to a jib hank to keep it clear of the bow wave when reaching.

The basic principle of reducing sail when reaching and beating is to keep a balanced sail plan so that the boat will develop neither lee nor

Figure 11-6. *Four identical U.S. Naval Academy yawls using different heavy weather sail combinations. From left to right these are: No. 2 genoa, reefed main, and mizzen; No. 2 genoa and mizzen; No. 1 genoa and storm trysail; and No. 3 genoa and full main. The extreme left and right boats seem to have the more powerful combinations and more effective slots between sails for driving to windward in the prevailing wind and sea conditions. (Courtesy U.S. Naval Institute)*

excessive weather helm. In theory, the total center of effort should be in about the same location for the reduced plan as when whole sail is carried, but in actuality it is usually advisable to move the center of effort slightly forward, because most boats develop extra weather helm when heeled. This means that a greater amount of sail will be carried forward than aft. A great advantage in reefing a sail is that its CE moves automatically forward as its area shrinks.

Roller reefing has one advantage over conventional (reef-point) reefing in that it allows variable sail reduction. There is always the possibility, however, that the roller mechanism at the gooseneck will break down during a lengthy passage, so offshore boats should have an alternate reefing system, such as rows of reef points or eyelets for lacing lines in their working sails. If the boom fitted with roller reefing is not tapered to prevent its after end from drooping, as was discussed earlier, then tapered shims (wedge-shaped battens of wood) might be inserted at the leech as the sail is wound around the boom. If this is done, don't let the shims fly out of the sail when it is unrolled. A better idea might be to secure the shims to the boom permanently when droop is a serious problem. If the mast is fitted with a gooseneck slide on a track, don't slack off the halyard until the boom has been rolled up to the top of the track. Though this will raise the center of effort slightly, it will also allow ample clearance for the after end of the boom. Remember that reef points of conventional reefing should be passed around the foot of the sail, not around the boom, thus allowing the sail's foot to provide some elasticity or "give" to distribute the strain evenly over reef points. If the sail's foot is attached to the boom with a bolt rope in a groove, use a continuous lacing line spirally wound around the boom through the reefing eyelets in the sail. On offshore boats, the tack and especially the clew earings (the pendants that hold down the luff and leech of the reefed sail) should be permanently rigged so that reefing can be done as quickly and easily as possible.

The modern trend in reefing is the so-called jiffy system, in which a simple clew earing holds the reefed leech to the boom while the luff is usually held down with a hook at the gooseneck. There are relatively few reef points, and often the bunt is left hanging. Another variation is to connect the clew earing with a multipurchase downhaul as in Figure 11-7 so that sail can be reduced with a single reefing line. The gear needs to be strong for extended offshore use, and I think the bunt and the middle of the sail should be lashed to the boom or secured with shock cord as illustrated unless the reef is only temporary. In prolonged heavy weather, always secure the leech grommet to the boom with a back-up lashing in case the earing or cheek block fails. Sometimes jiffy and roller reefing can be combined so that the bunt can be rolled around the boom, making a strong, neat job that prevents the bunt from filling with water.

You can reduce sail area conveniently by roller furling the headsail. The sail rolls up on the rod, head foil, or stay to which it is attached when you haul on a furling line wound around a drum near the tack. Roller furling is not always appropriate, however, for a lengthy thrash offshore, especially upwind, when specialized headsails will do a better job. Then too, many roller furling jibs are not designed for sailing with the jib partially furled. There is always the possibility that roller sails will jam or unroll or a luff foil might break. A major problem with a partially rolled headsail is that there is no way to tension the luff, leaving too

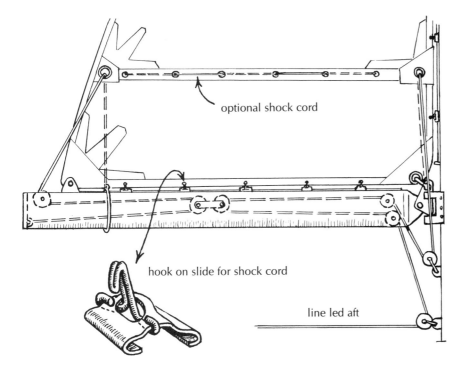

Figure 11-7. *Multipurchase one-line jiffy reefing.*

optional shock cord

hook on slide for shock cord

line led aft

Figure 11-8. *Jiffy reefing. In this photo sequence, first the mainsail is luffed and the halyard eased off until the reefing grommet at the tack is fitted on the hook above the gooseneck. Next, the tack is secured and the reef line taken in, after which the cockpit crew winches the first reef clew cringle down to the boom, and the halyard starts back up. Finally, the sail is trimmed after the luff tension is judged correct. The last photo shows the yawl under single-reefed mainsail, mizzen, and Number 2 genoa. (Photos by Bill Brooks; from* Sail and Power, *3rd edition, by Richard Henderson, Naval Institute Press, 1979)*

much draft too far aft. Partial solutions include North Sail's Aeroluff (a mid-luff rotating bolt rope), a foam-padded luff, and the double-swivel drum (allowing the head and tack to lag behind the foil as it turns) used in the Hood and Harken systems. Roller jibs seem most appropriate for off-the-wind sailing and when the vessel is cutter-rigged with a hanked-on inner staysail. Twin headsails that roller furl on wire luffs have been used successfully for easy downwind cruising and even trade-wind passages since 1930, when the rig was first introduced by Captain Otway Waller.

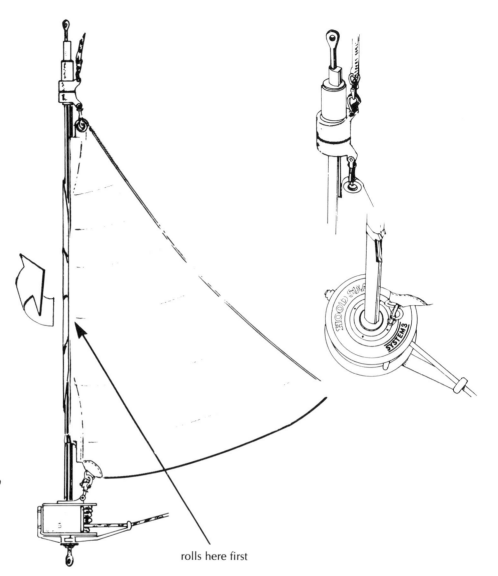

Figure 11-9. *A Sea Furl system with double swivel action permitting the foil to turn ahead of the tack and head, thereby removing a slight amount of camber. (Courtesy Hood Yacht Systems)*

rolls here first

When wind and seas necessitate a further reduction of sail, put in deeper reefs and bend on smaller headsails. A sloop without roller furling can carry a small, flat working jib or large storm jib forward of the mast, whereas a cutter might carry her working staysail without a jib. A modern yawl with a small mizzen sailing off the wind should probably have her mizzen furled and carry a reefed main and small jib, or a staysail if she is double-head rigged. A ketch might carry the same combination but with a reefed mizzen, but a double-head ketch may balance well under main and staysail, thereby avoiding the need to reef except in a hard blow. A schooner could carry a small jib, foresail or main staysail, and a deeply reefed mainsail. Many sail combinations are possible, and some experimentation is often necessary to find the best plan for each boat. In choosing the right combination bear in mind the sail-reduction principles: lower the center of effort and maintain balance; keep some sail bent to the after side of the mainmast to minimize pumping in head seas; try to keep the rig somewhat centralized (not spread out to the extent that no sail is amidships while large sails are at the boat's extremities); and raise the foot of any heavy-weather sail, particularly one at the bow or stern.

When sail reductions are necessary, don't delay. Not only does a boat lose speed and risk damage when she is overburdened, procrastination increases the difficulty of shortening down.

Further reduction of sail would require the storm trysail or Swedish mainsail (mentioned earlier) and a small storm jib, or spitfire as it is sometimes called. The Swedish mainsail is often the best sail when it is necessary to drive a long distance to windward or claw off a lee shore. The standard storm trysail may be sheeted to the main boom, and it will give some drive, but the sail is primarily for heaving-to. Storm jibs should be cut flat, with tack pendants of ample length to keep them well above the deck. In general, storm sails need not be much heavier than working sails because their areas are so small. Soft Dacron is the most suitable material, with triple-stitched and possibly glued seams when chafe is anticipated. It is better to tie the sheet to a storm sail with a bowline to eliminate the risk of a crewmember being struck in the head by a metal shackle. Avoid using snatch blocks for storm-jib sheet leads, as they have been known to open when the sail shakes.

When sailing in heavy weather, make frequent checks on the condition of the hull, rig, and fittings. Look at the bilge periodically to determine if the hull is leaking. Sight up the mast occasionally to make sure it is not whipping violently or bending seriously. An especially important part of the mast to check for bending is that point near the head of the storm trysail or reefed main, which may exert a considerable pull aft. It is best to raise the trysail or reef the main to a point where its head is nearly opposite a shroud or forestay that counteracts the pull aft. In addition, make frequent checks to see that spreaders are not sagging or working loose; turnbuckles are not coming unscrewed; mast and sheet lead tracks are not bending; halyards are not chafing, wrapping or fouling aloft; sail slides or hanks are not popping off; the jib is not scooping up waves; no sail seam is beginning to split; and so forth. If the motion permits, it is often a good plan to look at the heads of sails through binoculars. Headboards occasionally pull off, and then there is the devil to pay in retrieving the halyard. For this reason, it is sometimes wise to rig downhauls on the halyards before bad weather commences. Downhauls are also valuable in lowering jibs, which tend to blow upward due to the slant of the jibstay. By all means, do not let sails flog in a real breeze of wind as this is a sure way to damage them. A fairly new Dacron sail of proper weight and construction with unchafed seams will rarely blow out in almost any strength of wind if kept full and not allowed to flap. Carry ample heavy weather sails aboard in case it becomes necessary to replace blown-out or damaged sails.

Figure 11-10. *Adlard Coles's* Cohoe, *a Tumlare-type narrow double-ender using a double-slot heavy weather rig. (Bill Kuenzel photo)*

Sailing in a prolonged blow at sea is seldom pleasant, but it is made more bearable when the skipper and crew have confidence in the soundness of their sails and rigging. In general, a sound rig is one engineered with a large margin of safety and made of proven materials, with the primary emphasis on strength and reliability while low windage and light weight are merely secondary considerations. The skipper (or designer or builder) who chooses a flimsy rig over a strong one in hopes of gaining a slight advantage over his competition in fair-weather racing may sorely regret his choice when sailing in heavy weather offshore.

Chapter 12
SAILBOAT MANAGEMENT IN GALES OFFSHORE

Any boat that frequently ventures far offshore stands a good chance of encountering a real blow with heavy seas sooner or later. So far from shelter, the vessel has no recourse but to take her punishment, and her skipper faces a critical decision: What boat handling tactic will result in the least damage? The decision is rarely easy, and the variety of alternatives and advice given by seamanship manuals and experienced sailors often seems confusing and even conflicting. Hard and fast rules for offshore storm management are impossible given the variables involved: the design, displacement, rig, and construction of the boat; her location with respect to a lee shore, shoal water, offshore current, and the storm; the number and fitness of the crew; the nature and severity of the weather disturbance; and the size and character of the seas. Consider these five courses of action for sailboats in extremely heavy weather at sea: (1) pressing on under reduced sail, (2) heaving to under reduced sail, (3) lying a-hull under bare poles, (4) riding to a sea anchor (either from the bow or stern), and (5) scudding (running off with little or no sail and with or without drags astern). Each of these tactics will be discussed separately, with consideration of the conditions and circumstances that affect the choice. Still another course of action is "dodging," or driving slowly into the seas under auxiliary power, but in a severe storm this requires a sizable engine and prop. It is principally a powerboat tactic and will be discussed in the next chapter.

Pressing on Under Reduced Sail

Methods of progressively shortening sail in increasing wind and seas were discussed in the last chapter. A nonracing cruiser far offshore should reduce sail early, but a racing yacht will carry on under the fastest sail combination, without shortening down or heaving to, for the longest possible time. The task then is to determine the exact point at which high-speed sailing begins to involve an undue element of risk. Factors that influence the judgment were discussed in the last chapter. Some of today's ocean-racing skippers, sailing modern light-displacement boats, believe that there is safety in speed when the course is downwind, as we'll discuss later in the section entitled "Scudding."

With his normally large crew including a number of skilled helmsmen, the ocean racer is often able to press on under full or reduced sail for a much longer time than a cruising yacht of similar size. All skippers, however, must contend with sickness and fatigue. Seasickness can knock a crewmember off his or her feet, whereas fatigue can cause carelessness, an inability to steer and reef or change sails, and even hallucinations. The crew must get all the rest they can, take seasickness medication well in advance of bad weather, and have adequate nourishment in the form of quick energy food and hot drinks (preferably prepared before the blow and kept in thermos bottles). It is wise to stow warm articles of clothing in plastic bags to keep them dry during the blow. Other preparations for heavy weather were discussed in Chapter 9.

In deciding whether or not to press on, give primary consideration to the vessel's location. If she is near a lee shore with the weather deteriorating, then she must drive to weather in order to get all the sea room possible. This conveys at least one advantage in that the bow can be held fairly close to the seas to minimize the risk of being rolled over. On the other hand, the boat may heel and slam excessively or be swept by green water. Large, narrow boats with moderately fine, flared bows and an efficient lateral plane are usually best suited to the tactic. To reduce pounding and rooting, keep your speed no greater than that required for good steering control. Disadvantages of the tactic include violent motion, possible damage from seas breaking aboard, the risk of being thrown aback with possible damage to sails or rudder, and the need to man the helm continually. Sometimes a boat can be effectively motorsailed to windward, though great care must be taken to see that lines don't wash overboard and foul the prop.

Because the normal ocean racer is more weatherly and better able to claw off a lee shore than the average sailing cruiser, she may not need to alter course radically from the rhumb line. Facing the possibility of a full gale, however, even a racer will want to gain a decent offing. Some ocean racing sponsors provide escort vessels that may be able to aid a racer in trouble, but remember that even if signal contact (flares or radio) can be made, rescue at sea in a storm is extremely difficult, and it might be impossible for the escort to reach a yacht grounded on a lee shore.

As a matter of fact, in bad weather any shore can be dangerous, even one to windward that reduces fetch. A wind shift may put the shore to leeward, and if it is high and mountainous, it can produce strong gusts (called williwaws in cold areas) that fall on the water with tremendous force soon after passing over the mountains. Shoal water can turn relatively harmless deep-water waves into dangerously short breaking seas, and strong coastal currents can produce ugly seas in bad weather, especially when the wind opposes the current's flow.

Consider the vessel's location with respect to the track of the storm.

Figure 12-1. *The sequence of pictures on the following pages dramatically illustrates why the words ''lee shore'' fill the hearts of many coastal sailors with dread. The boat shown was reduced to kindling within an hour after grounding on the coast of Normandy. (Courtesy Edward Tadros)*

Sea Sense

Most severe storms are circular, and they usually travel in somewhat predictable paths. Listen to weather reports and continually observe the sky, barometer, and wind direction as outlined in Chapter 9. If the vessel is not headed for dangerously shoal water or a lee shore and she can keep sailing without undue risk of damage, then she should attempt to move away from the storm, out of its path and into the safest sector.

If you decide to press on, keep careful track of your position through dead reckoning and/or radio navigation (RDF, loran, satnav, GPS, or Decca). The weather will probably preclude celestial navigation. To assure reasonable dead reckoning accuracy, the helmsman should continually note the compass heading while the navigator consults the speed indicator or taffrail log (or estimates the boat's speed) and keeps track of the time spent on each heading. Make allowance for current, and estimate leeway. In heavy weather, it is almost impossible for the helmsman to hold a steady course on any point of sailing—after all, his primary concern is to avoid dangerous seas—but he can average his course changes by heading up briefly during a smooth after he has been forced to bear off, or bearing off after being forced to head up. Remember that leeway may be considerable in heavy winds and rough seas.

Heaving to Under Sail

When a boat is being damaged by shipping solid water and not merely spray, when the hull is leaking or showing signs of stress, when the sails or rigging are suffering strain or damaged, when steering is extremely difficult or any play begins to develop in the helm, when there is a strong tendency to broach-to or take extreme knockdowns, or when the crew is sick and exhausted, the skipper should reduce sail further and slow headway or almost stop. In such a case, unless the desired course lies downwind and the boat can be made to run off comfortably under bare poles or greatly reduced sail, she should probably heave-to. In a broad sense, heaving to implies stopping headway by any means other than anchoring or mooring. In the strictest sense, a vessel is said to be hove-to when she lies nearly dead in the water with the wind and seas between beam on and broad on the bow or somewhat farther ahead, while she carries a single storm sail or, most often, counteracting sails, one trimmed to work against another, so as to lessen headway or forereaching. Heaving to in this manner is very often the next step to take when it becomes too rough to press on, particularly when the desired course is to windward or there is insufficient sea room to run off.

The classic means of heaving to is to carry a small spitfire jib or storm staysail sheeted to windward, counteracting the drive of a deeply reefed mainsail or storm trysail (Figure 12-2). Normally, the helm is lashed down so that when the trysail or reefed main, which is sheeted in flat, drives the boat slowly ahead, the rudder turns her toward the wind. When the trysail or main begins to luff, the backed jib slows headway and forces the bow off until the main or trysail fills again. In the mean-

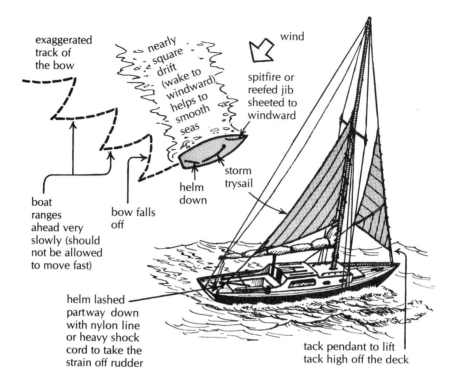

nearly square drift (wake to windward) helps to smooth seas

exaggerated track of the bow

wind

spitfire or reefed jib sheeted to windward

storm trysail

helm down

boat ranges ahead very slowly (should not be allowed to move fast)

bow falls off

helm lashed partway down with nylon line or heavy shock cord to take the strain off rudder

tack pendant to lift tack high off the deck

Figure 12-2. *Heaving to under sail. When there is an inner forestay, the spitfire should be used as a forestaysail.*

time, the boat makes substantial leeway because her headway is nearly stopped, she is heeled, and her keel is stalled (not supplying lift). This leaves a noticeable wake to windward, which in moderately heavy weather may smooth the seas slightly and possibly encourage them to break before they reach the boat. The less she forereaches and the more leeway she makes, the more effective her drift-wake to windward will be, but still the effect may be overrated in very heavy weather. I think the main advantages of heaving to are to reduce headway (in order to allow riding over rather than smashing into the seas), put the boat in an advantageous attitude to the waves, and allow her to retreat from or yield to the seas. Leeway or drift might be as much as two knots or more but will vary with the boat; a shoal-draft centerboarder with board up will make more leeway than a deep-keel boat with great lateral plane. A shoal-draft boat generally should be hove-to with the board up or only slightly down—no deeper than necessary for balance, because greater depth might cause the boat to trip on her board and suffer a knockdown or even bend the board. If the boat were rolled, a lowered board could fall into the well and cause damage. Most centerboard boats have short stability ranges and should not lie beam-to breaking seas.

The details of heaving to under sail vary greatly with individual boats and their rigs. Usually the center of effort (CE) of the reduced sail plan should be kept near or abaft the total center of effort (TCE, the center of effort of the full working sail plan). Seldom should the reduced CE be more than slightly forward of the TCE, or the boat may pay off and pick up speed even with the helm lashed down. Proper balance often dictates using a small staysail sheeted to windward rather than a storm jib; the staysail, being farther aft in the middle of the foredeck, is also easier for the crew to handle. Increased headway with the CE too far forward could deprive the hull of time needed to lift to the seas and would improve the keel's lateral resistance, thus reducing leeway and leaving the boat more vulnerable to beam seas. In other words, the boat would tend to plow into the seas and not yield to them.

This unhappy situation is exemplified by the experience of Fred M. Slavic's *Nightingale*, a 44-foot Sparkman-and-Stephens keel yawl, in a Force 9 gale (see the Beaufort scale in Appendix E). The *Nightingale* was comfortably hove-to in the Bay of Biscay under mizzen and backed storm jib, with her helm down, when suddenly she was rolled and damaged by a huge sea. The yawl had weathered several prior gales successfully under bare poles or with the storm trysail and spitfire, but on this occasion, Slavic theorized, the mizzen sheet let go, and the removal of wind pressure on the after sail (which moved the CE far forward) caused the boat to bear off and pick up headway. She then plunged her bow into a sea and was rolled down to an extreme angle of heel. The sea that did the damage may have been an unusually large rogue or freak wave, but still the *Nightingale* could have fared better with her bow closer to the wind and especially with less headway. This experience also shows us that if it is necessary to heave-to under two counteracting sails spread far apart on opposite sides of the designed CE, the after sail and its gear must be amply strong. If the forward sail blows out, there is probably little danger unless the boat turns so far that she lies head to wind, in which position the rudder could be damaged by the boat making sternway with the helm lashed down, or the mizzen could split from violent flogging. Any sail carried far aft or forward in extreme weather must be raised high enough to avoid a sea breaking against its foot.

Some boats will lie-to reasonably well with only a riding sail aft. A ketch might carry a reefed mizzen or storm trysail set on her mizzenmast. A yawl with a small, high-footed mizzen might carry it unreefed, but a smaller, strongly made storm mizzen cut very flat is usually better. Wright Britton, a winner of the Cruising Club of America's Blue Water Medal, claims that his yawl, *Delight*, a *Finisterre*-type centerboarder, will lie-to comfortably with her bow close to the wind under mizzen alone and with the helm loosely lashed amidships with shock cord. The *Delight* once weathered a 19-day succession of gales in this manner in waters east of Iceland. But again, this tactic is untenable if it causes the mizzen to flog violently or the boat to back down on her rudder.

Many a modern yawl with cut-away forefoot and small mizzen will not hold close to the wind under mizzen alone. Some will head little, if any, higher than beam to the wind and seas. Heaving to in this manner requires a high mizzen boom and strong rigging, stronger than that found on many racing yawls. Humphrey Barton has stated that when the mizzen is carried in extremely heavy weather, most yawls and ketches he

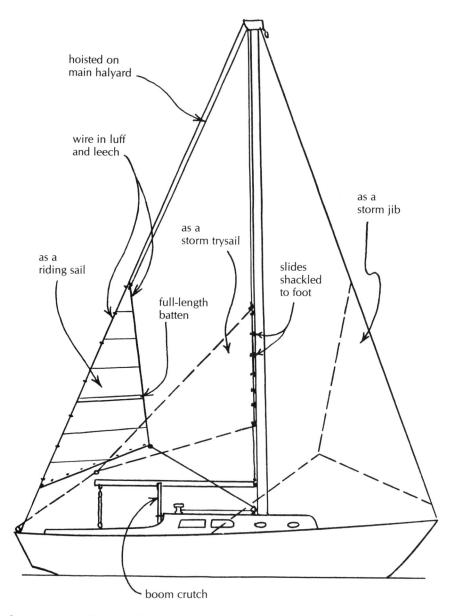

hoisted on
main halyard

wire in luff
and leech

as a
storm trysail

as a
storm jib

slides
shackled
to foot

as a
riding sail

full-length
batten

Figure 12-3. *A
triple-purpose storm sail.*

boom crutch

has seen need a special mizzen forestay to hold the mast forward and
counteract the mizzen's backward pull. A satisfactory substitute may be
a jumper stay to the mainmast head or a strut from the mizzenmast head
to the main permanent backstay, but on such rigs, if the mainmast ever
goes by the board it will probably take the mizzen with it.

On boats with no mizzenmast, a riding sail might be rigged on the
permanent backstay provided that stay is strong enough. The sail illustrated in Figure 12-3 is cut flat and has a full-length removable plastic or
fiberglass batten and wires in the luff and leech, all of which strengthen
the sail and keep it quiet. The hoped-for result is a versatile sail, one that

will serve primarily as a riding sail but can double as a storm trysail when its foot is secured to the mast or a spitfire jib when it is turned backward and hanked to the jibstay. I use this sail as a storm staysail. Some sailors object to battens in storm sails, but they help prevent flogging and the rapid leech flutter that can damage a sail in strong winds. Good flexible plastic or fiberglass battens are almost unbreakable, and short battens can be permanently sewn into a sail to prevent their working loose.

A great advantage of the storm trysail over a reefed mainsail is that it need not be secured to the main boom and thus may be trimmed similarly to a jib with a pair of sheets, one leading to the deck on either side of the boat. If a jibe were necessary in heavy weather, a boomless trysail would impose less strain and shock than a trysail sheeted to the boom. At other times, such as when the trysail is used in conjunction with other sails to impart headway while beating to windward, it may be advantageous to secure its clew to the boom and trim with the mainsheet, thus avoiding the necessity of casting off one sheet and hauling in the other on every tack. The weight of the boom and the leverage of a boom-end mainsheet can put quite a strain on the sail, so it is important to set up a bit on the topping lift. If the trysail is trimmed to the side decks, be sure that the lead blocks are secured to through-bolted eye straps. Some genoa tracks that are not through-bolted cannot accept the strain of a storm trysail sheet.

A trysail for really heavy weather should be considerably smaller than the deeply reefed mainsail. Its recommended size in square feet is .05 times the square of the mainsail's unreefed luff length. The head of the sail should come fairly close to the spreader sockets (given a single set of spreaders on the mainmast), or more generally to the point where forward lower shrouds (or a baby stay) attach to the mast, so that the head's after pull is opposed by the pull of the shrouds or stay to prevent the mast from bending. If the trysail is higher, then its head should probably be near the forestay attachment.

A tack pendant should keep the sail well above the furled mainsail, and the clew should be slightly higher than the main boom (in normal topped-up position) so that it can make fast there or, when sheeted to the deck, clear the boom in its crutch during tacks.

There are several ways to secure a trysail to the mast. Parrel lines were preferred once. Fitted with beads or wooden rollers to reduce friction when the sail was hoisted (see Figure 12-4), these lashings passed around the mast. Sometimes the beads were omitted, and the parrel lines were replaced by a single lacing line passed diagonally around the mast, back and forth (not in a spiral) between grommets as illustrated. The slant of the line in the latter method reduces friction, but not as much as do parrel beads. Nowadays, trysail luffs are usually secured to the mast with slides on a mast track.

Sometimes the trysail track is a short section, just long enough to accommodate all the luff slides when the sail is lowered, and a switch

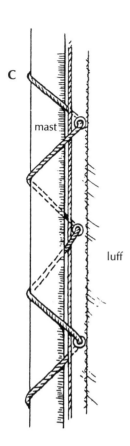

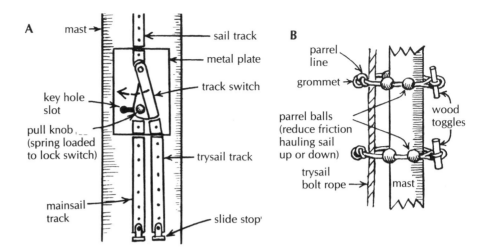

A

mast → | sail track
metal plate
track switch
key hole slot
pull knob (spring loaded to lock switch)
trysail track
mainsail track
slide stop

B

parrel line
grommet →
parrel balls (reduce friction hauling sail up or down)
wood toggles
trysail bolt rope →
mast

C

mast
luff

Figure 12-4. *Methods of attachment of a trysail to a mast.*

above routes the slides over to the main track after the mainsail has been lowered (see Figure 12-4). It is better, however, to have two full-length, side-by-side mast tracks, one for the mainsail and one for the trysail, thus decreasing the chance of the luff slides' jamming when sail is hoisted. Offshore you can leave the trysail permanently bent on its track and stowed in a small bag, immediately available. Most boats use the main halyard to hoist the trysail, but an extra halyard running through a block hung from the backstay crane permits the trysail to be hoisted before the main is lowered, saving time and keeping the mast continually well supported. If nylon slides are used, be sure they are extra-heavy. See that the trysail track is bolted to the mast at the normal position of the sail's head.

Traditionally, the storm trysail is cut vertically (with the cloth panels parallel to the leech) to give it great strength while minimizing bias stretch at the leech. Some modern trysails are miter-cut, with the panels at right angles to the foot and leech, minimizing bias stretch at the foot as well as the leech. This may create greater stress at some of the seams, so it is often good to have them glued as well as sewn. Because it is so small, a trysail need not be extremely heavy, and many sailmakers recommend a cloth weight similar to the mainsail's. By the same reasoning, the spitfire need not be extra-heavy when it is made of Dacron. The old-time storm sails of soft cotton were a delight to handle but lacked the strength of modern synthetic sails. Some years ago, after setting a cotton trysail, I was praising its softness and resistance to violent flogging when all at once it exploded into ribbons. Since then I have cheerfully put up with the comparatively slippery stiffness of Dacron, thankful for its extra strength and resistance to rot. If you are not overly concerned about stretch, and there is no reason you should be unless you are racing, then try unresinated Dacron (with relatively little resin filler); it is moderately soft and fairly easy to handle.

The most satisfactory method of heaving to can only be discovered with experimentation. The rig, the underwater shape of the hull, and the windage of the deckhouse and topsides all figure in the most effective reduced sail plan. Boats with keels that are cut away forward will normally tend to fall off the wind, prompting the helm to be lashed down farther and the CE of the storm sails to be moved farther aft. On my sloop, an Ohlson 38, which has a cut-away forefoot and her mast quite far aft, I rig a temporary stay to the mid-foredeck before going offshore. A small storm staysail can be hanked there in heavy weather, moving the CE farther aft to improve balance. Attached to the foredeck eye strap with a pelican hook, the stay can easily be disconnected when not in use and carried aft to lash to a shroud. Moderately heavy boats with long keels might heave-to easily and look after themselves, but lively fin-keelers are often hard to control, wanting to fall off the wind and fore-reach. Such a boat may need her helm lashed hard over, and her spitfire (storm headsail) should be very small: Rod Stephens recommends .025 times the square of the height of the foretriangle. The trysail should be trimmed in flat about 10 degrees off the boat's centerline.

A cutter or a modern sloop with a large foretriangle might lie-to under a backed spitfire or storm staysail in combination with a storm trysail. Alternatively, any single-masted boat might use the riding sail hanked to the backstay, either alone or in combination with a backed storm staysail. A schooner might carry a storm forestaysail with a main storm trysail, or a reefed foresail alone. A yawl or ketch might lie-to under the storm trysail alone, the storm mizzen alone, or (in the case of a modern yawl with a large base to her foretriangle) the storm staysail and trysail. All sorts of combinations are possible, especially when the rig is divided. Spaulding Dunbar, a naval architect, once told me that he hove-to successfully in a lengthy gale with a small jib hanked to the leeward lower shroud. The sail plan also depends on the wind velocity: Generally speaking, the stronger the wind, the less sail the boat should carry.

The main objectives are to reduce headway, hold the bow fairly high, and prevent the sails from flogging themselves to shreds. Experiment *before* you are caught in a gale, by taking your boat out in a moderate blow with a good crew and proper storm sails and trying out various sail combinations. Not only will you glean clues concerning your boat's heavy weather behavior, you'll get some sail-handling practice for the "real McCoy." In a gale at sea, especially when shorthanded, sail-changing experiments are extremely difficult. You should have at least some idea beforehand how your boat will behave.

Lying A-hull

When the wind increases to such an extent that sails cannot be carried or the boat's headway cannot be slowed, it is time to remove sail. At this point a common tactic is hulling, or lying a-hull, whereby the boat is simply left to drift and look after herself under bare poles. Since new, properly made Dacron sails will not easily blow out if they are not allowed to flog, the desire to depower and stop headway, rather than concern over sail damage, initiates this tactic, but the height of the seas and condition of the crew also affect the decision. High seas can blanket sails in the troughs and perhaps expose the boat to dangerous knockdowns on the crests, and bare-poling makes sense also when the vessel is shorthanded and her crew is sick or exhausted, because the helm can be abandoned after it is lashed alee while the crew battens down and then retires to the cabin.

Although hulling has been practiced since early times, some seamen, especially many longtime small-craft sailors, are opposed to letting a boat "wallow in the trough" or lie broadside to the seas, as most boats will do when left to drift freely. In this position, a small boat, especially one having a low stability range, is vulnerable to capsizing. Nevertheless, Tom Day, Marin-Marie, Jean Gau, John Guzzwell, Clare Francis, Maurice Cloughly, Chris Loehr, Chay Blyth, Bill Howell, Sheldon Kinney, Alec Rose, Adlard Coles, and other veteran sailors have endorsed the tactic. Coles, the author of *Heavy Weather Sailing* (3rd Edition, John de Graff, 1981), wrote: "It is difficult to draw the line between what is safe and what is dangerous, but countless yachts have weathered ordinary gales by lying a-hull and I personally propose to continue the practice up to the point where I consider the situation is getting out of hand." It is also interesting that most of the voyagers interviewed by Jimmy Cornell for his book *Ocean Cruising Survey* (Sheridan House, 1986) preferred the hulling tactic. Cornell wrote: "Every one of the skippers I spoke to, who had weathered extreme conditions by dropping all sail, lying a-hull, battening down, and leaving the boat to look after itself, stressed the wisdom of such an action and found this tactic more satisfactory than trying to battle the elements."

One of the first American yachtsmen to advocate and publicize hulling was Thomas Fleming Day, the editor of *Rudder* magazine, who made an early Atlantic crossing in the 25-foot yawl *Seabird*. In 1911 he wrote, "My long experience in small boats has taught me this: that if a boat is a good boat, when real trouble comes she is best let alone. She knows better what to do than you, and if you leave her alone, she will do the right thing; whereas nine times out of ten you will do the wrong." This same general philosophy is expressed in a different way by William Albert Robinson, the circumnavigator. In his book, *To the Great Southern Sea*, Robinson speaks of a vessel's "drift tendency," and how it is important in extremely heavy weather to let a boat drift the way she will, whether her attitude is beam-on or stern-to the wind and seas. He suggests that the best seamanship is that which encourages rather than fights this natural tendency. Drifting freely, a boat will back away and yield to the seas, as a boxer rolls with the punches.

A boat's natural drift attitude (I prefer the word *attitude* rather than *tendency* to describe a boat's position relative to the wind while she drifts freely) depends on her underwater shape and the windage of her hull, deckhouse, and rig, but is not always entirely predictable. Some boats that look as though they might fall off the wind and begin to run with the helm unattended will actually lie fairly close to beam-on. Naval architect and aerodynamicist Walter J. Bloemhard gives us a clue when he tells us that elongated bodies traveling in the direction of their longitudinal axis tend to be unstable, and the natural attitude of a flat plate in a flow is to lie across the flow. Bloemhard goes on to say that when the normal sailboat is brought broadside to the wind with her sails let completely out (with no forward and little side pressure on them), she is directionally stable and will not turn her bow to port or starboard. Commander D.A. Rayner, who wrote the book *Safety in Small Craft*, is more dogmatic. He says that an untended boat with normal hull shape, keel, masts, etc. will lie beam-on and "nothing on earth will stop her doing so." I think this is overstating it a little, since some boats with short keels located aft and considerable windage forward will undoubtedly lie with their quarters more or less up to the wind, and a very few with deep forefoots and windage aft will lie with the wind forward of the beam. As a matter of fact, some boats constantly change attitudes while hulling, but by and large the wind and seas are mostly on the beam.

Seamen who oppose lying a-hull in bad weather argue that when beam-on, a boat is more vulnerable to the seas because most of the hull is exposed, and she is in danger of being rolled by a large breaking sea. Some experienced blue-water sailors, such as Eric Hiscock, Erroll Bruce, and Humphrey Barton, have said that they approve of hulling up to a certain point, perhaps to Force 9 winds (depending on the type of boat and the particular weather and sea conditions). Not long ago, Hal Roth, author of *After 50,000 Miles*, wrote me that although he approves of lying a-hull in gales with regular waves, he likens a small boat using this tactic in irregular waves to a peanut under an elephant's foot.

Despite the arguments against it, there are sound reasons for using the tactic up to a whole gale when the seas are not extremely confused, and there are even arguments for hulling in survival conditions (the most extreme bad weather). The boat presents her maximum buoyancy to the seas; headway can be kept to a minimum, especially as compared with scudding; backing down on the rudder is minimal when compared with holding the bow up; sails are not subject to damage; there is little danger of broaching or pitch-poling (somersaulting end-over-end), as there is when running before it; the boat will yield to the seas by making leeway to a much greater extent than if she were held by a sea anchor; and drift is not extreme (a definite advantage when near shore), as compared with drift when running off. Buoyancy is obviously important in allowing the vessel to lift to the seas rather than shipping them aboard. Forereaching can be dangerous, because the boat may drive into a sea even if she lies beam-on, and headway tends to reduce leeway so that the boat will not readily yield to the seas.

Some boats (usually racing types) make considerable headway beam-on, even under bare poles, and if a boat tends to bear off with helm unattended, she will pick up forward speed; therefore, it is customary to lash the helm down when hulling. With the rudder turned to windward, any headway will make the boat turn toward the wind, slowing forward progress. A few boats have been known to make sternway when hulling; if such is the case, special precautions should be taken with lashing the tiller or even the rudder itself. We will return to this when we discuss riding to a sea anchor off the bow, a tactic which leaves the rudder especially vulnerable.

Comparing lying a-hull with broaching to, you might argue that a vessel is in approximately the same attitude with respect to wind and seas in both cases. There are important differences, however. A boat lying a-hull is in a directionally stable position drifting sideways, but a broach is associated with forward speed downwind, which results in a sudden turn to bring the boat broadside to the seas. The centrifugal force of the turn adds to the heeling moment produced by the wind and seas, and the vessel that broaches is often carrying at least some sail, which further adds to the heeling moment. Finally, her headway decreases leeway, giving her less opportunity to rise to the seas and reducing her ability to yield.

Some sailors fear structural damage on the exposed hull side, but at the crest of a wave a boat should heel sufficiently to present the rounded turn of her bilge to breaking water. This part of a vessel is usually very strong, and in taking the brunt of a sea it lessens the remaining force that would strike against a weaker part, such as the cabin house. Also, the boat will be side-slipping and yielding to wave smashes, while her drift wake will encourage the waves to break before they reach the boat.

The vessel may roll violently, and this is one reason for heaving to under sail while it is possible to do so. When the wind is so strong that carrying sail is impossible, however, there is often sufficient wind pressure on the masts and rigging to dampen rolling. Rod Stephens, Jr. wrote me, "It seems that lying a-hull is generally a satisfactory expedient when it is really too severe to carry any sail, but this presupposes a wind that will keep the boat pretty steady by virtue of the pressure on the spars, and in less than extreme conditions it would be very undesirable rolling to weather." In high, steep seas the vessel is apt to be becalmed in the troughs, and with her keel immersed in the backward-moving water particles she will roll to weather. The motion might be tolerable if the wave (or wavelet) period and the boat's period of roll do not coincide in such a way that accumulative or rhythmic rolling begins to develop. Unless normal (nonaccumulative) rolling is extreme, the motion will be more uncomfortable than dangerous. As with heaving to, a boat's behavior when lying beam-on in a particular wind and sea can only really be determined through trial.

Hulling seems most appropriate when the following conditions can be met: (1) the boat has a high range of stability; (2) she is strongly built with a round hull, low cabin trunk, and moderately high freeboard, and if she has a skeg or fin keel, the structure is nonvulnerable; (3) the keel is of such a shape and depth that it permits ample leeway when the boat has no headway; (4) the boat is directionally stable when lying beam-on, and her headway is controllable; (5) the seas are of the deep-water kind, long and with spilling rather than plunging breakers; (6) the wind is not strong enough to cause prolonged extreme heeling under bare poles; (7) the wave period and period of roll do not reinforce each other to produce accumulative rolling; (8) the boat has a tall mast with sufficient weight aloft to favorably affect her roll inertia; and (9) all of her heavy gear below and on deck is stowed with sufficient security to withstand a capsize. As to the first point, a boat has the least transverse stability (she is most tender) when beam-to wind and seas; therefore, it is of the utmost importance that she have a high range of stability if she is to lie a-hull. A range of 140 degrees or higher is most desirable, as this increases the chance of staying upright and helps assure prompt recovery in the event of a capsize. Think twice about hulling in breaking seas with a boat having a stability range less than 130 degrees. A fairly low initial stability is not dangerous, and it may even alleviate extremely quick rolling and help expose the sturdy turn of the bilge, but ultimate stability is vital.

A sailor who is unfortunate enough to be caught in the most extreme survival conditions at sea should be prepared for the worst. Although it is possible for seas to severely damage an upright boat, about the worst that could happen when running off is pitch-poling, but the worst when hulling is capsizing or turning turtle. The boat must have the necessary ballast and a sufficiently low center of gravity to recover from a bottom-up position; otherwise I don't think hulling in a severe storm is worth the risk. A boat lacking ultimate stability will probably stand a better chance of keeping her feet if she can be kept end-to the seas in such weather. When hulling, the crew should expect an occasional extreme, perhaps momentary, knockdown, even when the boat has ample stability. Many injuries have been inflicted in the cabin during knockdowns because heavy gear was not properly stowed or the crew not adequately secured in their bunks. In extreme conditions, ordinary bunk boards may not suffice. Bunks should perhaps be equipped with automobile-type seat belts.

When Jerry Cartwright was sailing the 29-foot Cascade sloop *Scuffler* in the 1969 Singlehander's Transpacific Race, he sustained a fractured skull and partial loss of memory from being thrown from his bunk. It is almost a miracle that he made it alone safely to Hawaii. The *Scuffler* is a light-displacement fin-keeler, and although somewhat tender, she lay a-hull successfully in winds up to 50 knots. On one occasion, she took a severe knockdown while hulling, but she recovered without damage to hull or rig.

A major problem in the 1979 Fastnet storm was lack of security in the cabin. When the racers were knocked down, heavy gear and other objects were thrown about to such an extent that cabins became uninhabitable. All heavy gear must be secured, and small items must be contained by well-fiddled shelves or latched lockers to withstand a 180-degree inversion. The vast majority of offshore boats are drastically deficient in this respect.

In considering the hull characteristics most suitable for lying a-hull, I think a low, strong cabin trunk with small windows is of tremendous importance. High deckhouses are especially vulnerable to seas breaking aboard, and surprisingly, the leeward side of the trunk is what is usually damaged during a violent knockdown. On seagoing boats, cabin trunks should be molded to the deck or strongly secured with bolts or metal straps, and it certainly helps if the trunk has a rounded shape. Many windows on modern yachts are dangerously large. They should be small, strongly secured with metal frames, equipped with storm shutters, and made of heavy Plexiglas, Lexan, safety glass, or even bullet-proof glass for the very worst conditions. Cabintops need a definite crown and should be heavily reinforced. On some boats, dodger coamings forward of the companionway add considerable strength to the roof. Full bulkheads and vertical grab posts also lend support and prevent oil-canning or inversion of the cabintop.

Excessive freeboard imposes a penalty in windage, weight above the waterline, and vulnerability to seas, but the topsides should be high enough for ample reserve buoyancy and reserve stability, which delays submerging the rail. I believe that if the rail is deeply buried when hulling, a well-placed sea against the boat's windward side and bottom could produce a capsizing force. The boat must be strongly built, an objective to which rounded topsides with moderate tumblehome contribute. One has only to observe how offshore lighthouses are rounded to stand up to years of awesome pounding. Another advantage of reasonably high freeboard (combined with a fairly straight or reversed sheer) is that it allows the use of a small cabin trunk in a small to medium-sized boat without sacrificing headroom below.

Many moderately light-displacement boats are suited to hulling because a light hull has great buoyancy and will rise easily and give to the seas. This certainly does not mean, however, that heavy boats are unsuited to the tactic. Sir Alex Rose, who made an outstanding one-stop solo circumnavigation in 1967 and 1968, is a great advocate of hulling, and his vessel, the 36-foot *Lively Lady*, was of considerable displacement. In accordance with the simple capsize screening formula given in Chapter 1, a heavy hull of narrow beam is highly resistant to capsizing, and its deeper underbody allows a lower cabin trunk without sacrifice to headroom below decks.

The combination of draft with the area and shape of the lateral plane also affects the success of lying a-hull. What we want is little lateral resistance (when there is no headway) combined with sufficient draft for deep placement of ballast, but not so deep as to result in an extremely low center of lateral resistance (CLR), which encourages tripping. As pointed out in Chapter 1, when there is great distance between the CLR and the center of wind pressure on the sails, the heeling moment is high; therefore, if a major consideration in hulling is the angle of heel, the CLR should be reasonably high. Draft alone does not determine the CLR's location; Figure 12-5 shows how keel shape plays a part. Stability

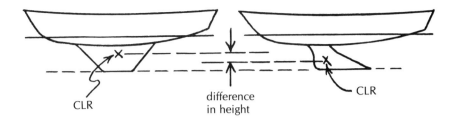

Figure 12-5. *Effect of keel shape on the center of lateral resistance.*

depends primarily on a vessel's beam and her ballast—the beam contributing stiffness at low angles of heel, and the ballast supplying the righting force at high angles of heel. The lower the ballast, the greater the range of stability; therefore, the ballasted keel must be reasonably deep to assure recovery from an extreme knockdown, but not deep enough (or large enough in area at its bottom) to make the CLR excessively low or prevent reasonable leeway when hulling.

Because shoal-draft boats generally make considerable leeway, sailors such as builder-designer Robert Derecktor feel that keel-centerboarders have a safety advantage over deep-keel boats when struck on the beam by extreme breaking seas. Since water particles move forward significantly only at the crest of a wave, a shallow hull is most likely to be carried sideways with the particles, taking little solid water over the deck and experiencing no great capsizing force. For this reason, centerboarders should usually lie a-hull with their boards fully retracted, unless a small amount of board is needed to correct balance. In 1964, the 39-foot centerboard yawl *Doubloon* was rolled over (through 360 degrees) twice in a gale off the coast of Georgia. The *Doubloon* was lying a-hull when the accident occurred, with her board down in an attempt to make her lie closer to the wind. Her owner-skipper, Joe Byars, later reflected that the lowered board tripped the yawl.

When Richard Carter tested the stability of his controversial retractable-keel design, the *Red Rooster*, in sailing trials, the boat could not be knocked down to any great extent with her keel up. She merely heeled over and slid off to leeward. Nevertheless, it could be dangerous to lie a-hull in a boat like *Red Rooster* with her keel retracted in extremely bad weather and heavy seas, because with so little draft, ultimate stability would suffer. Centerboarders and retractable-keel boats may have lower lateral resistance, but leeway should never be achieved at the expense of high ultimate stability. Normal, small seagoing centerboarders need a draft of at least one-seventh the load waterline length so that the rudder can be kept low (when it is not retractable) for good steering control and the ballast can be carried low for reserve stability. This is merely a rule of thumb, and the exact draft-to-LWL ratio would depend on hull shape, displacement, weight of ballast, and hull size (large boats requiring relatively less draft). Rod Stephens, Jr. wrote me, "In spite of a certain amount of propaganda from centerboard enthusiasts, I certainly feel a reasonable keel with the stability range provided would be my choice for bad weather offshore." Calculations of static stability ranges of

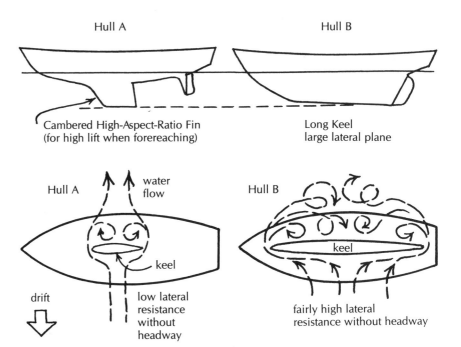

Figure 12-6. *Lateral plane and leeway without headway.*

Hull A

Hull B

Cambered High-Aspect-Ratio Fin
(for high lift when forereaching)

Long Keel
large lateral plane

Hull A

Hull B

water
flow

keel

keel

drift

low lateral
resistance
without
headway

fairly high lateral
resistance without headway

ocean racing centerboarders under the IMS (International Measurement System) handicap rule verify Rod's thinking. The classic Hinckley-built Bermuda 40, for instance, has positive stability to less than 110 degrees.

Although fin-keelers have traditionally been shunned for ocean cruising, principally because of their lack of directional stability, we see more and more of them offshore today. In modern transoceanic single-handed ocean races, most of the monohulls are fin-keelers of light or moderately light displacement. In one respect, a fin-keeler may have a special advantage. English author-designer Douglas Phillips-Birt tells us that when a keel is stalled, its lateral resistance depends on area rather than aspect ratio. When there is no headway (as when hulling) a fin-keeler will move sideways much as an airplane drops when its forward speed is reduced and its wings stall (see Figure 12-6). Thus a fin-keeler might give the greatest draft (to permit low placement of ballast provided the fin is not too short) for the least stalled lateral resistance (to help avoid tripping). Any difficulty from lying a-hull in a fin-keeler will most likely come from lack of directional stability. The boat might fall off the wind and forereach, but this fault can be corrected by lashing down the helm or, when conditions are not too extreme, by setting a very small riding sail aft. The stress on a fin keel is considerable in heavy weather offshore, so it must be carefully secured to the hull, and the hull's bottom must be heavily reinforced.

Although reasonable leeway is desirable when hulling, excessive leeway might not be, especially near a lee shore. In such a case, if hulling is still the preferred tactic, it might pay to stream warps or some sort of drag over the windward side, provided leeway is not slowed too much.

Warps might also help smooth the seas. John Guzzwell, who made a circumnavigation in the 20-foot light-displacement fin-keeler *Trekka*, wrote me that he usually lay a-hull, beam-on, with the helm down in bad weather. On one occasion in a lengthy gale off Queensland, Australia, he became worried about his offing, so he streamed to windward two long warps attached to an eight-foot piece of lumber. *Trekka*'s drift was noticeably lessened, but she did not lie-to as comfortably as when she had no drags to windward.

Since the first edition of this book, I have lain a-hull twice in our Ohlson 38, *Kelpie*. One gale was quite heavy, and the seas were certainly not regular, but the boat behaved very well, lying about beam-to the seas with the helm lashed down, making about two knots of leeway. I think *Kelpie* is well suited to this tactic in anything but horrendous conditions. Her suitability comes partly from her strong construction and deep keel. Its ample ballast contributes to a stability range of 134 degrees, but its abbreviated lateral plane allows plenty of leeway when the keel is stalled. I read that singlehander Clare Francis lay a-hull successfully in a sister boat during a gale that was as bad as or worse than ours. The seas she met were 35 feet high with breaking tops, but they were long. She described her boat as heeling on the crests, which caused the breaking wave tops to crash harmlessly against the topsides. *Kelpie* behaved similarly, although I think our drift-wake encouraged the seas to break before they struck the boat.

When hulling seems too dangerous, then the boat should be kept, as much as possible, end-to the seas. Her bow or stern will present the smallest target, and the hull will be in the position of greatest transverse stability. To be held in this position she must either run off before it or ride to a sea anchor.

Riding to a Sea Anchor

Although the term drogue is often used interchangeably with sea anchor, there is a distinction between the two. Each is a floating drag designed to slow a vessel's drift and help hold her in a desired attitude, but the sea anchor is intended to reduce drift to a bare minimum. The drogue provides less resistance and is intended merely to reduce the vessel's speed. The most familiar sea anchor is the conic cloth bag, the mouth of which is held open by an iron or steel hoop. This type and several other sea anchors and drogues are illustrated in Figure 12-7. Some designs, such as the Fenger type and Galerider, are specifically designed as drogues, but any kind of sea anchor can be used as a drogue if it is small enough.

The traditional way for a small boat to weather a storm at sea is to ride to a sea anchor streamed from her bow, but today this tactic is rarely used, with yachts at least. A great many sailors who have logged thousands of miles offshore have never used a sea anchor or even seen one in use. Is this tactic a lost art, or is there a good reason for abandoning the

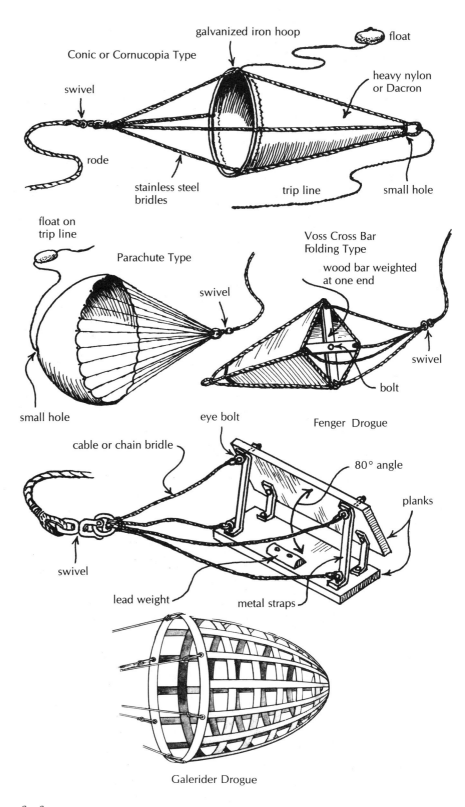

Figure 12-7. *Sea anchors and drogues. (Galerider courtesy Hathaway, Reiser, and Raymond)*

galvanized iron hoop

float

Conic or Cornucopia Type

heavy nylon or Dacron

swivel

rode

stainless steel bridles

trip line

small hole

float on trip line

Parachute Type

Voss Cross Bar Folding Type

wood bar weighted at one end

swivel

swivel

bolt

small hole

eye bolt

Fenger Drogue

cable or chain bridle

80° angle

planks

swivel

lead weight

metal straps

Galerider Drogue

Figure 12-8. *Captain John C. Voss at the helm of his Nootka Indian dugout canoe, the* Tilikum, *at Samoa in 1901. Voss, who sailed this craft across the Pacific, Indian, and Atlantic oceans, was a pioneer of small-boat blue-water sailing and a champion of the sea anchor. (Courtesy Provincial Archive, Victoria, B.C.)*

sea anchor? Perhaps there is some truth in the affirmative answer to both questions. It is certainly true that the typical modern yacht is not well adapted to riding to a sea anchor (especially off the bow), but on the other hand, there are at least two circumstances when a sea anchor might be valuable if not imperative: (1) for a small vessel caught near a lee shore in deep water and in conditions too severe to beat away under sail and power, and (2) when a boat with a very low stability range must be held end-to the seas yet lacks sea room to run off. It certainly seems advisable to carry a sea anchor and to practice handling it if you plan an extended coastal or offshore passage in a small boat.

The great champion of the sea anchor was Captain John C. Voss, who sailed the 37-foot Nootka dugout canoe *Tilikum* almost around the world in the early 1900s. His classic book, *Venturesome Voyages of Captain Voss*, contains a great deal of advice, some of which is still valuable, on handling small boats at sea. His small-boat seamanship theories are said to have greatly influenced polar explorer Ernest Shackleton, who made an incredible passage of 800 miles in an open boat through Antarctic seas after his ship, the *Endurance*, was crushed in the pack ice. In his book, Voss gives instructions on the use of a sea anchor and praises its effectiveness in helping to hold a vessel's bow up to the wind. Bear in mind, however, that most of the boats sailed by Voss were better able to lie bow-to the wind than are most contemporary boats. The *Tilikum* especially, with her long, shallow keel, low windage forward, and means of setting a satisfactory riding sail aft, was well suited to riding to a sea anchor off the bow. Lifeboats, dinghies, and other small, shoal-draft boats have successfully used this tactic (often without riding sails) to weather bad storms. When Robert Manry's 13½-foot dinghy *Tinkerbelle* encountered her first real blow during her Atlantic crossing in 1965, she did not keep her head up when a sea anchor was put over the bow. But when Manry unshipped her deep outboard rudder, she immediately swung head to wind and rode out the blow successfully.

Despite the success of many older, long-keeled boats and shoal-draft small craft streaming a sea anchor from the bow, most modern boats with short, deep keels and great windage forward cannot be held head to wind by this means alone. A riding sail aft in addition to the sea anchor forward might help, but severe jerking strains from the anchor line can pull the bow into the wind momentarily and cause the riding sail to flog violently at frequent intervals. In this case, the riding sail should be a specially made, flat-cut, extra-strong storm sail: possibly a storm mizzen on a yawl, but something similar to the type illustrated in Figure 12-3 on a sloop. Although it has been suggested that a small working jib hanked to the permanent backstay is a suitable riding sail, I don't think the usual jib is suitably made or cut flat enough to stand the punishment of a lengthy gale when set backward as a riding sail.

Even when a modern boat can be coaxed to lie reasonably well to a sea anchor forward and a riding sail aft, she will at times be thrown backward, quite possibly damaging her rudder. The 20-foot fin-keel yawl *Nova Espero* broke her rudder blade while riding to a sea anchor during an Atlantic gale in 1951, and even Voss broke his rudderpost on two occasions using this tactic. To alleviate the strain on the rudder caused by sternway, the rudder itself (instead of the helm) should be lashed amidships whenever possible, as in the case of an outboard rudder. Captain Voss suggested securing two blade ropes (he called them heel ropes) to a hole or eye in the above-water trailing edge of the rudder. The ropes are then pulled taut and secured to the deck, one at each quarter. Adlard Coles has suggested that such a hole in the rudder could be filled with soft putty that could be poked out easily in an emergency. Most rudders are deeply submerged and cannot be secured easily, but it might be possible to lash a spade rudder in the manner described. Since the top, after corner of many a spade rudder is close to or slightly above the waterline, blade ropes might be rigged just prior to bad weather or left attached to the rudder's corner when cruising offshore. They could be carried slack over the stern in fair weather as shown by the dashed line in Figure 12-9, but led to the quarters, hauled taut, and belayed in a storm. Propeller clearance permitting, some spade rudders might turn around backward to lessen strains due to sternway (see Figure 12-9). Blade ropes might also serve as jury steering lines in the event of a steering-gear failure.

One way to protect the rudder is to stream the sea anchor over the stern, thus bringing the stern up to the wind in an attitude more natural for a modern boat with her deepest draft aft and considerable windage forward. Keep in mind, however, that the sterns of some boats, especially those with long, overhanging counters, are less able to rise to the seas than their bows and may pound badly. A sea anchor should not be used astern unless the boat has a small, self-bailing cockpit. Cockpit scuppers must be large, the companionway must be high above the cockpit floor, and the companion hatch must be fitted with proper slides (not

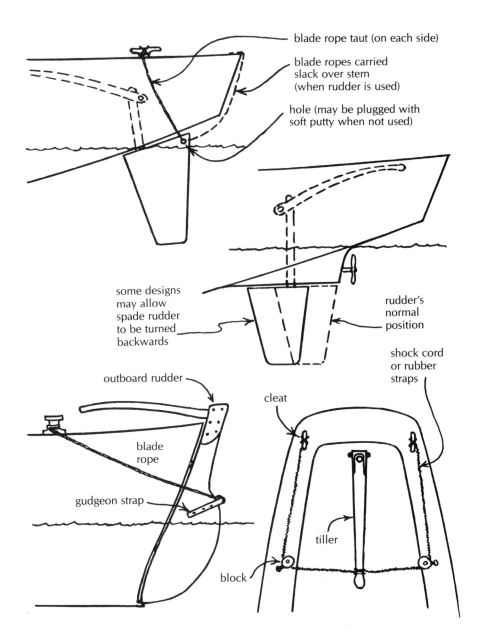

blade rope taut (on each side)

blade ropes carried slack over stern (when rudder is used)

hole (may be plugged with soft putty when not used)

some designs may allow spade rudder to be turned backwards

rudder's normal position

shock cord or rubber straps

outboard rudder

cleat

blade rope

gudgeon strap

tiller

block

Figure 12-9. Reducing rudder vulnerability when drifting backward at sea.

doors) of unquestionable strength. It is usually much easier to stream a sea anchor over the stern because the cockpit is more handy to work from than the foredeck, but the anchor should be secured to a very strong fitting, such as a heavy bitt located aft on the boat's centerline, or the mizzenmast of a yawl. The strains imposed by a sea anchor are so great that they can wrench off an ordinary cleat, and the anchor will often break up or part its bridle lines before a lengthy blow moderates. For this reason, the anchor and its gear must be tremendously strong and the rode extremely well parceled or protected with durable (perhaps rubber or neoprene) chafe guards at the chock. Authorities often recommend a short length of chain at the chock, or where the rode crosses the bobstay if the vessel has a bowsprit and the sea anchor is streamed from the bow. Most modern ocean racers are pathetically inadequate with regard to cleats, bitts, Samson posts, fairleads, or chocks for securing sea anchors or drogues.

Sometimes a sea anchor tethers a boat firmly against the seas so that she cannot yield, thus increasing the force of the waves against the hull and causing them to break aboard. When Humphrey Barton streamed a sea anchor over the starboard quarter of the *Vertue XXXV* during a storm near Bermuda in 1950, a sea broke aboard with such force that two cabin windows were smashed. Barton said that the anchor, a 21-inch-diameter conical type, had stopped his small boat "almost dead." It seems very possible that the force of the damaging sea was increased by tethering the boat to a nearly immovable sea anchor, and perhaps the sea would have caused less damage had the warp been secured on the boat's centerline instead of her quarter so that the stern would have been held more squarely to the seas. Apparently Barton himself, a knowledgeable and experienced blue-water sailor, yacht surveyor, and founder of the Ocean Cruising Club, believed that over-tethering was at least part of the problem. A standard rule of thumb for the diameter of a conical sea anchor is one-tenth the boat's waterline length, but a smaller size, perhaps one-twelfth or less, would lessen the tethering risk.

Another offshore sailor who has had experience with sea anchors, Dr. Paul Sheldon, recommends the parachute type (see Figure 12-7) when it is necessary to stop excessive drift in winds of up to 25 m.p.h. In stronger winds, he believes in towing astern the Fenger drogue (also shown in Figure 12-7), made from two heavy wooden planks, a type that allows more drift or give. Thomas Fleming Day suggested that an easily stowable drogue could be made by securing a plank across the flukes of an ordinary fisherman-type anchor. Most sea anchors made of planks will not overly tether a boat, as might a very large conical type and especially the parachute type. Indeed, some parachute anchors carry printed warnings against their use in extreme conditions because of their lack of "give" in heavy seas.

When I discussed this subject with Eric Hiscock years ago, he expressed concern over a boat being held too firmly to the seas and seemed to disapprove of sea anchors in general, especially when streamed from the bow. He said however that he believed in stowing a sea anchor for an emergency and in streaming it, nearly always from the stern, if it became essential to slow a vessel's drift. His *Wanderer III*, a 30-foot, transom-sterned sloop, once lay for four days in heavy weather to a sea anchor off the stern. Hiscock wanted to lessen drift away from a destination that lay to windward and to stay well clear of a small island and reef to leeward.

In order to minimize the jerking strains of a sea anchor, an ample length of springy nylon rode should be used. A leading maker of cloth sea anchors, Shewmon Incorporated of Dunedin, Florida, warns against an anchoring system that holds a vessel too firmly. Even though these specialists recommend a moderately large size to hold the vessel's end to the seas, the company's literature proclaims, "If a sea anchor is too large, it will not yield, causing rope and bow hardware overloading . . . . Steep, violent seas require long ropes with great springing action." Naval architect and author Juan Baader and others have suggested a scope as long as a wave or multiple thereof to synchronize as much as possible the motion of the boat and anchor. When anchor and boat are in wave crests simultaneously, both are carried forward by the water particles, and when both are in troughs at the same time, both are opposed by the orbiting water particles. On the other hand, Dag Pike, author of *Power Boats in Rough Seas*, recommends a scope of $1^1/2$, $2^1/2$, or $3^1/2$ wave lengths for drogues in short, steep seas to keep the device deeply immersed below the crests for maximum pull when the boat is about to be struck by a breaker. If the drogue is near the surface at the crest it will be thrown forward and lose its ability to pull.

The typical conical sea anchor is usually pictured with a float attached by a short float line and a trip line, as shown in Figure 12-7, yet some sailors who have had experience with drogues prefer not to use these extra lines because they not only add to the difficulty of streaming the drogue but can foul or twist badly if the drogue rotates on its rode. Shewmon recommends rodes of braided rather than twisted line and sea anchors that are weighted on one side to reduce rotation. Chapter 13's discussion of running inlets through surf will return to this point. Although a float might be needed in shallow water, it certainly seems desirable to avoid extra gear in deep water. It is not extremely difficult after using a sea anchor to bring it back aboard without a trip line. Simply haul in the rode or sail the boat up to her drogue when conditions moderate. When the drogue is alongside, its apex can be reached with a boathook, capsizing the bag to spill its water. A strong swivel between the rode and the drogue's bridle lines prevents twisting the bridles if the drogue starts spinning.

Two new drogue designs have received a fair amount of publicity. One of these, the Galerider, has already been mentioned and is illustrated in Figure 12-7. This device is a parobolic perforated bag with a wide mouth held open by a circle of 1×19 wire cable. Its widely spaced nylon webbing allows ample flow-through of water when the drogue is towed astern, offering enough resistance to slow a boat yet sufficient permeability to mitigate shock loading. Developed and manufactured by the sailmaking firm Hathaway, Reiser, and Raymond, the drogue was conceived by Frank Snyder, a vice-commodore of the New York Yacht Club, who commissioned the prototype after reading about close-mesh net sea anchors used successfully by the National Maritime Institute in England. Snyder had occasion to use his drogue during a heavy autumnal gale in 1984, and he praised its effectiveness in slowing his boat and preventing her from broaching to while she ran off before steep following seas. The Galerider has been extensively advertised and endorsed at American

Safety at Sea symposia. Many vessels now carry these drogues, including the U.S. Naval Academy's ocean racers.

The second new drogue design is perhaps more promising in helping to prevent a capsize. After the infamous Fastnet Race of 1979, a number of studies on vessel capsize were carried out by naval architects and marine engineers. Among the researchers using high-tech tank testing facilities were J.O. Salsich at the U.S. Naval Academy Hydromechanics Laboratory, J.A. Keuning at Delft University of Technology, G. Visinean at the University of California, Berkeley, E.D. Cokelet at the Pacific Marine Environmental Laboratory, P.G. Spens at the Stevens Institute of Technology, T. Nagel at the David Taylor Naval Research and Development Center, the Wolfson Unit at Southampton University, and Karl L. Kirkman, one of four directors of the Committee on Safety from Capsizing (sponsored by SNAME and the USYRU) at Hydronautics Ship Model Basin. One of the most constructive projects was carried out by consulting engineer Donald Jordan, working with the U.S. Coast Guard. Together, these studies have made significant contributions to the understanding of capsizing. The studies agree that narrow beam, heavy displacement, moderate freeboard, and a low center of gravity discourage capsizing, as does a tall, heavy mast through its considerable effect on the boat's roll moment of inertia. Kirkman observed little effect from keel depth and area, whereas Jordan's testing has shown that a boat with a large keel can indeed trip.

Jordan invented an entirely different type of drag, which he calls a series drogue, and it has been tested extensively over a period of years by Jordan and the Coast Guard with models and full-sized lifeboats. The sailboat models ranged from a traditional long-keel boat with a deep forefoot, to the classic New York 32 with a cut-away forefoot, to a fairly modern Standfast fin-keeler with a spade rudder, to trimarans with and without decking between the amas and main hull. These models were subjected to breaking seas with and without drogues, and their behavior was studied with the use of stroboscopic photography. The series drogue, consisting of many miniature conic sea anchors evenly spaced along the rode, maintains constant tension on all parts of the rode, thus holding the boat's end more quickly or constantly to the seas, lessening jerking and shock loading, and eliminating the danger of the drogue's tumbling or collapsing with passage of a wave as so often happens to a single parachute or cornucopia type.

Details of a series drogue for a small cruising trimaran are shown in Figure 12-10. Jordan suggests a 150-foot rode containing 90 cloth cones. The inboard end of the rode should be attached to a long bridle secured to each ama (or quarter of a monohull). A 25-pound conventional anchor is shackled to the very end of the rode, and the total length from vessel to anchor is 230 feet. He strongly urges towing the drogue astern, as his numerous tests verify that modern monohull sailing yachts will not consistently hold their bow to the seas no matter how large the sea anchor. (Notice how modern boats range or sail around even on their permanent

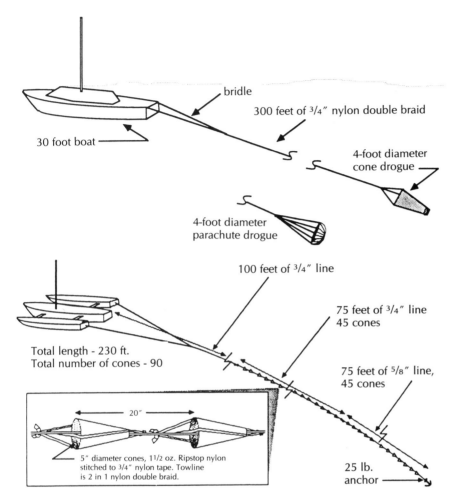

bridle

300 feet of ¾" nylon double braid

30 foot boat

4-foot diameter
cone drogue

4-foot diameter
parachute drogue

100 feet of ¾" line

75 feet of ¾" line
45 cones

Total length - 230 ft.
Total number of cones - 90

75 feet of ⅝" line,
45 cones

20"

5" diameter cones, 1½ oz. Ripstop nylon
stitched to ¾" nylon tape. Towline
is 2 in 1 nylon double braid.

25 lb.
anchor

Figure 12-10. *Deployment of single (top) or series (bottom) drogues as recommended by Donald Jordan and the U.S. Coast Guard.*

moorings during a storm.) In regard to acquiring this system, Jordan has written me: "Victor Shane, Para Anchors Int., Box 19, Summerland, CA 93067 will sell a kit for a series drogue as described in our report. This drogue has been thoroughly tested, and his particular cones have been tested above the design load." The exact number of cones needed will depend primarily on the boat's size and weight (see Figure 12-11).

My only reservation is the possible difficulty of deploying the series drogue. I can envision the cones snagging on a cleat or chock as the rode is paid out astern. When I mentioned this to Jordan he wrote back, "I completely agree with your comments on the need to have a simple, foolproof system for deploying the drogue in an emergency. Recently a crew deployed a parachute drogue under difficult conditions and it immediately was swept under the boat and fouled the propeller. I believe that the series drogue, if properly prerigged, should be easier to deploy than a four-foot cone. The 25-pound anchor is light enough for one man to slip over the stern. It will quickly sink and thus clear the boat. The series drogue does not build up large snatch loads, as does the cone or

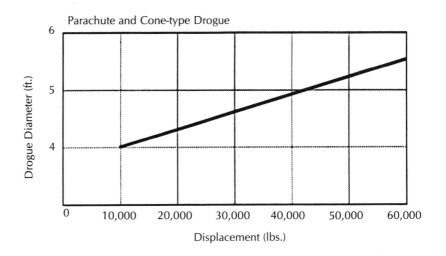

Parachute and Cone-type Drogue

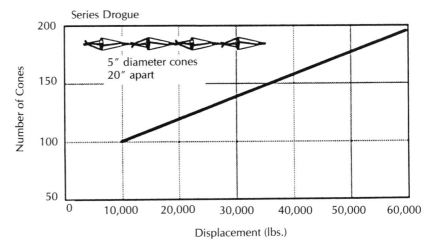

Series Drogue

Figure 12-11. *Recommended size of a single drogue (top) or number of series drogues (bottom) when deployed from the stern, from the findings of Donald Jordan and the U.S. Coast Guard.*

chute as soon as they enter the water, thus the rode can be paid out in a more orderly manner. The rode with the cones attached should be no more prone to foul than a simple rode. However, it is absolutely essential that the drogue be prerigged, properly stowed, and that the deployment be practiced under comfortable conditions until the crew is trained."

In a paper presented with Carol L. Hervey of the U.S. Coast Guard Research and Development Center, at the New England Sailing Yacht Symposium (1988), Jordan suggested prerigging and carrying the series drogue coiled in the stern lazarette. He advised deploying while the boat is lying a-hull or running off. To quote from the paper: "The anchor can be slipped over the stern and the line paid out. The drogue will build up load gradually as it feeds out. It is almost impossible to foul it or entangle it enough to make the drogue ineffective. The drogue rides beneath the waves and is not affected by the following sea even if a wave should break in the vicinity . . . . When the boat is in the trough of a large wave, the towline tends to go slack, thus permitting the boat to yaw. With the series drogue the anchor sinks, pulling the drogue backward and taking some unwanted slack out of the towline. The drogue does not collapse but retains its shape while moving backward."

Despite a great deal of confusion and controversy about sea anchors, the following conclusions seem reasonably safe:

- Sea anchors or drogues still have their place for small, very shoal-draft boats, especially open ones, whether motor, sail, or rowing. Boats of these types should carry some kind of drogue (even if it is only a *strong* bucket on a very small boat) when in unprotected waters. A partially decked or undecked boat should not be allowed to lie broadside to the seas in heavy weather. Keep any easily capsizable craft, no matter what her size or design, end-to breaking waves.

- Even when the vessel's attitude is not the major consideration, every offshore boat should carry a drogue, if only to help control speed and lessen drift toward a lee shore.

- The drogue or sea anchor should be tremendously strong to handle heavy loads, at least equal to the displacement of the boat, for 20 hours or more. The riding gear and rode should be as elastic as possible to reduce shock loading; the size of the drogue or sea anchor should be reasonably matched to the boat's displacement (see Figure 12-11); and the boat should have amply strong, properly bolted bitts or cleats on the stern to accept the rode or bridle.

- Since most modern boats with short keels, cut-away forefoots, and great windage forward will not lie close to the wind and seas (many will even yaw to the beam-on position) with a sea anchor over the bow, it is usually best to stream the anchor or drogue astern. This requires a small, self-draining cockpit with large scuppers and a high companionway hatch fitted with proper slides. The stern should be buoyant, preferably without a long overhanging counter or large flat (or open) transom.

- If a sea anchor is streamed from the bow, the average modern boat will require a strong, flat riding sail aft. With this method, the rudder blade should be lashed as described previously. If this is not possible, lash the helm with elastic shock cord or rubber straps to help alleviate jerking strains on the rudder caused by sternway (see Figure 12-9).

- In the most severe storms, the series drogue may offer the greatest hope for survival because it can most quickly turn a boat end-to after she has been struck by a breaking wave (more about this later in this chapter under "Survival Tactics").

- A drogue or sea anchor should be inspected periodically, and occasionally it should be used for practice in moderately bad weather.

Scudding

Although scudding—running before wind and seas with little or no sail set—has its dangers, contemporary sailors endorse it in the following circumstances: (1) when it is essential to vacate a dangerous area, (2) when the wind is favorable, the boat is completely manageable, and it is desirable to proceed toward one's destination, and (3) when conditions require that the boat be kept end-to the seas and yet, because of her drift attitude, vulnerable rudder, lack of proper riding sail, or some other reason, she cannot or should not be kept bow-to the seas. The dangers of scudding include the possibility of being pooped (i.e., a following sea breaking over the stern), broaching (inadvertently rounding up, beam-to the wind and seas), and pitch-poling (capsizing longitudinally, end over end).

To elaborate on these circumstances, you would certainly want to vacate an area if it had a strong current opposing a gale, if you were in the path or dangerous quadrant of the storm (see Chapter 9), or if you were on shoals that were producing dangerous seas. You would also want to run off to gain sea room if you anticipated a wind shift that would put a dangerous shore to leeward. When the wind is blowing toward your destination, it is desirable to gain all the distance possible in the right direction, provided there is no danger of closing with a lee shore before the bad weather dissipates.

If you choose scudding, fast or slow, you should continue only if the boat answers her helm and shows no tendency to yaw or root (bury her bow), broach-to, or pitch-pole. By all means shift tactics if heavy seas break over the stern or the stern begins to squat excessively or produce a significant stern wave that could reinforce the following seas. Scudding requires a small, self-bailing cockpit and a high companionway with proper slides. In severe weather with the threat of pooping seas, companion slides should be kept in and the sliding hatch closed when no one is entering or leaving the cabin. Conditions that might require keeping the vessel end-to the seas have been discussed, but to summarize briefly, they include a lack of reserve stability or ability to self-right; excessive draft and lateral plane, which might encourage tripping laterally on the keel; vulnerable topsides, cabin house, and especially windows; excessive rolling when lying a-hull; extreme initial tenderness of the boat and such a severe wind that beam-on and stripped of sail, she lies with her rail submerged in solid water; and seas that are dangerously irregular, short, and steep, with frequent breakers of the plunging type. In general, keeping the stern rather than the bow toward the seas entails fewer problems, especially if the bow tends to fall off the wind below beam-on when the vessel is allowed to assume her natural drift attitude (under bare poles with the helm free).

Although most offshore sailors agree that scudding is an entirely acceptable storm tactic under the right circumstances, there is considerable disagreement about the proper technique. Some advocate running off at fairly high speed, while others feel that speed must be kept low;

many recommend trailing lines or drags, while others do not; some believe in taking the seas on the quarter, while others insist on taking them squarely on the stern; and so forth. To a large extent, the boat, the size and character of the seas, and the severity of the weather will dictate technique.

The classic means of scudding is that first popularized by Joshua Slocum in his account of running off before a gale in the *Spray* near Cape Horn in 1896. The *Spray* carried no sail other than a reefed forestaysail sheeted flat, and she ran dead before it with her helm lashed amidships while towing two long hawsers over her stern. The small scrap of sail forward and the drags aft helped hold her off before the wind. This method of scudding was appropriate for the *Spray* because of her exceptionally good directional stability (mainly due to her flat run and long keel), and because she had ample buoyancy in her ends. Then too, the *Spray* did not have the ultimate stability of most modern boats, which suggests that Slocum was wise to avoid hulling in extremely bad weather, especially in the waters off Cape Horn. The big disadvantage of Slocum's method was that it carried him a little too rapidly toward a lee shore, and as a result he narrowly escaped being wrecked on a group of submerged rocks known as the Milky Way, off Cockburn Channel.

Although the subject of speed while scudding is controversial, I believe the weight of opinion favors going moderately slowly, or at least not extremely fast, when speed can be controlled. This is one of the main reasons for towing lines and drags astern. Even a single long, heavy line streaming astern causes a fair amount of friction, while tying many knots in the line and towing it in a bight increases the drag. Buckets, sails, anchors, spars towed sideways, or a swamped dinghy attached to the end of a line can create far more drag. Heavy floating objects, such as a dinghy or spars, should be towed far astern, because they can be thrown a considerable distance forward by a breaking crest. A swamped dinghy would probably break up, pull away from her painter, or part it in a lengthy gale, but would do better if towed in a cargo net. I have been told by quite a few blue-water sailors that weighted automobile tires make excellent drags. As discussed in the last section, drogues such as the Fenger type (Figure 12-7) will slow a boat without stopping her in the manner of a true sea anchor. Several experienced seamen have praised the Galerider for use when running off.

Lines or drags astern may also smooth the seas and help prevent the crests from breaking in weather less severe than survival conditions. Irving Johnson and others have suggested towing sails to help smooth the seas. Frik Potgieter, who sailed the 35-foot Piver-designed trimaran *Zulane* from South Africa to the West Indies, told me that he rode out a bad storm near the Cape of Good Hope by towing his mizzen boom with the mizzen attached while running off under bare poles. In addition to slowing the boat, the sail calmed the seas.

High-speed scudding in steep seas exacerbates the dangers mentioned above, especially for heavy-displacement vessels. A deep, heavy hull makes a large stern wave when traveling at hull speed (1.34 times the square root of her waterline length), and this might disturb a following sea and cause it to break over the stern. Furthermore, such a speed may cause the stern to squat or be sucked down, which would encourage being pooped. Scudding requires a buoyant stern, but not buoyant enough to depress the bow. High speed might cause the bow to dig in or root, which could lead to broaching or even pitch-poling in the most extreme case. The shape of the bow exerts a considerable influence, a buoyant bow with a shallow forefoot being probably best in this regard. The late professor of naval architecture at M.I.T., K.S.M. Davidson, pointed out some years ago that a deep forefoot can temporarily move a vessel's center of lateral resistance far forward when the stern is lifted while running before heavy seas. This disturbs directional stability and can lead to broaching. Although Dr. Davidson suggested that full, blunt bows have less tendency to dig in, high-speed scudding can be risky even for boats with this type of bow. Naval architect and author Howard Chapelle tells us, "The fallacy of the full entrance as a prevention of 'sailing under' by hard driving sailing craft was exploded by the middle of the last century. As a matter of fact, full-ended heavy-displacement sailing yachts tend to 'bore' if pushed."

If a vessel inadvertently broaches-to, her forward inertia will add to the capsizing force of the wind and seas when she turns beam-on. On the other hand, if the bow roots but the vessel does not turn, she may trip on her bow and somersault, or pitch-pole. The tendency to pitchpole or broach-to is aggravated not only by high speed, but also by the size and shape of the seas. A short, steep sea with a wave length about twice the vessel's length will not only lift her stern considerably higher than her bow, but will expose her stern to the forward-moving orbiting water particles at the very time her bow lies in the backward-moving particles of the trough (see Figure 12-12). A small headsail set forward might help hold the bow off the wind but would increase speed and perhaps depress the bows of some modern boats, adding to the danger of rooting.

Another argument in favor of slow-speed scudding says that the faster a vessel travels, the longer she stays on the crest of a sea. Even if the crest is not breaking, the forward-moving orbiting water particles are dangerous, and when a boat is on the crest she is supported amidships but not at her ends. In this position, she has minimal transverse stability. Tank tests have shown that a vessel's righting moment is generally greatest when she is in the trough while running before a following sea, but smallest when the crest is amidships. Furthermore, rudder control is tenuous on a crest due to the forward speed of the water particles and the likelihood of the rudder emerging. It seems desirable, therefore, to slow down and let the crest pass quickly.

Although the arguments against high-speed scudding (when this can be prevented) are convincing, most experienced offshore seamen favor enough speed for good steering control. The ideal compromise speed

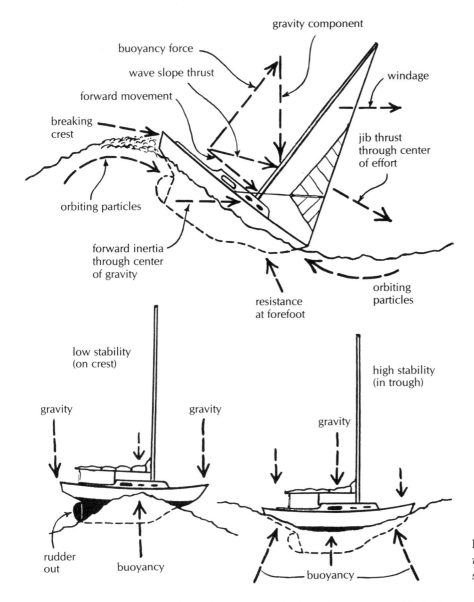

gravity component

buoyancy force

wave slope thrust

forward movement

breaking crest

windage

jib thrust through center of effort

orbiting particles

forward inertia through center of gravity

resistance at forefoot

orbiting particles

low stability (on crest)

high stability (in trough)

gravity

gravity

gravity

rudder out

buoyancy

buoyancy

Figure 12-12. *Forces at work when scudding in steep seas.*

allows the vessel to yield to the seas and gives her reasonable helm response without drawing a large stern wave, carrying excessive forward momentum, or driving her bow under. When there is enough headway to allow rudder control, breaking crests can sometimes be avoided, and the stern can be kept toward the seas. Just how fast a boat should run off, provided her speed can be controlled, depends to a large extent on her size, length of keel, hull shape, and rudder size and position, and especially on the wind and sea conditions. In general terms, the ideal speed for a small offshore boat (perhaps 25 feet on the waterline) might be 3 or 4 knots in moderately short seas but somewhat faster in long, regular seas. It could be dangerous to let a heavy-displacement hull exceed a speed-to-length ratio of 1.0 (5 knots for a 25-foot LWL) in steep seas, since beyond that speed a sizable quarter wave would develop.

While warps or drags will slow a boat, they may also hamper steering control. When one vessel tows another of comparable size, the helmsman of the towing vessel notices an adverse effect on steering when the towline is secured abaft his boat's rudderhead. This is why tugboats carry their towing bitts well forward of the rudder. Warps or drags secured to a boat's stern have a similar effect on steering. When the French circumnavigator Bernard Moitessier ran off his ketch, *Joshua*, before a gale in the South Pacific in 1965, he streamed lines and drags over the stern to slow his boat. But in the Roaring Forties between Tahiti and Cape Horn, the seas became so enormous, steep, and conducive to surfing that even a heavy steel 40-footer such as the *Joshua* could not be slowed. Moitessier claimed that in those conditions the drags (five long iron-ballasted hawsers and a heavy cargo net) failed to slow the boat and instead hampered steering as though he were towing a "motor boat." When the *Joshua* appeared in imminent danger of being overwhelmed, Moitessier cut loose the drags and immediately regained steering control. The successful technique he developed for these conditions was to strip the boat of sail and steer her, without drags astern, dead before the wind until she was overtaken by a steep following sea. At this time he would luff slightly, holding *Joshua*'s stern about 15 to 20 degrees from square to the approaching crest line in order to heel her somewhat and let the sea pass under her quarter. Although one might expect a quartering sea to exert a strong broaching force, Moitessier explained that the force was readily controlled by the rudder, that there was less tendency for the boat to plane, and that the slightly heeled hull presented the curve of its leeward bow to the trough "like a ski," thus helping to prevent rooting. Moitessier referred to himself as belonging to the "Vito Dumas school," because Argentinean circumnavigator Dumas often ran off at high speed (usually carrying sail) in his Colin Archer-type double-ender, *Lehg II*. However, this thinking should probably be called the Moitessier school, because Dumas gave few details of his technique, whereas Moitessier is explicit. Moitessier has told his story in his book, *Cape Horn: The Logical Route*.

While Moitessier's technique worked well for him, we must remember that he was in the great seas of the South Pacific, where the fetch is enormous and gales are often of unusual duration. He doubted that *Joshua* would lie a-hull without being rolled over, and he had no use for sea anchors in those conditions, so he elected to scud. Although the drags he trailed often hampered steering, they had "no more effect than a tuna line" in slowing the ketch; and Moitessier decided that if he had to run fast, he would do so in the manner allowing maximum steering control. Nevertheless, his technique is not necessarily suitable for all conditions. In lesser seas that are not so conducive to surfing, it would certainly seem prudent to attempt slowing the vessel at least to a speed equal to the square root of her waterline length, which would allow steering control but minimize most of the risks associated with high speeds. If the vessel could not be slowed, then the Moitessier technique might be considered. Aerohydrodynamicist and sailor C.A. Marchaj suggests that high-speed scudding is often suitable in long, fast-moving seas. When the waves are short, he recommends a slow speed and towing drags that will help hold the stern up when the boat is on a crest, at which time the rudder exerts little control.

There are ways to alleviate some of the steering problems imposed by drags. One is to attach the drag line forward of the rudderpost, as tugs do. A ketch towing a drogue (or drags attached to a single line) could make fast the line around the mizzenmast, high enough to avoid needing a chock aft (see Figure 12-13). This would require a very strong mizzen, and it would be desirable to have the mainmast's permanent backstay attached to the mizzenmast near the drogue line's point of attachment as shown in the illustration. This method would probably require removal of the mizzen sheet and perhaps the stern pulpit, and the drogue line would have to be protected against chafe at the point where it bears on the after rail.

In an article published in the *Cruising Club News* (December, 1968), E.F. Hanks suggested towing astern a heavy warp (or docklines made fast end to end) in a great bight, with the ends of the bight made fast to either side of the vessel near her maximum beam (nearly amidships) instead of on each quarter. I think that securing the warp on each side would not allow as much steering control as would a tugboat's single towline secured nearly amidships on the boat's centerline, but a line towed in a bight would tend to smooth the following seas. Hanks claimed that in trials in heavy seas the bight knocked down the crests of curling breakers, provided a steadying, controlling effect, and made a wide slick astern. Furthermore, he claimed that this technique allowed the stern to swing and did not unduly hamper steering. Hanks tested the method in shallow-water breakers as well as offshore, always with good results. Although he used power craft, Hanks recommended the method for sailboats as well. For best results, he specified a drag-line length of at least six boat lengths. Robin Knox-Johnston, the first man to make a nonstop antipodal circumnavigation alone, used the method successfully in winds as strong as Force 10 while scudding under a tiny storm jib set forward and sheeted flat on his 32-foot double-ender, *Suhaili*. The Hanks method seems worth trying, but I have reservations about its probable efficacy in the kind of conditions to which Moitessier was exposed, because the drag line could be thrown forward in the crests of those tremendous seas.

Drags might be added to a towed bight to help slow the vessel's speed. In Figure 12-13, an automobile tire is attached to the end of line number one, then the end of a second line is secured to the tire; a short distance (perhaps twice the beam of the boat) from the end of line number two, a second tire is secured. The drags are dropped over the stern, and each line is paid out and secured amidships. The bight would be

Figure 12-13. *Towing drags.*

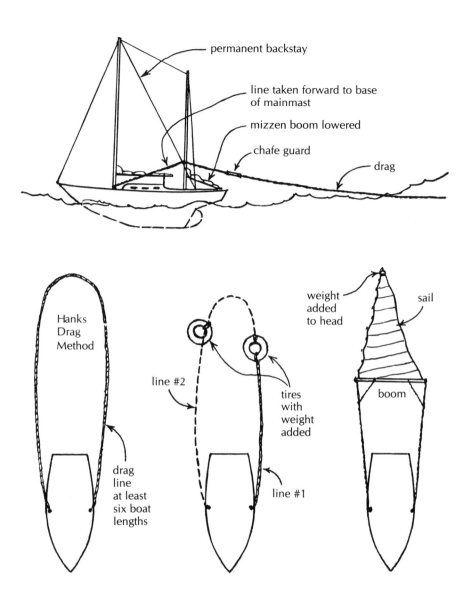

permanent backstay

line taken forward to base of mainmast

mizzen boom lowered

chafe guard

drag

Hanks Drag Method

drag line at least six boat lengths

line #2

tires with weight added

line #1

weight added to head

sail

boom

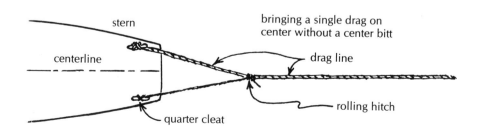

stern

bringing a single drag on center without a center bitt

centerline

drag line

rolling hitch

quarter cleat

narrow, but should be of some help. It might be necessary to add weight to the tires to keep them well submerged.

Dean H. Bergman, a veteran of towing vessels in heavy weather, suggested using what he calls a traveling snatch block. A rope bridle is rigged from one corner of the stern to the other, and a heavy snatch block is allowed to run freely along the rope. The towline is secured to the block's becket, and when the towboat yaws, the block travels along the bridle from side to side. This creates an artificial towing point, which is in effect some distance forward of the stern. The block must have good fairlead cheeks and be self-erecting if slack permits it to tumble.

Light-displacement boats are often better suited to high-speed scudding because they do not usually create the large stern waves that can reinforce following seas. Some designs also steer more easily and may gain dynamic stability when moving fast. High-speed scudding proved successful for some boats during the 1979 Fastnet storm, but many of those carried a number of exceptionally skilled helmsmen who could steer for hours with the necessary concentration to avoid the most dangerous breaking seas. The principal risk is that a momentary lapse in helmsmanship or failure to detect a particularly irregular breaker behind or hole in the water ahead (especially difficult to see at night) can lead to a devastating broach. Even if the boat is light and surfs without creating a large wave system, a sharp entrance and broad stern could leave her out of balance if she heels sharply on a wave slope. In the trough or wave's back, her bow may dig in and create a powerful broaching tendency.

Don Jordan wrote me as follows about high-speed scudding:

> Contrary to much nautical literature, our tests indicate that it should never be necessary to steer a boat in a severe storm. The boat should not be permitted to attain enough speed for steerage. A proper drogue is the best bet, and lying a-hull is the next, somewhat painful alternative. Any storm that you can survive by running off is one in which you could do better lying a-hull. There is no way you can realistically expect to dodge a breaking wave large enough to capsize the boat, although many sailors are deluded into believing that they have saved the boat by weaving a tortuous path through the storm for many hours. I know this sounds like heresy. Of course, large boats with ample, well-trained crew can run off successfully and be more comfortable than if they lay a-hull, but they would survive in either mode.

I can only add that Jordan's advice should not be taken lightly, but if you do decide to lie a-hull in plunging breakers, be prepared for a capsize. This is true even for a large boat, although she is much less likely to capsize than her small sister. (More on this subject in the next section.)

As with the sea anchor, the use of storm oil seems to be a dying art. In former times, few well-found boats would put to sea without a supply of oil that could be dripped overboard to help calm the seas in bad weather. Perhaps modern seamen have justification for abandoning the use of oil, because today's boats usually cannot be held head to the wind, and in most other attitudes they may run away from a slick unless a large amount of oil is used continuously. Oil is messy and can spill below, and seas washing it on board make the decks slippery. The highly effective fish oils have a nauseating smell that may encourage seasickness. However, oil can be valuable for brief periods of time when you enter an inlet in rough seas or when you have to board a wreck. If the wreck and the rescue vessel both spread oil, the technique is even more effective. Nevertheless, it seems doubtful that a small, modern boat weathering a severe, lengthy gale could carry enough oil for any sustained effect on the seas. To use oil in limited amounts, spread it from canvas bags pricked full of holes, filled with rags or oakum soaked in oil, and hung over the topsides or towed astern. If you use a sea anchor, an oil bag can be fastened to it. Modern mariners who have tried oil in heavy weather have most often used motor oil or other petroleum products, but oceanographer Willard Bascom tells us that these have relatively little effect as compared with fish or viscous animal oils.

Survival Tactics

Fortunately, the vast majority of blue-water sailors never experience survival weather or the ultimate storm. Nevertheless, the most optimistic offshore seaman can't be absolutely sure he will never be caught in such conditions, so it is important to give this contingency serious thought.

Since there is no sure way to guarantee survival in an ultimate storm at sea, avoid exposure if you can. In earlier chapters we discussed how careful routing, knowledge of regional weather patterns, and use of coast pilot books and pilot charts can minimize your chances of a storm encounter and lessen the impact of any you should happen to meet. A safe boat, soundly designed, constructed, and equipped, is no less important. If you absolutely insist on sailing in dangerous waters—off Cape Hatteras in the fall or winter, in the western North Atlantic during the hurricane season, off the "Cape of Storms" when the westerly winds oppose the Agulhas current, or in the South Pacific near Cape Horn—be prepared for the worst. As ocean sailor Edward Allcard said, "Assume that one day the boat will turn upside down."

When Marcel Bardiaux rounded Cape Horn in 1952 in the 30-foot sloop *Les 4 Vents*, sailing solo the "wrong way" (east to west) against gale-force winds opposing a 9-knot current, he expected the worst. His sloop was well built and fitted out to survive a capsizing, and it was just as well, because near Cape Horn she twice rolled bottomside up. Her recovery and survival were due largely to her extra-strong watertight construction, her rounded cabin house and decks designed to withstand solid water, small portholes instead of the large picture windows found on many modern boats, and the self-righting ability conferred by her outside lead ballast and the numerous buoyancy tanks bolted to her frames at a high level. The lesson for blue-water sailors seems clear: First, avoid exposure to survival conditions (they can usually be avoided with careful planning); but if you are compelled to take the ultimate risks, expect and be ready for anything, and this includes turning bottomside up. When you are really prepared, an inversion can be tolerable in a small boat. Cockleshell voyager Sven Lundin has called it "all part of the fun."

There are few ways for most modern boats to weather a lengthy ultimate storm at sea. In the most extreme conditions, it is doubtful that any sail could be carried, because even if the sail could survive it would impose too great a strain on the boat or her rig. Avoid using an unyielding sea anchor on the typical modern boat unless it is essential to slow your drift toward a lee shore, because the anchor will overly tether the boat and might pull itself to pieces or damage the hull. Dr. David Lewis nearly pulled the transom off his *Cardinal Vertue* with a sea anchor during a North Atlantic gale in 1960.

If we eliminate the tactics of heaving to and riding to a sea anchor, the remaining choices for a small to medium-size cruiser with limited crew are running off under bare poles or hulling. In either case, the chances of remaining upright could be improved with a series drogue over the stern. The drogue will slow the scudding boat and help hold her stern-to the seas. The hulling boat, lying beam-to the seas, would be thrown sideways if struck by a breaker, but the tug of the drogue may turn her hull sufficiently to prevent a roll-over. The tactic to use will depend on the state of the seas; wind strength; size, design, and construction of the boat; the skill and condition of the crew; and the need to evacuate the area. In the worst weather, downwind is probably the only direction in which motion is possible. Thus, if the boat is fairly close to a lee shore, hulling would be the better tactic to minimize drift. If there is ample sea room and it is necessary to vacate, running off would seem the best choice.

The boat's natural drift attitude should influence your tactical decision. Letting the boat do what she will naturally, rather than trying to make her resist overwhelming forces, is probably best. If the boat has buoyant ends, good directional stability when making headway downwind, a small, self-bailing cockpit (preferably located amidships), a moderately long keel without an excessively deep forefoot, a deep rudder (preferably with a nonvulnerable skeg when the keel and rudder are separated), moderate beam, a strong bridge deck or high companionway, strong, well-placed towing bitts aft, and the absence of a long, flat counter, she might be run off successfully. If the boat is large and light and well endowed with skillful helmsmen, she might run off with sufficient speed for good steering control in conditions approaching a survival storm, but a small, heavy boat with few or unskilled helmsmen should probably run off slowly with effective drags astern. For lying a-hull, the most important design virtues are plenty of reserve stability, self-righting ability, a low, strong, preferably rounded cabin trunk with a high, on-center companionway, small, strong ports or windows, a keel that allows adequate leeway when stalled (probably a short or moderately shoal-draft keel), a natural beam-on drift attitude, an adequately buoyant hull (preferably of moderate displacement) with moderate freeboard, and a round (rather than a flat-surfaced V-bottom) hull adequately strong at the turn of the bilge.

Some weather and sea conditions are so severe that no small boat can remain undamaged or stay upright, no matter how she is handled. After the 46-foot ketch *Tzu Hang* pitch-poled in the Roaring Forties about 1,000 miles from Cape Horn, many sailors offered suggestions on how the accident could have been prevented. Advice ranged from towing more drags or a sea anchor astern, to scudding with speed, to lying a-hull. Yet all of these methods have problems, as we have seen. A drogue might have helped if it had exerted sufficient drag to hold the boat's stern to the seas or quickly turn her stern-to when the breaking crest made contact. During a 1980 North Atlantic Force 10 gale in an 18-foot Goldeneye sloop, Bill Doherty had success towing a 15-pound mushroom anchor shackled to a swivel on a 12-foot length of chain and 200 feet of 3/8-inch nylon rode. But this kind of drogue probably would not supply sufficient drag for a larger boat.

Don Jordan is skeptical of the Galerider's effectiveness in really severe conditions. He wrote, "This drogue gained a good reputation because Mr. Snyder, Commodore of the New York Yacht Club, used it under moderate storm conditions and observed that it was effective in slowing the boat down and preventing surfing and broaching. Actually, the drogue he used was much too small to have prevented a capsize in the event of a large breaking wave strike. In general, the Galerider would behave like a cone or parachute drogue, except that a larger size would be required to provide the proper drag. This drogue, like the others, rides near the surface in a survival storm and would be subject to tumbling and fouling if struck by a breaking wave. I believe the Galerider is well made, but to my knowledge it has not been tested up to the high load that would be imposed in a breaking wave strike."

I have never used a series drogue, but I think that this device, together with an anchor to make it sink, would provide the most steady and continual drag without undue shock loading. There is no guarantee that a series drogue would have prevented the *Tzu Hang*'s capsize, but it most probably would have improved her chances of staying upright.

High-speed scudding might have worked in the Roaring Forties, but it can be dangerous. Dr. David Lewis capsized three times while using the Moitessier method during his remarkable 1972-73 voyage to Antarctica in the 32-foot steel sloop *Icebird*. Steering from below, Dr. Lewis ran off under a tiny storm jib at fast speeds before waves as high as 40 feet, which were taken at an angle of approximately 20 degrees from dead astern. The tactic failed utterly, and *Icebird* was rolled, dismasted, and suffered other damage, despite her exceptionally heavy construction. Dr. Lewis wrote, "I was greatly influenced by Moitessier. I thought it right to run her off before the wind, but I don't know . . . ."

Lying a-hull would probably have resulted in the *Tzu Hang*'s capsizing or turning turtle, as the seas were too steep and the ketch's deep draft, great lateral plane, and vulnerable cabin trunk made her unsuitable for hulling. Indeed, she did roll over while hulling on another occasion. No one can say with any certainty that any tactic could have kept her upright in the partical wave that tumbled her. John Guzzwell was aboard the *Tzu Hang* when she pitch-poled, and he contributed much to her survival by repairing the serious damage and constructing a jury rig that enabled her to make port in Chile. John suspects uncharted shoals in the area of the South Pacific where the pitch-poling took place. Oceanographers know that seamounts (isolated submarine mountains rising more than 500 fathoms) can drastically disturb the ocean surface. He described the state of the sea at that time as similar to "what would be encountered with a long swell passing over a shoal area: very steep seas, some of which toppled over and broke like surf." The ketch simply could not cope with those unusually bad seas.

If you meet a non-negotiable sea or conditions so bad that turning over is extremely probable, capsizing (turning over laterally) is better than pitch-poling end over end, and this is an argument for hulling in the worst possible conditions. The *Tzu Hang* was damaged far less when she rolled over while lying a-hull than when she somersaulted while scudding. Even Moitessier, the advocate of running off at high speed, maintains that the force of seas taken beam-on when hulling is softer and less damaging than when they are taken end-on with speed. He writes, "Even an enormous breaker taken full broadside reminds me of the image of the blow of a giant bludgeon made of foam rubber. The blow can be extremely powerful, but it will remain relatively soft, with very little breaking effect." There are more than a few records of seagoing boats capsizing offshore, and in most cases the rig was badly damaged. But when the hull, cabin, decks, and cockpit were properly designed and constructed, they were seldom seriously damaged, and in many cases the rig was not destroyed.

If the seas seem negotiable end-on (that is, without danger of pitch-poling), then try scudding with just enough speed (when it can be controlled) to provide good steerageway. It might be worthwhile trying the Hanks method of towing drags to control speed and help smooth the following seas with minimal harm to steering, or (if the boat is ketch-rigged) drags might be attached to the mizzen as suggested in Figure 12-13. When the seas do not seem negotiable end-on, or when the helm cannot be manned due to illness, injury, extreme fatigue, or weather that prevents prolonged exposure, then hulling (preferably with a series drogue dropped over the stern) may be the only answer. Carleton Mitchell has described the wind in the worst survival weather as "a raving, mad demon, totally unfamiliar, capable of picking up a man and throwing him down like an empty paper bag; of tearing off his clothes; of deafening, blinding, and smothering him." In conditions that bad, it seems doubtful that anyone could stay on deck for very long, much less steer effectively. The sailor should go below, batten down all hatches, stow and secure all movable objects, fasten himself in his bunk, and hope that the boat will look after herself. By this means Jean Gau, in the 30-foot Tahiti ketch *Atom*, weathered Hurricane Carrie, the same blow that sank the large training bark *Pamir*, drowning all but six of her 86 crewmembers. Don Jordan writes, "Our testing shows that almost any well-built sailing yacht will survive most storms if the crew retires to the cabin and leaves the boat to lie a-hull. In the rare instance of a dangerous breaking wave strike, a properly engineered drogue is the only equipment that can dramatically improve the chance of survival."

Before going below and leaving the boat to fend for herself, make careful preparations on deck. Make the boat completely watertight (this includes removing all vents, even Dorades). Thoroughly secure all gear that cannot be taken below, especially poles and booms that may have to serve as jury masts in the event of a dismasting. You may want to put oil bags over the windward bow and perhaps stream many lines or, preferably, a series drogue astern. To lessen windage, unbend working sails—perhaps even storm sails—unless it might be necessary later to attempt beating away from a lee shore. Also to reduce windage, you can remove halyards, except those that might be needed to set emergency storm sails when conditions moderate. If the boat's natural drift attitude is nearly beam-on or slightly stern-up, lash down the helm with shock cord to prevent forereaching. This advice is based on the premise that the risk of pitch-poling when scudding is high and that capsizing is the lesser of two evils. If the seas are not steep enough to induce surfing and serious rooting of the bow, which can result in broaching or pitch-poling, and the boat has a stern-up tendency, you may be wise to head off with the helm lashed amidships while towing all the drags possible—or drogues—astern. A tiny storm jib sheeted flat can help hold the bow off. When the helm cannot be manned, you have no need to be concerned about steering control. In this case, drags or a series drogue over the stern will help hold the stern to the seas, slow the boat, and smooth the sea. Again, avoid towing a sea anchor astern because of the strains and the risk of over-tethering.

In the past, knowledgeable sailors have suggested cutting down the masts when faced with the ultimate storm in order to reduce windage and weight aloft. Recent capsize studies, however, have shown conclusively that masts, especially tall and heavy ones, increase the boat's roll moment of inertia and therefore her dynamic stability and resistance to capsizing. Then too, wind pressure on the mast will help hold a boat steady and inhibit rolling when she lies a-hull. Furthermore, during a lull in the storm, a mast (or even a stump of the mast) may be needed to carry a stormsail while evacuating or clawing off a lee shore. And you will need sail to reach port after the blow has moderated. Boats often keep their rigs intact despite a capsizing, so you have far more to lose than to gain in a deliberate dismasting. About the only rationale for such a desperate tactic is that a boat which is very stable upside down will right more promptly when dismasted. This was demonstrated several

Figure 12-14. *Jean Gau's 30-foot Tahiti ketch* Atom *receives an assist from volunteers after she was blown ashore on Assateague Island, Maryland, in October 1971. The vessel was eventually refloated and towed in for repairs. (O.V. Wotton photo)*

times in the 1979 Fastnet Race. The 35-foot sloop *Ariadne*, for example, was slow to right after capsizing but took only 10 seconds to roll through 360 degrees after losing her mast.

One fact is encouraging for sailors caught in extremely bad conditions offshore: More than a few boats have survived after being left abandoned. This supports the theory of hulling and letting a boat assume her natural drift attitude. The survivors include *Black Duck, Dutch Treat, Curlew, Compass Rose, Water Witch,* and more recently, *Integrity* and *Irresistible.*

The old Crowninshield-designed schooner *Black Duck* broached while scudding before a gale in the Gulf Stream off Cape Hatteras in March 1948. The accident left her half swamped, with little more than a foot of freeboard, her main pump clogged and broken. She was repeatedly swept by seas while lying beam-on and appeared to be leaking badly. Her crew was taken off by a tanker, but the *Black Duck* did not sink until the next day, just before she was to be taken in tow by a freighter. Incidentally, there are few quicker ways of sinking a damaged vessel than towing her faster than her hull speed. Alain Gerbault's cutter *Firecrest* foundered while under tow.

The *Dutch Treat*, a 45-foot steel ketch designed by Al Mason, was abandoned during a blow off the coast of Charleston, South Carolina, in 1960. Although the wind in this case was not extreme, its direction opposed the flow of the Gulf Stream, building a dangerous sea. The boat wallowed in the trough and was swept by short, steep breaking waves.

Figure 12-15. *The steel ketch* Dutch Treat *is salvaged after eight days of drifting as a derelict. The boat was hardly damaged and had little water in her bilge. (Courtesy* Salt Water Sportsman)

Her crew sent out a distress signal and was soon rescued by a tanker. The abandoned ketch then proceeded to drift for eight days until she grounded on the sandbanks off Cape Hatteras. She sustained no serious damage and had very little water in her bilge.

The 67-foot schooner *Curlew* broached-to and was pooped while scudding under bare poles before a Force 12 storm near Bermuda in November 1962. Here crew was taken off by a U.S. Navy ship, and three days later she was found drifting, half swamped but still afloat, having cared for herself during the latter part of a real survival storm. In the case of the *Compass Rose*, a hard-chine keel yacht, abandonment occurred after grounding on a sandbar in the Bahamas during a gale in October 1967. Her skipper, the only crew, was rescued by helicopter. Somehow, the vessel refloated herself and drifted for six days, most of the time in gale-whipped seas. In November 1970, the 52-foot schooner *Integrity* was abandoned about 400 miles southeast of Cape Fear, South Carolina, after she had broached-to. Three weeks later she was still afloat and was towed to safety by a salvage tug.

Years ago, Shaw Mudge was kind enough to write me about the experience of the 49-foot Roue-designed and built schooner *Water Witch*, which was nearly lost during a horrendous storm below Cape Hatteras in October 1933. The crew was taken off by a tanker, but two weeks later the Coast Guard found *Water Witch* afloat and towed her to Charleston, where she was repaired. Not long afterward, Mr. Mudge's uncle, Theodore C. Wood, Jr., the boat's owner, took her to Florida and entered her in the first Miami-Nassau race, which turned out to be extremely rough. *Water Witch* was one of only three boats (out of 12 starters) to finish the race. Incidentally, the schooner had an off-center companionway, which added to her difficulties off Cape Hatteras.

In May 1986, the yawl-rigged Hinckley Sou'wester 42 *Irresistible* was rolled by a huge breaking sea after weathering a lengthy gale about 300 miles off Cape Cod, Massachusetts. While under power and creeping into the seas after the worst of the blow had subsided, *Irresistible* was inverted and probably rolled through 360 degrees. She righted promptly but in a battered condition, with her cabin windows smashed (probably from cabintop flexing), water almost up to the bunks, the liferaft swept away, and the mainmast crimped and teetering. The mast with its radio antennas soon went by the board, but not before the skipper, Preston Kelly, sent a Mayday. He and his crew were taken off the damaged yawl by a Coast Guard helicopter flying to the very limit of its range. The abandoned *Irresistible* drifted for three days but was then retrieved and towed to port. She was reconditioned by the Hinckley yard, and when I went aboard her about six months after the accident, she was in beautiful shape.

Some shortcomings and lessons to be learned from this incident are as follows: The bail on the mast for halyards was insufficiently strong and carried away, allowing the halyards to go adrift; the cabintop was insufficiently supported; the boat's stability range was lower than one would wish in such weather (the boat was a centerboarder); the liferaft stowage was weak (securing straps not through-bolted); the dogs securing cockpit seat lockers were inadequate; gear below was not stowed to withstand a severe knockdown; the bilge pumps were too small and the deck pump was in the wrong location; all hatches and vents (including the Dorades, which were installed with the cowl ahead of the deck hole) leaked; the bulkhead taping failed; the dodger was insufficiently strong; the boat had no sea anchor or drogue; the cabin sole, icebox lid, and bunk bottom lift-outs had no hold-downs; and the radio antennas depended on the mast. These deficiencies are especially interesting in that Hinckley boats are among the best American-built yachts. *Irresistable's* good points included prompt righting, the strength to survive, well-bolted winches strong enough to be used for tow lines, a cockpit drain time of about one minute, drawers that remained shut, a mast that stood long enough for a Mayday call (one shroud pulled out of a swaged fitting), an electrical system that performed well, an engine that still ran after a roll-over, an absence of gelcoat cracks, storm shutters that were available though not used, and a good skipper.

With the exception of the *Black Duck* all of these boats were saved. The skipper of a damaged craft can hardly be blamed for a decision to abandon ship when a rescue ship or aircraft is available and there is a real possibility of foundering. It is better not to gamble with human life. Nevertheless, these incidents show clearly how well a vessel can look out for herself, even in the worst conditions.

During the 1979 Fastnet storm, a total of 24 yachts were abandoned because they were considered uninhabitable. The main faults or deficiencies that led to their abandonment are as follows:

- **Unseaworthy designs.** Vulnerability to capsize resulting from an inadequate range of stability, due primarily to light displacement, excessive beam, and a high center of gravity.

- **Lack of proper storm gear.** No storm trysail, or a storm jib that was too large, or both. No proper drogue, no adequate cleating arrangements for rodes, or both.

- **Inadequate security for the crew, leading to injury or fear of injury.** Lack of bunk belts and secure attachment eyes for belts. Flimsy companionway slides that could easily fall out and could not be locked in place.

Despite these faults, 20 of the 24 abandoned yachts were later recovered, and one of the unrecovered boats sank only after being towed.

Abandonment

Rescue by Ship

Abandoning at sea in the middle of a survival storm can be tremendously difficult. It is generally agreed that the rescue ship should go to windward of the boat being abandoned to create a lee, but the rescuer will make more leeway and will soon drift down on the boat and damage her. Despite the risk, I think this approach is nearly always preferable to one on the lee side of the boat unless, perhaps, the ship has a Lyle gun (line-throwing gun) that can shoot a line a considerable distance. In this case the ship might stand clear to leeward, shoot a line to the boat, and transfer the crew in a rubber raft. But when the rescue ship is close aboard to leeward, she not only fails to make a lee, but waves reflecting off her windward side can make a dangerously steep and confused sea. It has been suggested that the ship could go some distance to windward of the boat and, at the end of a long line, float down to her a rubber raft or rescue mat (a floating mat usually made of buoyant PVC). It seems to me, however, that this operation would be next to impossible when the vessels lie beam-to-beam in water too deep for anchoring, because a raft or mat would drift very little, if any, faster than the ship. The two vessels would likely collide and perhaps even crush the abandoning crew before they could be taken aboard the ship. Better to approach the distressed boat from the windward side, then turn into the wind and try to hold position while a raft or mat is drifted down, though great care must be taken not to foul the propeller. A faster and more certain means of rescue, even though the distressed boat will probably be damaged, is for the ship to come alongside to windward of the boat. When side by side, the two vessels can be lashed together while the crew of the boat climb, or are hauled up the side of the ship. This is a dangerous operation because the man going up can be crushed between the vessels, thrown against the side of the ship, or struck by the boat's rigging when the ship rolls. David Q. Scott, who was taken off the *Black Duck* when she was abandoned, told me that he considered it far safer to be hauled up the ship's side rather than climb up on a rope ladder or cargo net. He said that when the rescue ship came alongside the apparently sinking schooner, lines were thrown down with bowlines on the bight tied in their ends. The *Black Duck*'s crew were able to slip into the loops of the bowlines and be pulled aloft quickly before they could be smashed by either vessel. It is even better to be lifted by a horseshoe lifesling like that used by a Coast Guard cutter to lift off the crew of the trimaran *Gonzo* after she capsized in the Atlantic in 1982. The ascent, whether climbing or being pulled, should begin when the boat is on the crest of a wave, so that she will drop away from the crew going aloft, who should be as far as possible from the masts so as not to be struck by the rigging or speared by a spreader. When the boat being abandoned is a trimaran with her awkward amas, the rescue might be effected more easily from the rescue ship's lifeboat.

Rescue by Helicopter

When a boat is abandoned close to shore, the crew are often taken off by helicopter. The U.S. Coast Guard has stated that 250 miles is near the limit for helicopter rescue, but the crew of *Irresistible* was lifted off nearly 300 miles offshore. Every rescue is an individual operation, and hard and fast rules are difficult. The following general advice is based mainly on Coast Guard experience:

- The stricken vessel should have a radio antenna independent of the mast in case of dismasting.

- Once good communication is established with the helicopter, normally over VHF radio, keep in contact and don't shift frequency, as the rescuers may attempt to talk you through the operation.

- Lash down all objects and stop all sails (downdraft from the rotor can be about 90 miles per hour). Clear an area away from masts (often on the stern of a sloop) for evacuation. Lower all masts or booms that can be lowered. During evacuation, see that all unnecessary crew are out of the way.

- When the helicopter arrives, the boat should be headed under power if possible, 45 to 20 degrees off the wind with seas on the port bow. Alternate headings may come from the helicopter pilot via radio or other signals. The vessel's helmsman should power slowly and hold a steady course. When the engine is not running, a drogue may have to be used, possibly over the stern since many sailboats will not hold their heads to wind.

- Crew should don personal flotation devices and be prepared to jump overboard if there is danger of snagging the mast. In rough seas, fouling a lifting basket in the rigging could cause the helicopter to crash.

- The helicopter will normally lower a sling, basket, or litter attached to the hoisting cable with a hook. Victims should not touch the hoisting devices until they have been grounded by touching the deck or water in order to discharge static electricity.

- If the basket or other rescue device has to be moved from the cleared area to evacuate a person, unhook it from the hoisting cable. When a cable is unhooked, don't attach the hook or cable to any part of the boat. Don't throw anything in the direction of the rotor.

- At night, illuminate the deck but don't shine a light directly at the helicopter.

- To rescue a victim from the water, the Coast Guard will often drop a "swimmer" to help. Even a medic may be dropped when the victim is seriously injured.

- When early radio contact can be made with the Coast Guard, it can drop pumps, liferafts, survival suits, and other helpful gear.

- Read instructions on the lifting device and assist the person being lifted, but keep clear when possible in case of a sudden movement. A steadying line is often used to keep the device from swinging excessively.

- Show a "thumbs up" signal when ready for the helicopter to hoist.

Multihulls in Heavy Weather

Chapter 3 offered arguments for and against using multihulled craft for blue-water sailing. Although multihull enthusiasts abound and have completed many successful voyages in these craft, more than a few have been unsuccessful. The inherent drawbacks of multihulls are capsizability and inability to self-right. The debate over multihulls extends to the manner in which they should be handled in heavy weather. Some experienced multihull sailors believe in scudding, others prefer lying to a sea anchor, and more than a few recommend lying a-hull. Some racers opt for carrying on under greatly reduced sail.

The last tactic is based on the premise that it is better to have controlled maneuverability with headway, but for some racers this may be a rationale masking a strong desire to win. Chay Blyth and Rob James, sailing a large trimaran, determined that they should keep sailing rather than lie a-hull when they were forced to lower sail to reeve an earing during the double-handed transatlantic race in 1981. After nearly being flipped by a wave on the beam, they resolved to "never stop again—whatever the weather." Bill Homewood, who has done so well in solo transatlantic races in his smaller trimaran, has come to about the same conclusion. After nearly capsizing while lying to a sea anchor in the 1980 OSTAR, he now favors keeping his boat moving at moderate speed under a triple-reefed main. Speed does provide rudder control to help

Figure 12-16. *Bill Homewood's speedy Val trimaran* Third Turtle, *temporarily named* British Airways *for the 1984 OSTAR race. (Courtesy Bill Homewood)*

avoid or steer through breaking seas, but the helmsman had better be skilled and alert, and the speed should be kept down, particularly when bashing against head seas. Taking breakers on the beam, especially when centerboards are down, could trip the boat, and heeling forces are greatest when the wind is abeam. If the choice were to keep sailing, I would want to run, reach off, or sail close-hauled under the smallest possible sail that would provide steering control.

Proponents of lying a-hull feel that it is without high risk because of the usual multihull's great righting moment and shallow draft, which allows the boat to be thrown to leeward sideways without tripping. When a multihull has a greater-than-normal stability range or resistance to capsizing due to large size, ballast, a specially placed sponson, or widely separated hulls, she might lie a-hull in weather that is quite heavy. Indeed, Dr. David Lewis so weathered an Atlantic gale in 1964 in his heavily ballasted catamaran, *Rehu Moana*. Likewise, the unballasted catamaran *Golden Cockerel* lay a-hull in the 1968 Singlehander's Transatlantic Race during a lengthy gale. Her skipper, Bill Howell, retracted her daggerboards to avoid tripping, and he reported that one sea lifted the catamaran and threw her 50 yards to leeward. Centerboards should be retracted not only to avoid tripping but to lessen stress on the hull. Despite many successful hulling experiences, however, it seems safest to keep a capsizable and non-self-righting multihull, especially a small one, end-to the wind and seas in extremely bad weather. The 25-foot trimaran, *Clipper One*, turned turtle while lying a-hull, stripped of all sail,

Figure 12-17. *Dr. David Lewis's* Rehu Moana, *a heavily ballasted catamaran intended for around-the-world cruising. Her heavy displacement detracted greatly from her sailing performance. (Eileen Ramsay photo)*

not far from the Cape of Good Hope during a gale in 1968. Her skipper, singlehander Tom Corkill, survived the accident after extricating himself from the cabin and clinging to the upturned boat for 18 hours before he was rescued. Despite the *Clipper One*'s tremendous initial stability—a result of her above-normal beam and the fact that she had no sail set—she was capsized by a sea breaking on her beam. It seems likely that she would have had a better chance lying end-to such seas.

Some multihull enthusiasts advocate running off at high speed in bad weather. A champion of the tactic was Arthur Piver, who claimed that a light-displacement trimaran can surf down the faces of storm waves and stay ahead of their breaking crests. Although it is true that a well-designed, directionally stable multihull can surf for hours in heavy winds and large seas with attentive handling of the helm, many sailors oppose the high-speed running technique in extremely bad weather with confused seas. Piver was lost at sea in March 1968 while single-handing a trimaran of his design. Although no one knows how he disappeared, it seems conceivable that he might have been overwhelmed while testing his high-speed theory. When Walter Greene capsized in the trimaran *Gonzo* in 1982, he was scudding at considerable speed, and he stated that in the future he would do anything but run. "I think you get a false sense of security running," Greene said. Although it is sometimes argued that multihulls are less subject than monohulls to pitch-poling and being pooped when running off at high speeds, these accidents are always possible with any boat in the worst conditions. Some cats, and tris especially, are subject to capsizing diagonally—that is, capsizing and pitch-poling simultaneously. This can happen when the bow of the leeward hull or ama roots while the stern of the windward ama is lifted. Risk of diagonal capsizing can be minimized by keeping the mast and center of effort of the sail plan reasonably far aft and, according to trimaran designer Jim Brown, by amas of sufficient length forward with adequate buoyancy in their bows. On the other hand, trimaran designer Lock Crowther warns that excessively buoyant bows with a lot of flare can encourage a tendency to broach-to. When the lee bow begins to bury and the seas are irregular and confused, it certainly seems prudent to reduce sail, slow down, and in extreme conditions keep the sterns square to the waves.

Catamaran designer Rudy Choy has suggested running a cat dead before it under bare poles in the heaviest weather. He advocates towing all possible warps, lines, and drags astern to slow her speed. If she still tends to surf, he suggests plugging the self-bailing cockpit and filling it or letter it fill with water in order to weigh her down and further reduce speed. Designer James Wharram, a V-hulled catamaran enthusiast, advocates running off in bad weather and suggests slowing speed by towing automobile tires from each stern. However, he recommends a speed sufficient for good steering control so that the stern can be held square to the seas. This seems a good plan in regular waves, but with extremely confused seas coming from several directions at once, the helmsman might fail to keep all waves dead astern. If a single drogue is towed astern to slow a cat, a bridle will be needed to keep the drogue halfway between the hulls, and this bridle will help pull the stern toward the seas.

Perhaps the most favored tactic among offshore cruising multihullers is lying to a sea anchor or drogue. Advocates of this method include Joan and John Casanova, experienced blue-water trimaran sailors, who contributed to the book *The Parachute Anchoring System*. The Casanovas believe in using a large parachute anchor with plenty of scope from the bow. Designer Dick Newick had success in exceptionally steep seas aboard his 31-foot trimaran deploying two conic sea anchors, a large one from the bow of the central hull and a smaller one from the windward ama on a shorter, weighted rode. Although the system worked well and was effective against the odd wave from a different direction, he admitted that it might possibly permit the boat to turn so that the ama without the anchor faces the waves. Many of Newick's recent offshore trimarans are designed to take seas from astern, and he writes that on these boats he would stream a sea anchor from the stern."

The extensive drogue testing program conducted by Donald Jordan with the U.S. Coast Guard and described earlier in this chapter included tests on model trimarans as well as on monohulls. The conclusions are interesting and promising. Of considerable value to offshore multihull sailors is the following quote from the technical paper by Jordan and Carol Hervey:

> The monohull models did not behave well with a drogue (or sea anchor) deployed from the bow. It took a large parachute to pull the bow into the wind, and even with this large chute, the bow would quickly fall off when the towline became slack, which it did whenever the boat passed through the trough of a large wave. This is an important observation in that it accounts for the failure of a number of actual attempts to use a sea anchor in survival storms.
>
> The multihull models behaved very well with a drogue deployed from the bow or the stern, better in some respects than the monohulls. There are several reasons for this. The bridle which attaches the drogue to a multihull has a wide base, as much as 40 feet from ama to ama. Such a bridle can impose a very powerful turning moment on the boat and thus prevent broaching. Also, since it has a long narrow hull in contact with the water, the multihull does not fall off rapidly when the towline goes slack. Finally, the light weight of the multihull reduces the inertia loads, and the low hull drag reduces the drag loads as the drogue pulls the boat through the breaking crests.
>
> Unlike a monohull, a multihull rode well with a drogue (sea anchor) deployed from the bow, as well as from the stern. However, a large parachute was required to pull the bow into the wind initially. We feel that a drogue from the stern is preferable because it can be smaller and will impose lower loads. Also, in the process of pulling the bow into the wind, a multihull is vulnerable to capsize, whereas it easily swings downwind as the drogue is deployed from the stern.

If caught in a very heavy blow during a coastal passage, a shoal-draft multihull might have an advantage over a deep-keeled monohull in that the former can more easily be run ashore and beached. However, such a tactic is usually one of final desperation, and every attempt should be made to claw off a lee shore before the vessel is deliberately grounded, regardless of her draft. On the subject of beaching in heavy seas, my feelings are similar to those of Captain A.J. Kenealy. In an early (1905) manual on seamanship, *Boat Sailing in Fair Weather and Foul*, the Captain wrote: "Now praying on shipboard is not to be scoffed at, but it should be delayed until man has exhausted every possible means of saving the ship."

Chapter 13
POWERBOAT MANAGEMENT IN HEAVY SEAS

Powerboats Offshore

A powerboat designed for long-distance runs offshore should share many characteristics in common with the offshore sailboat. Motorboats that have nearly opposite characteristics, such as many high-speed, low-deadrise planing boats and especially houseboats, with their flat bottoms, low freeboard, and lofty deckhouses, should not expose themselves to heavy weather in unprotected waters. A low stability range, very hard bilges, extremely unbalanced hull (sharp forward, broad and flat aft), tiny rudders (often ineffective at low speeds), and a large open cockpit are all unsuitable for rough going. Displacement offshore motorboats of the MFV (motor fishing vessel) type must be completely watertight, should have a low center of gravity to assure reasonable stability, modest-sized windows, sufficient draft to assure good propeller and rudder depth, and a reasonably balanced hull (in the fore-and-aft distribution of buoyancy). The one outstanding drawback of the heavy, round-bottomed, relatively narrow-stern type is its tendency to roll. Such a vessel should have some means to damp rolling, preferably a small sail that can also be used for emergency locomotion in the event of engine failure. Naval architect William Garden has suggested that when a steadying sail is to serve as occasional propulsion, it should be located far forward so that the powerboat can be made to run off satisfactorily before the wind. It is also advisable to have a means of setting a small riding sail aft when and if it becomes desirable to hold the vessel's bow toward the seas.

Some permanent or built-in means of preventing severe rolling were mentioned in Chapter 3. The paravane or fisherman stabilizer is a temporary or removable roll preventer (Figure 13-1). This device, sometimes called a "flopper-stopper," was refined for yacht use by noted powerboat seaman Robert Beebe. The antirolling system comprises two heavy metal plates shaped like delta wings, suspended well below the water on wire or rope pendants from the ends of two booms rigged one on each side of the boat. Although the paravanes are designed for rough water, they

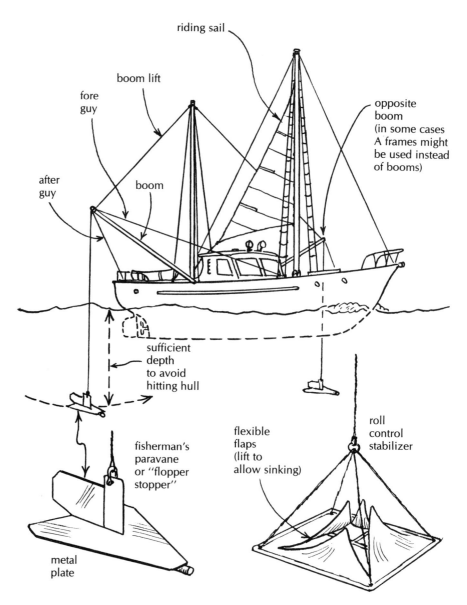

riding sail

boom lift

fore guy

opposite boom (in some cases A frames might be used instead of booms)

after guy

boom

sufficient depth to avoid hitting hull

fisherman's paravane or "flopper stopper"

flexible flaps (lift to allow sinking)

roll control stabilizer

Figure 13-1. *Removable roll stabilizers.*

metal plate

could be dangerous in the most extreme weather offshore because a boom or guy may break or the heavy plates be thrown against the hull. Nevertheless, Beebe claimed to have carried his flopper-stoppers in gale-force winds, and felt that they contribute to safety when it is desirable to run off with the seas on the quarter. A similar roll-damper called the Roll Control is also shown in Figure 13-1. This device has a valve flap that opens to let the plate sink but closes to resist rolling when the plate is lifted. Unlike the flopper-stopper, the Roll Control is not designed to be towed when the boat is moving with any speed, but is intended merely for boats at anchor or possibly when drifting slowly.

As for high-speed boats at sea, you are not at any great risk in a fast,

Figure 13-2. *A large MFV type cruiser. Note her "flopper-stopper" booms and roller furling headsails.* (*Courtesy* National Fisherman)

decked, and buoyant motorboat making a short run offshore in fair weather or a careful passage along a coast with numerous accessible inlets. Such a boat should have some means to call for help or have emergency propulsion, such as an auxiliary outboard motor, in case of engine failure. The Coast Guard strongly urges "a secondary means of propulsion on small boats." Few, if any, small planing motor craft, especially those with low freeboard and large open cockpits, should make extended passages a great distance offshore. These boats are vulnerable to swamping or capsizing and turning turtle if caught in extremely heavy weather, and they don't have the fuel capacity to power into or run before a lengthy gale. As long as the high-speed boat stays reasonably close to shore, however, she can make a dash for port when bad weather threatens. This requires a reliable engine regularly serviced and a vigilant weather eye and frequent checks on radio weather reports. Some fast boats, usually offshore sport fishermen or those with fairly deep-V bottoms having the V carried well aft, are quite well designed to withstand pounding into rough head seas. This type of hull is often used for offshore powerboat racing. Nevertheless, keep in mind that such a boat is by no means intended to cope with a lengthy survival storm far offshore.

If a small planing motorboat is unfortunate enough to be caught offshore in heavy weather, keep her end-on, preferably bow-to, the seas. She should proceed toward shelter if possible, but her course might be a zigzag one in the interest of avoiding or minimizing the dangers of heavy breaking seas. A wave breaking on the beam could easily capsize or swamp the normal high-speed boat. Thus, a course parallel to the crests of the waves (normally at right angles to the wind) might be negotiated in a weaving manner that first brings the crests broad on the bow and

Figure 13-3. *This Maine lobsterboat type is quite seaworthy for coastal work, and her high speed allows her to reach shelter quickly in the event of heavy weather. Her large cockpit and low freeboard aft, however, make her unsuitable for coping with a bad storm at sea. (Courtesy* National Fisherman)

then on the quarter. The speed should be quite slow, but fast enough for good steerageway. In extremely heavy weather, even a skillfully steered zigzag course might be too dangerous, so most motorboats should be held end-to the seas by powering slowly into them (a tactic sometimes termed "dodging"), lying to a sea anchor, or possibly running off.

When the course lies dead to windward, the fast motorboat should power slowly into the seas with just enough speed to prevent her bow from being blown or knocked off. Some experienced powerboaters say that the seas should be taken at a slight angle to the bow (up to 30 degrees), but the angle should not be broad enough to create rolling problems or require great speed to hold up the bow. When the bow begins to fall off, the throttle should be opened only momentarily for steering control. Too much speed can damage the hull through pounding or can cause the seas to break into the cockpit and swamp an undecked boat. Remember that even a self-draining cockpit usually drains very slowly. Even when a boat has ample flotation, the shifting of water in a large, filled cockpit during a roll can seriously affect her stability. Driving with speed into a head sea puts a greater strain on the hull than many people realize. Many years ago, I was aboard an 85-foot air-sea rescue crash-boat that cracked six frames while driving toward port at a moderate speed into a head sea. After discovering the damage, we were forced to run off, which we did successfully at moderately low speed until the weather improved.

Some motorboats, usually the heavy seagoing types, will run off fairly well in heavy weather, but many small high-speed types with sharp bows, little deadrise aft, and tiny rudders can be extremely difficult in following seas. The latter type, designed to plane easily in smooth water, has far more buoyancy aft than forward. This makes the bow root when scudding at low speed in heavy weather, and rooting could lead to broaching or even pitch-poling. One school of thought advocates running off at high speed in order to keep the bow high and stay ahead of wave crests. According to this theory, the boat should ride on the back of a wave and travel at the exact speed of the wave. This can work in regular waves and when running through a short stretch of regular breakers— say to a nearby port. The throttle(s) will have to be played carefully so that the boat will stay on the back of a wave, and also to change the boat's trim; open the throttles momentarily when the bow drops, and close them momentarily when the bow lifts too high. If the boat has trim tabs, they should be adjusted to keep the bow from rooting. But running at wave speed can be dangerous in heavy weather at sea. Storm waves at sea can run at 25 to 35 knots or faster, and it would be exceedingly difficult to ride them hour after hour, even in a high-speed boat. Fuel consumption is great at high speeds, and fast boats normally have a short cruising range. Waves at sea are frequently confused, with wave trains mixing and seas crossing other seas or swells from several directions. In such a case, the boat could easily poke her bow into a hollow, and her high-speed momentum could cause her to broach and capsize or pitchpole. Tank tests have shown that a boat running off at nearly the same speed as the waves is in a position of great instability when she is overtaken by a crest. Furthermore, many shoal-draft powerboats run the risk of lifting the rudder and propeller clear of the water and temporarily losing steering control. When you are overtaken by a crest, slow down and let the wave pass by in the quickest possible time. The noted yacht deliverer Peter Hayward wrote of doing considerable damage to a fast 36-foot motorboat by going faster than the seas and running into the back of a wave.

While scudding under power might be an effective tactic for a heavy seagoing motor craft with a relatively balanced hull, I suggest a slow-to-moderate speed, just enough for steering control, because the vessel's own wave system can reinforce the following seas when she is going fast. Furthermore, too much speed would keep the boat on the crest for a dangerous length of time.

If running off is too risky for a small planing boat in confused seas, you might be wise to cut power and stream a sea anchor when progress cannot be made safely against the seas. Some shallow hulls with low windage forward and a small propeller may ride to a sea anchor over the bow if weight is kept forward. If the engine is an outboard and can be raised, lifting the prop clear of the water may help keep the bow toward the seas. In the event the bow cannot be held up, however, the sea anchor might be streamed astern, but only if the boat has plenty of freeboard aft so that waves will not break over the stern. The heavy MFV or even the decked-over express cruiser or offshore sport fisherman might have success with the Hanks method (described earlier) of towing the bight of a warp astern to help slow speed and smooth the seas with minimal hampering of steering control. Another technique sometimes recommended is towing a drogue astern with its rode secured all the way aft and the engine revved up to keep a good strain on the line. This will hamper steering control but will hold the stern up to following seas when they are not too irregular. The technique is most commonly used when running a stretch of surf, and it will be further discussed in the next section. Take great care when towing drags not to let lines foul the propeller.

Seamen such as Thomas Fleming Day and Humphrey Barton have suggested hulling in seagoing motor craft, but this tactic requires many of the characteristics of an offshore sailer. For instance, the powerboat should have a reasonable stability range and some means to damp rolling. A small riding sail can alleviate rolling but requires ample reserve stability if it is not to contribute to a capsizing in very heavy weather. Even a short mast without sail will contribute somewhat to the boat's roll moment of inertia to increase dynamic stability. One definite drawback to powerboats lying a-hull is that such craft often have vulnerable deckhouses with large glass windows. Only if such windows are of heavy plastic or safety glass or are fitted with storm shutters would it be sensible to come broadside to heavy seas. Pilothouse windows should be heavily glazed, preferably with polycarbonates (Lexan or Tuffak), or vulnerable windows should be protected with a fine-mesh wire screen or sheet plywood with vision ports. The success of hulling will depend not only on the suitability of the boat but on the nature of the seas. Long, fairly regular deep-water waves might allow safe and reasonably comfortable hulling, but short, steep shallow-water waves with frequently breaking crests of the plunging variety taken beam-on could be disastrous.

Running Inlets

On coastal passages when bad weather threatens, harbors are often available, but sometimes they can only be reached by negotiating a treacherous inlet. These inlets usually consist of narrow, sometimes twisting channels that pass through shoals over which surf breaks continually. In most cases, a seaworthy sailboat with an able crew should head offshore into deep water and get all the sea room possible to weather the blow, rather than attempt running a dangerous inlet. A maneuverable powerboat not specifically designed for heavy weather offshore, however, might be well advised to run the inlet and reach shelter provided certain precautions are taken. These include carefully studying the approaches on the chart and reading about the inlet in the coast pilot; studying the inlet visually to determine the state of sea and the location of breakers; studying tables and especially observing channel markers to determine the state of tide and current; preparing the boat and crew (donning life jackets) for heavy seas; and, if possible, contacting the Coast Guard for a report on the condition of the inlet. Enter treacherous inlets on slack water or preferably a flood tide, but only under the most urgent circumstances when the current is flowing against the seas. Cross the entrance (where the worst seas are usually located) during a lull in the seas, as might occur after the seventh or eleventh wave or some other numerical spacing that seems to produce an especially high wave due to the mixing of wave trains. Make every attempt to avoid breaking crests. The boat should be held end-to (usually stern-to) the seas, and she must be carefully steered and handled to prevent

Figure 13-4. *Two fishing boats entering an inlet. Notice the bar opposite the entrance and the offset channel that leads in from the right-hand side. (Edward D. Hipple photo)*

broaching or turning sideways to breakers. Direct the passage through the deepest part of the channel in the smoothest water. Preparations include making the boat watertight (closing hatches, ports, vents, all seacocks except those on scuppers, etc.) and checking to see that the engine is running smoothly, the liferaft is available, all crewmembers have donned life jackets, and all equipment that might be needed is ready for use. Such equipment includes an anchor and drogue with neatly coiled line, a bucket, a loud horn, and a strong searchlight and flares if the inlet is approached at night.

You might consider three methods of entering an inlet through breaking seas: (1) running before the seas at high speed, (2) running at low speed (with or without a drogue), and (3) entering backward, bow to the seas. The first method is dangerous but can be successful when the boat is reasonably fast, of light displacement, and is directionally stable with highly controllable steering. She should pass through the breakers at the exact speed of the waves, perhaps about 15 knots, so that she can remain in the trough or on the back of a sea (never on its face). Too little speed will allow the crest to overtake the boat, which will adversely affect her stability and subject her to the possibilities of broaching or being pooped by the break. Too much speed will cause her to overrun the crest, slide down the wave face, and perhaps root her bow and broach or pitch-pole. On a wave's crest, a shoal-draft boat's propeller and rudder are apt to emerge, depriving her of steering control.

It is seldom advisable to run before steep seas in a heavy displacement craft, because she will not have sufficient speed to keep up with the waves, and her own wave system may disturb the following seas and encourage them to break over the stern.

Method two, sometimes referred to as "washing in," is generally a wetter but safer method of running breakers. Boat speed should be just fast enough for good steerageway, but you should throttle down the engine to idling speed when a crest overtakes the boat. When this is done, the chance of the bow rooting is minimized, and the sea passes in the quickest possible time. However, a good deal of water may come over

Figure 13-5. *A Coast Guard 44-foot lifeboat negotiating a breaker at the entrance to the Umpqua River, Oregon. She is self-righting and has been rolled over twice by the seas at this entrance. On each occasion she lost a man overboard and recovered him. On the second occasion, she also rescued all four occupants of a 16-foot outboard boat that had been broken into three pieces by the wave that capsized the lifeboat. (Courtesy U.S. Coast Guard)*

the stern; thus, the boat should have a self-bailing cockpit with large drains or a very effective bilge pump. After the crest has passed, it may be necessary to speed up momentarily, throwing propeller wash against the rudder to turn the boat's stern square to the seas. Motor craft with twin screws are highly controllable when handled by skilled operators.

Some authorities advocate towing a conic sea anchor astern to help hold the stern to the seas, but this suggestion is not very practical for the average skipper. Towing a sea anchor astern in surf is tricky. The drogue must be allowed to fill and therefore cause a drag precisely when the boat speeds up as the crest overtakes her. At this time, there is a tremendous strain on the rode, and after the crest passes, it is necessary to spill the drogue with a special tripping line, the handling of which requires skill and practice. Also, the average modern motorboat is not fitted with proper bitts and fairleads for the heavy loads of powering against a large drogue or conic sea anchor deployed from the stern. Improperly handled, the device can spin and twist its lines, pull off a cleat or break its lines, dive and dredge up mud, porpoise (jump out of water), hamper steering, or foul the propeller. On the other hand, a simple drag (or drags) towed astern, such as the bight of a heavy line towed in the manner suggested by Hanks (see Chapter 12), may be easy to handle and could be of some help in controlling the boat's speed. It is also likely that the Galerider or series drogue discussed earlier could be effective.

Method three, entering the inlet stern first, is the one used least, and this is not surprising as it requires a strong flooding current and a boat that can be maneuvered easily in reverse. The boat is backed when she is in the trough but given slow speed ahead on the crests to hold her bow up to the seas. Meanwhile, she is being swept into the inlet by the current. The principal danger of the method is in losing steering control of the boat while she is backed. Skillful engine operation and helmsmanship are required to keep the boat on her proper heading with her bow square to the waves.

Along some coasts with sandbars off their beaches, onshore winds help concentrate current pathways called rip currents. These flow toward the sea approximately at right angles to the shore, providing escape routes for high water piled up by the wind and seas behind the bars that run parallel to the beach. A boat moving toward shore should avoid these rips, because small, choppy, spilling-type breakers may develop. If it becomes necessary to land on the beach or pass through the bars, however, there will be fewer large breakers in the rip current channels because water in the channels will be deeper than over the bars. Of course, there is the additional danger of grounding when crossing a bar. Should it be necessary to pass through a short stretch of surf, you may want to drop an anchor over the stern (or bow if the boat is backing) so that the rode can be hauled on as each sea passes to help keep the boat end-to the seas. This technique requires a considerable length of anchor rode even when the surf runs over a very narrow shoal.

When crossing a bar or entering a rough inlet, a powerboater might spread oil to help calm the seas, but a considerable quantity would be needed to have any effect at all on shallow-water breakers. Oil might be spread by pumping it through forward outlets, such as the head discharge, or it could be poured through a hose leading over the bow (when the boat is moving ahead). A very slow boat speed will be needed for maximum benefit.

Although contrary to my intentions, the last two chapters may have been a little frightening. It is my contention, however, that a seaworthy, well-found, and properly handled boat can live through extremely bad conditions at sea. Although boats are occasionally lost, the reason nearly always lies in some deficiency of the vessel's design and construction or a serious mistake in seamanship or grave error in judgment by her master. One hears talk of gigantic "freak" waves at sea, which no vessel can possibly negotiate in the upright position, and it is true that such waves exist, but they are rare. Monstrous freaks are nearly always born in regions where high, steady winds combine with almost limitless fetch and where uncharted (or charted) shoals, seamounts, or fast-moving currents oppose the winds as, for example, off Cape Agulhas, South Africa. The sailor of a sizable, stable, and seaworthy boat who carefully charts his passages over the safest routes when favorable weather is expected could spend a lifetime at sea without meeting a non-negotiable wave. Indeed, I think that a well-planned offshore passage in a suitable boat is far safer than a lengthy automobile trip.

Appendix A / United States Coast Guard Auxiliary Courtesy Examination

The Coast Guard Auxiliary offers a Courtesy Marine Examination as a service to boatowners. While not a comprehensive survey, the examination helps the boatowner determine whether his boat is safe, and if not, what should be done to improve it. The following summary of examination should help you run safety checks on your own boat.

A Courtesy Marine Examination cannot be performed while the boat is underway. Boats longer than 26 feet must be observed safely waterborne and moored. Boats of less than 26 feet in length and of known stock design can be examined out of the water, provided they are built of materials which are not subject to warping or shrinkage. All through-hull fittings on boats so examined must be properly installed in order for a decal to be awarded.

Use the following paragraphs as a check-off list to help you determine if your boat meets the requirements of federal law and the additional safety standards recommended by the Auxiliary. Legal requirements are based upon the class of the motorboat or auxiliary-powered sailboat, which is in turn determined by its length. The length is measured in a straight line along the centerline from the foremost part of the boat to the aftermost part of the boat. Bowsprits, outboard motor brackets, and similar attachments are not included in this measurement.

Class A - less than 16 feet in length
Class 1 - 16 feet or over in length and less than 26 feet
Class 2 - 26 feet or over in length and less than 40 feet
Class 3 - 40 feet or over in length and not more than 65 feet

Numbering

Vessels equipped with propulsion machinery of any type are required to be numbered by the Coast Guard or by the state. In some states, boats not in this category must also be numbered. Check your state for its requirements.

The number must be properly displayed and the registration must be available for examination.

Natural Ventilation

All motorboats (including auxiliary sailboats) using gasoline or other fuel with a flash point less than 110°F., configured so that explosive or flammable vapors could be entrapped, must have at least two ventilator ducts fitted with cowls or the equivalent leading to each engine or fuel tank compartment for the efficient removal of explosive gases. The exhaust ducts shall lead from the lower portion of the bilge, and the intake ducts shall lead at least midway to the bilge below the carburetor air intake. Cowls shall be located and trimmed for maximum effectiveness and to prevent displaced fumes from being recirculated.

- Classes A, 1, 2, and 3—required on all motorboats using fuel with a flash point less than 110° F. the construction or decking over of which was commenced after April 25, 1940.

Powered Ventilation

Vessels built after July 31, 1980 that have gasoline engines with a cranking motor (starter) for electrical generation, mechanical power, or propulsion in a closed compartment are required to have a powered ventilation system. This includes each compartment with such an engine.

No person may operate a vessel built after July 31, 1980 with a gasoline engine in a closed compartment unless it is equipped with an operable ventilation system that meets Coast Guard standards. The operator is required to keep the system in operating condition and ensure cowls and ducting are not blocked or torn.

Backfire Flame Control

Efficient means of backfire flame control is required for each carburetor on every inboard engine installed after April 25, 1940. Acceptable means of backfire flame control are:

- A Coast Guard-approved backfire flame arrestor secured to the air intake of each carburetor; or
- Engine and fuel intake system which provides equivalent protection and is labeled to indicate Coast Guard acceptance; or
- Any attachment firmly secured to the carburetor or arrangement of the air intake by means of which flames caused by backfire will be dispersed to the atmosphere in such a way as not to endanger the vessel or persons on board.

Fire Extinguishers

Fire extinguishers are classed according to their size and type. Extinguishers must bear Coast Guard and/or Underwriters Laboratory "Marine Type" approved labels. Type B fire extinguishers, designed for extinguishing flammable liquids, are required on motorboats. Equivalent sizes and extinguishing agent are shown on this table:

Minimum Number of
Type B Fire Extinguishers Required

Classification (type size)	Foam (minimum gallons)	Carbon Dioxide (minimum pounds)	Dry Chemical (minimum pounds)	Halon (minimum pounds)
B-I	$1^{1}/_{4}$	4	2	$2^{1}/_{2}$
B-II	$2^{1}/_{2}$	15	10	None

Note: Carbon tetrachloride extinguishers and others of the toxic vaporizing-liquid type such as chlorobromomethane are no longer approved and are not accepted as required fire extinguishers.

The number of approved extinguishers required depends upon the class of the motorboat. One B-II extinguisher may be substituted for two B-I extinguishers. When the engine compartment of the motorboat is equipped with a fixed (built-in) extinguisher system, one less hand-portable B-I extinguisher is required.

Classes A & 1 *outboard motorboats* so constructed that entrapment of flammable vapors *cannot occur* are not required to carry fire extinguishers. Classes A & 1 motorboats which do not meet the above exception, and all Classes 2 & 3 motorboats must be equipped with fire extinguishers according to the table on the following page:

Minimum Number of
Hand-Portable Fire Extinguishers Required

	No fixed system in machinery space	Fixed fire extinguishing system in machinery space
Class A	1 B-I	None
Class 1	1 B-I	None
Class 2	2 B-I or 1 B-II	1 B-I
Class 3	3 B-I or 1 B-II and 1 B-I	2 B-I or 1 B-II

Bell, Whistle, or Horn

The requirement to carry a bell depends upon the class of boat. All bells must emit a clear bell-like tone when struck. The type of whistle or horn required differs with the class of boat. All horns or whistles must be capable of producing a blast of 2 seconds or more duration. The requirements for bell, whistle or horn are shown in this table:

Bell	Whistle or Horn
Class A none required	none required (except where International Rules apply)
Class 1 none required	mouth-, hand- or power-operated, audible at least $1/2$ mile
Class 2 required	hand- or power-operated, audible at least 1 mile
Class 3 required	power-operated, audible at least 1 mile

Note: While it is not required that all classes of boat carry the bell, whistle, or horn, the Rules of the Road require all vessels to give proper signals if a signaling situation develops.

Navigation Lights

All motorboats are required to display navigation lights prescribed for the class when operated between the hours of sunset and sunrise. The International configuration may be displayed on the high seas and on all United States waters. The Motorboat Act of 1940 configuration *cannot* be displayed on the high seas.

Lifesaving Devices

Every motorboat must have one approved lifesaving device in acceptable condition for each person on board or in tow (waterskier, surfboats, etc.). Lifesaving devices must be readily accessible. Kapok and fiberglass lifesaving devices which do not have plastic-covered buoyant pads are not acceptable.

- CLASSES 1, 2, and 3 motorboats must carry one approved Type I, II, or III PFD for each person on board and one Type IV PFD.
- CLASS A motorboats must carry an approved Type I, II, III, or IV PFD for each person on board.

Visual Distress Signals

All vessels, used on coastal waters, the Great Lakes, territorial seas and those waters connected directly to them, up to a point where a body of water is less than two miles wide, must be equipped with visual distress signals. Vessels owned in the United States operating on the high seas must be equipped with visual distress signals. The following vessels are not required to carry day signals but must carry night signals when operating from sunset to sunrise.

- Recreational boats less than 16 feet in length.
- Boats participating in organized events such as races, regattas or marine parades.
- Open sailboats less than 26 feet in length not equipped with propulsion machinery.
- Manually propelled boats

Pyrotechnic visual distress signals must be Coast Guard Approved, in serviceable condition and readily accessible. They are marked with a date showing the service life, which must not be expired. Launchers manufactured before January 1, 1981, intended for use with approved signals, are not required to be Coast Guard Approved. If pyrotechnic devices are selected, a minimum of three are required. That is three signals for day use and three signals for night. Some pyrotechnic signals meet both day and night use requirements. Pyrotechnic devices should be stored in a cool, dry location. A watertight container painted red or orange and prominently marked "DISTRESS SIGNALS" is recommended.

USCG Approved Pyrotechnic Visual Distress Signals and Associated Devices include:

- Pyrotechnic red flares, hand-held or aerial.
- Pyrotechnic orange smoke, hand-held or floating.
- Launchers for aerial red meteors or parachute flares.

Nonpyrotechnic visual distress signals must be in serviceable condition, readily accessible and certified by the manufacturer as complying with USCG requirements, they include:

- Orange distress flag
- Electric distress light

The distress flag is a day signal only. It must be at least 3×3 feet with a black square and ball on an orange background. It is most distinctive when attached and waved on a paddle or boathook or flown from a mast.

The electric distress light is accepted for night use only and must automatically flash the international SOS distress signal (···— — —···). This is an unmistakable distress signal. A standard flashlight is not acceptable as a visual distress signal.

Under Inland Navigation Rules, a high intensity white light flashing at regular intervals from 50-70 times per minute is considered a distress signal. Strobe lights used in inland waters shall only be used as a distress signal.

Regulations prohibit display of visual distress signals on the water under any circumstances except when assistance is required to prevent immediate or potential danger to persons on board a vessel.

All distress signals have distinct advantages and disadvantages, no single device is ideal under all conditions or suitable for all purposes. Pyrotechnics are excellent distress signals, universally recognized. However, there is potential for injury and property damage if not properly handled. These devices produce a very hot flame, the residue can cause burns and ignite flammable material. Pistol launched and handheld parachute flares and meteors have many characteristics of a firearm and must be handled with caution.

Auxiliary Standards for Award of Decal

Before a boat can be awarded the Courtesy Marine Examination decal, it must meet all the foregoing requirements of the federal law, and in addition it must meet the following standards considered necessary for safe operation:

- *Lifesaving devices*. There must be at least as many approved lifesaving devices, of the type required for the class of boat, as there are berths. A boat with fewer than two bunks must have at least two approved lifesaving devices aboard. Lifesaving devices must be readily accessible.
- *Fire extinguishers*. All Class A and Class 1 motorboats, whether or not they are equipped with a fixed fire extinguishing system, must carry one hand-portable fire extinguisher of approved type.
- *Navigation lights* must be of a configuration specified for the class of boat and must be operative and fully visible through the required arc.
- *Distress signals*. Recreational boats 16 feet or longer (with a few exceptions) must carry distress signals (see above).
- *Galley stove*. If carried, the galley stove must be securely mounted so that it cannot shift position. Stoves must be installed so that no flammable materials in the vicinity can be ignited. Any of the common types of fuel may be used *except* gasoline.
- *Permanently installed fuel tanks* must be securely mounted so that they cannot shift position.
- *Fuel tank vent*. A vent terminating outboard of the hull and compartments must lead to each permanently installed fuel tank.
- A *fuel tank fill pipe* leading to permanently installed fuel tanks must fit into a filling plate located on deck outside the cockpit to insure that spilled fuel flows overboard.
- *Portable fuel tanks and spare fuel containers*. Tanks and containers which exceed 7 gallons are not classed as portable tanks, and must meet all requirements for permanently installed tanks. Tanks and spare fuel containers of less than 7 gallons must be tight and sufficiently sturdy to withstand ordinary usage. Glass or other breakable materials may not be used for portable fuel tanks or containers.
- *Carburetor drip pan*. A drip pan must be installed under all side-draft or up-draft carburetors not provided with an effective sump.
- *Backfire flame control*. All inboard motorboats, regardless of date of construction or engine installation, must meet current federal requirements for backfire flame control.
- *Whistle or sound producing device*. All Class A boats must carry a whistle or sound-producing device capable of producing a blast of 2 seconds or more duration and audible at least $1/2$ mile.
- *Ventilation*. All motorboats regardless of class or date of construction must meet the current federal requirements for ventilation.
- *Electrical installation*. Wiring must be in good condition and properly installed. There should be no open knife switches located in the bilge.
- *Anchor and anchor line*. The boat must be equipped with an adequate anchor and line of suitable size and length for the locality.
- *General condition*. The vessel must be in good overall condition, the hull sound, fuel lines intact and properly installed. The decal will not be awarded to a vessel which is not generally shipshape and in seaworthy condition.

Class A motorboats must carry the following additional equipment.

- Pump or bailer
- Paddle or oar
- Distress signals (when operating at night).

Recommended Condition and Equipment Standards

While not cause of withholding the decal, the Auxiliary recommends the following standards of condition and equipment. Your boating pleasure depends upon the condition of your craft and how you outfit and maintain her.

- Through-hull fittings should have shut-off valves or wooden plugs accessible for use.
- Fuel lines should lead from the top of the tank and be equipped with shut-off valves at the tank and engine.
- Auxiliary generators should have separate fuel tanks.
- All switches located in the bilges should be designed for submerged use.
- Distress signaling equipment should be carried on every boat.
- A manual bilge pump should be carried on every boat irrespective of any mechanical pumping devices.
- Handrails should be secured with through bolts.
- Spare canisters should be carried for horns or whistles which operate from compressed gas.
- Spare batteries and spare bulbs should be carried for battery-operated lights.
- A fully equipped first-aid kit should be carried in every boat.
- Have tools and spare parts on board in usable condition.
- The safe loading plate affixed at the time of manufacture should be legible, and the load capacities indicated thereon should not be exceeded.

Appendix B / *Offshore Rating Council Regulations Governing Minimum Equipment and Accommodations Standards*

(Reproduced with the permission of the Offshore Racing Council)

1.0   PURPOSE AND USE

1.1   It is the purpose of these special regulations to establish uniform minimum equipment and accommodations standards for monohull yachts racing offshore.
N.B.   Monohull: Hull in which the hull depth in any section does not decrease towards the centre-line.

1.2   These regulations do not replace, but rather supplement, the requirements of governmental authority and the Racing Rules.   The attention of owners is called to restrictions in the rules on the location and movement of equipment.

1.3   The Offshore Racing Council strongly recommends the use of these special regulations by all organisations sponsoring offshore races.   Race Committees may select the category deemed most suitable for the type of race to be sailed.

2.0   OWNER'S RESPONSIBILITY

2.1   The safety of a yacht and her crew is the sole and inescapable responsibility of the owner, or owner's representative who must do his best to ensure that the yacht is fully found, thoroughly seaworthy and manned by an experienced crew who are physically fit to face bad weather.   He must be satisfied as to the soundness of hull, spars, rigging, sails and all gear.   He must ensure that all safety equipment is properly maintained and stowed and that the crew know where it is kept and how it is to be used.

2.2   Neither the establishment of these special regulations, their use by sponsoring organisations, nor the inspection of a yacht under these regulations in any way limits or reduces the complete and unlimited responsibility of the owner or owner's representative.

2.3   It is the sole and exclusive responsibility of each yacht to decide whether or not to start or continue to race.

3.0 INSPECTION

3.1 A yacht may be inspected at any time. If she does not comply with these special regulations her entry may be rejected, or she will be liable to disqualification or such other penalty as may be prescribed by the national authority or the sponsoring organisation.

4.0 CATEGORIES OF OFFSHORE EVENTS

4.1 In many types of races, ranging from long-distance ocean races sailed under adverse conditions to short-course day races sailed in protected waters, five categories of races are established, as follows, to provide for the differences in the standards of safety and accommodation required for such varying circumstances.

4.2 Category 0 race. Trans-Ocean races, where yachts must be completely self-sufficient for very extended periods of time, capable of withstanding heavy storms and prepared to meet serious emergencies without the expectation of outside assistance.

4.3 Category 1 race. Races of long distance and well offshore, where yachts must be completely self-sufficient for extended periods of time, capable of withstanding heavy storm and prepared to meet serious emergencies without the expectation of outside assistance.

4.4 Category 2 race. Races of extended duration along or not far removed from shorelines or in large unprotected bays or lakes, where a high degree of self-sufficiency is required of the yachts but with the reasonable probability that outside assistance could be called upon for aid in the event of serious emergencies.

4.5 Category 3 race. Races across open water, most of which is relatively protected or close to shorelines, including races for small yachts.

4.6 Category 4 race. Short races, close to shore in relatively warm or protected waters normally held in daylight.

5.0 BASIC REQUIREMENTS

RACE
CATEGORY

5.1 All required equipment shall:
Function properly
Be readily accessible
Be of a type, size and capacity suitable and adequate
    for the intended use and size of the yacht

| 0 | 1 | 2 | 3 | 4 |

5.2   Yachts shall be self-righting (see I.O.R. Part XII). They shall be strongly built, watertight and, particularly with regard to hulls, decks and cabin trunks capable of withstanding solid water and knockdowns.   They must be properly rigged and ballasted, be fully seaworthy and must meet the standards set forth herein.   "Properly rigged" means (inter alia) that shrouds shall never be disconnected.

Race Category: 0 1 2 3 4

5.3   Inboard engine installations shall be such that the engine when running can be securely covered, and that the exhaust and fuel supply systems are securely installed and adequately protected from the effects of heavy weather.   When an electric starter is the only provision for starting the engine, a separate battery shall be carried, the primary purpose of which is to start the engine.

Race Category: 0 1 2 3 4

Each yacht fitted with a propulsion engine shall carry a minimum amount of fuel in a permanently installed fuel tank. This minimum amount of fuel may be specified in the Notice of Race but if not, shall be sufficient to be able to meet charging requirements for the duration of the race and to motor at $L(\sqrt{LWL})$ knots for at least 8 hours.

Race Category: 1 2 3 4

Organising clubs are recommended to apply their own minimum fuel requirements.

Race Category: 0

5.4   Ballast and Heavy Equipment.   All heavy items including inside ballast and internal fittings (such as batteries, stoves, gas bottles, tanks, engines, outboard motors etc.) and anchors and chains (see 8.31 and 8.32) shall be securely fastened so as to remain in position should the yacht be capsized 180 degrees.

Race Category: 0 1 2 3

5.5   Yacht equipment and fittings shall be securely fastened.

Race Category: 4

5.6   Sail Numbers shall be in accordance with IYRR 25.

Race Category: 0 1 2 3 4

A yacht shall carry on all mainsails, all spinnakers and all jibs with LPG greater than 1.3xJ (Longest perpendicular greater that 1.3 x Base of foretriangle):

(a) A letter or letters showing her nationality except that National letters need not be carried in home waters, except in an international championship.

(b) A sail number allotted to her by her national or state authority.

The sail numbers and letters of the size shown on the mainsail must be displayed by alternative means if none of the numbered sails is set. (See SR 10.52)

6.0 STRUCTURAL FEATURES

<table>
<tr><td colspan="2" align="center">RACE
CATEGORY</td></tr>
</table>

Yachts shall have been built in accordance with ABS approved plans according to the ABS Guide for Building and Classing Offshore Racing Yachts.

Age or Series date (whichever is earlier) of 1/1986 or later. **[0 1]**

Age or Series date (whichever is earlier) of 1/1987 or later and LOA of 40ft. (12.19m) and above. **[2]**

Age or Series Dte (whichever is earlier) of 1/1988 or later and LOA of less than 40ft. (12.19m). **[2]**

Age Date is not otherwise specified shall be the month and year of launch and the Series Date shall be the launch date of the first yacht of the production series. **[0 1 2]**

6.1 The hull, including deck, coach roof and all other parts, shall form an integral, essentially watertight, unit and any openings in it shall be capable of being immediately secured to maintain this integrity (see 5.1). For example, running rigging or control lines shall not compromise this watertight unit. Centerboard and daggerboard trunks shall not open into the interior of the hull. **[0 1 2 3 4]**

6.12 Hatches. No hatches forward of the BMAX (maximum beam) station shall open inwards excepting ports having an area of less than 110 sq. in. (710 sq.cm.) Hatches shall be so arranged as to be above the water when the hull is heeled 90°. All hatches shall be permanently fitted so that they can be closed immediately and will remain firmly shut in a 180° capsize. The main companionway hatch shall be fitted with a strong securing arrangement which shall be operable from above and below. **[0 1 2 3 4]**

6.13 Companionways. All blocking arrangements (washboards, hatch-boards, etc.) shall be capable of being secured in position with the hatch open or shut and shall be secured to the yacht by lanyard or other mechanical means to prevent their being lost overboard. **[0 1 2 3 4]**

6.14 Cockpit companionways, if extended below main deck level, must be capable of being blocked off to the level of the main deck at the sheer line abreast the opening. When such blocking arrangements are in place this companionway (or hatch) shall continue to give access to the interior of the hull. **[0 1 2 3 4]**

6.21 Cockpits shall be structurally strong, self draining and permanently incorporated as an integral part of the hull. They must be essentially watertight, that is, all openings to the hull must be capable of being strongly and rigidly secured. Any bow, lateral central or stern well will be considered as a cockpit for the purposes of 6.21, 6.22, 6.23 and 6.31. **[0 1 2 3 4]**

6.22 Cockpits opening aft to the sea. The lower edge of the companionway shall not be below main deck level as measured above. The openings shall not be less than 50% of maximum cockpit depth multiplied by maximum cockpit width. The requirement in 6.31 that cockpits must drain at all angles of heel applies.

0	1	2	3	4

6.23 Cockpit Volume

6.23.1 The maximum volume of all cockpits below lowest coamings shall not exceed 6% L x B x FA (6% loaded water line x maximum beam x freeboard abreast the cockpit). The cockpit sole must be at least 2% L above LWL (2% length overall above loaded water line).

0	1			

6.23.2 The maximum volume of all cockpits below lowest coamings shall not exceed 9% L x B x FA (9% loaded water line x maximum beam x freeboard abreast the cockpit). The cockpit sole must be at least 2% L above LWL (2% length overall above loaded water line).

		2	3	4

6.31 Cockpit drains.

6.31.1 For yachts 28 feet/8.53m length overall and over. Cockpit drains adequate to drain cockpits quickly but with a combined area (after allowance for screens, if attached) of not less than the equivalent of four .75in. (19mm) diameter drains. Yachts built before 1-1-72 must have drains with a combined area (after allowance for screens, if attached) of not less than the equivalent of two 1 in. (25mm) drains. Cockpits shall drain at all angles of heel.
    Yachts built before 1-1-77 may conform to 6.31.2 for races in Categories 3 and 4.

0	1	2	3	4

6.31.2 For yachts under 28 feet/8.53m length overall. Cockpit drains adequate to drain cockpits quickly but not less in combined area (after allowance for screens, if attached) than the equivalent of two 1 in.(25mm) diameter drains. Cockpits shall drain at all angles of heel.

0	1	2	3	4

6.4 Storm covering for all windows more than two square feet in area (1858 sq. cm.)

0	1	2	3	

6.51 Sea cocks or valves on all through-hull openings below LWL, except integral deck scuppers, shaft log, speed indicators, depth finders and the like, however a means of closing such openings, when necessary to do so, shall be provided.
Does not apply in Category 4 races to yachts built before 1-1-76.

0	1	2	3	4

6.52 Soft wood plugs, tapered and of the correct size, to be attached to, or adjacent to, the appropriate fitting.

0	1	2	3	4

6.53   Sheet winches shall be mounted in such a way that no operator is required to be substantially below deck.

| 0 | 1 | 2 | 3 | 4 |

6.54   Mast Step. The heel of a keel stepped mast shall be securely fastened to the mast step or adjoining structure.

| 0 | 1 | 2 | 3 | 4 |

6.55   Bulkhead.   The hull shall have a watertight bulkhead within 15% of the vessel's length from the bow and abaft the forward perpendicular.

| 0 |

6.6   LIFELINES, STANCHIONS, PULPITS AND JACKSTAYS

6.61   For all yachts.

6.61.1   Life-line terminals and life-line material.   All life-lines shall comprise 1 x 19 stainless steel wire or a stranded stainless steel wire of the same or greater strength (see also 6.62.1 and IYRR 62).   A taut lanyard of synthetic rope may be used to secure life-lines, provided that when in position its length does not exceed 4 in. (100mm).   The lanyard(s) and end fittings shall have an equivalent strength to that of the wire life-line.

| 0 | 1 | 2 | 3 | 4 |

6.61.2   Stanchions shall not be angled at more than ten degrees from the vertical at any point above 50mm from the deck nor within the first 50mm from the deck, may they be displaced horizontally from the point at which they emerge from the deck or base by more than 10mm.   For yachts with an Age Date of 1/1988 or later, stanchions shall be straight, except that one bend is permitted in the first 50mm above deck.   For yachts with an Age Date of 1/1987 or later, stanchions, pulpits, and lifelines shall not be made of carbon fibre.

| 0 | 1 | 2 | 3 | 4 |

6.61.3   Overlapping pulpits.   Lifelines need not be affixed to the bow pulpit if they terminate at, or pass through, adequately braced stanchions 2 ft. (610mm) ⌊18 in. (457mm) for yachts 28 feet/8.53 m length overall⌋ above the working deck, set inside and overlapping the bow pulpit. provided that the gap between the upper lifeline and the bow pulpit does not exceed 6 ins. (152mm).

| 0 | 1 | 2 | 3 | 4 |

6.61.4   Pulpit and stanchion fixing.   Pulpits and stanchions shall be securely attached.
a) When there are sockets or studs, these shall be through-bolted, bonded or welded.   The pulpit(s) and/or stanchions fitted to these shall be mechanically retained without the help of the lifelines.
b) Without sockets or studs, pulpits and/or stanchions shall be through-bolted, bonded or welded.
The bases of pulpits and stanchions shall not be further inboard from the edge of the working deck than 5% of BMAX (maximum beam) or 6in. (152mm), whichever is greater. Stanchion bases shall not be situated outboard of the working deck.

| 0 | 1 | 2 | 3 | 4 |

6.62   For yachts of 28 feet/8.53m length overall and over.

6.62.1   Taut double lifelines, with upper lifeline of wire at a height of not less than 2 ft. (609mm) above the working deck, to be permanently supported at intervals of not more than 7 ft. (2.13 m).   When the cockpit opens aft to the sea, additional lifelines must be fitted so that no opening is greater in height than 22 in. (560mm).   For yachts of 28ft./8.53m LOA or over, all life-lines shall comprise wire of minimum diameter 5mm.

`0 | 1 | 2 | 3 | 4`

6.62.2   Pulpits.   Fixed bow pulpit (forward of headstay) and stern pulpit (unless lifelines are arranged as to adequately substitute for a stern pulpit).   Lower lifelines need not extend through the bow pulpit.   Upper rails of pulpits shall be at not less height above the working deck than upper lifelines.   Upper rails in bow pulpits shall be securely closed while racing.   Any lifeline attachment point will be considered as a stanchion in so far as its base shall not be situated outboard of the working deck.*

`0 | 1 | 2 | 3 | 4`

6.63   For yachts under 28 feet/8.53m length overall.

6.63.1   Taut single wire lifeline, at a height of not less than 18 ins. (457mm) above the working deck, to be permanently supported at intervals of not more than 7 ft. (2.13m).   If the lifeline is at any point more than 22 ins. (560mm) above the rail cap, a second intermediate lifeline must be fitted.   If the cockpit opens aft to the sea additional lifelines must be fitted so that no opening is greater in height than 22 ins. (560mm).   Life-lines shall comprise wire of minimum diameter 4mm.

`0 | 1 | 2 | 3 | 4`

6.63.2   Pulpits.   Fixed bow pulpit and stern pulpit (unless lifelines are arranged as to adequately substitute for a stern pulpit).   Lower lifelines need not extend through the bow pulpit.   Upper rails of pulpits must be at no less height above the working deck than upper lifelines.   Upper rails in bow pulpits shall be securely closed while racing.   The bow pulpit may be fitted abaft the forestay with its bases secured at any points on deck, but a point on its upper rail must be within 16 ins. (406mm) of the forestay on which the foremost headsail is hanked.
    Provided the complete lifeline enclosure is supported by stanchions and pulpit bases within the working deck, lifeline terminals and support struts may be fixed to the hull aft of the working deck.

`0 | 1 | 2 | 3 | 4`

*Provided the complete lifeline enclosure is supported by stanchions and pulpit bases within the working deck, lifeline terminals and support struts may be fixed to the hull aft of the working deck.

	0	1	2	3	4
6.64 Toe Rails. A toe-rail of not less than 1 in. (25mm) shall be permanently fitted around the deck forward of the mast, except in way of fittings. Location to be not further inboard from the edge of the working deck than one third of the local beam. A third lifeline (or second for yachts under 28 feet/8.53m length overall at a height of not less than 1 in. (25mm) or more than 2 ins. (50mm) above the working deck will be accepted in place of a toe-rail. In yachts built before 1 January 1981 a toe-rail of 0.75in. (19mm) will be accepted.	0	1	2	3	

6.65 JACKSTAYS

Jackstays must be fitted on deck, port and starboard of the yacht's centre line to provide secure attachments for safety harnesses.   Jackstays shall comprise stainless steel 1 x 19 wire of minimum diameter 5mm, or webbing of equivalent strength.   Jackstays must be attached to through-bolted or welded deck plates, or other suitable and strong anchorages. The jackstays must, if possible, be fitted in such a way that a crew member, when clipped on, can move from a cockpit to the forward and to the after end of the main deck without unclipping the harness.   If the deck lay-out renders this impossible, additional lines must be fitted so that a crew member can move as described with a minimum of clipping operations.

A crew member must be able to clip on before coming on deck, unclip after going below and remain clipped on while moving laterally across the yacht on the foredeck, the afterdeck, and amidships.   If necessary additional jackstays and/or through-bolted or welded anchorage points must be provided for this purpose.

Through-bolted or welded anchorage points, or other suitable and strong anchorage, for safety harnesses must be provided adjacent to stations such as the helm, sheet winches and masts, where crew members work for long periods.   Jackstays should be sited in such a way that the safety harness lanyard can be kept as short as possible.

7.0 ACCOMMODATIONS

	0	1	2	3	4
7.11 Toilet, securely installed	0	1	2		
7.12 Toilet, securely installed, or fitted bucket				3	4
7.2 Bunks, securely installed	0	1	2	3	4
7.3 Cooking stove,'securely installed against a capsize with safe accessible fuel shutoff control capable of being safely operatedin a seaway.	0	1	2	3	
7.4 Galley facilities.	0	1	2	3	4

	0	1	2	3	4
7.51 Water tank(s), securely installed and capable of dividing the water supply into at least three compartments and discharging through a pump. The quantity of water to be taken aboard is left to the discretion of the organising authority, but two gallons (nine litres) per person per one thousand miles shall be taken as the absolute minimum.	0				
7.52 Water tank(s), securely installed and capable of dividing the water supply into at least two compartments and discharging through a pump.		1			
7.53 At least one securely installed water tank discharging through a pump.			2	3	

8.0 GENERAL EQUIPMENT

	0	1	2	3	4
8.1 Fire extinguishers, at least two, readily accessible in suitable and different parts of the boat.	0	1	2	3	4
8.21.1 Bilge Pumps, at least two manually operated, securely fitted to the yacht's structure, one operable above, the other below deck. Each pump shall be operable with all cockpit seats, hatches and companionways shut.	0	1	2		
8.21.2 Each bilge pump shall be provided with permanently fitted discharge pipe(s) of sufficient capacity to accommodate simultaneously both pumps.	0	1	2		
8.21.3 No bilge pumps may discharge into a cockpit unless that cockpit opens aft to the sea. Bilge pumps shall not be connected to cockpit drains.	0	1	2	3	4
8.21.4 Unless permanently fitted, each bilge pump handle shall be provided with a lanyard or catch or similar device to prevent accidental loss.	0	1	2	3	4
8.22 One manual bilge pump operable with all cockpit seats, hatches and companionways closed.				3	
8.23 One manual bilge pump.					4
8.24 Two buckets of stout construction each with at least 2 gallons (9 litres) capacity. Each bucket to have a lanyard.	0	1	2	3	4
8.31 Anchors. Two with cables except yachts under 28 feet/8.53m length overall which shall carry at least one anchor and cable. Anchors and any chain shall be securely fastened in the position recorded on the Rating Certificate when not in use.	0	1	2	3	
8.32 One anchor and cable. Anchor(s) and any chain shall be securely fastened in the position recorded on the Rating Certificate when not in use.					4

	0	1	2	3	4
8.41 Flashlights, one of which is suitable for signalling, water resistant, with spare batteries and bulbs.	0	1	2	3	
8.42 At least one flashlight, water resistant, with spare batteries and bulb.					4
8.5 First aid kit and manual.	0	1	2	3	4
8.6 Foghorn.	0	1	2	3	4
8.7 Radar reflector. If a radar reflector is octahedral it must have a minimum diagonal measurement of 18 ins. (457mm), or if not octahedral must have a documented "equivalent echoing area" of not less than 10 sq.m.	0	1	2	3	4
8.8 Set of international code flags and international code book.	0	1			
8.9 Shutoff valves on all fuel tanks.	0	1	2	3	4

9.0 **NAVIGATION EQUIPMENT**

	0	1	2	3	4
9.1 Compass, marine type, properly installed and adjusted.	0	1	2	3	4
9.2 Spare compass.	0	1	2	3	
9.3 Charts, light list and piloting equipment.	0	1	2	3	
9.4 Sextant, tables and accurate time piece.	0	1			
9.5 Radio direction finder or an automatic position fixing device.	0	1	2		
9.6 Lead line or echo sounder.	0	1	2	3	4
9.7 Speedometer or distance measuring instrument.	0	1	2	3	
9.8 Navigation lights, to be shown as required by the International Regulations for Preventing Collision at Sea, mounted so that they will not be masked by sails or the heeling of the yacht. Yachts under 7m LOA shall comply with the regulations for those between 12m and 7m LOA (i.e. they shall exhibit sidelights and a sternlight). Navigation lights shall not be mounted below deck level. Spare bulbs for navigation lights shall be carried. A a guide, minimum bulb wattage in navigation lights for yachts under sail should be as follows: (a) yachts less than 12m (39.6 ft) LOA - 10 watts (b) yachts of 12m (39.6 ft) LOA and greater - 25 watts. Attention is drawn to Part C and Technical Annex I of International Regulations for Preventing Collisions at Sea, 1972.	0	1	2	3	4

10.0 EMERGENCY EQUIPMENT

10.1 Emergency navigation lights and power source.
Emergency navigation lights shall have the same minimum specifications as the navigation lights in 9.8 and a power source and wiring separate from that used for the normal navigation lights.
Emergency navigation lights shall not be used if the normal navigation lights (under Rule 9.8) are operable.

0	1	2	3

10.21 The following specifications for mandatory sails give maximum areas; smaller areas may well suit some yachts. Appropriate sheeting positions on deck shall be provided for these sails.

10.21.1 One storm trysail not larger than $0.175 \times P \times E$ in area. It shall be sheeted independently of the boom and shall have neither a headboard nor battens and be of suitable strength for the purpose. The yacht's sail number and letter(s) shall be placed on both sides of the trysail in as large a size as is practicable.
Aromatic polyamides, carbon fibres and other high modulous fibres shall not be used in the storm trysail.

0	1	2

10.21.2 One storm jib of not more than $0.05 \times IG \times IG$ (5% height of the foretriangle squared) in area, the luff of which does not exceed $0.65 \times IG$ (65% height of the foretriangle), and of suitable strength for the purpose.
Aromatic polyamides, carbon fibres and other high modulous fibres shall not be used in the storm jib.

0	1	2

10.21.3 One heavy-weather jib of suitable strength for the purpose with area not greater than $0.135 \times IG \times IG$ (13.5% height of the foretriangle squared) and which does not contain reef points.

0	1	2

10.22 One heavy-weather jib as in 10.21.3 (or heavy-weather sail in a boat with no forestay) and either:
(a) a storm trysail as in 10.21.1 or
(b) mainsail reefing equipment capable of reducing the effective luff to 60% P or less when aromatic polyamides, carbon fibres and other high modulous fibres shall not be used.

3	4

10.23 Any storm or heavy-weather jib if designed for a seastay or luff-groove device shall have an alternative method of attachment to the stay.

0	1	2	3	4

10.24 No mast shall have less than two halyards each capable of hoisting a sail.

0	1	2	3	4

10.3 Emergency Steering Equipment

10.31 An emergency tiller capable of being fitted to the rudder stock. `0 1 2 3`

10.32 Crews must be aware of alternative methods of steering the yacht in any sea condition in the event of rudder failure. At least one method must have been proven to work on board the yacht. An inspector may require that this method be demonstrated. `0 1 2 3 4`

10.4 Tools and spare parts, including adequate means to disconnect or sever the standing rigging from the hull in the case of need. `0 1 2 3 4`

10.5   Yacht's name on miscellaneous buoyant equipment, such as life jackets, oars, cushions, lifebuoys and lifeslings, etc. `0 1 2 3 4`

10.51 Life-buoys, lifeslings, life-rafts, and life-jackets shall be fitted with marine grade retro-reflective material. `0 1 2 3 4`

10.52   Sail numbers, either portable or displayed on each side of the hull and meeting the requirements for mainsail numbers. `0 1 2 3`

10.61 Marine radio transmitter and receiver.   If the regular antenna depends upon the mast, an emergency antenna must be provided.
    Yachts fitted with VHF transceivers are recommended to install VHF Channel 72 (156.625 MHZ Simplex).   This is an international ship-ship channel which, by "common use", could become an accepted yacht-yacht channel for all ocean racing yachts anywhere in the world. `0 1 2`

10.62   In addition to 10.61, a waterproof hand held VHF transceiver is recommended. `0 1`

10.63 Radio receiver capable of receiving weather bulletins. `0 1 2 3 4`

10.64 EPIRBs
Emergency indicator beacon transmitting on 121.5, 243 or 406 MHz. `0 1`

10.7 At least 2 gallons (9 litres) of water for emergency use carried in one or more containers. `0 1 2 3`

11.0 SAFETY EQUIPMENT

11.1 Life jackets, one for each crew member.
In the absence of any specification, the following definition of a life jacket is recommended:
"A life jacket should be of a form which is capable of providing not less than 16kg. of buoyancy, arranged so that an unconscious man will be securely suspended face upwards at approximately 45 degrees to the water surface." `0 1 2 3 4`

11.2 Whistles attached to life jackets.

0	1	2	3

11.3 Safety belt (harness type) one for each crew member.
      Each yacht may be required to demonstrate that two thirds
of the crew can be adequately attached to strong points on the
yacht.

0	1	2	3

11.4   Life raft(s)   capable of carrying the entire crew and
meeting the following requirements:

0	1	2

A. Must be carried on the working deck or in a special stowage
opening immediately to the working deck containing the life-
raft(s) only.

B.   For yachts built after 1.7.83
     Life-raft(s) may only be stowed under the working deck
provided:
     (a) the stowage compartment is water tight or self
draining
     (b) if the stowage compartment is not watertight, then the
floor of the special stowage is defined as the cockpit sole for
the purposes of rule 6.23.2
     (c) the cover of this compartment shall be capable of
being opened under water pressure.

C. Life-raft(s) packed in a valise and not exceeding 40 kg. may
be securely stowed below deck adjacent to the companionway.

D. Each raft shall be capable of being got to the lifelines
within 15 seconds.

E. Must have a valid annual certificate from the manufacturer
or an approved servicing agent certifying that it has been
inspected, that it complies with the above requirements and
stating the official capacity of the raft which shall not be
exceeded.   The certificate, or a copy thereof, to be carried
on board the yacht.

11.51 Lifebuoy with a drogue, or lifesling, equipped with a
self-igniting light within reach of the helmsman and ready for
instant use.

0	1	2	3	4

	0	1	2	3	4
11.52 In addition to 11.51. One lifebuoy, within reach of the helmsman and ready for instant use and equipped with a whistle, dye marker, drogue, a self-igniting light, and a pole and flag. The pole shall be either permanently extended or be capable of being fully automatically extended in less than 5 seconds. It shall be attached to the lifebuoy with 10ft. (3.048m) of floating line and is to be of a length and so ballasted that the flag will fly at least 6ft. (1.828m) off the water.	0	1	2		
11.61 Distress signals conforming to the current International Convention for the Safety of Life at Sea (SOLAS) regulations (chapter III Visual Signals) to be stowed in a waterproof container or containers, as indicated.	0	1	2	3	4
11.62 Twelve red parachute flares. (SOLAS regulation 35)	0	1			
11.63 Four red parachute flares. (SOLAS regulation 35)			2	3	
11.64 Four red hand flares. (SOLAS regulation 36)	0	1	2	3	4
11.65 Four white hand flares. Although not specified by SOLAS, it is recommended that design criteria, excepting colour and candela rating, be in accordance with SOLAS regulation 36.	0	1	2	3	4
11.66 Two orange smoke day signals. (SOLAS regulation 37)	0	1	2	3	
11.67 Distress signals which are more than 3 years old (as indicated by the date of manufacture) or of which the date of expiry has passed are not acceptable.	0	1	2	3	4
11.7 Heaving line (50 ft. (15.24m) minimum length) readily accessible to cockpit.	0	1	2	3	4
12. Weight jackets (IYRR 61.2) shall not be permitted.	0	1	2	3	4

Appendix C / *Distress Signals*

International Rules of the Road
1. The following signals, used or exhibited either together or separately, indicate distress and need of assistance:
   a a gun or other explosive signal fired at intervals of about a minute;
   b a continuous sounding with any fog-signalling apparatus;
   c rockets or shells, throwing red stars fired one at a time at short intervals;
   d a signal made by radiotelegraphy or by any other signalling method consisting of the group ···— — —··· (SOS) in the Morse code;
   e a signal sent by radiotelephony consisting of the spoken word "Mayday";
   f the International Code Signal of distress indicated by N.C.;
   g a signal consisting of a square flag having above or below it a ball or anything resembling a ball;
   h flames on the vessel (as from a burning tar barrel, oil barrel, etc.);
   i a rocket parachute flare or a hand flare showing a red light;
   j a smoke signal giving off orange-coloured smoke;
   k slowly and repeatedly raising and lowering arms outstretched to each side;
   l the radiotelegraph alarm signal;
   m the radiotelephone alarm signal;
   n signals transmitted by emergency position-indicating radio beacons.
2. The use or exhibition of any of the foregoing signals except for the purpose of indicating distress and need of assistance and the use of other signals which may be confused with any of the above signals is prohibited.
3. Attention is drawn to the relevant sections of the International Code of Signals, the Merchant Ship Search and Rescue Manual, and the following signals:
   a a piece of orange-coloured canvas with either a black square and circle or other appropriate symbol (for identification from the air);
   b a dye marker.

Inland Rules of the Road
Note: The distress signals for inland waters are the same as those for international waters. Inland rules, however, also include an additional signal: a high-intensity white light flashing at regular intervals from 50 to 70 times per minute.

Appendix D / Storm Warning Signals

SMALL CRAFT*

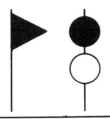

DAYTIME: Red Pennant.

NIGHTTIME: Red Light Over White Light.

Indicates: Forecast winds as high as 33 knots and sea conditions considered dangerous to small-craft operations.

GALE

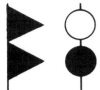

DAYTIME: Two Red Pennants.

NIGHTTIME: White Light Over Red Light.

Indicates: Forecast winds in the range 34-47 knots.

STORM

DAYTIME: Square Red Flag With Black Square Centered.

NIGHTTIME: Two Red Lights.

Indicates: Forecast winds 48 knots and above no matter how high the wind speed. If the winds are associated with a tropical cyclone (hurricane), storm warnings indicate forecast winds of 48-63 knots.

HURRICANE

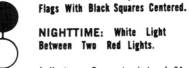

DAYTIME: Two Square Red Flags With Black Squares Centered.

NIGHTTIME: White Light Between Two Red Lights.

Indicates: Forecast winds of 64 knots and above, displayed only in connection with a hurricane.

Appendix E / *Beaufort Scale*

Beaufort Number	Wind speed		Seaman's Terms	Estimating wind speed	
	Knots	mph		Observations at sea	Observations on land
0	under 1	under 1	Calm	Sea like mirror.	Calm; smoke rises vertically.
1	1–3	1–3	Light air	Ripples with appearance of scales; no foam crests.	Smoke drift indicates wind direction; vanes do not move.
2	4–6	4–7	Light breeze	Small wavelets; crests of glassy appearance, not breaking.	Wind felt on face; leaves rustle; vanes begin to move.
3	7–10	8–12	Gentle breeze	Large wavelets; crests begin to break; scattered whitecaps.	Leaves, small twigs in constant motion; light flags extended.
4	11–16	13–18	Moderate breeze	Small waves, becoming longer; numerous whitecaps.	Dust, leaves, and loose paper raised up; small branches move.
5	17–21	19–24	Fresh breeze	Moderate waves, taking longer form; many whitecaps; some spray.	Small trees in leaf begin to sway.
6	22–27	25–31	Strong breeze	Larger waves forming; whitecaps everywhere; more spray.	Larger branches of trees in motion; whistling heard in wires
7	28–33	32–38	Moderate gale	Sea heaps up; white foam from breaking waves begins to be blown in streaks.	Whole trees in motion; resistance felt in walking against wind.
8	34–40	39–46	Fresh gale	Moderately high waves of greater length; edges of crests begin to break into spindrift; foam is blown in well-marked streaks.	Twigs and small branches broken off trees; progress generally impeded.
9	41–47	47–54	Strong gale	High waves; sea begins to roll; dense streaks of foam; spray may reduce visibility.	Slight structural damage occurs; slate blown from roofs.
10	48–55	55–63	Whole gale	Very high waves with overhanging crests; sea takes white appearance as foam is blown in very dense streaks; rolling is heavy and visibility reduced.	Seldom experienced on land; trees broken or uprooted; considerable structural damage occurs.
11	56–63	64–72	Storm	Exceptionally high waves; sea covered with white foam patches; visibility still more reduced.	
12	64–71	73–82	Hurricane	Air filled with foam; sea completely white with driving spray; visibility greatly reduced.	Very rarely experienced on land; usually accompanied by widespread damage.
13	72–80	83–92			
14	81–89	93–103			
15	90–99	104–114			
16	100–108	115–125			
17	109–118	126–136			

(U. S. Naval Institute)

Appendix F / Sea State Table

Hydrographic Office		International	
Term and height of waves, in feet	Code	Term and height of waves, in feet	Code
Calm, 0	0	Calm, glassy, 0	0
Smooth, less than 1	1		
Slight, 1–3	2	Rippled, 0–1	1
Moderate, 3–5	3	Smooth, 1–2	2
Rough, 5–8	4	Slight, 2–4	3
		Moderate, 4–8	4
		Rough, 8–13	5
Very rough, 8–12	5	Very rough, 13–20	6
High, 12–20	6		
Very high, 20–40	7	High, 20–30	7
Mountainous, 40 and higher	8	Very high, 30–45	8
Confused	9	Phenomenal, over 45	9

(*U. S. Naval Institute*)

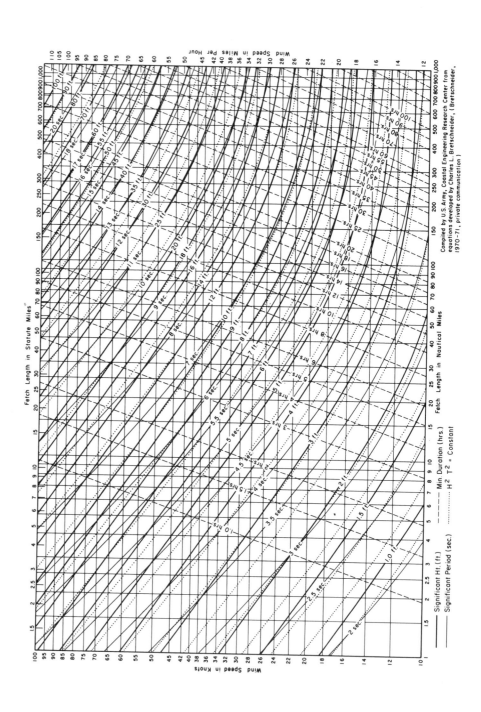

Compiled by U.S. Army, Coastal Engineering Research Center from
equations developed by Charles L. Bretschneider, (Bretschneider,
1970–71, private communication)

Appendix H / Treatment of Injury or Illness at Sea

by George H.A. Clowes, Jr., M.D. Fleet Surgeon

Among the healthy people who are usually found in the crews of yachts at sea, illness is relatively uncommon. They are far more likely to contract gastrointestinal and other diseases in port, where medical help can be obtained if urgently needed. Injuries are more common than sickness, but sickness may occur, especially among the elderly members of the crew. Illnesses range from coronary heart attacks to prostatic obstruction of the urinary tract.

Of course, prevention of injury by foresight and recognition of hazards in rig, machinery, etc., is far better than treatment after the fact. The same may be said for preventive measures against disease, such as appropriate inoculations to develop immunity against diseases current in ports to be visited or by avoidance of uncooked food likely to transmit bacillary dysentery in certain regions of the world.

Despite all precautions, injury or illness may strike, and it may become necessary to treat the patient at sea, far from land-based medical facilities. If you do not have a doctor on board, medical advice can be obtained by radio from the U.S. Public Health Service through the Coast Guard, through the medical service of the British Shipping Board, and from other private or public sources. A doctor may be aboard a nearby vessel who might be able to advise or come to your assistance. In any case, certain basic equipment, supplies, and drugs will be required. The appended list of essentials is compiled with this problem in mind. It is obvious that the needs for every contingency cannot be provided, yet an effort has been made to satisfy essential requirements for the most common injuries or illnesses.

In seeking medical assistance by radio, it is necessary to report clearly the clinical problem and to answer the doctor's questions to help him make a diagnosis and formulate suggestions for treatment. One must then request instructions on how to carry out treatment. The appropriate drugs and medical equipment available must be discussed in order that the doctor may know what is at hand.

Certain other sources of information on medical problems at sea are available in the form of books or first-aid manuals.

In the limited space available here, we shall make no attempt to present an outline of treatment, except to indicate the general field in which the drugs or equipment may be used.

In considering the items in the list of drugs an attempt has been made not to include dangerous drugs. When they are included, only small quantities of narcotics or toxic antibiotics are suggested. These will be sufficient for several days, when presumably some help may become available.

The common injuries to be dealt with require compression bandages for sprains, splints for fractures, and instruments, sutures, and local anesthetics for stopping hemorrhage or suturing lacerations. A syringe and large-bore needle (#19) may be essential to relieve a tension pneumothorax or accumulation of air between the lung and the chest wall, if fractured ribs perforate the lung. Betadine ointment is good for preventing or reducing infection in serious burns, which are all too frequent when cooking at sea. Surfacaine can relieve the pain of severe sunburn, but it is better to prevent sunburn by an effective sunshield ointment.

For the eyes, foreign bodies can be removed from the cunjunctiva with the help of a drop of local anesthetic Ophthaine. On the other hand, never use an anesthetic eye ointment, for permanent corneal injury may result. Rely on an eye ointment containing Bacitracin or other potent antibiotic. Colyrium or some other eye wash may be very helpful, as are dark glasses or eye patches.

Paregoric to control diarrhea may be supplemented by codeine. The laxatives are obvious but a far better system is to prevent constipation by a rough diet and adequate daily water intake by mouth. Bacillary dysenteries respond well to sulfadiazine or sulfathalidine. With the exception of adrenalin, the cardiovascular drugs are included only to assist in control of unusual heart rhythm in the event of a heart attack. Digitalis purposely is not included, since this is a drug requiring dosage close to the toxic level, and would be very hard to regulate at sea.

This brings up the subject of crewmembers who are on chronic medication with digitalis, diuretics, or insulin. Each should be encouraged to bring their own drugs in supply sufficient for the voyage. Most such patients are fully aware of their own requirements and will deal with them.

A skipper or other person responsible for outfitting a vessel for sea who is desirous of securing the items on this list should consult his own doctor to obtain prescriptions for certain of the drugs and syringes. Your doctor may also have valuable suggestions both in terms of other supplies or immunizations you or your crew should have for your special voyage. In any case, don't worry about the possibility of a sickness that is uncommon at sea. It is easier to prepare with a few essentials if injury or illness should strike.

Suggested Medical Supplies and Drugs for Offshore Voyages

Instruments and Equipment

1	Scalpel with 6 disposable blades
1	Surgical Mayo scissors, curved
1	Surgical straight scissors
1	Surgical thumb forceps, medium smooth
1	Surgical thumb forceps, medium toothed
1	Splinter forceps
1	Fine nail scissors
1	Needle holder, medium
1	Needle holder, small
4	Hemostats
4	Kelly hemostats
1	Laryngeal forceps for removal of foreign bodies (meat, etc.) from cricopharynx
1	Urethral catheter rubber, Fr#18
1	Urethral catheter rubber, Fr#16
1	Urethral catheter rubber, Fr#14
2	Foley urethral catheters, Fr#16
3	Intravenous administration sets to fit i.v. solution containers
2	Levine nasogastric tubes
1	Oral airway tube
	Disposable plastic hypodermic syringes (sterile):
	3 2cc

> 3   10cc
>
> 3   25cc

Intravenous and hypodermic needles, disposable (sterile):

> 12 #21 needles, 1$^{1}/_{2}$"
>
> 12 #20 needles, 2"
>
> 12 #19 needles, 2"
>
> 4 Pairs surgical gloves (sterile), size 8
>
> Selection of curved and straight surgical needles

Supplies

Ringer lactate solution (sterile for intravenous administration), each 1 liter, 3 bags

Gauze bandages: 1", 2", 3", 6 of each

Gauze sponges: 4"×4", 3"×3", 2 dozen of each

Adhesive tapes: 1", 2", 3", 3 rolls of each

Bandaids: Selection of sizes, 2 containers

Elastic bandages: 3", 4", 6 of each

Curlex gauze bandages: 1 dozen

Cotton-tipped applicators (sterile): 2 dozen

Wooden tongue depressors

Splints (sail battens may be used)

Sutures (sterilized):

Subcutaneous:	00 chromic catgut curved round 1" needles
	000 chromic catgut with curved 1" needles
Skin:	00 silk curved cutting 1" needles
	000 silk straight cutting needles
Ligatures:	000 silk spool
	00 silk spool

Lubricating Jelly, sterile

Sterile cotton

Fever thermometer

Drugs

Antibiotics

Keflex (cephalosporin) capsules 250 mg (milligrams), #50

Chloromycetin (chloramphenicol) capsules 250 mg, #50 (not to be used except on direction and for no more than one week)

Terramycin (tetracycline) capsules 250 mg, #50 (for urinary tract infections, etc.)

Amcill-S (ampicillin) vials 250 mg, #12 (for intravenous or intramuscular injection. Warning: danger of anaphylactic reaction if penicillin sensitivity present in patient.)

Bactrim tablets (standard size) 40 tablets (dose: 2 tablets every 12 hours) for urinary tract infection, diarrhea

Mefoxin (Cefoxitin): 1-gram vials, #12, with sterile water for mixing (dose: 1 gram every 8 hours) for intramuscular injection to treat peritonitis, appendicitis, etc.

Antifungal Agents

Desenex powder (feet, etc.)

Cruex powder, aerosol (groin, etc.)

Tinactin cream 1% (athlete's foot)

Antihistamine

Benadryl capsules 50 mg, #50

Chlor-trimetron tablets 4 mg, #50

Pain (Analgesics)

    Morphine sulfate: 15 mg, 10 doses (to be injected subcutaneously, not more often than every 4 hours. Comes in a Tubex-prefilled cartridge needle unit with Tubex syringe. To be used only with medical consultation)

    Codeine: tablets 30 mg, #50 (dose: 1 not more often than every four hours. For toothache, headache, or other severe pain)

    Aspirin: tablets 325 mg, #100 (may be used with codeine)

Motion Sickness

    Dramamine (1 tablet not more often than every four hours)

    Bonine (1 or 2 tablets every 24 hours)

Local Anesthetic

    Procaine hydrochloride 1%, 10 vials 10 cc

    Xylocaine solution 1% (without epinephrine), 50 cc vial

    Sedatives (Not to be used for personnel on duty at sea):

    Valium: tablets 5 mg, #25 (not more than 1 tablet twice daily, for severe psychological disorders)

    Dalmane: tablets 15 mg, #25 (for sleep—one tablet at bedtime)

Cardiovascular

    Quinidine sulfate: 3 grain tablets, #50

    Adrenalin (Epinephrine) Solution (1:1000), one vial 10 cc

    Pronestyl (Procaine amide): capsules 250 mg, #50

    Nitroglycerine: sublingual tablets 0.4 mg, #20

Ear, Nose and Throat

    Afrin (nasal) solution 0.5%, 30 cc bottle with dropper (Dose: not more than 4 drops twice daily. Relieves nasal congestion and sinus or ear pain.)

Eye

    Bacitracin ophthalmic ointment, 1 tube

    Ophthaine solution 0.5%, 1 squeeze bottle with dropper 15 cc (To be used only as anesthetic for removal of foreign bodies. *Do not use ophthalmic anesthetic solution or ointment for more than a brief period.*)

Gastro-Intestinal

    Laxatives: Cascara sagrada, Epsom salts; Milk of magnesia

    Atropine (Belladenal tablets, #50: 2 to 4 tablets/day)

    Sulfathalidine: tablets 500 mg, #100 (1 gram each 4 hours); or Sulfadiazine: tablets 500 mg, #100

    Maalox (for gastritis or ulcer pain)

    Anusol suppositories (for painful hemorrhoids)

    Paregoric (dose: 1 teaspoon 4 times daily)

Genito-Urinary

    Gantricin: tablets 500 mg, #50 (1 gm./day cystitis)

    Urispas: tablets 100 mg, #50 (1 tablet 4 times daily)

Musculo-Skeletal

    Norflex-tabs, #50 (1 tablet every 4 hours) or Parafon Forte, #100 (2 tablets 4 times daily)

Skin

    Betadine solution, 16 oz. (skin sterilizing for surgery, etc.)

    Betadine ointment, 16 oz. jar (for burns)

    Sunburn preventive: Sunshield, Piz Buin, etc.

    Silvadene cream, 50-gram jar (for burns—keep burned area covered with layer of cream 1/16″ thick)

Appendix I / Glossary of Terms
As Used in This Book

(In many cases definitions are no longer than necessary for an understanding of how the term is used in this book.)

Abaft—The proper expression for "aft of." Farther toward the stern.

ABS—American Bureau of Shipping.

ABYC—American Boat and Yacht Council.

All-standing jibe—An inadvertent or accidental jibe during which the sheet is not shortened and the boom slams across the boat, occasionally causing damage.

Ama—An outrigger hull on a trimaran or proa.

Backing wind—Wind shifting in a counterclockwise direction, as from east to northeast.

Ballot's Law—A law conceived by meteorologist Buys Ballot, which provides the approximate location of a high or low from wind direction. When the observer stands with his back to the wind, low pressure is to his left and high pressure is to his right in the northern hemisphere.

Bare poling—Sailing downwind with no sails set.

Bermuda Triangle—An area, roughly between Florida, Bermuda, and the Virgin Islands, that is noted for the loss of vessels and aircraft. Although a number of sensational books and articles have attempted to make mysteries of these Bermuda Triangle losses, the vast majority can be logically explained and attributed to severe weather.

Boater—Properly a hat but increasingly (and improperly), a substitute for boatman.

Bobstay—Stay or chain attached to a vessel's stem, under her bowsprit, to counteract the upward pull of her forestay or headstay.

Bonding—"The electrical connection of the exposed, metallic, non-current-carrying parts to the ground (negative) side of the direct current system." (ABYC definition)

Boom vang—A tackle or spring-loaded or hydraulically controlled rod, which holds down the boom to control sail twist.

Bowline on the bight—A bowline knot with two loops, which can serve as an emergency bosun's chair (see illustration in Chapter 7).

Broach (broach-to)—To inadvertently round up into the wind and expose the boat's beam to wind and seas after running off.

Bruce number—A simplified sail area-to-displacement ratio obtained by dividing the square root of the sail area (in square feet) by the cube root of the displacement (in pounds).

Bunt—The lower or middle part of a sail that is loose when the sail is reefed.

Buttock lines—Vertical, longitudinal sections through a hull running parallel to the centerline and appearing as straight lines on the body and half-breadth plans but as curved lines on the sheer or profile plan.

By the lee—Sailing beyond dead before the wind without jibing so that the wind gets behind the mainsail (or other boomed sail), increasing the risk of an accidental all-standing jibe.

Cabin trunk—A low deckhouse, normally between side decks, to increase headroom below and to afford a base for handrails.

Cat ketch—see Periauger.

CCA—Cruising Club of America

Center of effort—The geometric center of a sail, used in figuring a vessel's helm balance and sail-carrying power.

Cocked hat—The triangle formed by the crossing of three lines of position that don't precisely agree.

Coriolis effect—The deflection of a moving body such as the wind or a weather system to the right in the northern hemisphere and to the left in the southern hemisphere, due to the earth's rotation on its axis.

Counter—On a boat with overhang aft, the underpart of her stern between the transom and the load waterline.

Crossed winds—Upper- and lower-level winds blowing from different directions. Observations of crossed winds can provide information as to the observer's location with respect to a low pressure system.

Cruising-racer—Primarily a racing sailboat with cruising accommodations. More extreme, usually less seakindly, and often less seaworthy than the more conservative racing-cruiser.

Cumulonimbus—The "thunderhead" or thunderstorm cloud, normally a puffy-looking vertical cloud with darkish base, which can rear up to 25,000 feet or higher. When fully developed or past that stage it flares out aloft to form an anvil-shaped top.

Deadrise—The vertical distance of the upward slant of a boat's bottom. Often described by the angle between a horizontal at the top of the keel and the chine or turn of the bilge. Flat-bottomed boats have no deadrise. Deep-V boats usually have 20 to 25 degrees of deadrise.

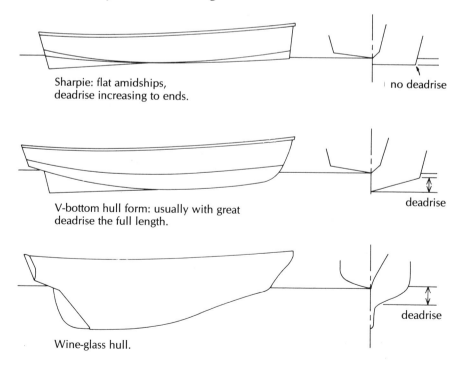

Sharpie: flat amidships, deadrise increasing to ends.

no deadrise

V-bottom hull form: usually with great deadrise the full length.

deadrise

Wine-glass hull.

deadrise

Deckhouse—A raised cabin or shelter that does not extend to the sides of the vessel.

Dodging—Powering, sailing, or motorsailing slowly into heavy seas to prevent being rolled down by waves taken on the beam.

Doghouse—The raised portion of a cabin trunk, usually near the companionway. Normally, a doghouse is for the purpose of improving headroom below or to afford shelter at the forward end of the cockpit.

Dorades—Ventilators mounted on water trap boxes, with the ventilator offset abaft the deck hole to prevent any water entering the vent from going below. There are drains at the low end of the water trap box and a raised pipe in the deck hole. Used on and named after the famous yawl *Dorade*.

Downflooding—The flooding of a vessel through hatches or other deck openings.

Drogue—A miniature or perforated sea anchor or other drag usually towed astern, intended to slow a vessel's way or her drift.

Drop keel—A ballasted keel that can be raised or lowered. It is usually moved vertically, or almost so, in the manner of a daggerboard.

Earing—Line or pendant used to hold down a reef grommet or cringle of a reefed sail.

Electrolysis—"The production of chemical changes by the passage of current from an electrode to an electrolyte or visa versa." (ABYC definition) The term is often loosely applied to stray-current corrosion resulting not from self-generation, as in galvanic corrosion, but from leaks in a DC or AC power system.

Entrance—Forward part of a hull's underbody. The immersed part of the hull between the forward load waterline ending and greatest waterline beam.

EPIRB—Emergency position-indicating radiobeacon.

Fetch—Distance of open water over which the wind blows to produce seas. (Also, to lay a mark or destination when close-hauled.)

Fiddles—Low rails around tables or shelves to prevent objects from sliding off when the vessel heels.

Flare—Outward turning of the topsides near the deck edge, gunwale, or toerail, usually near the bow, to deflect spray and provide reserve buoyancy.

Flasher—An asymmetrical, poleless spinnaker used on cruising boats.

Flotsam—Wreckage, driftwood, cargo lost overboard, or other objects floating on or just under the surface of the water.

Forefoot—Forward part of a boat's underbody directly abaft and beneath the above-water part of her stem. It can be deep and fairly sharp, or more shallow and flat.

Forestay—On a fractionally rigged sailboat, when the foremost stay or *headstay* doesn't go to the masthead, it is called the *forestay*. A shorter stay with its base farther aft on the foredeck and usually supporting a staysail is called an inner forestay or staysail stay. An even shorter forestay used to control mast bend is usually called a babystay.

Fractional rig—A rig with its jibstay not reaching the masthead (see *Forestay*).

Freeboard—Vertical distance from the waterline to the gunwale, deck edge, or toerail.

Free-surface effect—Movement of liquid within a partially filled tank, often adversely affecting a vessel's stability.

Fujiwhara effect—The rotating of two low-pressure systems about a point between them.

Fully developed wave—One that is not limited in size by fetch or duration of the wind.

Galerider—A modern version of the Chinese basket drogue, consisting of a bag comprising loosely woven strips of heavy cloth.

Gallows frame—A permanent frame across the vessel to support her boom when sail is lowered.

Galvanic action—Galvanic corrosion, which is defined as follows by the ABYC: "The increased corrosion above normal corrosion resulting from electrical current flow between two metals which have different tendencies to go into solution, are connected electrically, and are in contact with the same electrolyte saltwater."

Garboards—Originally the strake (plank) next to the keel. Now the term is also used with vessels made of materials other than wood when referring to the area of the bottom just above the keel.

Gooseneck—Fitting which holds the boom to the mast and allows movement in all directions.

Green water—Solid water, not merely spray, taken on deck when a vessel plows into a sea.

Ground (electrical)—Electrically connecting the hull and its equipment with a conductor to the earth to equalize potential or degree of electrification.

Gunwale (pronounced gun'l)—Top edge along the sheer of an open boat.

Half-winder—An experimental spinnaker with ventilating holes near the after leech.

Hammerlock moor—A two-anchor system of mooring a vessel with one anchor at short scope and out of tandem with the other.

Headstay—Foremost stay on a sailboat for mast or jib support, running from the bow or end of the bowsprit to the masthead.

Heave-to—To stop or nearly stop a vessel's headway with small opposing sails. Normally, one or more sails are backed to oppose the forward driving sail(s).

Hole in the sea—An unusually deep trough between waves.

Hulling—See *Lying a-hull*.

Hypothermia—A dangerous condition of exposure to the cold in which the core temperature of the human body drops below 95 degrees Fahrenheit.

IMS—International Measurement System, a non-type-forming handicap rule designed to encourage the racing of dual-purpose yachts.

IOR—International Offshore Rule, a type-forming yacht racing handicap rule predominant in the 1970s and early 1980s.

In irons (or In stays)—Loss of way and steering control, normally resulting when a sailboat fails to complete a tack and becomes caught in the eye of the wind with her sails luffing or aback. In this predicament she eventually makes sternway (drifts backward) and the helm must be reversed to fall off on the desired tack.

Initial stability—A vessel's resistance to heeling at low angles of heel.

IYRU—International Yacht Racing Union.

Jacklines—Lines or wire rope fastened to the deck or cabin trunk and running fore and aft, to which a safety harness tether may be attached to allow uninterrupted crew movement along the deck. (Also, a relieving line for slides or hanks at the bottom of a sail's luff.)

Jiffy reefing—A simplified variation on the old-fashioned points reefing whereby the sail is held down mainly by a clew earing and most often with a tack hook at the gooseneck.

Keel-centerboarder—A boat with a shallow keel that houses a centerboard, the primary purpose of which is to improve windward ability. The keel is usually ballasted.

Lateral plane—Underbody of a boat and its immersed parts such as keel, skeg, centerboard, and rudder that resist leeway. Its profile is shown beneath the load waterline on a vessel's sheer plan.

Law of storms—Standard advice first given by Henry Piddington describing the structure and movement of a tropical storm and providing advice to the shipmaster on how to avoid the worst of it (see Chapter 9).

Lee shore—The shore onto which the wind is blowing and which should be avoided by a vessel in a storm. Sometimes confused (once even by Webster of dictionary fame) with the windward shore, which may form a protective lee for a vessel.

Lifesling—A shorthanded man-overboard recovery device/system using a flexible horsecollar buoy thrown overboard and towed astern on a long floating line while the victim is circled by the boat.

Lying a-hull—Allowing a vessel to drift freely and look out for herself in heavy weather. In this condition sailboats usually have sails furled and lie about beam-to the seas with the helm lashed alee.

Mackerel sky—Lumpy, rippled masses of high-altitude clouds (over 20,000 feet), which can predict the approach of a warm front in unstable air.

Main bulkhead—A near-amidships transverse partition affording structural support, cabin space division, and sometimes watertightness. On a sloop, cutter, yawl, or ketch the main bulkhead is normally in way of the mainmast.

Mares' tails—High-altitude cirrus clouds, normally seen as wispy white streaks. When thick, these are often forerunners of a front.

Metacenter—The point at which a line corresponding to the stem line when a boat is viewed from ahead intersects a vertical line through her heeled center of buoyancy at a moderate angle of heel.

Metacentric height (often referred to as GM)—The distance between a boat's center of gravity and her metacenter.

MFV—Motor fishing vessel.

Microburst—A low-level wind shear that generates a powerful downdraft and outflow over a concentrated area.

Millibar—A unit of barometric pressure. One inch of mercury is equal to 33.86 millibars.

NAMS—National Association of Marine Surveyors.

Navigable semicircle—The left side of a tropical storm (if you are facing the direction in which it is moving). In general, less dangerous than the right side, partly because the storm's forward movement is subtracted from the spiralling wind velocity.

Negative stability—the stability of a vessel when she is inverted or upside down.

ORC—Offshore Racing Council, the international offshore yacht racing regulatory authority.

Overfalls—Breaking seas occurring where there is an abrupt change in water depth or where opposing currents meet.

PFD—Personal flotation device.

Parbuckle—A method of lifting a somewhat cylindrical object with line (usually) by fastening one end of the line and passing the other end under the object, then hauling on the free end to lift.

Partners—Structural support, originally horizontal knees, at the deck hole of a keel-stepped mast.

Pendant—A length of rope, wire, or chain attached to the tack or head of a sail, spar, centerboard, etc. Pronounced "pennant" and often confused with a pennant, which is properly a kind of flag.

Periauger—A two-masted rig with mainmast stepped far forward as on the early two-masted sharpies. Known today as the cat-ketch rig.

Pilot charts—Charts published by the Defense Mapping Agency which provide oceanic information in percentage form about gales, calms, wind direction and strength, current, fog, ice limits, pressure, magnetic variation, etc.

Pitch—A vessel's turning about her transverse axis, usually resulting from encountering head seas.

Pitch-pole—The capsizing of a vessel end-over-end.

Plunging breaker—A breaking wave, usually in relatively shallow water or running against a current, which tumbles forward from its base with great destructive force. See also *Spilling breaker*.

Pooped—A vessel is pooped when a large wave breaks over her stern, filling her cockpit. In former times, vessels were often built with raised afterdecks called poop decks to prevent this.

Precursor lines—Bands of cumulonimbus clouds perhaps a day ahead of a hurricane.

Preventer—A line rigged temporarily for support or to prevent an accident; for example, a jibing preventer rigged as a foreguy on the main boom to prevent an inadvertent flying jibe.

Proa—A boat with two hulls having bows at each end and the rig on one hull. The outrigger hull is always kept to windward or leeward, and the proa changes tacks by sailing forward and then, in effect, "backward."

Prismatic coefficient—A measure of the fineness of a vessel's ends in comparison with her midship section.

Quarter wave—Transverse or divergent waves near the vessel's quarter, caused by a displacement (heavy) hull moving through the water.

Racetrack turn—A powerboat man-overboard recovery maneuver used in good visibility, whereby the vessel makes two 180-degree turns, describing a course similar to a racetrack.

Racing-cruiser—A fast sailing cruiser most often used for moderate-distance cruising and club racing. Usually suitable for offshore use when properly equipped.

Reef points—Short lines (not the eyes) secured to a sail in a line parallel to the boom, and used to tie down the sail when reefing.

Reel winch—A winch, potentially dangerous to handle, that has a brake and self-stores the wire rope (normally a halyard) it services.

Riding sail—a small, flat sail normally set aft and sheeted flat to help hold a vessel steady, usually with her head into the wind or nearly so.

Rode—Anchor line.

Roll—A vessel's turning about her longitudinal axis, usually resulting from encountering beam seas.

Roller reefing—Reducing a sail's area by winding its luff around itself or around a boom, rod, or foil.

Rollout—The lifting of a hull as a result of increased buoyancy on her leeward side as she heels. (See "Running Aground" in Chapter 6 and accompanying illustration.)

Rooting—Burying the bow in a heavy sea.

Run—After part of a hull's underbody, defined by the buttock lines, between the greatest waterline beam and the after load waterline ending. The term also refers to a vessel's point of sailing when approximately dead before the wind, or her distance covered in a given time or route.

Scantlings—Dimensions and specifications of structural members and other components used in shipbuilding. Scantlings are usually drawn up by classification societies such as Lloyds, American Bureau of Shipping, or Det Norske Veritas.

Scope—Length of anchor rode. Recommended scope for heavy weather is six or seven times the depth of water.

Scudding—Running off, usually at reduced speed and often towing drags, before heavy seas.

Sea anchor—A floating anchor, usually a conic bag or parachute type, intended to hold a vessel's end to the seas and reduce drift to the bare minimum.

Seacock—A shut-off valve in way of through-hull fittings, which operates with a handle that is rotated a quarter of a turn to open or close.

Seakindly—Said of a boat with a relatively easy motion in rough seas. Moderately heavy vessels usually have a slower, gentler motion, which is more tolerable to most sailors (not all) than light-displacement craft.

Seamount—A hill-like elevation rising from the bottom of the sea, which may alter wave characteristics above it.

Series drogue—A drogue comprising several small conic sea anchors evenly spaced along the rode.

Sheer (or sheerline)—Curvature of the toerail or gunwale as viewed from the vessel's side. Normal sheer is concave, with the lowest freeboard just abaft amidships, but some boats have reverse (convex) or powderhorn (a combination of concave and convex) sheer.

Shrouds—Members of the standing rigging that support the mast in the athwartship direction.

Skeg—Underwater appendage near the stern, most often existing for the purpose of providing directional stability, improving rudder efficiency, and protecting and/or supporting the rudder. Some powerboats use skegs for propeller protection.

SNAME—Society of Naval Architects and Marine Engineers.

Spilling breaker—Normally, a deep-water breaking wave with a whitecap that breaks only at the crest.

Spitfire—A very small storm jib or staysail.

Sponson—A flotation chamber projecting outboard of the hull at deck level.

Spreaders—Arms cocked up slightly from a right angle to the mast, which hold the shrouds away from the mast to reduce compression loads.

Squatting—Burying the stern as a result of being in a wave trough or lacking buoyancy aft.

Stability range—The heeling angle at which a vessel will lose positive stability and capsize.

Stays—members of the standing rigging that support the mast in the fore-and-aft direction.

Stuffing box—Packing gland to prevent leakage where a prop shaft or rudderstock enters the hull.

Swedish mainsail—A tall, narrow, small mainsail with hollow leech for windward efficiency in heavy weather.

Tail splice—A wire-to-rope splice for the primary purpose of enabling cleating, usually of a halyard or topping lift.

Tangs—Strong metal straps secured to the mast, to which the standing rigging is attached.

Terminal fitting—An eye or fork, normally swaged to the end of a shroud or stay.

Toggle—A metal fitting at the end of a shroud or stay, which acts as a universal joint to alleviate metal fatigue.

Trim—The angle a vessel's designed waterline makes with the water surface, indicating a bow-up or stern-up (or down) flotation. (Also, the inward adjustment of a sail with its sheet.)

Trim tabs—Adjustable flaps at the stern of a powerboat, used to change her trim. (On a sailboat, a trim tab is a keel flap similar to a rudder, used primarily to enhance keel lift.)

Tumblehome—Inward turning of a vessel's topsides near her deck edge, gunwale, or toerail.

Turn turtle—To capsize and remain, at least temporarily, upside down.

USYRU—United States Yacht Racing Union.

Veering wind—A clockwise wind shift, as from east to southeast.

Virga—High-altitude rain that mostly evaporates before reaching the ground.

Warning pieces—Fatigue-indicating fittings that include a part that breaks away before the fitting fails, in order to warn of potential weakness.

Warps—Heavy lines used for mooring, towing, or warping (moving a vessel by hauling on her lines). Warps are sometimes towed astern to slow her speed in heavy weather.

Waterlines—Horizontal, longitudinal sections through a hull which show as straight lines on the body and sheer plans but as curved lines on the half-breadth plan. These lines are parallel to the load waterline on which the hull floats.

Wave train—a group or system of related waves moving at approximately half the speed of the individual waves.

Wave refraction—The bending of a wave line as a result of shoals on one side of the line as the wave moves past a point, peninsula, or island.

Wave reflection—The bouncing back of a wave so that it reverses direction after striking a solid vertical object such as a seawall.

Wear ship—To change tacks on a sailing vessel by jibing around.

Weather helm—Tendency for a sailboat to turn into the wind when her helm is released. A moderate weather helm in moderate to fresh winds is desirable for safety and sailing efficiency.

Weather bomb—An explosively developing extratropical cyclone (low), in which the barometer falls at least one millibar per hour for 24 hours.

Weatherliness—The ability of a sailboat to make progress to windward.

Wetted surface—Immersed area of the hull, accounting for skin friction, the principal source of drag at low speeds.

White squall—An extremely powerful gust of wind from a cloudless sky.

Williamson turn—A powerboat man-overboard recovery turn used in reduced visibility because it makes good the original track. The rudder is put full over in the direction the victim fell until the heading is about 60 degrees beyond the original course. Then the vessel is turned onto her reciprocal course.

Yaw—A vessel's turning or tendency to turn around her vertical axis. Correctable with the helm when the vessel is underway.

INDEX

Metal construction, 38-40: aluminum, 39, 40; dissimilar metals and, 38-39, 40; electrolysis/galvanic action, 38, 40; hydrogen embrittlement and, 39; protective voltage and, 39; steel, 39

Monohull sailboat safety, 64

Motor Fishing Vessels (MFVs): ballast and, 83-84; deckhouses, 83; definition of, 76-77; emergency propulsion and, 85-86, 88; engine placement, 84-85; fuel tanks, 85; hull design, 78-80; in heavy seas, 311; roll damping, 86-88; windows, 80, 83

Motorsailers: vs. powerboats, 88-90; sail plan and, 89-90

Multihulls, in heavy weather, 306-310

Navigation: charts, 130, 131; currents/tides, 131; depth sounder, 131; electronic navigation, 131-132; erroneous navigation, 130-132; heavy seas and, 263; lines of position (LOP), 131, 132; piloting tools, 130-131

Offshore multihull sailboats, 67-76; capsizing and, 69, 70-73; hull strength, 73; masthead flotation, 71-72; performance and Bruce number, 69; reducing sail, 72; safety considerations, 67-69; stability and, 70; watertightness, 72, 74

Offshore powerboats. See Motor Fishing Vessels (MFVs); Motorsailers

Offshore Rating Council (ORC), 16; Offshore Equipment Lists, 105; Governing Minimum Equipment and Accommodations Standards, 326-328

Offshore sailing craft, 42-67: cabin trunks, 65; centerboarders, 54; companionways/hatches, 66; diagram of types, 44; heavy double-under type, 44-45, 47; hull design, 45, 49, 51-52, 54-56, 64-65; monohull sailboat safety, 4; overhangs, 64; racing cruiser handicap rating rules, 66-67; rudder considerations, 62-64; stability and, 48-49, 54, 59; steering and, 49, 51-52, 54-56; windows, 65-66

Overhangs in offshore sailing craft, 64

Personal flotation devices (PFDs), 105, 112-113

Powerboats. See Motor Fishing Vessels

Protective voltage, metal construction and, 39

Radar deflector, 117

Radio equipment, 110-111

Reducing sail in offshore multihull sailboats, 72

Rigging: center of effort (CE), 234, 236; Chinese lug rig, 239, 240, 241; determining size, 225; mitigation of

chafe, 241; offshore rig, 233-241; running rigging and fittings, 230-233; standing rigging and fittings, 222-230; stock boat faults and, 220-222

Righting craft. See Capsizing

Rudder considerations, offshore sailing craft, 62-64

Running aground, 132-136; centerboards and, 135; heeling, 133-134, 135; kedging off, 133, 134; tides and, 135; towing, 135

Running rigging and fittings, 230-233

Safety: Beaufort Scale, 342; cockpit guidelines, 17; deficiencies in stock boats, 2-3; designs for open waters, 9-20; distress signals, 340; flotation and, 3-6; helmsman's view guidelines, 7-8; monohull sailboat safety, 64; offshore multihull sailboats, 67-69; Offshore Rating Council Regulations Governing Minimum Equipment and Accommodations Standards, 326-328; Sailing School Vessel Regulations, 13; small craft design and, 3-9; storm warning signals, 341; U.S. Coast Guard Auxiliary Courtesy Examination, 320-325. See also Crew security/welfare; Emergencies

Safety equipment: bilge pump, 105-107; companionway slides, locking, 107-108; compass, 108-110; distress signaling equipment, 117-119; emergency position-indicating radio beams (EPIRBs), 111-112; first-aid supplies/information, 122; lifelines, 108; liferafts, 113-116; lighting, 110, 117; Offshore Rating Council (ORC) equipment list, 105; personal flotation devices (PFDs), 105, 112-113; radar deflector, 117; radio communication equipment, 110-111; repair kits, 119-120; safety belts, 116-117; spare parts, 119, 120-121, 122; tools, 119, 122

Sailing in a blow: heavy-weather sails and, 255-256; hull inspection and, 255; jiffy reefing, 251, 252; mast inspection and, 255; reducing sail, 244-246, 249-251, 253-255; roller reefing vs. conventional reefing, 250; spinnaker knockdowns, 246, 248; spinnaker types and, 246-247

Sailing in a gale: abandonment and rescue, 304-306; center of effort (CE) and, 264-265; courses of action, 257-258; drift attitude and, 270-271; heaving-to under sail, 263-269; heavy-weather sails and, 265-268; lying a-hull, 269-277; multihulls in heavy weather, 306-310; navigation and, 263; racer vs. cruiser in, 257-258; under reduced sail, 257-263; riding to

a sea anchor, 277-287, 310; scudding, 288-296; survival tactics, 296-304; total center of effort (TCE) and, 264-265

Sailing School Vessel Regulations, 13

Scudding, 288-296; conditions for, 288; sea oil and, 295-296; speed and, 289-292, 295; steering control and drags, 292-295; techniques for, 288-289

Sea anchors, 277-287; rudder vulnerability and, 280-282; series drogue, 284-287

Seacocks, maintenance of, 19

Sea oil, scudding and, 295-296

Series drogue, 284-287

Shrinkage, wood construction and, 35

Small craft: flotation and, 3-6; heavy seas and, 313-316; safety features for, 6-9

Stability: elements of heeling motion, 14; low negative stability, 12; offshore multihull sailboats and, 70; offshore sailing craft and, 48-49, 54, 59; static stability, 275-276; static stability range, 10, 12, 13, 54; of stock centerboarders, 54. See also Capsizing

Standing rigging and fittings, 222-230

Static stability, lying a-hull and, 275-276

Steering, offshore sailing craft and, 49, 51-52, 54-56

Storms, 193-201; anchors and, 217-218; avoidance planning, 207; coastal waters and, 214-215; extratropical lows, 208-209; preparing for in port, 216-219; preparing for at sea, 215-216; tropical storm strategy, 209-214. See also Weather

Storm warning signals, 341

Stowage plan, 120, 121

Stray-current corrosion, 38, 40; definition of, 97; prevention of, 99-100, 101

Survival tactics, heavy seas, 296-304

Total center of effort (TCE), heavy seas and, 264-265

Tropical storm strategy, 209-214

U.S. Coast Guard: Auxiliary Courtesy Examination, 320-325; loading capacity guidelines, 6-7

Watertightness: cockpits and, 17; considerations for, 16-20; offshore multihull sailboats, 72, 74

Waves: weather and, 201-206

Weather: basis of, 191-193; publications related to, 207; radio advisories, 195, 208; storms, 193-201; waves and, 201-206; wind systems, 191-192

Windows in offshore sailing craft, 65-66

Wind vane self-steerer, 49, 52

Wood construction, 34-38; composite construction, 37-38; dry rot and, 34-35; shrinkage and, 35